OCR GOVERNMENT AND POLITICS

US Government and Politics

OCR and Heinemann are working together to provide better support for you

Diane Canwell
Jonathan Sutherland
Consultant: Mike Simpson

Heinemann is an imprint of Pearson Education Limited, a company incorporated in England and Wales, having its registered office at Edinburgh Gate, Harlow, Essex, CM20 2JE. Registered company number: 872828

www.heinemann.co.uk

Heinemann is a registered trademark of Pearson Education Limited

First published 2009

13 12 11 10 09
10 9 8 7 6 5 4 3 2

British Library Cataloguing in Publication Data
A catalogue record for this book is available from the British Library.

ISBN 978 0 435 33182 5

Edited by Alexander Gray
Typeset by TechType
Original illustrations © TechType
Cover photo/illustration © Jon Helgason/Alamy
Printed in China(EPC/02)

Acknowledgements
The author and publisher would like to thank the following individuals and organisations for permission to reproduce photographs:
Getty Images p56(r.); Library of Congress pp 16, 21, 23, 26, 48, 53, 54, 56 (l.), 69, 73, 122, 127, 130, 133, 138, 173, 184; Daniel Acker/Landov/Pa Photos p 193; Jay Laprete/Landov/Pa Photos p 193

Every effort has been made to contact copyright holders of material reproduced in this book. Any omissions will be rectified in subsequent printings if notice is given to the publishers.

Websites
There are links to relevant websites in this book. In order to ensure that the links are up to date, that the links work, and that the sites are not inadvertently linked to sites that could be considered offensive, we have made the links available on the Heinemann website at www.heinemann.co.uk/hotlinks. When you access the site, the express code is 1825P

Contents

Introduction

This textbook has been written and designed specifically to help you deal with the requirements of the OCR A2 Optional Units focusing on US Government and Politics examinations. You should find that, together with some background reading and getting into the habit of paying attention to political stories in the media, this book will prepare you for anything the examiners might want to throw at you. The book is structured so that it successively deals with each of the two parts of the A2 syllabus related to US Government and Politics (units F853 and F855). You will find all the key terms and phrases defined and important concepts highlighted and illustrated with examples. Each of the topics within the syllabus is dealt with either in single or double sections. The book has several key features, which include:

- specific learning objectives for every section
- key words or phrases defined
- links to additional reading and research
- an exam café feature at the end of each topic, with expert knowledge and guidance.

Each of the chapters is structured so that you will be first introduced to new ideas, concepts, mechanisms and features of US Government and Politics. Following this there is a series of typical and recurring F853 and F855 examination questions. These contain new material, in addition to that of the topics in the first part of each chapter. The purpose of these is to illustrate how examiners may structure questions and to indicate the kind of material and detail that you will need in order to answer essay questions and incorporate synoptic aspects.

F853 and F855

The A2 is the second half of the complete A Level. It is made up of two optional units, both of which are externally assessed. The units are:

- A2 Unit F853: Contemporary US Government and Politics
- A2 Unit F855: US Government and Politics

Unit F853 is worth 25 per cent of the overall A Level mark. You will be required to sit a two-hour written paper with 100 marks available. You will have to answer question 1, which is a structured question and contains stimulus material. The questions could require you to provide answers from any of the topic areas in the unit. You will then have to choose three questions from a range of seven to show your understanding of:

- elections, presidential and congressional
- the Constitution
- the presidency
- civil rights and liberties
- political parties, pressure groups
- Congress
- the Supreme Court.

Unit F855 is also worth 25 per cent of the total A Level mark. It is also a two-hour paper with 100 marks available. It is important to note that this unit is synoptic. Synoptic means that the examinations test your understanding of the connections between different elements of government and politics. You will be required to answer two questions from a choice of eight. You will be expected to draw on your knowledge of:

- elections
- civil rights and liberties
- legislatures
- judiciaries
- political parties and pressure groups
- constitutions
- executives.

Exam cafés

In our exam café pages you will find plenty of ideas to help you prepare for the exams. You will find an exam café at the end of each chapter. Our first exam café shows you how to relax and prepare to write US Government and Politics essays and how to allocate your time. There is also a vital section showing you what to avoid doing when you write an essay and handy revision advice from teachers and examiners. All of the other exam cafés have a **Relax and prepare** feature and a **Refresh your memory** feature, with exercises that will help you to revise, structure your notes and guide you on what you need to know for different papers. **Get the Results!** includes hints and tips on revision and keeping up to date to help you achieve the best grades.

The exam café explains the assessment objectives for US Government and Politics to you. These are the assessment objectives.

- A01 – You are required to demonstrate knowledge and understanding of relevant institutions, processes, political concepts, theories and debates.
- A02 – You are required to analyse and evaluate political information, arguments and explanations, and where appropriate identify parallels, connections, similarities and differences between aspects of the political systems studied, including the EU.
- A03 – You are required to construct and communicate coherent arguments making use of a range of appropriate political vocabulary.

The more assessment objectives you can cover in your answers, the greater the chance you have of achieving a high grade in the examinations. Each of the assessment objectives has four levels, ranging from Level 1 – a basic attempt to achieve the assessment objective, through to Level 4 – a more thorough interpretation in which you integrate and interpret information.

Exam cafés will also show you how the examiner allocates marks for each question. You should get into the habit of offering more than just facts, as this will only gain you A01 marks (for demonstrating knowledge and understanding). You need to argue, analyse and evaluate in order to achieve A02 (for analysing and evaluating). To achieve A03 (for communicating) your English needs to be as precise as possible and your sentences and arguments must be well structured. The exam cafés will also give you an idea about hot topics and the style of questions that may crop up. The unique essay questions at the end of each topic are also designed to reinforce your awareness of recurring questions that examiners love to ask.

The final exam café at the end of the book gives you key ideas to help prepare you for the exams, covering the rights and wrongs of revision and how to impress the examiner. You will also find a list of other books that may be useful in preparing for the F853 and F855 examinations.

Organising your notes and keeping up to date

Over the duration of the course you should try to organise your notes in the best way possible, making sure that you note down any useful contemporary examples. Make sure you understand what the syllabus is asking you to do. There is a high probability that any part of it could form the basis of a question, and it is a difficult and dangerous business to try to predict what the examiner may or may not ask. However, certain topics lend themselves to particular types of questions and all of these have been identified. You need to know the topics thoroughly and answer the questions. A common complaint from examiners is that students simply write down everything they know about a particular topic and do not pay attention to the question.

US Government and Politics is a constantly developing subject. Politics is never out of the media, and there is always something new happening. New political personalities, as well as political ideas, constantly emerge and others disappear. While we were writing this book the US elected a new president, ending eight years of a Republican presidency. Make sure that you do not use out-of-date examples when more recent ones are always available in the news.

Try to follow stories through. See who is involved, who makes the decisions, why those decisions have been made and what their consequences are. Develop your own strategy for keeping up to date. As the primary focus is on US Government and Politics you will need to get used to visiting websites, such as CNN, ABC and NBC. Wherever possible we have identified ideal websites with political commentary and constant updates. There are also a number of websites where you can download US political programmes that have appeared on television or cable networks. Although the BBC does have some US political coverage and some stories are featured in newspapers and magazines, it is wise to look at US magazines, such as *Time,* and perhaps ask your school or college library to take out a subscription to one of the major US newspapers.

The course and the book

For this course the units of F853: Contemporary US Government and Politics and F855: US Government and Politics fit together perfectly so that you can first discover how the US political system was established and then how it has developed; you can then turn your attention to the workings and realities of the US system and how it has similarities and differences with other political systems, such as Britain and the European Union.

F853 gives you an opportunity to study the role and functions of elections, political parties, pressure groups, Congress, the presidency and the Supreme Court, as well as the development of the US Constitution and civil rights and liberties.

In F855 you will examine all of these aspects and institutions in practice and you can compare and contrast US politics with British and European Union practices.

There are six chapters in this book. Each of them examines both F853 and F855. The different aspects of each chapter are covered by a series of topics, at the end of which there will be a series of essay question topics; these are identified as F853 and F855. We have tried to present the functional and role aspects in the F853 essay question topics and the more practical application and examples in the F855 ones.

Essay question topics

The radically new feature is that we present the information relating to F853 and F855 at the beginning of each of the chapters and then specifically turn our attention to structuring the rest of the information, so that it directly relates to the typical essay questions that you will find in the examination paper.

The essay topic questions are designed to focus your attention on recurring essay questions that feature in the majority of the examination papers. We have researched and studied examination papers stretching back over several years and identified key essay topics. There is no absolute guarantee that these essay topics will appear, but given the structure of the two units there are only so many different angles and potential areas of questioning that the examiners can use. You should be aware, however, that the essay-focused topics are not written in essay format, but they will introduce new ideas, concepts, institutions and practices you should think about.

The F853 essay question topics are followed by the F855 ones in each chapter. The F855 essay question topics are more complex, as they have incorporated synoptic aspects to them and provide a valuable starting point to help you understand the way in which you should structure your arguments. You will also discover that the essay topic spreads have tables and charts. This does not imply that you should use these in your essays, but they have been used in order to present information in a clear and succinct way.

Bear in mind that you need to be able to give the examiners up-to-date examples and in a fast-moving subject such as US politics relevant examples are always emerging. You should make note of any contemporary examples that you come across in your reading of the subject.

About American politics

The United States is a multiracial, multilingual, socially diverse country. However it has an intense sense of national unity, shared values and common culture. Dating back to the Founding Fathers who wrote the US Constitution, Americans have a faith in democracy and representative government. They favour limited government, equality, liberty, the rule of law, and opportunity (perhaps no more so than their view of the American dream, where anyone can prosper if they use their talents). They also favour a free-market system, individual rights and freedom of speech. Americans are strongly attached to liberty and tolerance and although there have been and continue to be huge differences in income and wealth, America does not have the deep class system that is so obvious in many other countries.

In many respects the US government and its systems aim to represent liberalism and democracy alongside one another. Americans have a deep interest in how power is exercised, they accept majority rule and accept popular sovereignty. They are strong supporters of the rule of law, where individual rights are protected and all citizens are required to abide by codes of behaviour. They dislike excessive authority and they have a strong inclination to support politicians who are able to articulate the feelings and experiences of ordinary people.

Unlike Britain, for example, there is a strong religious feeling running through US society and religion was a key feature in the campaign for civil rights and more recently in the power of the religious right. Citizens are very patriotic and are proud of their constitution and other signs of their nation. They respect the office of president. Socialism is almost absent in US politics and it has never taken root.

The US has a written constitution, nevertheless it is a flexible one, which has rarely been amended but has the ability to be interpreted in different ways for different generations in different circumstances. The method of selecting presidential candidates has evolved over 200 years and certainly the system favours the two dominant parties: the Democrats and the Republicans.

In the US there is an even greater focus on the separation of powers than in even Britain. Each element of government is not only independent, and either elected or appointed in different ways, it also jealously guards that independence and its role to act as a check or balance against the other two elements of government. US political parties are both stronger and weaker than in Britain. They are stronger in the sense of their ability to be able to raise finance, but weaker in their ability to control and direct candidates or elected individuals who have achieved power via the party's support.

The recent US presidential election in 2008 brought US politics into far sharper focus, with a truly exciting and potentially groundbreaking election campaign, with a radical choice of candidates. It saw the first African-American to stand as president and ultimately win. It also saw the first female vice-presidential candidate, plucked from obscurity to act as a running mate for a more traditional, white, conservative Republican presidential candidate.

Further reading

No single book on US Government and Politics could possibly provide you with everything you need for studying this subject or for what you can expect in the examination. So, it is vital that you read as widely as possible. Do try to read as broadly as you can on US politics. This will help you understand different points of view, standpoints and policies, some of which become legislation. This book should provide you with most of the information that you will need to appreciate the complexities of US government and politics and how their system has developed in a relatively short period of time. Above all, you should remember that politics is a constantly changing discipline and that ideas and practices in the US, while often based on key constitutional understandings, may be interpreted and viewed in many different ways by many different people.

US Government and Politics is a fast-moving subject, with new institutions and power groups to understand. So much that happens in Washington DC and in the state capitals around the United States impacts upon all our lives.

INTERNET RESEARCH

Throughout the chapters you will be directed to useful websites. Follow the links to investigate topics more fully by going to www.heinemann.co.uk/hotlinks. Insert the express code 1825P and click on the relevant link.

Exam Café

Relax and prepare

How to use the exam cafés

At the end of each chapter there will be an opportunity for you to think more closely about how to use the information you have just read. In each exam café there are hints on how to focus on the key issues; guidance will be given on how to revise the different topic areas, including several essay questions of a type that could occur in your exams, sample essay plans and answers, and also suggestions for additional reading. The first of these exam cafés is about how to write essays on US government and politics and for the synoptic paper, something that will be very new to you and possibly quite daunting. So pour yourself an invigorating espresso and let's get started.

Relax and prepare

Below are suggestions for how to structure your essays for the two US politics and government units. When writing future essays for these units use them as a guide.

In Focus – F853

For unit F853 you will need to answer a compulsory two-part question, based around the reading of a source and then three further essay-style questions. Overall you should spend 30 minutes on each question, making the exam two hours in length.

Compulsory questions

Carefully read the short source accompanying the question – it may contain hints on what to focus upon in your answers. Give yourself approximately 5 minutes to make sure you understand the source and the questions before you start writing.

Part A questions (worth 10 marks)

All that is required is knowledge and understanding (examiners refer to this as Assessment Objective 1 – AO1 for short) of an institution/branch of government/party ideology etc. raised in the source. Give a clear definition and extend where possible by providing information not evident in the source. Use contemporary examples whenever possible. Avoid getting sidetracked into debates (this is required in part B). Above all keep your answer fairly short and to the point as you will have only about 10 minutes to write it.

Part B questions (worth 15 marks)

All the marks are for analysis and evaluation (Assessment Objective 2 – AO2), thus your answer must focus on debate. Depending on the specific question asked, this could be comparing and contrasting, evaluating the strengths and weaknesses of a particular institution, or considering the relative importance of key factors. Here you will have slightly longer to develop your ideas, 15 minutes in all but still not long enough to get sidetracked into irrelevant arguments. There will be no need to give extensive supporting evidence.

Optional questions (each worth 25 marks)

The following suggestions will help you improve your answers to the exam questions.

- Make sure you read all seven questions before you choose which to answer. Sometimes you may regret your choice of questions when there may be others further down that you would have felt more comfortable answering.
- Plan out your answer – don't be afraid to spend approximately five minutes planning each answer and making sure that you fully understand the question set.
- At the beginning of each essay clearly define any key words or technical terms in the question.
- Make sure you also show the examiner that you fully understand what the question requires you to do by outlining the key areas you intend to cover, by briefly stating the two sides to the argument in view.
- Deal with each relevant argument in a separate paragraph – this may be a point of comparison, strength or a weakness, or relevant perspective.
- Try to illustrate each argument with an example. The more recent this example is, the better. There is no need to learn extensive quotes, accurate paraphrasing is just as good. Good quotes should be attributed to their source.
- Avoid just listing or describing points, but instead consider issues such as the extent of similarity/difference, the relative importance of each factor, or whether the strengths outweigh the weaknesses in a particular idea.
- Conclude by outlining the most important factors you have considered in a manner that directly addresses the question set and give, where appropriate, some personal, reasoned perspective upon the topic – this shows evaluation of the arguments.

Exam tips

The following are tips on how to improve your chances of doing well in the exam.

- Focus on the key words in the questions set and *do not* offer pre-prepared answers to other questions.
- Provide contemporary examples in your essay and give a clear understanding of the constitutional arrangements in the US.
- Use paragraphs to separate each individual argument and provide a balanced viewpoint by giving both sides of the argument in order to access the higher mark levels. So, avoid writing one-sided essays or essays from a single viewpoint, especially avoid essays that constantly use 'I think ...'

In Focus – F855

For unit F855, once again you will have two hours to answer the questions, however here you only have to write two essays, thus spending an hour on each.

The following suggestions for writing each essay will help you improve your answers to these exam questions.

- Make sure you read all eight questions before you choose which to answer. Sometimes you may regret your choice of questions when there may be others further down that you would have felt more comfortable answering.
- Plan out your answer – having an hour to write each essay you should be able to spend between 5 and 10 minutes planning each answer and making sure that you fully understand the question set.
- Many of the techniques detailed above can be used for a synoptic essay. Remember though, you will need examples from both the US and UK, and where possible from the EU and other countries.
- Furthermore, the following points can also help in the planning and writing of an essay on both papers.

Exam tips

These are suggestions on how to write an essay for the exam.

- It is useful to start an essay with a relevant quote or recent event. This might serve to illustrate the saliency of an issue or a relevant argument relating to the question. It is also a useful way to catch the examiner's eye.
- As a general rule try to avoid rewriting the question in its entirety. It is worth remembering that the introduction is the first thing the examiner reads and so it can make an impact.
- With practice, it is possible that you will not need to write out an essay plan as this could be done in the introduction, and so you can avoid wasting time. Plans should be short and as much time as possible should be spent writing the essay, as this is what the marks are awarded for. A good introduction can provide you with a basic framework that will allow you to think on your feet as you write.
- Avoid making judgements at this stage; this can be done in the conclusion. Similarly, avoid going into too much detail. Again, this can be done later.
- It might be useful to use a court case analogy for considering how this sort of essay might be structured. In the introduction we could have the opening arguments from the prosecution and the defence. At A2, the importance of words such as 'Discuss' and 'Assess' is that they require a **balanced approach**. You must therefore argue both for and against.
- The construct above allows you to remain neutral and lends itself to a clear separation of these arguments.
- To show that there is to be a clear change in the line of argument with a movement from arguments for to those against, you could leave five lines to clearly flag the change in tack.
- The conclusion is where it is possible to change roles once more. From prosecuting lawyer to defence lawyer, you now become judge and jury. You reach a verdict. Having outlined the case both for and against, you can now reach your verdict and decide which of the arguments have been the most persuasive.

Exam tips

A visual plan for a two-sided essay

The following is a suggestion for setting up your plan for writing a two-sided essay for the exam.

Introduction
Start with recent event or quote.
Briefly outline the two sides of the argument.

Arguments in favour of the view expressed in the question.
Paragraph
1.
2.
3.
4.
5.

Arguments against the view expressed in the question.
Paragraph
1.
2.
3.
4.
5.

Conclusion
Which of the arguments for and against are the strongest?
Is there a particular argument that outweighs the others?
Reach a decision. Answer the question.

For the sake of simplicity, other questions might be considered to be **list questions**, where you have to identify relevant factors. The mental image you might apply here is more along the lines of the following.

Mental image of a list essay

Introduction
Start with recent event or quote.
Briefly outline the various factors that are relevant.

Factor 1

Factor 2

Factor 3

Factor 4

Factor 5

Conclusion
Which factor is the most important?

1 The Constitution

Unlike Britain, the United States has a written constitution. It was specifically designed to be a flexible document, which incorporated a clear separation of powers between the executive (president), the legislature (two houses of Congress) and the judiciary (the courts and the Supreme Court).

The Constitution itself has developed over the past two centuries and has had a number of amendments attached to it, which have become integral parts. The Constitution and the rights of individual citizens of the United States are at the heart of the document. The Constitution clearly sets down the limits of power of the three main parts of government and has been variously interpreted so that the federal government in Washington and the states' governments across the US have clearly defined powers and responsibilities. The Constitution not only determines the clear separation of powers, but also sets in place a series of checks and balances, in order to ensure that the rule of law and constitutional rights are not infringed or threatened.

The US Constitution is also the basis of the nation's federal system of government, under which the powers of government are separated into two levels – federal and state. Each of these levels of government are sovereign in their own right, in that they are free to govern according to their constitutional rights.

The Constitution is a flexible and resilient document that was drawn up so that it could be amended or developed over time as the US changed. Various types of federalism have developed since the Constitution came into force. Among them are dual federalism, cooperative federalism, creative federalism, new federalism and fiscal federalism.

Making changes to the Constitution by amendment can be a long and difficult process and the vast majority of proposed amendments have failed.

There are five key themes in this chapter.

- The making of the Constitution
- Separation of powers
- Federal constitutions
- Unitary and devolved constitutions
- Constitutional reform and amendments

These are represented by the first five topics, and are supported by two question topics for F853, looking at the most common essay titles, and three F855 question topics, which again look at popular essay themes in the examination.

This chapter contains 10 topics in total, representing the following.

The chapter is rounded off with an exam café feature on page 42.

1.1 The Making of the Constitution

Learning objectives

- What was the government like before the US Constitution?
- How did the US Constitution come into existence?
- What are the key features of the US Constitution?
- How can the Constitution be amended?

A stained glass representation of the Founding Fathers

What was the government like before the US Constitution?

In 1776 the 13 existing British colonies in America declared independence from Great Britain. For the next eight years there was a War of Independence, but in 1781 the colonies established a loose association, or confederacy, with much of the political power in the hands of each of the states.

Until 1787 this remained as the status quo. A congress existed, but only as a debating chamber; it could not pass laws. In order to achieve some kind of clarity as to the relationships between the states something needed to be done. Taxes were different, as was the currency. There was no national court and no president.

How did the US Constitution come into existence?

Delegates from all of the states were invited to attend the Philadelphia Convention in May 1787. Delegates from all the states, except Rhode Island, attended. Chairing the convention was George Washington.

Starting with the premise that they simply wished to amend the Articles of Confederation, the decision was made to create a new constitution. There were two opposing plans: the Virginia Plan was essentially in favour of framing a constitution that would give the more highly populated states an advantage. The New Jersey Plan tried to address the concerns of the lesser populated states. At the time Virginia had the largest population and Rhode Island had not attended out of fear that it would lose many of the new freedoms obtained by gaining independence.

The basis for agreement was framed and is known as the Connecticut Compromise, or the Great Compromise. As a result, a new constitution was created, written by the 55 delegates who attended the convention; from then on they would be known as the Founding Fathers.

The Constitution and the compromises needed for it to be acceptable reflect the way in which American government and politics works. The three key compromises in the new Constitution are outlined in the following table.

Compromise	Reasons and implications
Type of government	In a very short period of time the American colonies had shifted from a **unitary** form of government through a **confederal** system to a **federal** type of system. The federal form was the compromise. It gave powers to the national government, and equal powers to the state governments.
How the states are represented	In a system where states are represented in proportion to their population in Congress, it would mean that the larger states had considerably more power than the lesser populated states. The smaller population states demanded equal representation. The compromise was made so that in the House of Representatives representation would reflect population, but in the Senate each state would have equal representation.
How the president is selected	Some states favoured an appointed president. Others wanted a president who was directly elected by the population. The compromise was an indirectly elected president. This meant the creation of an electoral college. The population would elect that electoral college and those electors in the electoral college would select the president.

What are the key features of the US Constitution?

The Constitution divides law-making, law-enforcing and law-interpreting, which we more commonly know as legislative, executive and judicial. The US Constitution has strict written definitions of the powers of both federal and state levels of government.

The original Constitution set out seven articles, as can be seen in the following table.

Article	Implications
I	Legislative branch. This describes the Congress as a **bicameral** body, the lower house being the House of Representatives and the upper house being the Senate. It covers elections, powers and limits, as well as responsibilities.
II	Executive branch. This describes the presidency, the election process, the qualifications of the president, the role of the vice-president and how a president can be removed from office.
III	Judicial branch. This describes the court system and the Supreme Court, trial by jury, how cases are heard and how appeals are handled.
IV	Federalism. This sets out the relationship between the states and between the states and federal government. It sets out citizens' rights, freedom of movement and how states should be governed.
V	Amendments procedure. This sets out the two ways in which the constitution can be amended, either by Congress or by national convention. It sets out that the two-thirds vote is required for an amendment and how amendments are ratified.
VI	Supremacy clause. This establishes federal laws over state laws and prohibits religious tests for office holders.
VII	Ratification. This sets up the conditions needed for the initial ratification of the Constitution.

In 1791 the Bill of Rights was passed, which at a stroke made 10 amendments to the Constitution, from underpinning the freedom of religion, speech, press and assembly (1st Amendment) to the right to jury trial in civil cases (7th Amendment). Since then there have been another 17 amendments to the Constitution, although only 26 of the 27 amendments are currently in effect because the 18th Amendment prohibited the manufacture or sale of alcohol (1919), but this was repealed by the 21st Amendment in 1933.

This is not to say that there have not been attempts to make other amendments. In fact since 1789 there have been over 10,000 attempts.

How can the Constitution be amended?

As we have seen, there are two ways in which the Constitution can be amended. The first is a proposal to amend by Congress, which needs to be passed with a two-thirds majority in both houses. The second is by a constitutional convention in which two-thirds of the states are in favour of the amendment. In practice the latter has never occurred.

An amendment needs to be ratified by three-quarters of the state legislatures, or three-quarters of the states that are present at a constitutional convention. This latter ratification method has only happened once and that was in 1933 for the 21st Amendment.

Unitary
A system by which power is held by one central authority. In such a state the central authority or government can assign or recall power from regions or local parliaments or assemblies. This is the case in Britain.

Confederal
An association of empowered states or communities in which membership is usually voluntary. An example is a confederation of sovereign states acting in common purpose, such as the EU, in which the relationships are bound by a treaty.

Federal
A system in which the states' self-governing status is protected and cannot be changed unilaterally by the federal or national government.

Bicameral
This is a system of government in which there are two chambers or houses. In the US the system is divided into the Senate and the House of Representatives.

INTERNET RESEARCH

Be wary of the many thousands of websites that purport to tell you about the US Constitution. A good place to look is the website of the US House of Representatives. To see this, go to www.heinemann.co.uk/hotlinks, insert the express code 1825P and click on the relevant link. Click on 'Education resources' and you will find all the key historical documents, the Bill of Rights, ratified amendments to the Constitution and a list of proposed amendments to the Constitution that were not ratified.

Learning objectives

- The separation of powers
- Checks and balances within the system

The separation of powers

Britain is a parliamentary democracy in which the powers of the executive and the legislature are not separate. This means that the members of the cabinet, (the executive), are also members of the parliament, (the legistature). In such a system the powers are said to be fused.

In America there is a clear separation of powers. Heads of executive bodies and departments do not sit in Congress, and members of Congress cannot hold an executive office. The president is, of course, answerable to Congress, but the president's main responsibility is to the people, rather than the legislature.

As you will recall there are three key functions of government, as can be seen in the following table.

Function of government	Branch	Function	US body	UK body
Legislating	Legislature	To make the law	Congress	Houses of Parliament
Executing	Executive	To carry out the law	President and the federal bureaucracy	Prime minister and cabinet
Enforcing	Judiciary	To enforce and interpret the law	Supreme Court, Appeal Court and Trial Court	Criminal and civil courts, Court of Appeal and Supreme Court

The following diagram outlines how the separation of powers operates in the United States.

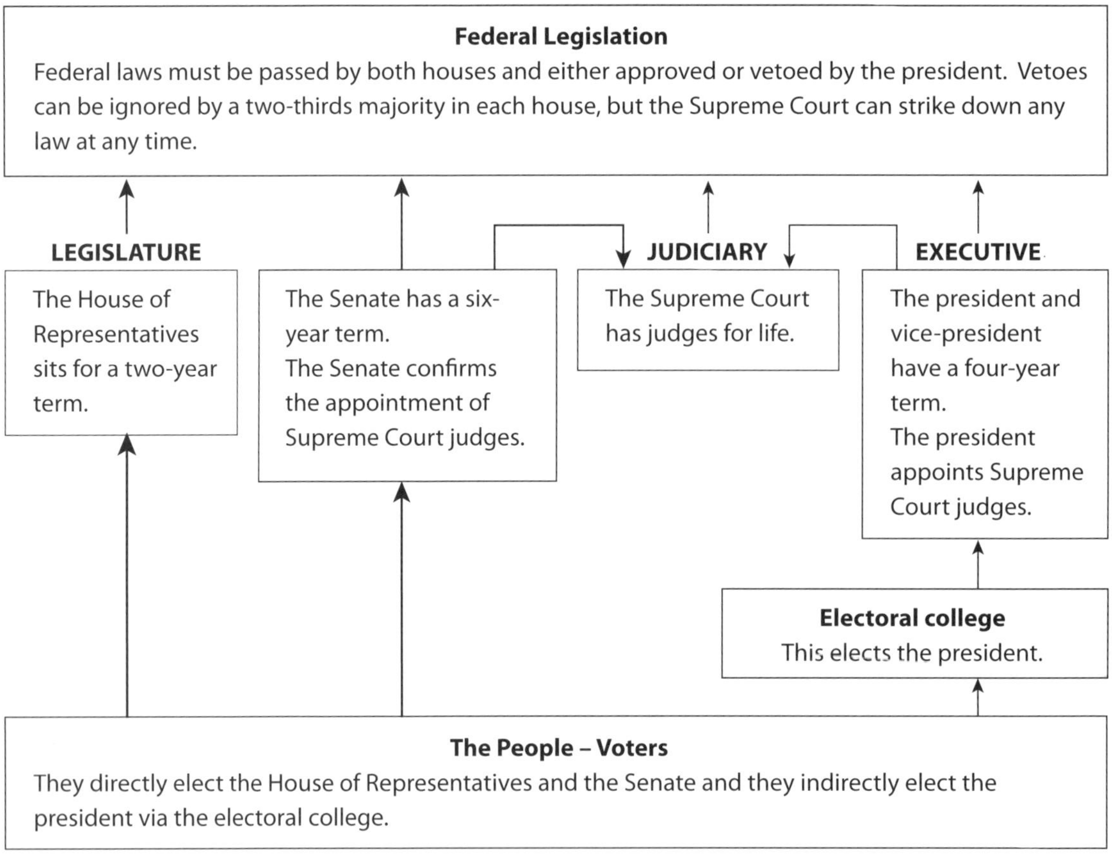

Federal Legislation
Federal laws must be passed by both houses and either approved or vetoed by the president. Vetoes can be ignored by a two-thirds majority in each house, but the Supreme Court can strike down any law at any time.

LEGISLATURE

The House of Representatives sits for a two-year term.

The Senate has a six-year term.
The Senate confirms the appointment of Supreme Court judges.

JUDICIARY

The Supreme Court has judges for life.

EXECUTIVE

The president and vice-president have a four-year term.
The president appoints Supreme Court judges.

Electoral college
This elects the president.

The People – Voters
They directly elect the House of Representatives and the Senate and they indirectly elect the president via the electoral college.

Although the Philadelphia Convention may have aimed to establish a separation of powers, it failed. The US government system is more accurately described as separate institutions that share power. Although the presidency, Congress and the courts are separate, they share their powers, which gives the US system a series of valuable checks and balances, so each can monitor and limit the powers and the actions of the other two.

Checks and balances in action

An example of the checks and balances in action occurred in 2007 over the war in Iraq. In the previous November, elections had brought a Democratic majority to both houses of Congress. On 10 January, President George W. Bush announced that he would be deploying over 20,000 more US troops in Iraq to deal with Sunni resistance. On 6 February, the House of Representatives passed a resolution disapproving of the decision. It was seen as the beginning of a move by Congress to prevent escalating military commitments in Iraq.

Checks and balances within the system

The way the US Constitution was created means that each of the three branches are dependent upon one another and must, therefore, cooperate. Without cooperation very little can be achieved. The Founding Fathers, in their desire to avoid creating a tyranny, made the president's power subject to sweeping checks and balances. This becomes increasingly complex when the majority in Congress and the president are from different political parties. This was the state of affairs between 1969 and 2001 and from 2006 to 2008. If Congress and the president cannot agree or cooperate then this can lead to **gridlock**. In 1995 President Clinton had enormous problems with the House of Representatives over the federal budget and this resulted in a temporary shutdown of federal government. Conflict between the majority in Congress and the president is frequent, even when they are from the same party, due to the relative weakness of the US party system; this weakness prevents the building of strong ties between the legislature and the executive.

Gridlock

This is a political stalemate, where it is difficult for either Congress or the president to create law. From 2006 to 2008 there was gridlock on issues of health care, Iraq and energy.

The different powers that each branch of government possesses creates the tendency towards making compromises in order to get government business done. These powers are indicated in the diagram.

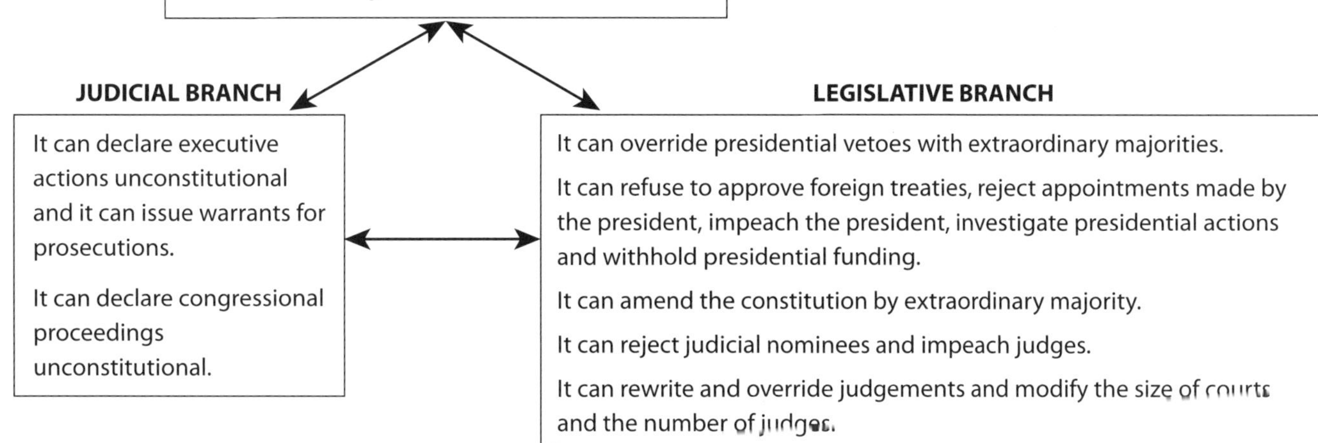

Many would argue that the US Constitution is deliberately inefficient, as each of the branches has particular powers and the powers that they have are both checked and limited by the other branches. By forcing each of the branches to be accountable to one another no one branch can gain enough power to become dominant.

Even the legislature (Congress) itself, because it has two houses (the Senate and the House of Representatives), is self-checking: bills have to be passed by both houses. The House of Representatives has the power to originate revenue bills and to impeach any official who has been accused of criminal behaviour. The Senate is responsible for rectifying treaties and approving presidential appointments, and for trying anyone who has been impeached.

1.3 Federal Constitutions

Learning objectives

- What is federalism?
- Federalism and the US Constitution
- The development of federalism

Länder system

This is a system in which powers are devolved to the separate states but in which the federal legislative remains supreme on national unity, identity, sovereignty and defence.

What is federalism?

Federalism is a political system that divides power between two tiers of government. In the US, Australia, Canada and India this means there is a federal government (national government) and state governments (subnational governments). In other words this means that there has been a degree of decentralisation. Again it reflects the nature of the compromises that were made in 1787 and in practice, as America has grown and more states have been added, it is an ideal form of government. On the one hand there is national unity through the federal or national government, yet there is diversity or regional identity through the power of the states.

It is important to note that each level of government is sovereign within its own sphere of influence. In fact the US system has many of the characteristics of the German **Länder system**.

Federalism and the US Constitution

Neither federal nor federalism is explicitly mentioned in the US Constitution, but it is implicit, as the following list explains.

- Articles I, II and III detail the precise powers of national government.
- The 10th Amendment (1791) reserves unlisted powers for the states or for the people.

As we have seen, the US Constitution was a compromise, as well as a reaction to what the colonists had seen as an autocratic, remote and centralised government that had controlled their lives until the War of Independence. The colonies had experimented with allowing states to rule their own affairs, but this was clearly a failure. The Constitution therefore represented a way in which national unity could be forged, while the freedoms and interests of each of the states could be protected. This means that there are a series of problems, as the arrangements were not exactly perfect.

- The states had to relinquish some of their powers to the new federal government. They could no longer print their own money, enter into treaties, levy taxes on imports and exports or have their own troops.
- The Constitution had to guarantee the rights of states, which meant that no matter how small in terms of population or size a state may be, it would have equal representation in the Senate. It also meant that the Constitution could not be changed unless three-quarters of the states agreed.
- In exchange for the guarantee of certain states' rights, states were expected to take responsibility. They had to recognise the laws of the other states and to grant other states leave to demand the return of fugitives.

Although, as we will see, the US Constitution is a written one, it is still a flexible one. There are no definitive lines of power between the federal and the state governments. As a result, the federal system has been able to develop over the years to cope with the shifting demands and complexities associated with a large country with a large number of semi-independent states. The key clause is Article I, which is often referred to as the Elastic Clause because it allows the relative powers of federal and state government to change (clauses such as the interstate commerce clause Article I Section 8 are referred to as elastic due to the scope for interpretation but not the article as a whole).

The development of federalism

Alexander Hamilton

James Madison

The concept of federalism was established in the *Federalist Papers* and early decisions by the Supreme Court. Alexander Hamilton wrote in the *Federalist Papers* No. 9:

> *This form of government is a convention by which several smaller states agree to become members of a larger one, which they intend to form. It is a kind of assemblage of societies that constitutes a new one, capable of increasing, by means of new associations, until they arrive to such a degree of power as to be able to provide for the security of the united body.*

James Madison wrote:

> *In the first place it is to be remembered that the general government is not to be charged with the whole power of making and administering laws. The subordinate governments, which can extend their care to all those other objects which can be separately provided for, will retain their due authority and activity.*

These writings, plus early judgements, such as McCulloch vs Maryland (1819), Gibbons vs Ogden (1824) and Fletcher vs Peck (1810), effectively set the course of federalism.

Throughout US history it has often been difficult to be clear about the lines that divide national or federal government and the states. In practice, the balance of powers between them is constantly changing, but at some points in time, it is possible to identify distinct periods or trends in federalism.

- Dual federalism, often known as 'layer-cake federalism', involves clearly enumerated powers between the national and state governments, and sovereignty in equal spheres. This was the relationship from the 1790s to 1930. The 13th, 14th and 15th amendments (1865–70) were attempts by the federal government to exert more influence on states. This type of federalism is characterised by national governments exerting their powers independently from state governments.
- Cooperative federalism, referred to as 'marble-cake federalism', involved the national and state governments sharing functions and collaborating on major national priorities. This was the relationship between 1930 and 1960. President Roosevelt's New Deal made federal government more intrusive. Local institutions were reformed and there was a federal relief and recovery programme as a result of the Great Depression. National governments would provide money and state governments would administer programmes. This cooperation existed until after the Second World War.
- Creative federalism, or 'picket-fence federalism', was dominant during the period of 1960 to 1980. This was characterised by overloaded cooperation and cross-cutting regulations. With increased civil rights legislation in the 1960s states were becoming more reliant on federally funded programmes. Federal and state governments would share costs, but the rules and guidelines were set by federal government and there was dual administration for programmes such as the US government-run health insurance programme, Medicaid.
- New federalism, critically referred to as 'on your own federalism', was characterised by further devolution of power from national to state governments and deregulation. There is also increased difficulty for states to fulfil their new mandates. This period began in 1981 and continues to the present. President Richard Nixon wanted to decentralise. He called it New

Fiscal federalism

Fiscal federalism involves the offer of money from the national government to the states in the form of grants to promote national ends such as public welfare, environmental standards and educational improvements.

Categorical grants, in which the national government provides money to the states for specific purposes, became a major policy tool of the national government during the New Deal era, and expanded rapidly during the 1960s' Great Society.

Beginning in the mid-1960s, block grants, which combined several categorical grants in broad policy areas into one general grant, became increasingly popular. States prefer block grants because they allow state officials to adapt the grants to their particular needs.

Revenue sharing was developed during the Nixon administration as a way to provide monies to states with no strings attached. Using statistical formulas to account for differences among states, the national government provided billions of dollars to the states until the programme was abolished in 1986.

Federalism, which was followed by President Ronald Reagan in 1980. The aim of competitive federalism was to give states more responsibility, providing they accepted conditions set upon them by the federal government. Large numbers of federal programmes had restrictions and required compliance in order to receive funding. An ideal example was that states had to agree highway speed limits in exchange for money to pay for the repairs of highways. Federal government provides a different range of grants to states, usually with strings attached. Funds are for specific purposes, but the state can decide where and how the money is spent. For example, welfare responsibility was transferred to the states, which then had to develop their own programmes to move people out of welfare and into work.

INTERNET RESEARCH

To see the scope and the powers of federal government in the United States, go to www.heinemann.co.uk/hotlinks, insert the express code 1825P and click on the relevant link. There is information on all types of funding and policy.

The following diagram shows the US system of dual federalism, the basis upon which many of the forms of federalism that have been introduced over the years. It indicates which powers are reserved for the federal and state governments, and which are shared by them, and how they have been constitutionally established.

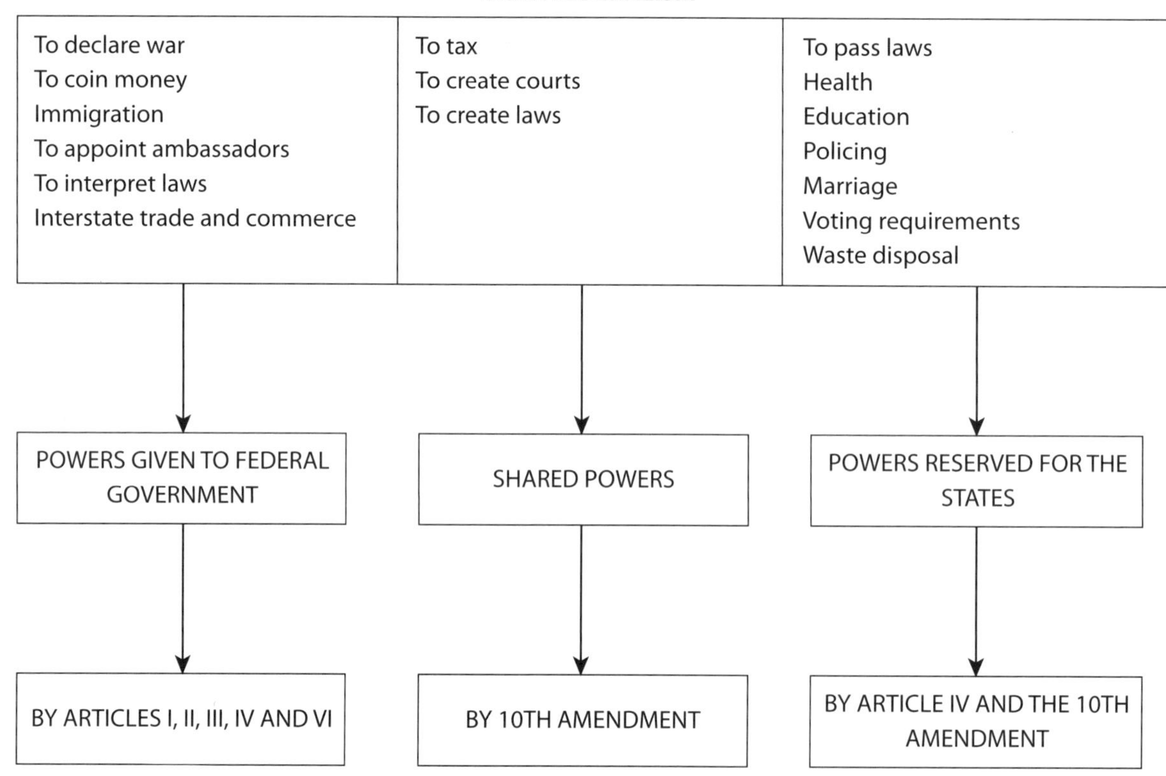

Learning objectives

- Unitary systems
- Federal and unitary constitutions
- Arguments for and against unitary, devolved and federal governments

Unitary systems

Unitary systems of government can be found in Britain, Norway, Sweden, Spain and France, among others. They differ in the level of concentration of power. Although the political power of government may have been transferred to lower levels of government, such as regional or local elected assemblies, or even devolved government, the central government retains the option to cancel and reassume this delegated power.

In unitary states, sub-governmental units can be created, abolished, have their powers varied or amended by central government. In effect, any national or regional governments may have devolved powers, but the scope of their powers can always be broadened or narrowed at the discretion of central government without the permission of those devolved units.

In a federal system, the states have constitutional protection, a series of clearly defined functions, and these cannot be changed unilaterally by central government. In the US, the federal government only has powers that have been allocated to it according to the Constitution. The situation is that the overarching governmental system is federal, while the states themselves are unitary. The states devolve power down to counties and municipalities, but this power can be taken back if the state sees fit.

Any of the devolved powers and laws that might emanate from a devolved unit can also be overridden by central government. In the case of the Scottish Parliament the following is the case.

- The Scottish Parliament cannot challenge the constitutional legality of laws passed by the national parliament in Westminster.
- If Westminster sees fit, it can override legislation passed by the Scottish Parliament.
- If Westminster sees fit, it can either revoke or reduce the powers devolved to the Scottish Parliament (in fact the prime minister also has this ability).

The White House, Washington DC, the centre of US presidential power

The situation is altogether different for Northern Ireland. It has devolved powers, but these powers can (and have been) suspended by Westminster or the executive.

These are examples of situations when different regions of a country are given different levels of power and status, or asymmetric devolution. In a federation such as the US, devolution is symmetrical as each of the states has the same powers and the same status.

Federal and unitary constitutions

Prior to the creation of the US Constitution political systems tended to be unitary, which meant that political power was at the centre of the system. The US Constitution separated sovereignty and had constituent states and a central authority. This federal approach can now be seen in Germany, India, Australia, Belgium and Russia. In Europe the Scandinavian countries are perhaps the best examples of unitary states. Spain and Great Britain lie somewhere between the unitary and federal, as in these countries power has been devolved to local assemblies, giving them some independence while retaining a central sovereignty. Spain is perhaps closer to being federal as it has autonomous regions such as Catalonia. To a lesser extent France and Italy have also done this.

Britain, however, is one of the more complex examples, as the degree of devolution differs in various parts of the country. Scotland has considerable power, including the ability to make primary legislation and to vary income tax. The Welsh Assembly has nowhere near that amount of power. England has no assembly of its own, but there is a London Assembly and a London mayor with executive power. The Isle of Man has its own parliament, taxes and currency, as do the Channel Islands. They are not represented in the British parliament, but Britain manages their foreign relations.

Even the European Union is not a true federal system and neither is it a confederacy. The member states have their own sovereignty, but more and more of their power is being surrendered to the European Union. The European Court of Justice, the EU version of a Supreme Court, focuses on interpreting the Constitution (although there is no constitution), but more clearly ensures that member states observe treaties. The European Commission can make decisions that bind member states and there is no clear way in which member states can withdraw from the European Union, although a simple of Act of parliament would be sufficient.

While in Europe there has been a movement of power from the centre to the periphery, this has also been reflected in the US where states have taken on a greater role, although federal government is still important.

Arguments for and against unitary, devolved and federal governments

Federal states usually involve a full constitutional sharing of powers and coexistence of sovereignties. It is invariably the case that the regional government consists of an elected parliament and will have limited budgetary powers. Crucially, it cannot be abolished or restructured by the central government.

Unitary states in devolving have a directly elected tier of regional government with constitutional status. They will have a measure of autonomy and legislative powers. They tend to be financed by central government even though they may have limited tax revenue raising powers. The main difference from federal states is the absence of a set of exclusive competencies and a sovereignty protected by constitutional status. In classic unitary states, the power tends to remain at the centre, with administrative functions only at regional level.

There are many differing views on devolved, federal and unitary government. The key points are outlined in the following table.

INTERNET RESEARCH

There is useful material on the functioning of the European Union and the relative powers of each of the institutions. To see this, go to heinemann.co.uk/hotlinks, insert the express code 1825P and click on the relevant link.

View	Key points
Pro-federal government	Federalism deals with the problem in large countries where government seems remote. People with cultural or ethnic differences can enjoy a level of relative self-government while being part of a larger country, for example the Quebecois in Canada. It is a compromise between economic and military advantages. There is structure, interdependence yet diversity. Sub-national governments can tackle new and innovative approaches to policy without affecting the whole country (so-called laboratories of democracy).
Anti-federal government	It is difficult to create a national policy where views may differ widely across the different states. In the 1950s and 1960s US states made use of the 10th Amendment and their independence to hold back on giving African-Americans civil rights. What may be legal in one state may not be legal in another, which causes confusion. It is difficult to be sure which level of government is responsible for successes and failures. A handful of states can block reforms. National political parties can be weak.
Pro-devolution government	It allows distinct communities to govern themselves. It retains unitary government and the advantages and the central government can address inequalities.
Anti-devolution government	There can be conflict over policies, particularly in revenue raising and economic management. The laws will differ.
Pro-unitary government	Forming national policies is simpler. Economic issues and redistribution can be more easily handled. There are no political or legal confusions. There can be national responses. There is clear accountability.
Anti-unitary government	Minorities seldom have the ability to express themselves. Local issues can be ignored. Central government can reorganise political institutions as they please. Political parties can dominate areas in which they have little or no support.

Learning objectives

- The Constitution and amendments
- How amendments happen and why

Thomas Jefferson was elected president by the House of Representatives on 17 February 1801, after a tie with Aaron Burr in the electoral college.

The Constitution and amendments

Back in the latter part of the 18th century the US Constitution applied to some 3.5 million people in a handful of states. Now it applies to a highly industrialised, wealthy world power with almost a hundred times more people than it had over 200 years ago. The 17 amendments to the Constitution that have been accepted are not as significant as the changes in the interpretation of the Constitution. In fact two of the amendments cancel one another out.

Arguably the most important amendment was the 12th, which aimed to simplify the election of the electoral college, and was born out of an impasse when there was a tie between the presidential candidates Thomas Jefferson and Aaron Burr in the electoral college in 1800. The House of Representatives, after a number of ballots, declared Jefferson the winner. The 12th Amendment established how things would work from then on; that there would be a run-off election in the House of Representatives and that the votes for the president and vice-president were combined.

The electoral college system still favours the larger states and any talk of reforming the system is always a hot and current topic. However, the mechanism as it stands is likely to remain, as there are only two main parties in the United States.

Some of the amendments to the Constitution have focused on improving the democratic element of the Constitution, such as the 15th Amendment extending voting rights to all races. Others amendments, such as the 22nd, limited individuals from holding the presidential office for more than two terms. The powers of the federal government have also been affected by amendments. The 13th Amendment imposed federal power over states that permitted slavery, the 14th imposed a Bill of Rights and the 16th gave federal government the power to introduce a national income tax.

Changes in the interpretation of the Constitution tend to reflect how America and its economy have developed, rather than what the actual wording of the Constitution is. There have been four key areas of change in how the Constitution has been interpreted.

- The assertion of federal over state power.
- The assertion of the executive over the legislative.
- The way in which the Supreme Court has become the final arbiter of the Constitution.
- The way that federal government takes a lead in the protection of individual rights.

The first two were not intended by the Founding Fathers. The third was probably implied and the fourth was not an issue considered by the Founding Fathers in 1787.

In the US, the federal government is involved in every part of the affairs of the nation. The 10th Amendment stated: 'The powers not delegated to the United States by the Constitution, nor prohibited by it to the states, are reserved to the states respectively, or to the people.'

However, it has been the federal government that has taken the powers, not the states. The US government has become larger, more centralised and more concentrated, specifically in the executive rather than the legislature. This has also been a trend in many countries that have grown quickly, both economically and socially. However, there is still inertia and although the 13th and 14th amendments outlawed slavery and discrimination, the Supreme Court did not enforce the 14th Amendment until after the Second World War.

Institutions and processes have evolved in the US that could not have been predicted when the Constitution was written. Political mobilisation is driven by political parties, interest groups have enormous political power and influence, and public opinion is moulded by a sophisticated media. Those relationships between institutions have changed, but the Constitution retains the separation of powers between Congress and the presidency. Congress is still independent, as are the courts, and the states are still important as political units even though they are less autonomous and more interdependent.

The way in which politics is conducted in America does not reflect badly on the Constitution. The gradual erosion of the powers of the states has far more to do with their inability to deal with social and economic issues as separate units.

The Founding Fathers understood they had to create a document that stood the test of time and produced good government that reconciled differences between competing groups and interests. This is not to say that the Constitution will never change; some believe that the division of power between the executive and the legislature is too inefficient and confrontational, yet it survives more or less intact and is seen as a success by many.

The Supreme Court and constitutional amendments

The US Constitution is also influenced by the courts, particularly the Supreme Court which has made decisions in the past that have now become precedents in law. A prime example is the Marbury vs Madison case in 1803 which established the concept and practice of judicial review. In this, the court has the right to look at legislation and Acts of Congress and then assess their relationship with the Constitution and how they will be applied in practice. In effect, these interpretations (such as the rights of the accused in criminal cases) have affected the understanding and the application of constitutional clauses, but not the text of them.

How amendments happen and why

The US Constitution can only ever be amended after a long and involved deliberation. Article V of the Constitution states:

> *The Congress, whenever two-thirds of both houses shall deem it necessary, shall propose amendments to this constitution, or, on the application of the legislatures of two-thirds of the several states, shall convene a convention for proposing amendments, which in either case shall be valid to all intents and purposes as part of this constitution, when ratified by the legislatures of three-fourths of the several states, or by conventions in three-fourths thereof, as one or other mode of ratification may be proposed by Congress.*

In fact no national constitutional convention has ever been summoned. Of the 27 amendments to the Constitution, 26 of them have been brought about by congressional action and state legislature ratification. The 21st Amendment repealed the 18th and this too was proposed by Congress and ratified by state conventions.

The following list shows some examples of amendments that were considered to be inappropriate.

- 1878 – the abolition of the office of president and the replacement with an executive council of three
- 1914 – prohibition of divorce
- 1916 – acts of war should be put to the national vote and all of those that vote in favour of the war should be registered as a volunteer for services in the US armed forces
- 1938 – drunkenness in the United States to be forbidden
- 1947 – an individual's income should be taxed at a rate of no more than 25 per cent.

INTERNET RESEARCH

The full text of the US Constitution and the 27 constitutional amendments can be found as original documents. To see this, go to heinemann.co.uk/hotlinks, insert the express code 1825P and click on the relevant link. Click on 'Exhibits' and select 'Charters of Freedom'.

1.6 The Constitution and Checks and Balances

Learning objectives

- Why is the US Constitution so rarely amended?
- What are the checks and balances between the president and Congress and the dangers of gridlock?
- What constitutional checks and balances exist in different political systems?

Why is the US Constitution so rarely amended?

As we know, many thousands of amendments have been proposed to the US Constitution, but there have only been 27 amendments to it since 1787. The US Constitution has survived over 200 years of rapid and significant change, in terms of the economy, technology, population and immigration, wars and industrialisation. The Constitution and the principles upon which it was based still remain largely intact.

US Senator Robert C. Byrd (2006) said: 'Given the hurdles that were deliberately established by Article V, it is no surprise that so few amendments to the Constitution have been approved.'

Although the US Constitution is written, it is a flexible document that at 7000 words is short and full of what is known as elastic clauses. Because it is so short it does not go into massive detail and is not prescriptive, allowing it to be flexible.

Some key Supreme Court decisions that illustrate the reason why amendments are unnecessary when interpretations can cope with changing circumstances are listed below.

Case	Constitutional implications
Marbury vs Madison (1803)	This was a landmark case that established the exercise of judicial reviews in the United States, under Article III of the US constitution.
Brown vs Board of Education (1954)	This declared that 'separated educational facilities are inherently unequal'. Separate schooling for ethnic groups was seen to be in violation of the 14th Amendment (constitutional rights and equal protection).
Gideon vs Wainwright (1963)	This established that state courts are required under the 6th Amendment to provide a defence lawyer in criminal cases where the defendant cannot afford their own lawyer.
Miranda vs Arizona (1966)	This ruled that unless a suspect is made aware of the consequences, a confession is not admissible in court under the 5th Amendment (self-incrimination clause) and the 6th Amendment (right to a lawyer). Evidence is only admissible if the suspect has waived these rights.
US vs Katz (1967)	This extended the 4th Amendment from unreasonable search and seizure to protect people using public telephones from wire tapping (eavesdropping).
Reno vs ACLU (1996)	This ruled that the Communications Decency Act (1996), which had sought to regulate material on the internet, was in fact an unconstitutional abridgement of the 1st and 5th amendments. It confirmed that the Act had violated the 1st Amendment's guarantee of freedom of speech.
Hamdan vs Rumsfeld (2004)	This was an important ruling on executive power. The Supreme Court invalidated President Bush's system of trying accused war criminals at Guantanamo Bay in Cuba.

It was clear that when the US Constitution was written that the Founding Fathers wanted the underlying principles to be difficult to reform. It requires two-thirds of the House of Representatives and of the Senate, plus three-quarters of the states themselves, to approve an amendment. This is often incredibly difficult. There have been numerous attempts to push through the Equal Rights Amendment since the 1980s. It had originally been written in 1923. This is possibly due to the fragmented nature of Congress.

Some of the amendments, such as the 18th, have been adopted and then required another amendment (21st) to reject them. The US is cautious about all amendment proposals and it is the role of the Supreme Court to provide new interpretations of the Constitution to maintain the flexibility and to avoid the need for amendments.

What are the checks and balances between the president and Congress and the dangers of gridlock?

The Constitution clearly defines three separate branches of government, along with their powers and how positions in each are filled. The system of checks and balances aims to ensure the distribution of powers between the three branches. In other words, each branch can exercise some power over the others.

Justices in the Supreme Court (the judiciary) are appointed by the president (the executive), but their appointments must have the consent of the US Senate (legislative). On a number of occasions the Supreme Court has also struck down unconstitutional laws that have been passed by Congress and approved by the president.

The first 10 amendments of the Constitution (or Bill of Rights) aim to guarantee the key freedoms to American citizens, including the freedom of speech, press and religion, trial by jury and the right to be free from unreasonable search. The Constitution guarantees these rights and powers of the people. It limits the power that the executive and the legislature have at all levels. If a law or part of a law is judged by the Supreme Court to be in conflict with the Constitution it is struck down.

The states also have key provisions and powers, and the power of the federal government is limited only to those areas that have been granted to it by the Constitution (national defence, creating money, immigration and naturalisation, and foreign treaties). This does not mean that the federal government does not have the power to influence states. In the 1970s it threatened to withhold money for road projects if states did not agree to lower speed limits.

In the US there is often political gridlock, as bills stall because either side will not compromise. Larry Sabato, the director the University of Virginia's Center for Politics, said: 'Gridlock is not necessarily a bad thing. It limits government and party excesses.'

This is often the state of affairs when the president represents one party and the majority of Congress another party. A prime example was President Bush's proposals to bolster the financial markets with an unprecedented rescue plan in September and October 2008. The bill was rejected initially by the House of Representatives, but then as the financial markets plummeted once more and there was greater uncertainty, the $700 billion plan was amended and accepted.

INTERNET RESEARCH

There are a number of articles and opinions related to checks, balances and gridlock in the US. To see these, go to heinemann.co.uk/hotlinks, insert the express code 1825P and click on the relevant link. Use the search engine to find current stories.

What constitutional checks and balances exist in different political systems?

There are a number of different models of political systems around the world in which checks and balances can be observed. The following table outlines the key ones.

Country	Checks and balances in political systems
EU	There are five main parts: the European Commission is executive, the Council of Ministers is both legislative and executive, the European Parliament is legislative, the European Court of Justice is judicial and the European Court of Auditors is auditory and independent.
France	Government agencies and the civil service are controlled by the cabinet, but some agencies are independent and excluded from the executive's authority, even though they are part of the executive branch. These agencies have regulatory powers, executive power and some judicial power. The executive branch, for example, includes the president and the government, the legislative national assembly and senate, and the judicial order, administrative order and constitutional council.
Germany	This has six branches: the federal president and cabinet executive, the federal diet and federal council, which are legislative, the federal assembly which is the presidential electoral college, the federal constitutional court and the judicial branch with five supreme courts and state-based courts.
Australia	Ministers must sit in parliament, so they have both executive and legislative powers. The Australian constitution specifically identifies parliament, executive government and the judiciary, each with powers along with checks and balances.
People's Republic of China	The National People's Congress is the highest state body and the only legislative house. The president and vice-president are elected by this congress. Judges of the Supreme People's Court are also appointed by congress and governors of provinces and autonomous regions are appointed by central government (state council) after receiving consent from congress.

The US has a codified constitution and it can be considered to be sovereign and the highest authority. It is the supreme law. Enshrined within the US Constitution are principles such as separation of powers and checks and balances. It is arguable whether there are more than four key principles of the US Constitution, but certainly they could be taken to be the following.

Popular sovereignty – it is the people who hold the ultimate authority and the representative democracy allows the people to elect leaders to make decisions on their behalf.
Limited government – the framers of the Constitution were keen to ensure that the country was guarded against tyranny. As a result the government is limited to the power that is given to them by the Constitution. The Constitution also explicitly states how leaders can be removed if they overstep their power.
Federalism – this indicates the division of power between state and the national government. Although the national government has supreme power some powers are shared.
Separation of powers – no one branch holds an overwhelming amount of power. The legislature makes the laws, the executive carries out the laws and the judiciary interprets the laws.

It is important to appreciate that the US Constitution is far more than a single document. It can be at times rigid and at other times flexible. It incorporates innumerable laws, administrative and judicial decisions, customs and habits. Formal amendments are possible but these require a two-third majority vote from each house. This formal amendment process has allowed the Constitution to develop or evolve, but there have only been a handful of these amendments, which shows the inherent flexibility of the Constitution itself and how it has been interpreted in different ways over time.

There has of course been informal growth and amendment, with legislation enacted by Congress or by state legislatures, which has placed emphasis on particular features of the Constitution. There have been executive and administrative actions, which have also altered the emphasis or interpretation of the law. Judicial decisions have also played an important role and these have made significant changes to the Constitution. All law, once executed, is subject to being challenged and brought before the courts for interpretation in connection with a case. In the US each of these judgements is a step in the development of the Constitution.

Separation of Powers

Learning objectives

- Discuss whether American government is best described as a system of separated powers or shared powers.
- Is the US still federal?

Discuss whether American government is best described as a system of separated powers or shared powers

The US Constitution sets up a federal system that divides power between both national and state governments, as well as separating the power among the three independent branches: the executive, the legislative and the judiciary.

The executive branch, or the president, enforces national laws, Congress as the legislative branch makes national laws and the Supreme Court and other federal courts, as the judicial branch, both apply and interpret the laws in deciding legal disputes.

The idea is that the separation of power protects both liberty and democracy. The three elements slow down the process of law-making and enforcement, so as to protect against excessive executive power.

Back in 1885 President Woodrow Wilson warned that it would be difficult for the executive and the legislature, in their attempts to cooperate and have confidence in one another, to avoid colluding with one another.

According to Richard Neustadt, an American political scientist, the constitutional convention of 1787 did not create a government of separated powers. In his view it actually created a government of separated institutions that shared power.

At that Philadelphia Convention no one really knew how much separation there should be. Some prerogatives that now rest with the president were originally with Congress. Originally the judiciary would be chosen by the legislature, but then it became the role solely of the Senate.

Justice Robert H. Jackson, the former US Attorney General, suggested that the Constitution diffuses power in order to secure liberty, the assumption being that in working practice it will integrate those dispersed powers, so that government is workable. It also aims to ensure that the branches are separate but interdependent, autonomous but reliant on the mutual exchange of privileges.

Alexander Hamilton, writing in the *Federalist Papers*, said that separation was 'entirely compatible with partial intermixture' and that overlapping was 'proper, but necessary to the mutual defense of the several members of the government, against each other'.

When the first Congress debated what would become the Bill of Rights it actually rejected a proposal that would have strictly allocated power among the three branches.

Some might say that the separation of powers and the system of checks and balances are irreconcilable and contradictory, but they do actually support one another. None of the three institutions can check on another unless it has some independence and it cannot keep that independence unless it has the ability to check.

Over time the Supreme Court has not been so sure about the sharing of power. In 1974 it said that the power that federal courts had by virtue of Article III of the Constitution 'can no more be shared with the executive branch than the chief executive, for example, can share with the judiciary the veto power, or the Congress share with the judiciary the power to override a presidential veto'.

Separation is clear in Article I Section 6: no member of Congress can hold an appointed office. Each branch has exclusive powers. The president's exclusive powers are the power to nominate, negotiate with foreign countries and to pardon. But this does not mean that the executive powers can operate without legislative support. Congress can limit all three powers. Foreign policy and shared powers is a potentially complex mix.

- The president negotiates treaties with overseas nations, subject to advice and the consent of the Senate.
- Treaties only come into force if they are ratified by two-thirds of the Senate.
- The president is commander-in-chief of the US armed forces, but Congress has the sole authority to declare war.
- The US Secretary of State and US ambassadors are appointed by the president and are instrumental in diplomacy. The Senate assists the president in making appointments through advice and consent, but it is Congress that has the power to regulate trade deals.

Is the US still federal?

Although the term federal, or federalism, was never used in the US Constitution, there is a sense that the Founding Fathers wanted to create a balance between central government and the states. For a significant period of time the federal government was the junior partner in the relationship between states and federal affairs. The two world wars and the Great Depression can be seen as having contributed to the growth in federal government. During the Great Depression the federal government claimed vast new powers and created hundreds of programmes.

There are numerous examples where federal government cannot provide a solution. After the attack on the Twin Towers, the federal government took control of airport security. It was a disaster and costs increased by over 700 per cent. Private companies did a better job. Federal government spends a staggering $2,500,000,000,000 (2005) per year, which suggests that it is involved in an enormous number of projects and activities that would have at one point in time been under the control of individual states. There is an enormous federal bureaucracy: an estimated 17 million Americans work directly or indirectly for the federal government.

Federalism in the United States has been defined in different ways throughout its history. Layer-cake federalism and marble-cake federalism are two examples.

Layer-cake federalism is often referred to as dual federalism. The way it operated was that the federal government played a limited role and the states had considerable antonomy. It is so-called because the separate roles of the federal and state governments were rather like a layer-cake. The period when it operated is usually taken to be from the 1790s to the 1920s.

Out of the Wall Street Crash of the late 1920s and the Great Depression there emerged greater cooperation between the federal government and the state government. This was known as marble-cake federalism, which is often referred to as cooperative federalism. It's aim was to try to solve social problems such as poverty and unemployment. It led to the creation of the Federal Health and Welfare Department in 1953 and the Housing Department in 1965. It became an important part of the apparatus of government and by the 1990s the states were receiving federal funds in excess of $200,000,000,000 each year.

American Federalism – Marble-cake or Layer-cake?

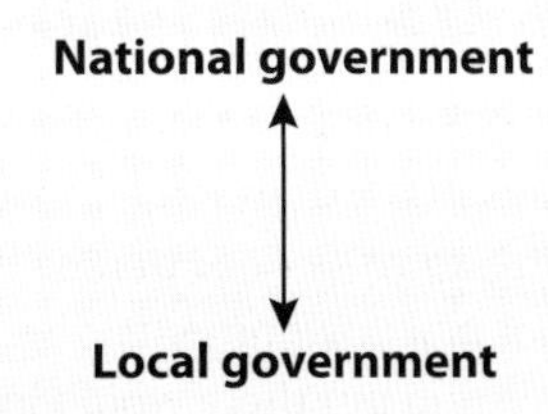

Marble-cake federalism: authority and programmes arise from multiple interactions between national, state and local governments

Layer-cake federalism: no interactions and clear delineation of authority and programmes between the levels of government

There have been a number of stages at which the question as to whether or not the US is still federal has been asked. Civil rights legislation saw a shift away from state power, however Richard Nixon, the president in the early1970s, tried to reverse the shift towards federal government. He largely failed but since the 1980s there have been changes. President Reagan cut grants to states from federal government. He attempted to give states more power. States were now taxing more and spending more. President Clinton, in 1996, ended the federal commitment to minimum incomes for the poor, which had existed since being introduced by the New Deal in the 1930s.

Some believe that while there has been an increase in state power it has been offset by an increase in federal power. The federal government in recent years has imposed cross-state driving licence laws, extended the scope of federal crimes and introduced federal education law.

The US could be considered to not be totally federal, and the relationship between the states and the federal government is always likely to change over time.

For many years federal support paid for infrastructure projects and initiatives at state level. But this has declined in favour of block grants given to states, who can then, within limitations, distribute the funds. The Federal Emergency Management Agency (FEMA) was an independent organisation that had direct access to the president. But after the attack on the Twin Towers it reported to Homeland Security, showing a shift in the role of federal government. Also multi-level governance through the federal system has been shown to be ineffective in dealing with natural disasters and their aftermath, such as Hurricane Katrina, which struck New Orleans in August 2005.

INTERNET RESEARCH

Good places to look for examples of state independence, particularly in courts, are the US vs Lopez case, which argued that federal law regulating firearms in schools was unconstitutional, and the US vs Printz, which challenged the constitutional nature of the Brady Handgun Violence Prevention Act (1993). Go to the National Center for Public Policy Research. To do this, go to heinemann.co.uk/hotlinks, insert the express code 1825P and click on the relevant link and use the search tool.

1.8 Resilience and Reform of Constitutions

Learning objectives

- Why is the US Constitution so resilient?
- Should constitutions be difficult to reform?

Why is the US Constitution so resilient?

In September 2005 US Secretary of State Condoleezza Rice suggested that one of the best things that the writers of the draft Iraqi Constitution had done was leave room for that nation's next elected assembly to write rules that will further define the respective roles of a central government and regional governments. She went on to add that the new Constitution was based on a federal system but there would inevitably be debate as to what that actually meant. It was her opinion that any definition of the precise nature of the Constitution had to be left to the Iraqis themselves. She then pointed out that the US Constitution was amended numerous times since its initial approval and that the Iraqi Constitution will also likely evolve over time.

President Bush also drew parallels between the framing of the Iraq Constitution and the US Constitution by noting that it was a difficult process that had involved an enormous amount of debate and ultimately compromise. He made the point that the US Constitutional Convention had seen political rivalry and regional disagreements. In the end, what came out of the Convention was not and had never intended to be the definitive word on the Constitution and that it was amended on several subsequent occasions. By implication, he suggested that this would be the case with the Iraqi Constitution.

The 1781 Articles of Confederation had left most power to the 13 states, so much so that they operated almost like independent countries. When the War of Independence ended, the US had a unicameral Congress and no president. It was also flawed because Congress could not raise taxes or enforce the law. Congress and the US were powerless until there was a call for state delegates to meet in Philadelphia in 1787 'to devise such further provisions as shall appear to them necessary to render the constitution of the federal government adequate to the exigencies of the Union'.

Most of the delegates were lawyers, farmers or merchants, with differing political philosophies and agendas, there were no women, African-Americans or men without property. There were disputes and compromises lasting nearly four months. The key compromise was proposed by Connecticut's Roger Sherman. He suggested that each state have one vote in a Senate, and the population would determine the number of representatives in a House of Representatives.

Since it was created, the US Constitution has proved to be a dynamic document, which over time has been amended to suit the needs of the country while retaining its principles. The Bill of Rights in 1789 introduced the first 10 amendments to the Constitution, but in all there have only been 27 amendments, that range from granting women the right to vote and prohibiting slavery.

Some of the key reasons why the Constitution has been so resilient and has been allowed to evolve rather than rewritten as circumstances change can be found in the table opposite.

Key reason	Resilience of Constitution
Based on popular consent	The Constitution, with its explicit reference to its being ordained by 'We the people', stands for government based on popular consent.
Invalidating unconstitutional laws	The Constitution declares that it, and laws enacted 'in pursuance thereof', shall be the 'supreme law of the land'. Implemented by judicial review, the courts' power to invalidate laws was found to be in conflict with the Constitution. This ensures that constitutional guarantees protect minority rights and liberty even against democratically elected majorities.
The text itself	The Constitution aims to balance society's need for order with individual liberty. The separation of powers and checks and balances, enable the apportionment of real power and authority among the executive, the legislative and judicial branches of government.
Compromise	The Constitution created a central government with sufficient power, while preserving citizens' ability to address local issues at the local level. Retaining state and local governments as well as the structure of a federal government has largely managed to balance national and local needs.

Should constitutions be difficult to reform?

US system

Amending the US Constitution is difficult and has only taken place 27 times since it was written. An example of calls for reform and amendment is that of the electoral college. The close presidential contest between Republican George W. Bush and Democrat Al Gore in Florida in 2000 and its impact on the outcome stimulated calls for reform of the electoral college. Many Democrats are of the opinion that the loss of their candidate in the 2000 presidential election shows the urgent need for reform; Al Gore received 500,000 more votes than George W. Bush and still lost. Republicans view efforts to change the system as an effort to discredit the victory of their candidate. Despite some support across party lines, there is no consensus in favour of reform.

When the US Constitution was written, there was a clear awareness that changes to the Constitution might be needed from time to time. Built into the Constitution was a system that would not allow quick and easy, and perhaps ill-conceived, changes. On the other hand, a system was put in place to try to ensure that it was clear that if changes to the Constitution were demanded by the bulk of the population, that this too could happen. In other words, two ways were created to change the Constitution.

Amendments need to be proposed and then ratified, regardless of the route. Although there are two routes by which the US Constitution can be amended, only one way has been used to date. This has been by achieving a two-thirds majority in both houses of Congress. The other route, requiring two-thirds of the state legislatures to approve the amendment at a Constitutional Convention, has not been used and it is unclear exactly how this might work if it ever became the case.

Assuming that the amendment is proposed and passed in Congress, it still needs to be approved by three-quarters of the states (ratification). Depending on the nature of the amendment, either the state legislatures or special state conventions are needed to approve the amendment by a majority vote. In all of the 27 amendments, only the 21st Amendment has ever called for special state conventions.

When an amendment is ratified it is appended to the existing Constitution and does not alter or delete what is already there. The US Constitution does not have a process in place to delete text and that includes text that relates to material that is contradicted or rescinded by newer amendments.

In Finley vs US (1989) the Supreme Court expressed the interest 'that Congress be able to legislate against a background of clear interpretive rules, so that it may know the effect of the language it adopts'. The Supreme Court will have to interpret the meaning of any statutes and will make presumptions as to the meaning. Executive Order 12988 (1996) provides guidance to executive agencies on preparing legislation. It gives them a checklist of topics and alerts them to the fact that court decisions are often made at variance with the intention of the legislation because there is unclear statutory guidance. When the court interprets statutes it does recognise that legislative power remains with Congress. It is aware that Congress can legislate away interpretations with which the court disagrees. Congress can revisit statutory issues to override or counter the court's interpretation. However this can be a lengthy and time-consuming process, so it is in Congress's interest to ensure that the intent is clear from the outset.

Judicial review is probably the US Supreme Court's most potent power. In just two centuries it has overturned in whole or in part over 1500 laws and ordnances passed by elected bodies in the United States as being unconstitutional. Approximately 155 of these laws were congressional statutes.

The dominant trend across the Supreme Court's history is actually one of supporting Congress (the 1960s and 1990s were notable decades when they did not do this). Many of the cases that they have nullified or reversed relate to civil rights and the 1st Amendment.

For more on the Supreme Court and the Constitution, see Topic 5.8, pages 235–36.

British system

In Britain, we have an uncodified constitution, which means that there is no single document. Britain has a series of documents, conventions, and Acts of parliament, EU directives and documents relating to devolution. In Britain, it is now the role of the Ministry of Justice to put forward ideas for constitutional reform, its aims being:

- to invigorate our democracy, with citizens given the means to participate in decision-making at every level
- to clarify the role of government, both central and local
- to rebalance power between parliament and government, and give parliament greater ability to hold government to account
- to give the British people a stronger sense of what it means to be British, and to include them in a debate on the future of the country's constitution.

In late 2008, a draft Constitutional Renewal Bill was released containing a series of proposed reforms that aim to renew Britain's constitutional arrangements. The reforms would limit the government's power on certain matters and hand more power to parliament.

Written and Unwritten Constitutions

Is there nothing to be gained from a written constitution?

It is highly unlikely that the British Constitution will be written down in the foreseeable future. There appears to be no significant support for a written constitution among the major political parties, nor among the electorate. If it was ever written down, the British Constitution would need to be sufficiently short and clear so that the powers, constraints, processes, procedures and structures could be understood by most people. As it is there is considerable ambiguity about the current rules and there is likely to be a good deal of disagreement as to which rules to write down and which to leave to tradition or convention. The risk is that the constitution would be an extensive and unwieldy document that would be too complex for many to understand.

For Britain to have a written constitution would involve setting up a body of people with the knowledge, expertise and trustworthiness to ensure that the constitution document would be drawn up free from political party, or any other special interests, influence and would be properly embedded in an appropriate legal framework.

The British Constitution, unlike that of the US one or the rejected European one, is unwritten. Supporters of the unwritten constitution suggest that it allows flexibility and change. Those in favour of a written constitution suggest that it should be codified so that it is accessible and understandable to the public, so that they don't have to rely on constitutional experts in order to understand and interpret it. It is also pointed out that amendments to the unwritten constitution are carried out in a very similar way to those of written ones. Both houses of parliament would have to approve it (by a simple majority) and it would have to gain royal assent – this is a markedly different process to that of presidential approval.

If the only purpose of a constitution is to create a framework within which government functions, incorporating how it functions and what powers it has been given, then that framework could over time become outdated and inappropriate.

If a nation has a flexible constitution, whether it is written or unwritten, then the role of government and its powers can be kept up to date. The political system will have a chance to develop, and not be fixed or trapped in outdated ways that are no longer appropriate. In the 1990s, New Zealand's Constitution allowed for the electoral system to be updated. In recent years, the British Constitution allowed for the creation of devolved assemblies. In the US, with its written constitution, there are difficulties over foreign policy, for example. The Senate must approve (with a two-thirds majority) treaties with other nations. Congress, however, has the power to deploy the US military in a declaration of war. The root of this system dates back to the 18th century when shared responsibility was thought to be the most important aspect of the Constitution. This is no longer the case and the executive could seek more power to make foreign policy.

A written constitution should mean that it is difficult to change aspects of the political system that were expedient at the time it was conceived, which in the longer term became injurious to the country and its people. An independent judiciary, especially a Supreme Court or equivalent (such as Germany's Constitutional Court), can rule on whether any measure taken by the legislature or the executive is in contravention to the constitution.

Where there is no written constitution as such, elements of the constitution, including the rights, liberties and freedoms of the individual, can be taken apart piecemeal by a government and not

Learning objectives

- Is there nothing to be gained from a written constitution?
- Are the important features of a constitution to be found in statutes, conventions and judicial precedence?

Framing the EU Constitution

Those drafting the EU Constitution compared themselves with the Founding Fathers who held a convention in Philadelphia in 1787 to work out the constitutional foundation of the United States. Debate over the US Constitution raged at all levels and was thoroughly analysed and dissected. The EU Constitution was written by a group of constitutional experts led by a former French president, Valery Giscard D'Estaing, who had a reputation for not being swayed by public opinion. It is clear that opposing views on the Constitution were ignored and there was no public debate.

be considered as unconstitutional, as it would be if there was a written constitution. An example is the Criminal Justice and Public Order Act (1994), which was seen as a major attack on human rights in Britain. Under it, suspects who remained silent when questioned by the police could find when they were brought to trial their non-cooperation being brought to the attention of the court. Had this Act been proposed in the US, the Supreme Court would have rejected it as being unconstitutional as it breached the 5th Amendment.

Are the important features of a constitution to be found in statutes, conventions and judicial precedence?

Not having a single written constitutional document means that the various rules and principles that determine the British political system have been derived from a number of different sources created at different times. The sources include prerogative powers, judicial decisions, statutes and conventions. As we will see, there are also a number of secondary authorities.

Prerogative powers are those held by the monarch, derived from a historical basis. Britain is a monarchy, but over time the powers of the monarch have diminished, however they have not disappeared or been removed, it is simply that the monarch no longer exercises those powers. The government, including ministers and their departments, in the modern context is the Crown. It exercises its powers on behalf of the monarch. Technically it does not operate in the public interest or for the people, but operates as agents of the Crown. Of course in practice, if it does not operate in the public interest in the view of voters, it is unlikely to be re-elected.

In criminal cases, the royal prerogative of mercy is exercised on behalf of the monarch by the Home Secretary. Similarly, the royal prerogative to declare war or conduct foreign policy is handled by ministers on behalf of the monarch. Prerogative powers give the executive independent legislative power (Orders in Council). This power tends to be used to generate legislation that would waste parliamentary time, as it is non-contentious. Only two prerogatives are used directly by the monarch in practice: the dissolution of parliament and the appointment of the prime minister.

Judicial decisions have been a key source of the Constitution, particularly from the 17th to the 19th century, when courts acted to protect the individual liberties of the people. Theoretically the judiciary maintained the position that an individual had the right to do anything they wanted, provided it was not expressly forbidden by law. These were known as residual rights. However, as government has become increasingly powerful the courts have been less significant as a source for the Constitution. Despite this, common law to a large extent embodies the concept of the rule of law.

Given that Britain has no constitutional law, the statutes of parliament are the ultimate source of law. So, unlike in the United States, the judiciary cannot strike down statutes on the basis that they are unconstitutional.

Finally, there are a number of texts and commentaries that form part of Britain's unwritten Constitution. These include those of A. V. Dicey and Walter Bagehot. They do not provide comprehensive guides to the way in which the political system works and, to some extent, they reflect the particular points of view of the authors. More modern authors, such as Robert Hazell, are often viewed as having written material based on what they have observed and that this may only relate to what practices and procedures were used at that time.

Human Rights Act and the Constitution

All legislation (past, present and future) has to be read and implemented in a way which is compatible with the Convention on Human Rights. The Act does not permit the convention to be used by the courts to strike out inconsistent primary legislation or secondary legislation, but the courts are obliged to interpret existing and future laws so that they are consistent with the convention and Strasbourg case law. If not they can make a 'declaration of incompatibility'. Parliament then needs to fast-track a remedy through the legislative process.

Conventions are also important, as they govern conduct and procedure. They are not legally enforceable, but are integral parts of the political process. They are flexible and allow for differing interpretations when it is questionable whether a convention has or has not been correctly applied.

Administrative law

These are laws relating to the power and control of government agencies that have been given statutory powers of administration. These statutory powers are based on those needed to make the agency work, along with making quasi-judicial decisions (e.g. tax liability, dealing with complaints etc.).

1.10 Federalism and Devolution

Learning objectives

- Do federal and devolved systems of government enhance democracy?
- Is it the case that devolved government has all the benefits of federalism without the disadvantages?
- How do constitutions and other factors limit the power of the executive?

Do federal and devolved systems of government enhance democracy?

It is often argued that federalism and devolved systems are more democratic because power has been decentralised and it is closer to the people. However, just having the institutions geographically close has nothing to do with democracy; it requires information to attain political closeness and democracy.

Generally speaking, the more power a particular level of government may have, the more interest voters will take in it. It may be the case that when power is concentrated in central government it will come under greater scrutiny, while if it is decentralised and spread then voters' interest in it is less marked. There were low voter turnouts in Britain in 2001 and 2005 which point to voter apathy.

It is said that federalism in particular makes it difficult to follow politics, as it is difficult to ensure that a specific group of politicians is held accountable for their actions. Simply there is too much opportunity to pass on responsibility. In order to properly regulate different levels of government, a clear constitution is often necessary and this constitution should not be subject to the national government, as it would have the ultimate power to repeal it. The constitution is, therefore, interpreted by an undemocratic institution, the judiciary, and they are not directly responsible to the electorate.

James Madison, in *Federalist Papers* No. 10, argued that in a federal type of government:

> *The influence of factious leaders may kindle a flame within their particular states, but will be unable to spread a general conflagration through the other states. A rage for paper money, for an abolition of debts, for an equal diversion of property, or for any other improper or wicked project, will be less apt to persuade the whole body of the Union than a particular member of it; [just as] it is more likely to taint a particular country or district than an entire state.*

In other words, by subdividing voters into geographical areas obstacles are placed in the way of new ideas or radical solutions, whether they are good or whether they are bad.

Is it the case that devolved government has all the benefits of federalism without the disadvantages?

Many view devolution as a more modern form of federalism. Countries such as Britain and Spain had unitary systems and devolved government has created what is in effect a quasi-federation.

As the United States discovered, a confederacy tends to mean a weak federal government, whereas a federation allows a strong federal government.

Devolution allows varying levels of autonomies for different areas still within a single nation state. Federalism tends to imply that all such areas would have the same powers.

In Britain, with an unwritten constitution, referenda were used to implement what was seen by many as a radical constitutional change, that is, devolution. In Spain, which has a written constitution, the right to devolution is specifically written; powers are agreed. In theory, the US and Australian state systems and the German Länder system are more straightforward to understand and to operate; each area has precisely the same powers and level of autonomy. This can be compared directly to the issue in Britain, where Scotland, Wales and Northern Ireland have differing levels of power and autonomy, yet England itself does not have any devolved institutions. It is argued that traditional federalism, such as the US system, would not work well in Britain. It would have been difficult to have struck the right balance. Scotland would have wanted a weak federal government and to have had the maximum autonomy. The Welsh did not want that degree of autonomy, and with a fragile peace agreement in Northern Ireland it would not have been appropriate to have given that level of autonomy to that part of Britain. Devolution allows Scotland to run its own affairs, to pass laws and to vary taxes; Wales and Northern Ireland have less power.

Another key consideration was the disproportionate distribution of population in England. With around 50 million of the 60 million, an English government could prove to be more powerful than a federal British government. The only other alternative would have been to have broken England up into a number of regions, with each region becoming a federal state. Devolution was seen as an ideal compromise.

One of the key problems, however, is that Scottish and Welsh MPs have the right to vote on issues that only apply to England. This is seen as being undemocratic. It is also important to appreciate that devolution, as it has been developed in Britain, is asymmetrical. In other words devolution has not been equally applied across the regions. In Canada, French-speaking Quebec argues for asymmetric autonomy, as it wants more powers than the nine English-speaking provinces.

How do constitutions and other factors limit the power of the executive?

Both the British and the Israeli constitutions have legislative supremacy. In other words, parliament says what the constitution means. However, parliaments tend to be controlled by executives through the party system and in practice there are limited checks on the powers of the executive. Lord Hailsham (1976) described this as an elective dictatorship. It caused considerable problems in 2001 when Britain, against the wishes of some parliamentary members, sent troops to Afghanistan. The executive used the royal prerogative, which is not subject to parliamentary checks, as a means of pursuing foreign policy.

The US Constitution expressly limits the power of the executive and when the US sent troops to liberate Kuwait in the early 1990s, Congress supported President George H.W. Bush's decision, but it was clear that Bush would have sent troops anyway and determined the meaning of the Constitution himself. As commander-in-chief, the president would also be able to make use of the War Powers Act (1973).

Constitutions can fail countries where democracy and political culture are not embedded or fully supported. In both India and Pakistan the constitutions have been set aside when the executive has declared states of emergency.

Just because there is a constitution there is no guarantee of a constitutional government. A British prime minister has greater power through the royal prerogative and being the leader of the majority party in parliament than the more limited set of powers that a US president enjoys. In the EU there are few ways in which to check the power of the European Council or European Commission.

Political culture is important; if there are groups and institutions that want to uphold the rule of law and if there is strong support for the constitution then the power of executives can be kept in check.

Exam Café

Relax, refresh, result!

Relax and prepare

Questions for the exam are likely to be drawn from the following topic areas or similar. Use these to help focus on what areas of the subject you should be revising.

- The amendment process and the reasons why there have been so few amendments.
- The merits and demerits of a written constitution.
- Federalism and changes in relations between state and federal government over time.
- Federal and devolved systems of government.

Refresh your memory

When revising this topic, try the following exercises. They will help you structure your notes and will provide a guide as to what you will need to know for the different papers. Remember to work through unit F853 first as this will provide the base you will need for F855.

You should have an understanding of:

- the historical context of the Philadelphia Convention and the aims of the Founding Fathers
- Beard's revisionist view of the Constitution
- the Constitution itself and what each article deals with
- the separation of powers and checks and balances
- the process of constitutional amendments
- details of failed amendments in the recent past
- changes in the relationship between federal and state government over time.

Copy out the following table and for each of the following areas, try to identify relevant examples from the recent past.

For this and other tables, it would be a good idea to complete the table on a word processor so that detail can be added at various times and a complete revision sheet prepared for the exam.

The constitutional checks between the branches of government

	Constitutional checks	Examples
Congress upon the president	Congress can reject presidential legislation	Congress initially rejected the financial rescue package of 2008.
Congress upon the Supreme Court		
The president upon the Congress		
The president upon the Supreme Court		
The Supreme Court upon the president		
The Supreme Court upon the Congress		

Keep an eye on contemporary developments in US politics and see if fresh examples can be added to the examples detailed.

The changing relationship between federal and state

Copy out and complete the following table.

	Definition and cause	Impact upon federal-state relations
Dual/classical federalism		
Cooperative federalism		
Coercive federalism		
New federalism		
Fiscal revival		
Institutional revival		
Permissive federalism		
Kaleidoscopic federalism		

Exam tips

These are some reasons why students do badly in exams. They provide a guide to what you need to avoid and by implication what you need to do to perform well in the exam.

- They are not able to separate and rank the relative importance of factors in explaining why the Constitution has been so rarely amended.
- The discussion of recent amendment attempts is limited. The failure of equal rights, balanced budget, same-sex unions and flag-burning amendments provides plenty of scope for excellent discussion in this regard.
- In essays on federalism, candidates frequently take too historical an approach and may fail to recognise that the question may only require a discussion of more recent developments.

Get the result!

These are some ideas to help you in your revision and to keep up to date with the latest developments in US politics.

- You might prioritise the study of the US Constitution as it underlies every other topic in the paper.
- There are particularly close links to this topic and the Supreme Court and the issue of rights.
- The same extends to the synoptic paper where these three topics, constitutions, judiciaries and rights, may be studied collectively.
- Essays on the president and Congress too could well feature some reference to constitutional arrangements and the adequacy of checks and balances within the Constitution.
- Be aware of the 'elastic clauses' of the Constitution and the notion of the 'living constitution' whose organic evolution over time can be assisted by judicial review and precedent from the Supreme Court.
- Examine the fiscal and institutional revival of the states from the 1960s onwards. The former refers to the increasing independence of the states from federal government finances from the 1980s onwards. The latter refers to the increased professionalism of state government particularly at the legislative and executive level.
- The impact of the 'credit crunch' and its impact on government spending plans could have a major impact upon federal–state relations as it did during the 1980s. This therefore would be a good area to focus on.
- In this regard keep an eye out for policy initiatives from the states that support the 'states as laboratories' idea. California under Schwarzenegger might be a good start given its innovative environmental policies.
- Use the National Governors Association website to keep abreast of contemporary developments and issues in federal state relations.
- See if rulings from the Supreme Court continue in the same vein as the 'federalism revolution' under the Rehnquist Court, which greatly enhanced state powers.

In Focus – F855

The following will help you in revising and in developing your knowledge at this level in order to gain a higher mark. Make sure you have an understanding of:

- the role of constitutions in different political systems
- the differences between written and unwritten constitutions
- the differences in the method of amendment
- the advantages and disadvantages of each type of constitution
- constitutional developments in the UK, EU and other countries. The debate surrounding the EU Constitution provides an excellent basis upon which to develop discussion. This can extend to the drafting of the Constitution and problems of interpretation, length and detail as opposed to brevity and ambiguity, the need for consensus and problems of ratification.

Copy out and complete the table below including as much detail as you can from the UK, US, EU and any other countries you may have examined.

- Students sometimes complete case studies of an individual country, such as Israel or New Zealand, to determine their constitutional arrangements and incorporate these examples into their essays, not only on constitutions and unitary vs federal arrangements but also their discussion of legislatures and executives.

The advantages of a written constitution	The disadvantages of a written constitution

- Try to incorporate the debate surrounding the proposed EU Constitution. Issues such as who drafted it, the content, the meaning of content, the role of the ECJ (European Court of Justice) in its future interpretation will provide much scope for relevant discussion here.
- Monitor the work of the Scottish Parliament, Welsh Assembly and Northern Ireland Assembly and issues surrounding devolution.
- By the same token, see how the demands for regional assemblies and an English parliament fare and consider the arguments both for and against.
- Compare and contrast federalist and unitary systems of government, including asymmetric devolution in the UK and developments in countries such as Belgium, Spain and Germany.

2 The Executive and Legislature

Although the US political system has a two-house legislature like the British system, there are marked differences between them. In the US both houses are elected, unlike in Britain, and they have clear, defined functions, responsibilities and powers; they are also considered to be equal. The Senate is not simply a revising chamber.

Again, unlike the British parliamentary system, the president is not drawn from the ranks of the majority party in Congress; instead the president is separately elected and has a different role and sets of powers, compared to a prime minister. The president is supported by a cabinet of officials who tend not to be elected members of the congress; they are appointed by the president. In Britain the cabinet is made up of elected members of parliament.

At the heart of US politics is the committee system, a series of specialist groups that examine proposed legislation, filter it and hone it before it is presented to Congress. They also have a vital role in the oversight of the executive.

As the executive and the legislature is so separated by the Constitution and by different electoral systems occurring at different times in the calendar, there is often a problem of coordination and cooperation between the two branches. Both the executive and the legislature have relationships with the judicial branches of government. There are often complications, as the judiciary may interpret legislation in such a way as to declare it unconstitutional. Therefore the broadest possible examination of legislation is vital before it is presented to Congress for approval.

There are 16 key themes in this chapter.

- The executive
- Powers of the president
- The presidents
- Efficiency of the executive and the executive office of the president
- Executive branch and government
- Policymaking
- Relationships
- Presidential power and contemporary issues
- Functions of the legislatures
- US Congress
- Membership, leadership and committees
- Political parties
- Presidential persuasion and power
- The legislative process
- Oversight and relationships
- Contemporary issues and voting behaviour

These are represented by the first 16 topics, which are supported by two question topics for F853, looking at the most common essay types, and 12 F855 question topics, which again look at popular essay themes in the examination.

This chapter contains 30 topics in total, representing the following.

The chapter is rounded off with an exam café feature on page 112.

Learning objectives

- Executive power and functions
- Presidential, prime ministerial and cabinet government

President Gerald Ford and some of his cabinet, in the cabinet room at the White House

Executive power and functions

As we have seen, government has three key functions: legislative, judicial and executive. The executive is not directly involved with the making of law, but is involved in decision-making and implementing those laws that have been approved by the legislature.

Most executives are made up of elected politicians and non-elected appointees who often operate as administrative bureaucrats. The presidential executive in the US is based on a separation of powers. In Britain, on the other hand, there is a cabinet executive and a fusion of powers, in which there is no clear separation between the legislative and the executive. In some other countries there is no fusion of the two; for example in the Republic of Ireland the president has a ceremonial role, with the business of government being carried out by a cabinet executive. The president acts as a non-political, non-partisan head of state.

Executive government directly controls enforcement agencies, such as the military and the police. In the US there are also organisations under indirect control of the executive, including the Federal Reserve Board. These tend to be described as independent regulatory commissions or agencies. In Britain they are known as next-step executive agencies.

In the US the president functions as a distinct entity from the Congress. He is the chief executive with separate powers and is directly elected by the people. He therefore has a direct mandate from the electorate. In Britain the prime minister is not directly elected; they are the leader of their party which is elected to govern by the electorate. By being leader of the successful party they become prime minister.

Unlike the British cabinet, the cabinet in the US is purely advisory and has limited powers. This means that the president represents a singular, separate executive. This makes it difficult to remove the president from office; for this to happen he would have to be **impeached**.

Given the distinct separation between the executive and the legislature in the US, presidents are often frustrated in their attempts to push through policy, because of the independence of the legislature. The key functions of executives are outlined in the following table.

Function	Explanation	Examples
Ceremonial duties	Where there is a singular executive the president will operate as the head of state.	In Britain, where there is a parliamentary system in which the political head of government is separate from the ceremonial leader.
Initiating policy	The executive is elected on the basis of a manifesto, identifying priorities, but these need to be approved by the legislature.	In the US, because of Congress's independence, a president's proposals may not be approved. In Britain, the royal prerogative can be used and the EU Commission plays an important role in policy initiation. In Britain governments ensure their success by using the party whip and their majority.
Political leadership	This involves securing support of key decision-makers, pressure groups and the public to ensure cooperation.	The prime minister, Gordon Brown, has sought consolidated support in dealing with the financial crisis of 2008. A previous prime minister, Margaret Thatcher, failed to obtain cooperation for the poll tax, which ultimately led to her downfall.

Function	Explanation	Examples
Administration and execution of policy	The executive must direct the bureaucracy and manage it. Often they do not have the experience needed for this and government departments may have their own agendas.	In the US, government departments are often linked to interest groups (known as iron triangles). In Britain politicians as diverse as Tony Benn and Margaret Thatcher suspected that the civil service had failed to be loyal to them.
Decisive leadership	The executive needs to take a leading role in times of crisis and be decisive.	Gordon Brown showed this decisiveness in handling the 2008 financial crisis by securing international agreements, as did George W. Bush after negotiating with Congress.

Presidential, prime ministerial and cabinet government

In the US the president's powers are limited by the Constitution, in a similar way to those in Germany and the Republic of Ireland. There are different theories about US presidential power. Originally the role of the president was probably perceived as having the ability to act decisively when needed, but subject to checks and balances. When the president made a decision the legislature would then reconcile any conflicting interests through debate. In recent times US presidents have been referred to as being activists, that is, they have taken positive government action on issues.

In Britain, with its cabinet form of government, prime ministers from Harold Wilson to Tony Blair have been accused of being presidential. However even Margaret Thatcher, a strident presidential leader, was removed from power in 1990 by lack of cabinet support, indicating the power of the cabinet.

The following table identifies the key characteristics and differences between presidential, prime ministerial and cabinet government.

Impeachment

This occurs when a criminal accusation is made by the legislature against the president. This is not the same as removal from office. It is a power that Congress exercises. It has only been used 13 times but never followed through. Only two presidents have been impeached, but both were acquitted.

US executive	British prime minister	British cabinet
It is often the case that the US president is more likely to receive the support of Congress on foreign policy than domestic. This is known as the two presidencies theory. George W. Bush took swift action in his role as commander-in-chief after the terrorist attacks in 2001. But Congress was less willing to allow him to take a lead on domestic responses. In 1993 President Clinton proposed a health care reform package, but it was rejected by a Democrat-controlled Congress.	Prime ministers such as Thatcher and Blair have been described as being presidential, reflecting the trend of the weakening of cabinet government.	The cabinet represents a link between the executive and the legislature. They are senior policymakers. They share responsibility with the prime minister, who is viewed as 'first amongst equals'.
Arthur M. Schlesinger, the US historian, believed that the role of commander-in-chief gave the president too much power and described President Nixon's administration as being imperial. Roosevelt had used this to see the US through the Second World War. Truman had used it to strike decisively against Japan. Presidents were seen to be more activist in nature.	The British prime minister has few of the characteristics of a US president. They are not separately elected, have no personal mandate and have a limited personal bureaucracy. They are dependent on the cabinet and on the party members in the legislature to retain their position.	The work of each cabinet member and their department is scrutinised by the others, which sometimes means ministers spend more time defending themselves than policymaking.

US executive	British prime minister	British cabinet
In the 1970s the positions switched to an imperial (or resurgent) Congress, particularly during the administration of Gerald Ford. During this time presidents found it difficult to operate without Congress's support and they needed to make concessions to achieve their objectives.	The prime minister's office has approximately100 staff, many civil servants. The US president appoints approximately 6000.	As most cabinet members are from the legislature there is a strong democratic accountability. Most democracies have a cabinet structure, even though the structure may be different.
President Clinton took office intending to focus on domestic issues, but due to his lack of power in this area it has been suggested that he focused on international policies, where he had greater freedom. This notion has persisted, as in recent elections the president has emerged with only a marginal majority of the vote.	The British prime minister has a Commons majority and a largely united party and can use royal prerogatives.	The role of the cabinet has developed over time but there is still a sense of collective leadership and responsibility.
The president also has to contend with large bureaucracies that are difficult to manage and may often make mistakes. In 1998 the Supreme Court used judicial review in the Clinton vs City of New York case to block the Line Item Veto Act (1996), which allowed the president to cancel certain laws that had been passed by Congress.	The British prime minister may often make direct appeals for support to the public via the media, rather than working through the legislature. A popular party leader is often seen as the key to success and party discipline is demanded. The cabinet is dominated by the prime minister and cabinet meetings are brief. The royal prerogative is not subject to parliamentary scrutiny and as the prime minister does not have departmental responsibilities they can meddle in any area of government power.	Ministers have more work as the state has become involved in more areas of life.

The US cabinet, sometimes called the president's cabinet, consists of the senior appointed officers of the executive branch of the federal government. It has been a long-standing tradition, as far as the cabinet is concerned, dating back to the first US president, George Washington, who had a four-member cabinet. The cabinet officers are nominated by the president and presented to the Senate for either confirmation or rejection by a simple majority. When Barack Obama formed his initial cabinet, Hillary Clinton became Secretary of State. Other key positions were filled throughout January and February 2009.

It is important to note that an elected vice-president does not require Senate confirmation and neither do White House staff (such as the Chief of Staff). The Secretary of Defense, Robert Gates, acted as President George W. Bush's Secretary of Defense and he was confirmed by the Senate in December 2006, and therefore did not need reconfirmation.

The cabinet is seated according to order of precedence at meetings, with the higher ranking officers sitting closer to the centre of the table. The order of precedence also indicates the line of succession in the event of the death or resignation of the president or vice-president.

Arguably, there has been a major decline in the influence of the cabinet and the Secretary of State, Secretary of the Treasury, Secretary of Defense and Attorney General, often referred to as the Big Four. They are the inner circle of the cabinet.

Presidential tasks, functions and duties

The powers, tasks, functions and duties of the president are outlined in Article II of the US Constitution. In effect, the following 10 key powers have remained the same since the election of the first US president, George Washington, to the newly-elected president, Barack Obama.

Propose legislation to Congress

Each January the president addresses Congress and outlines the legislative agenda for the coming year. This falls under Article II, Section 3 of the US Congress: 'He shall from time to time give to the Congress information of the state of the union and recommend to their consideration such measures as he shall judge necessary and expedient.' This is known as the 'state of the union address'. In addition to the state of the union address the president will often call press conferences or make announcements.

Submit the annual budget to Congress

The Office of Management and the Budget draws up the annual federal budget on behalf of the president. The president presents this to Congress. There is then bargaining between Congress and the president in order to approve elements of the budget. This is particularly problematic if Congress is controlled by one party and the president represents another party.

Sign legislation that has been approved by Congress

Having deliberated and finally passed bills, Congress will then present the bill to the president for approval. It is only when the president has signed the bill that it becomes law. The president is not obliged to sign the bill, but in the majority of cases the president will sign it and take some of the credit. The bills are signed in a ceremony attended by members of Congress and those who will be directly affected by the new laws.

Act as the chief executive of the United States

The president derives this role from Article II of the US Constitution, effectively making the president the chief executive and responsible for running the executive branch of federal government. In practice much of the power is delegated to departments and agencies.

Nominate officials to the executive branch of government

The George W. Bush second administration had 15 executive departments, possibly the best known being the Department of State, run by Condoleezza Rice. The president nominates the heads of these executive departments (which includes treasury, justice, education and defense) and presents the nominations to the Senate for approval. The nominations are then confirmed by the Senate by a simple majority vote.

Nominate judges

The president will make hundreds of appointments, as this power extends to trial and appeal courts in federal government. The judicial appointments are for life. In George W. Bush's second term of office he nominated John G. Roberts as the 17th Chief Justice of the Supreme Court, and in the same year nominated Harriet Miers as a justice of the Supreme Court, but withdrew her name after opposition and instead nominated Samuel Alito, who was confirmed as the 110th Supreme Court justice in January 2006.

Negotiate treaties on behalf of the United States

The presidential seal of office reflects the dual nature of the president in terms of the role of commander-in-chief, which is symbolised by the arrows and the holding of an olive branch, which symbolises peace. Presidents negotiate treaties on behalf of the nation. Ronald Reagan,

Learning objectives

- Presidential tasks, functions and duties

State of the Union

The last state of the union address made by President George W. Bush was on 28 January 2008. He proposed tax relief and the reform of the housing market, health care, education, work on trade and investment, crime, energy, immigration, and various initiatives on foreign policy and affairs.

for instance, negotiated the Strategic Arms Reduction Treaty, primarily with the Russians. The Senate, however, has the power to ratify any treaty negotiated by the president. On seven occasions in the past hundred years the Senate has rejected a treaty, under the rule that required a two-thirds majority for ratification.

Act as commander-in-chief

Since the Second World War in particular, this role has been of significance, from the presidency of Franklin D. Roosevelt to the present. This role incorporates providing clear and inspirational leadership and directly influencing the effort of the nation in times of war and crisis. It is important to remember that the president, however, is restricted by Congress's power to declare wars (only four have ever been made: George W. Bush convinced Congress to pass a resolution rather than a declaration of war against Afghanistan and Iraq), determine whether budgets are allocated to conflicts and crises, and to initiate investigations into the conduct of the president and the executive departments in handling these issues.

To pardon felons

Presidents have the power to grant a pardon, mainly in uncontroversial cases. Sometimes the pardon has been granted in very controversial circumstances, such as President Ford pardoning former president Nixon in 1974, or George H. W. Bush pardoning former Defense Secretary Caspar Weinberger in 1992.

Veto legislation that has been approved by Congress

If a president does not wish to sign a bill he can choose to veto it, or at least threaten to veto it. Many bills have been vetoed over the years. George W. Bush between July 2006 and July 2008 vetoed 12 bills. In order to veto a bill the whole bill has to be vetoed. When this happens it is returned to the house that first considered it, along with a note explaining the president's objections. Congress then has two options: it can do nothing and therefore allow the bill to die, or it can attempt to override the president's veto (this requires a two-third majority in both chambers, which is difficult to achieve, and is therefore rare). The table on below shows how the vetoes were handled during George W. Bush's administration.

Bill	Outcome of override
Stem Cell Research Enhancement Act (2005)	Failed
US Troop Readiness, Veterans Care, Katrina Recovery and Iraq Accountability Appropriations Act (2007)	Failed, although a later version was approved by the president
Stem Cell Research Enhancement Act (2007)	Override not attempted
Children's Health Insurance Program Reauthorisation Act (2007)	Failed
Water Resources Development Act (2007)	Overridden
Departments of Labor, Health and Human Services, and Education, and Related Agencies Appropriations Act (2008)	Failed
Children's Health Insurance Program Reauthorisation Act (2007)	Failed for the second time
National Defense Authorisation Act for Fiscal Year 2008	Minor changes made and later approved by the president
Intelligence Authorisation Act for Fiscal Year 2008	Failed
2007 US Farm Bill	Overridden
2007 US Farm Bill	Re-passed due to a clerical error. Vetoed then overridden
Medicare Improvements for Patients and Providers Act (2008)	Overridden

Presidents from John F. Kennedy to George W. Bush

During this period each president faced their own series of problems and had their own specific domestic and foreign agendas. The following table outlines the key issues for each president.

President and terms(s)	Party	Issues	Domestic policy	Foreign policy
J. F. Kennedy 1961–63	Democrat	In his inaugural address he said: 'Ask not what your country can do for you – ask what you can do for your country.' This was in the midst of the Cold War. Kennedy wanted to slow down the arms race, leading to a test ban treaty in 1963. He wanted 'a world of law and free choice, banishing the world of war and coercion'. Kennedy was assassinated in November 1963.	Supported equal rights and called for civil rights legislation. He launched economic programmes that would see the US go through its longest period of sustained expansion. He planned to tackle poverty in the US head on.	With the Alliance for Progress and the Peace Corps he promoted human rights throughout the world. He faced the Cuban missile crisis in 1962, the blockade of Berlin and strove to deal with the arms race, which was spiraling out of control.
Lyndon B. Johnson 1963–69	Democrat	Became president after Kennedy's assassination and won the presidency in his own right in 1964 with 61 per cent of the vote. His key set of legislative programmes was framed around what is dubbed 'a great society'. He chose not to stand for re-election in 1968.	His programmes looked for funding in education, disease, Medicare, urban renewal, conservation, anti-poverty, anti-crime and removing obstacles to voting.	Dominated by the conflict in Vietnam. He strove to reach a settlement but by 1968 the fighting was out of control.
Richard M. Nixon 1969–74	Republican	Reconciliation was his key theme to deal with what was now a nation divided over domestic and foreign affairs. His campaign in 1972 was rocked by the Watergate scandal, focusing on a break-in to the Democratic Party offices in Washington. Nixon resigned in 1974. He was the first president to do so.	He ended the draft, supported revenue sharing, anti-crime laws and environmental programmes.	He focused on achieving world stability, reducing tensions with the USSR and China and ending direct US involvement in Vietnam.

Learning objectives

- Presidents from John F. Kennedy to George W. Bush

John F. Kennedy was the 35th President of the United States. He served for only two years as he was assassinated in 1963

President Lyndon B. Johnson became the 36th President of the United States. As vice-president he succeeded JFK but became president in his own right by beating Barry M. Goldwater in the 1964 presidential election

President Jimmy Carter entered state politics in 1962, becoming governor of Georgia. He became president in 1977 beating Gerald Ford with 297 electoral votes to 241

President George H. W. Bush was a former US Navy pilot who served two terms in the House of Representatives. He became Ronald Reagan's vice-president and then ran for the presidency himself in 1988 with Dan Quayle, beating Massachusetts governor Michael Dukakis

President and terms(s)	Party	Issues	Domestic policy	Foreign policy
Gerald Ford 1974–77	Republican	He was the first president chosen under the terms of the 25th Amendment (succeeding the first ever president to resign). Inflation, a depressed economy, energy shortages and world peace were all major problems he had to face.	He sought to curb government market intervention and spending. He granted Nixon a full pardon. He vetoed 39 bills and aimed to stimulate the economy.	He sought to maintain US prestige on the world stage, set limitations with the USSR on nuclear weapons and sought a peace settlement in the Middle East.
Jimmy Carter 1977–81	Democrat	He sought to make government 'competent and compassionate' and focused on high energy costs, inflation and tensions. His main worries were unemployment and inflation, as the country was in recession.	He deregulated industry, reformed the civil service and created a Department of Education.	He championed human rights, tried to bring peace to the Middle East, established relations with China, negotiated nuclear limitations with the USSR and faced a major challenge when 52 US embassy staff in Iran were seized by militants (they were released on the day he left office).
Ronald Reagan 1981–89	Republican	His campaign pledge was to restore 'the great, confident roar of American progress and growth and optimism'. He wanted to reinvigorate the country and reduce peoples' reliance on government. His programme was known as the 'Reagan Revolution'.	He dealt in a skilful way with Congress, he managed to get legislation passed to stimulate economic growth, curb inflation, cut taxes and government expenditure, and increased national defence. He overhauled the income tax system, creating US's longest period of prosperity.	His approach was 'peace through strength'. He increased defence spending, but improved relations with the USSR. He waged war against international terrorists. His speech in Berlin in June 1987 is directly credited with the pulling down of the Berlin Wall two years later.
George H. W. Bush 1989–93	Republican	He was dedicated to traditional American values and to making the US 'a kinder and gentler nation'. He promised to use American strength as a 'force of good'. He faced a changing world with the Cold War at an end, despite which he favoured restraint in US policy abroad (even though this involved the first Gulf War).	Bush is seen as far more of a foreign affairs president than a domestic one. He did little to deal with a poor US economy, violent inner cities and high deficit spending.	He sent troops to Panama and into Kuwait, the latter to liberate the country from the Iraqi dictator, Saddam Hussein. Bush was militarily and diplomatically triumphant.

President and terms(s)	Party	Issues	Domestic policy	Foreign policy
William J. Clinton 1993–2001	Democrat	The US enjoyed peace and economic prosperity. Clinton was the first Democrat since Roosevelt to win a second term. The US had low unemployment and inflation and falling crime. As a result of personal indiscretions he was the second US president to be impeached, but found not guilty.	He planned to balance the budget and managed to achieve a budget surplus. He wanted to end racial discrimination at home, reform health care and education and declare that 'the era of big government is over'.	Supported an expanded NATO, increased international trade and campaigned against drug trafficking. Sent peace-keepers to Bosnia and ordered Iraq to be bombed for non-compliance with the United Nations.
George W. Bush 2001–08	Republican	He had a reputation as a compassionate conservative in favour of limited government, but with strong families and local control. His first major issue was the terrorist attacks in September 2001. He took unprecedented steps in response.	He aimed to create a home ownership society with lower taxes, education reforms (notably the No Child Left Behind Act (2001)). He favoured accountability, improved health care, increased home ownership and increased military strength.	Bush beefed up homeland security and then launched a series of campaigns against terrorist movements across the globe. The US attacked Afghanistan in response to the attack on the twin towers in New York on 9/11 and a US-led coalition attacked Iraq and deposed Saddam Hussein. Elsewhere, Bush has been active in developing a global alliance against terrorists.

2.4 Efficiency of the Executive and the Executive Office of the President

Learning objectives

- Efficiency of the executive
- The executive office of the president

During President Bill Clinton's administration Al Gore was given special status in the White House, which made him appear to be the heir-apparent to Clinton. He was active in a number of policy initiatives

Efficiency of the executive

As we have seen, the president does not have wide ranging and unrestrained power because the separation of powers divides the executive from the legislature and the checks and balances limit the power of the president.

The immense size of the executive branch means that it has to be managed in an efficient manner to support the president. However, there have been many occasions when a president's appointments to run the executive branch have led to failures in efficiency or to a lack of ability. Some parts of the executive are not under the direct control of the president, such as the Federal Reserve Board (FRB), which sets US interest rates, and there have been many occasions when the chief of the FRB and a president have been in conflict over policy.

Collective responsibility is not an aspect of the US executive, which has led to open disagreements between members of the cabinet; this has caused serious problems. More often than not, the efficiency of the executive can be undermined when the president and Congress are controlled by different parties. In the period 1952 to 1998, 16 of the congressional terms experienced divided government, leading to gridlock. However, even in such circumstances, in which a government is divided, legislation can be passed due to weak discipline among the opposition and the tendency among some of its members to support the president.

President George W. Bush's vice-president was Dick Cheney. Cheney had a reputation for being the hard man of the administration and was a surprise running mate. He was a mentor to Bush, highly influential and a key Washington insider

The president's relationship with Congress is vitally important, given that Congress has the sole power to make law. Coalitions are therefore necessary to pass laws; the coalitions almost always are cross-party ones.

The Supreme Court also obstructs or influences the efficiency of the executive by declaring laws to be unconstitutional, and judicial review reinforces this, but only occasionally does it rule against the executive. Presidents find it difficult to influence the Supreme Court, as the only opportunity they have to appoint a sympathetic judge is when a vacancy arises.

The US media may also influence the effectiveness of a presidency. The media played a powerful role in undermining Richard Nixon over the Watergate affair, and relentlessly pursued President Clinton over the Lewinsky affair and the Whitewater scandal.

In comparison, British cabinets contain ministers with large departments and who are overburdened with responsibilities. As a result, overarching policy is often left to the prime minister and selected ministers. In Germany governments also face the problem of having a workable majority in parliament. This is not so much the case in Britain, however John Major faced this problem from 1992 when his government had a tiny majority and relied on the Ulster Unionists for support. When contentious issues arose in 1995, Major faced a party leader re-election battle, with 111 Conservative MPs failing to support him.

The executive office of the president (EOP)

The staff of the executive office support the president, not members of his party or members of Congress. The EOP has grown significantly over time and often has a difficult relationship with Congress.

When a British prime minister has a considerable majority, as Tony Blair had in 1997, even policies that are unpopular or contentious can be pushed through parliament, such as the building of the Millennium Dome and making the Bank of England independent. Perhaps the key was not Blair's Commons majority but his overwhelming popularity with the voters. In 1997 he had a majority of 179 and in 2001 it was167. Along with party discipline, which was a feature of New Labour, electoral support helped the government considerably.

It would be wrong to assume that the prime minister's office, and other offices that directly support the prime minister, are like the executive office of the US president. The British equivalent is very limited by comparison. The prime minister has to answer directly to the legislature through prime minister's questions and through select committees. This is also true of cabinet ministers. Because Britain has a parliamentary sovereignty, the British courts cannot declare Acts of parliament to be unconstitutional. However, some executive actions based on the royal prerogative powers have been challenged by the courts.

The executive office of the president

The executive office of the president aims to provide advice, assistance, coordination and administrative support. It was created in 1939 at the suggestion of the Brownlow Committee, which recognised that the president needed support in running his administration. The EOP provides key support and staff, working in both the White House and the Eisenhower Executive Office Building.

The White House staff comprises of the president's closest advisers. They provide advice and administrative support on policy, personnel, management, liaison with the federal bureaucracy and Congress, the day-to-day running of the White House, organising the president's schedule and assisting the president in organising his workload. These individuals are not policymakers and tend to shun the limelight.

The executive office of the president employs upwards of 2000 people and it also includes the National Security Council, which was established in 1947 in order to coordinate defence and foreign policy. Currently, in March 2009, this is headed by General James L. Jones, who was appointed in January when Barack Obama became president.

Another key part of the executive office is the Office of Management and Budget, which was created in 1970 to advise the president on the allocation of federal funds and to oversee federal government departments and agencies' spending. It is headed by a director (currently Peter Orszag).

The logic behind the executive office is to ensure that the president has influence over the bureaucracy via his personally chosen senior staff. These staff aim to ensure that the president's views and ideas are foremost in policy and to assert their influence over the executive. The idea is that the president can be assured that his personal staff will ensure that executive departments are doing what is expected, as it is impossible for the president to control it all without this help.

In *Politics and the Oval Office,* Hugh Heclo was of the opinion that bureaucracies will inevitably impede the president, whatever the style or nature of that president. Bureaucracies often serve their own purpose. The president must delegate responsibility to aides, but the problem is that none of them take the president's oath of office or have the president's responsibilities. Ultimately the president is the one who will be held accountable for the actions of any aides or bureaucrats, regardless of how much that president may trust personal friends, loyal allies or technocrats.

The EOP

The EOP is overseen by the White House chief-of-staff. It actually consists of a number of different councils, offices and boards.

- Council of Economic Advisers
- Council on Environmental Quality
- Domestic Policy Council
- National Economic Council
- National Security Council
- Office of Administration
- Office of Management and Budget
- Office of National AIDS Policy
- Office of National Drug Control Policy
- Office of Science and Technology Policy
- Office of the United States Trade Representative
- President's Intelligence Advisory Board and Intelligence Oversight Board
- Privacy and Civil Liberties Oversight Board
- White House Military Office

There are also other groups and organisations that exist within the White House executive office of the president, such as the Office of the First Lady, Office of Political Affairs, Office of Social Innovation and Homeland Security Council.

INTERNET RESEARCH

For more on the specific responsibilities and roles of offices within the executive office of the president and the White House office, go to www.heinemann.co.uk/hotlinks, insert the express code 1825P and click on the relevant link.

Learning objectives

- Coordinating the executive branch
- Key government departments and authorities

Coordinating the executive branch

The federal bureaucracy is a monolithic organisation and attracts considerable criticism. Indeed, the terms 'federal government' and 'bureaucracy' are often tinged with negative connotations. Americans tend to be prejudiced towards government and against bureaucracy, regulation, the civil service and Washington.

Theoretically, the bureaucrats are simply empowered to carry out duties or orders that have been delegated to them by elected individuals. However, the reality is that bureaucrats have considerable control over policy. They are administrative gatekeepers, with the role of discovering what is and what is not achievable when laws have been created either by the executive or by the legislature. Politicians turn to them for advice and information, as it would be impossible for a president or a secretary to deal with all the necessary information required for making decisions.

Constant calls are made to reduce the size and complexity of the bureaucracy of the executive branch. The numbers of federal employees declined in the 1970s and the early 1980s, but since then they have been rising again. Attempts have also been made to simplify federal regulations, such as the Paperwork Reduction Act (1980). Calls have been made for agencies and programmes to be reviewed on an annual basis, and if they were failing to achieve their objectives, they would effectively cease to exist. Bill Clinton certainly wanted to streamline the executive branch and make it more responsive and more representative of the population. His intention was never to weaken executive power, just to make it more efficient and more responsive.

Real coordination still remains elusive, as the federal bureaucracy is complex, autonomous and fragmented. Many parts have overlapping jurisdictions, which only serves to make coordination all the more difficult.

Key government departments and authorities

As we have already seen, the federal executive branch consists of the executive office of the president, the White House staff and a number of executive departments. There are also a number of independent agencies and government corporations, such as the Central Intelligence Agency (CIA), the Federal Trade Commission (FTC) and the United States Postal Service (USPS); and there are boards, commissions and committees, such as the Endangered Species Committee, Social Security Advisory Board and the American Battle Monuments Commission. There are also quasi-official agencies that are not officially government agencies, but are required by law to publish information about their programmes and activities in the **Federal Register.** These include the Smithsonian Institute and the Legal Services Corporation. The following figure lists the various bodies that make up the government of the United States.

Federal Register

This is a daily publication of proposed and final regulations, legal notices, presidential proclamations and executive orders and information on the activities of branches of the federal government.

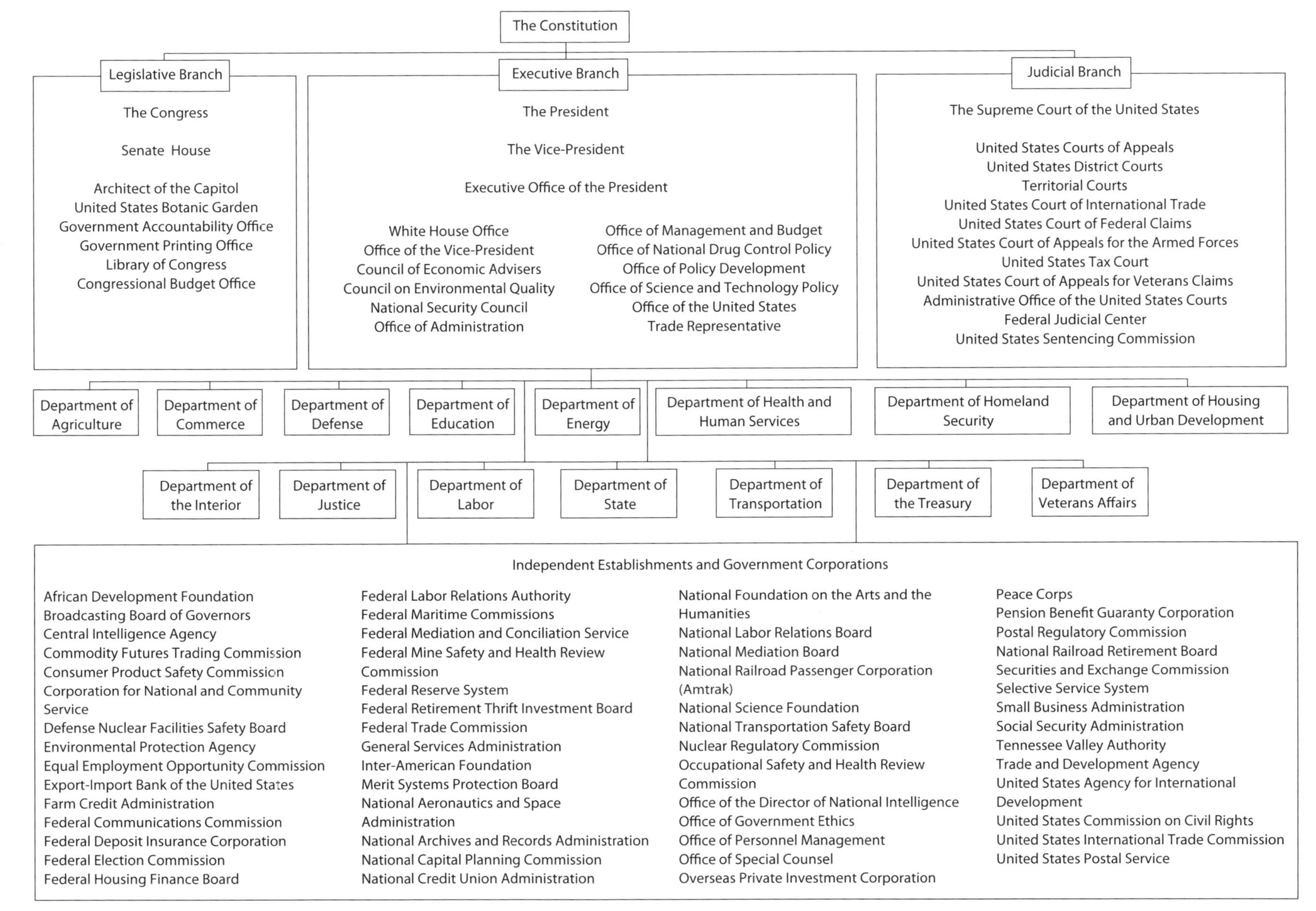
THE GOVERNMENT OF THE UNITED STATES
The Constitution
Legislative Branch
The Congress
Senate House
Architect of the Capitol
United States Botanic Garden
Government Accountability Office
Government Printing Office
Library of Congress
Congressional Budget Office
Executive Branch
The President
The Vice-President
Executive Office of the President
White House Office
Office of the Vice-President
Council of Economic Advisers
Council on Environmental Quality
National Security Council
Office of Administration
Office of Management and Budget
Office of National Drug Control Policy
Office of Policy Development
Office of Science and Technology Policy
Office of the United States Trade Representative
Judicial Branch
The Supreme Court of the United States
United States Courts of Appeals
United States District Courts
Territorial Courts
United States Court of International Trade
United States Court of Federal Claims
United States Court of Appeals for the Armed Forces
United States Tax Court
United States Court of Appeals for Veterans Claims
Administrative Office of the United States Courts
Federal Judicial Center
United States Sentencing Commission
Department of Agriculture
Department of Commerce
Department of Defense
Department of Education
Department of Energy
Department of Health and Human Services
Department of Homeland Security
Department of Housing and Urban Development
Department of the Interior
Department of Justice
Department of Labor
Department of State
Department of Transportation
Department of the Treasury
Department of Veterans Affairs
Independent Establishments and Government Corporations
African Development Foundation
Broadcasting Board of Governors
Central Intelligence Agency
Commodity Futures Trading Commission
Consumer Product Safety Commission
Corporation for National and Community Service
Defense Nuclear Facilities Safety Board
Environmental Protection Agency
Equal Employment Opportunity Commission
Export-Import Bank of the United States
Farm Credit Administration
Federal Communications Commission
Federal Deposit Insurance Corporation
Federal Election Commission
Federal Housing Finance Board
Federal Labor Relations Authority
Federal Maritime Commissions
Federal Mediation and Conciliation Service
Federal Mine Safety and Health Review Commission
Federal Reserve System
Federal Retirement Thrift Investment Board
Federal Trade Commission
General Services Administration
Inter-American Foundation
Merit Systems Protection Board
National Aeronautics and Space Administration
National Archives and Records Administration
National Capital Planning Commission
National Credit Union Administration
National Foundation on the Arts and the Humanities
National Labor Relations Board
National Mediation Board
National Railroad Passenger Corporation (Amtrak)
National Science Foundation
National Transportation Safety Board
Nuclear Regulatory Commission
Occupational Safety and Health Review Commission
Office of the Director of National Intelligence
Office of Government Ethics
Office of Personnel Management
Office of Special Counsel
Overseas Private Investment Corporation
Peace Corps
Pension Benefit Guaranty Corporation
Postal Regulatory Commission
National Railroad Retirement Board
Securities and Exchange Commission
Selective Service System
Small Business Administration
Social Security Administration
Tennessee Valley Authority
Trade and Development Agency
United States Agency for International Development
United States Commission on Civil Rights
United States International Trade Commission
United States Postal Service

Learning objectives

- Formulation of domestic policy
- Formulation of foreign policy

The US cabinet

The tradition of the US cabinet was established in Article II, Section 2, of the US Constitution, which says that the president '...shall nominate, and by and with the Advice and Consent of the Senate, shall appoint Ambassadors, other public Ministers and Consuls, Judges of the Supreme Court, and all other Officers of the United States, whose Appointments are not herein otherwise provided for, and which shall be established by Law: but the Congress may by Law vest the Appointment of such inferior Officers, as they think proper, in the President alone, in the Courts of Law, or in the Heads of Departments.'

The cabinet's role is to advise the president on any subject relating to the duties of each member's respective office. The cabinet includes the vice president and the heads of 15 executive departments (the Secretaries of Agriculture, Commerce, Defense, Education, Energy, Health and Human Services, Homeland Security, Housing and Urban Development, Interior, Labor, State, Transportation, Treasury, Veterans Affairs and the Attorney General).

Formulation of domestic policy

Domestic policy is a term used to describe a massive range of policy areas and in recent years has seen bitter battles over policy on education, welfare, homeland security and health care.

In theory at least 13 of the 15 members of the president's cabinet can be directly or indirectly involved in the formulation and implementation of domestic policy. In response to the terrorist attacks in September 2001, the Department of Homeland Security was created, which meant the reorganisation of no fewer than 170,000 federal employees.

Successive presidents have tried to centralise mechanisms to coordinate the development of domestic policy and then to oversee its implementation. The process began in the 1930s with the Bureau of the Budget, which Richard Nixon later replaced with the Office of Management and Budget. This examined legislation destined for Congress and aimed to establish a central clearance system. In 1939 the executive office of the president was created, and later Dwight D. Eisenhower created interdepartmental groups to deal with public works, airways modernisation and agriculture.

The White House domestic staff was enlarged during the administration of Lyndon Johnson, who was keen to push through domestic policy changes. Apart from the Office of Management and Budget, Richard Nixon also created the Domestic Council in the White House. This was a forum for cabinet-level members, chaired by the president. In the Nixon administration John Ehrlichman was in charge of the forum, and after Nixon's resignation his successor Gerald Ford appointed his vice-president Nelson Rockefeller.

Ford also created the Economic Policy Board, a parallel cabinet-level working group. Later Jimmy Carter replaced the Domestic Council with the Domestic Policy Staff. Then Ronald Reagan reasserted the importance of the Office of Management and Budget, appointing seven cabinet councils under a new Office of Policy Development. To a large extent this model has remained intact, although it has undergone some name changes and is now known as the Domestic Policy Council. Under George W. Bush it had over 20 professional members.

The president has the power to affect domestic policy without going through Congress. He can reorganise agencies and make appointments so as to gain more power over them. He can direct executive agencies in their interpretation of the law and how laws are implemented. Legislation is often vague or fails to cover a particular set of circumstances. To overcome this, George W. Bush, for example, issued an executive order in 2001 to create military tribunals outside of the US court system in order to deal with foreign nationals suspected of terrorist activities.

The formulation of domestic policy and its ultimate implementation means that the president has to contend with legislators, interest groups and the bureaucratic establishment. The executive office of the president provides the president with a stable organisational means of coordinating policy development, enactment and implementation.

Formulation of foreign policy

The most influential players in the development of US foreign policy are the president, the Secretary of State, the National Security Adviser to the president, the Secretary of Defense, the Chairman of the Joint Chiefs of Staff and the Director of Central Intelligence. These individuals are the core of the National Security Council, America's highest-level foreign policymaking body.

The Secretary of State takes the primary role of being the foremost advisor to the president on foreign policy issues. The other individuals offer different dimensions and considerations. The Secretary of Defense offers national security considerations and the National Security Advisor to the president coordinates the activities of the members of the foreign policy team.

One of the main difficulties is how much Congress needs to be told, that is, how important their opinions and views are on policy. The president will always be concerned as to how foreign policy will be received by Congress. He will look at the views of individual members, congressional leaders and committee chairs. Ultimately Congress has a vital part to play, as it will approve funding for government programmes. Congress can legislate on foreign policy issues, so the quandary facing the president is whether Congress will cooperate or oppose a policy. Added to this is whether legislation is actually required. The president takes the lead in consulting with Congress, but the Secretary of State will also canvas the opinions of senior members of Congress.

Foreign policy may also be determined by opinions in the UN Security Council. Domestically a number of different agencies will be directly or indirectly involved in foreign policy affairs and objectives, and will have their own opinions.

Consultation with foreign governments is also important, even though the US views itself the world leader in foreign policy. It will often need the support of friends, allies and sometimes even enemies. Therefore direct contact and forums, such as the United Nations, will be used to lobby key overseas decision-makers.

As for the media, it is the president and the Secretary of State who articulate US foreign policy. It is vital that foreign policy appears to be supported by a national consensus, therefore efforts are made to keep the media on side. The framing of US foreign policy is assisted by vital information gained through a network of American missions and ambassadors across the world.

As a former Under Secretary of State for Political Affairs, Thomas R. Pickering, said: 'When working in Washington, one of the things one learns is to be alert to and aware of the domestic factors that play a role in foreign policymaking. The Secretary has a primary responsibility for that.'

The ability of the United States to shape international events that will advance US interests is dependent upon the Department of State, the Department of Defense and other agencies, and how creative and cooperative they are to respond to the challenges.

INTERNET RESEARCH

For more on the formulation of domestic and foreign policy, go to www.heinemann.co.uk/hotlinks, insert the express code 1825P and click on the relevant link.

US cabinet and policymaking

Although there is no official schedule for cabinet meetings, presidents generally try to meet with their cabinets on a weekly basis. In addition to the president and department secretaries, cabinet meetings are usually attended by the vice president, the US ambassador to the United Nations, and other top-level officials, as determined by the president.

In recent years, the cabinet has generally declined in importance as a policy- making body. From the presidency of Franklin Roosevelt (1933-1945), the trend has been for presidents to act through the executive office of the president. This has led to a situation where non-cabinet officials (such as the White House Chief of Staff, the Director of the Office of Management and Budget, or the National Security Adviser) have significantly more power than some of the cabinet officials.

Learning objectives

- The executive's relationship with the legislature
- The executive's relationship with the judiciary

Recess appointment

This is when a president fills a vacant federal position during a recess in the Senate, making it less likely that it will be challenged. However, the appointment must then be approved by the Senate by the end of the next session. If it isn't then the position is vacant again.

The executive's relationship with the legislature

Many commentators argue that the powers of the presidency have been eroded since the Watergate scandal and during the administration of President Clinton. President George W. Bush was determined to reassert presidential prerogatives and to protect the post from scandals in order to regain respect and authority. Bush used executive orders, proclamations, statements, memoranda and national security directives. Executive orders are used to bypass Congress, particularly in situations when the president has difficulties with that body. They allow the president to act unilaterally and take the lead in policy formulation. They can, however, be challenged by both Congress and the courts. However, the president's ability to use executive orders is seen as an antidote in a system where the legislative process is often slow.

Bush used executive orders to establish military tribunals, freeze the assets of suspected terrorist organisations and undermine environmental and industrial regulation. He also used proclamations, such as creating a Life Day, which was seen as his commitment to the anti-abortion movement. He also used signing statements, where he made statements when he signed a bill into law. These encompassed his presidential objectives, objections and directions to courts to interpret the new law in a particular way.

Another way of working around Congress is to use **recess appointments**. Initially the Senate blocked the appointment of John Bolton to become the Ambassador to the United Nations, but Bush got around this by using a recess appointment.

The relationship between the president and Congress is often seen as the key determining factor in the success of a presidential term. Due to the electoral cycles of the president and Congress, it is likely that there will be a fundamental change in the make-up of Congress during the presidential term. Each Congress will obviously be different, with a different composition and set of internal politics. When George W. Bush became president in 2000, Republicans were dominant in the Senate. In the mid-term elections of 2002 the Republicans gained control of both houses. Nonetheless, Bush had to compromise over his educational reform (the No Child Left Behind Act); actually compromise was a dominant feature of George W. Bush's relationship with Congress throughout both terms. However, even when he had to make compromises and concessions, he claimed victory.

When Bush won his second term in 2004 he had the advantage of greater Republican control of Congress. He no longer faced Democrat opposition to his judicial nominations and many of his legislative ideas. However, by 2007 the Democrats had regained control of the House of Representatives and the Senate and by this stage, with a presidential election looming in 2008, Bush was generally seen to be a lame duck president, with his radical reforms doomed to failure through Democrat opposition.

The executive's relationship with the judiciary

Through appointments presidents can stamp their philosophy on the courts at all levels of the federal judiciary. The president has considerable influence over the Supreme Court, however his power to change the composition of the court depends on vacancies for the court arising.

Presidents can influence the courts in other ways, by using the office of the Solicitor General to advance their agendas, to push for constitutional amendments to overturn decisions, or to initiate new legislation. To a large extent the president can determine how the courts implement the law.

In theory, once a justice has been nominated by the president and confirmed by the Senate, they are no longer directly accountable to the other branches of government (although the constitution allows the impeachment of federal judges). Given its stability and lifetime appointments, the Supreme Court is insulated from the influence of the executive. However, given the checks and balances within the constitution, the court is not as independent as it may appear. For example, it is powerless to ensure compliance with decisions that they have made without the cooperation of the executive and the legislature. This is due to the separation of powers.

Some commentators suggest that the Constitution created a situation where there would always be a struggle for power within the US political system. Presidents have always tried to push the boundaries of their power, relative to Congress and to the Supreme Court. They have the power to make unilateral decisions; neither Congress nor the court has this ability or power. Congress can pass laws contrary to the wishes of the president, but only if they can create a veto-proof super majority. Presidents have discretion over decisions, a power not shared by Congress or the courts.

Presidential appointments to the court give the president an influence that outlives their own term of office. A prime example was the situation that confronted Franklin D. Roosevelt. In his 12 years in the White House he was only able to appoint one Supreme Court judge. The other judges were Republicans, who had no interest in supporting his economic policies or ideas on civil liberties and rights.

Robert Scigliano, a leading authority on the US Constitution, suggested that the executive and judicial branches of the government were always designed to be 'an informal and limited alliance against Congress'. To support this, Scigliano suggested that the rise of presidential and judicial power has always been at the expense of Congress. The court has been complicit in allowing the expansion of presidential power, as historically they have been unwilling to challenge the exercise of executive power.

In early October 2008 a federal district judge, Ricardo Urbina, ruled that the imprisonment of 17 Chinese Muslims held in Guantanamo Bay was unlawful under the Constitution and ordered the Bush administration to release them. The Bush administration responded by asking the court to put the release on hold while they proceeded with the appeal against the judgement. The men in question were cleared for release in 2004, but no country was willing to accept them and it was feared that they would face persecution if they were returned to China.

INTERNET RESEARCH

To follow the continuing story of the Chinese detainees, go to www.heinemann.co.uk/hotlinks, insert the express code 1825P and click on the relevant link. Then type in 'Ricardo Urbina'.

Learning objectives

- The role and power of the executive in theory and in practice
- The authority and accountability of the executive in theory and in practice

The role and power of the executive in theory and in practice

On May 6 2008, in a speech on judicial philosophy at Wake Forest University, presidential candidate John McCain suggested that the Constitutional restraint on power was as fundamental to the American system as the exercise of that power. He recognised the fact that the Founding Fathers were aware that these constitutional restraints would not always be observed. They knew that there would be abuses of power by the executive and that there needed to be checks put in place in order to deal with these situations. In McCain's view, American democracy had been born out of their experiences with tyranny. It had left them with an ingrained suspicion of power and had woven that suspicion into the American Constitution itself. McCain went on to say that the three key areas of the US government are wary of one another and each seeks to keep the others within the bounds of their given powers. In McCain's view, the Founding Fathers knew precisely what they were doing and that the system with checks and balances built into the Constitution invariably worked.

Despite McCain's views on the checks and balances that frame the role and the power of the executive, many other commentators would suggest that George W. Bush in particular had acted on many occasions without meaningful constraints and checks by Congress and, for that matter, by the judiciary.

Many of course refer to the memorandum written by the then Deputy Assistant Attorney General, John Yoo, on September 25, 2001. Yoo pointed out that Congress recognised that the president had authority to use force in certain circumstances, such as those that had been created by the September 11 terrorist attacks. The War Powers Resolution and the Joint Resolution could not put limits on the president's ability to deal with terrorist threats, and neither could they limit the military force that the president could use in response to terrorist attacks. This included the timing and the nature of that response. Yoo was clear that under the US Constitution these decisions were for the president, and only the president, to make.

The memorandum also went on to declare that in matters of national defence, war and foreign policy, the president alone had authority, although it welcomed Congressional support.

Barack Obama, in response to the question whether the Bush administration had used its executive power in an unconstitutional manner, rejected the view suggested in Department of Justice memoranda that the president should be able to do whatever he feels is necessary to protect national security. In Obama's view the president should not torture people regardless of the views of Congress and that Bush's use of executive authority to over-classify information to ensure that it remained secret was wrong. Obama held the view that a balance needed to be struck between what needed to be secret and what needed to be open and clear in a democracy.

The author Gene Healy, in his book *The Cult of the Presidency: America's Dangerous Devotion to Executive Power,* argues that the US political system has been undermined by an unchecked executive and that the president has become a central and all-powerful figure of authority, the view being that Bush in particular had operated outside the law and exploited a climate where there had been no constraint or checks.

The authority and accountability of the executive in theory and in practice

In late December 2005 George W. Bush's vice-president, Dick Cheney, complained that the president of the United States needed to have unimpaired constitutional powers and that in the five years they had been working together they had been trying to make sure that those powers were unimpaired. Cheney pointed to the 1973 War Powers Act, which put restrictions on the president's authority to launch military action without the support of Congress. Cheney believed it to be an infringement on the authority of the president and probably unconstitutional.

In the wake of the Watergate scandal in the 1970s, the political scientist Charles Hardin suggested nine proposals that would aim to give greater presidential accountability and control.

- The president and Congress should be elected at the same time for four-year terms.
- The creation of 'at large' members of the House of Representatives, not linked to geographical areas.
- The members of the House of Representatives to nominate presidential candidates and there would be no vice-president.
- There should be a reduction in the power of the Senate, much along the lines of the House of Lords.
- The House of Representatives to override presidential vetoes by a majority.
- The members of Congress should be allowed to serve in the president's cabinet.
- A defeated presidential candidate would have a seat in the House of Representatives.
- The presidency would go to the party winning the largest national share of the vote.
- The repeal of the two-term presidential limit (22nd Amendment).

This would have made much of the US system very similar to Britain, where the House of Commons is paramount and the prime minister is effectively nominated by party members alone by virtue of being party leader. Also there are no restrictions for cabinet membership or number of terms that the prime minister can hold the post.

One of the key questions, however, which links power, authority and accountability, is how can the executive lead if they have to be continually accountable? Certainly both Margaret Thatcher and Tony Blair were described as being presidential and at worst elected dictators. Certain US presidents have been accused of being imperial. Both negative descriptions imply excessive use of power, with little constraint and a desire not to be held accountable. As democratic countries, however, both Britain and the US have an inbuilt means by which leaders are ultimately accountable. They can be voted out by the electorate and while in power there are checks and balances, along with restraints.

In the US the Constitution created an executive that had sufficient powers to be able to carry out the wishes of the nation, but to offset this the president requires consent of Congress for appointments and treaties, and must present the state of the union report to Congress. Modern-day US presidents find that the restraints placed upon them make it difficult to fulfil the expectations of the public and ask for new powers. Powers such as the line-item veto can give the president more authority and it increases accountability. Much of US politics relies on consensus and compromise, which works well if policies are successful. The problem of accountability arises if the policy fails.

INS vs Chadha (1983)

This was a Supreme Court ruling that stated that legislative vetoes on executive acts were unconstitutional, as they violated the separation of powers.

INTERNET RESEARCH

There has been a long-standing debate about presidential accountability with regard to the continued presence of US troops in Iraq. Even now after Bush's term of office has ended the debate is likely to continue for some time. Search for current views on presidential accountability. To do this, go to www.heinemann.co.uk/hotlinks, insert the express code 1825P and click on the relevant link.

Learning objectives

- Representation, participation and accountability

Representation, participation and accountability

There are many different views on the range of functions that are fulfilled by the legislatures. Certainly the most recurrent themes are:

- the creation of legislation
- representation of the broader population
- scrutiny of the executive
- political recruitment
- providing a sense of legitimacy to the political system.

It is difficult to be precise about the full range of functions of the legislature, since clearly there are different perspectives and there are also slightly different sets of expectations from country to country and in different political systems. Law-making, scrutiny, confirmation of government appointments, raising issues of both local and national importance and instituting constitutional change can probably be agreed as a list of the more common functions.

In the United States, for example, investigation into the actions of the executive and supervision, or oversight, is a function which aims to monitor federal bureaucracy. Also, in the US there is a judicial function in as much as it is Congress that impeaches a president. Perhaps the main functions of Congress are representation, legislation, oversight of the executive and the right to veto.

As we will see, the role of the legislature has been the primary source of the initiation of policies and laws, but this has largely been superseded by the executive branch. Nonetheless, Congress is still perceived as being a law-making body. It is independent and largely retains its powers to initiate and to approve laws. It would therefore, perhaps, be more valuable to identify the functions of the US Congress in a manner in which Robert McKeever suggested in 1999, as outlined in the following table.

Primary function	Major function	Minor function
Law-making	Oversight	Judicial (impeachment)
	Political education of the public	Leadership selection (preparation for higher office)
	Representation	

Just as there are disagreements regarding the functions of Congress, there are also inevitably similar differences of opinion with regard to the British parliament and its functions. One of the most commonly held views is that it is not necessarily the role of parliament to govern; instead it is to hold those who do govern to account and scrutinise their behaviour. We can therefore see that the basic functions of the House of Commons, for example, would be legislation, approving spending, and examining and criticising the activities of government. Since the government effectively controls business in the House of Commons by determining the timetable (and in effect the time allocated to particular discussions), added to which they have a majority in the House, all that the House of Commons can do with regard to legislation is to discuss it and then to approve it.

In the view of many the House of Commons has a far broader range of functions. It needs to be able to represent the people and to express their grievances. It effectively sustains the government in office and it legitimises their activities. It is a major vehicle for discussion and debate. It has a role to inform and educate the electorate and it also provides an environment in which talented individuals can flourish and eventually become ministers. It is important to remember that in a system such as the British one there are in fact two houses, and the House of Lords has many similar functions to those of the House of Commons, but it still retains a partial judicial responsibility.

In practice, both houses of Congress have the power to introduce legislation (with the exception of revenue rising; this has to come from the House of Representatives). The House of Representatives also has the sole right to begin proceedings that can lead to impeachment, but it is the Senate that tries those impeachment cases. Article I of the US Constitution spells out the broad powers of the whole of Congress as being to:

- levy and collect taxes
- borrow money for the public treasury
- make rules and regulations governing commerce among the states and with foreign countries
- make uniform rules for the naturalisation of foreign citizens
- coin money, state its value, and provide for the punishment of counterfeiters
- set the standards for weights and measures
- establish bankruptcy laws
- establish post offices and post roads
- issue patents and copyrights
- set up a system of federal courts
- punish piracy
- declare war
- raise and support armies
- provide for a navy
- call out the militia to enforce federal laws, suppress lawlessness, or repel invasions
- make all laws for the seat of government
- make all laws necessary to enforce the Constitution.

Although a number of these powers are now outdated they still remain in effect. Under the terms of the 10th Amendment there are limits on congressional authority, by providing that powers that have not been delegated to the national government are reserved to the states or to the people.

Alexander Hamilton writing in the *Federalist Papers* (1787–88) proclaimed: 'Government implies the power of making laws.' Indeed Article I of the Constitution granted all legislative powers of federal government to a two-chamber Congress. Although members of the House

INTERNET RESEARCH

A good primer on US government can be found by going to www.heinemann.co.uk/hotlinks, inserting the express code 1825P and clicking on the relevant link. Go to the publications section and look for 'Outline of US government'.

of Representatives were elected for 100 years after the adoption of the Constitution, senators were chosen by their state legislatures and their primary responsibility was to make sure that their state received equal treatment in all legislation. The idea was sound in the creation of two different groups: one would represent the state governments (senators) and the other would represent the people (House of Representatives). Both groups would have to approve each law. This meant that Congress would never pass laws without due deliberation. Each of the houses could serve as checks on one another, and even when the 17th Amendment was adopted in 1913 to allow for direct elections to the Senate, this did not necessarily change the relationship.

Initially the delegates at the Constitutional Convention back in the 18th century believed that Congress would spend much of its time deliberating foreign affairs. Domestic matters would be left to the states and to local government. As it transpired, they were wrong. Congress, with its broad powers and authority, has been involved in all law-making, and although Congress's power has changed over the years, it still cannot be considered to be simply a rubber stamp for decisions made by the president.

US cabinet or EU Commission – which is more democratic?

There are constant accusations that the EU is not democratic, particularly given the fact that the EU Commission, one of the most powerful EU bodies, is unelected. However, this is not unusual and has been the case in the US for some years. Although the president is the most powerful member of the executive, the US voters do not directly vote for the president, it is the electoral college that actually makes the final decision on who shall become president. It is perfectly possible (as in 2000 with Al Gore), that a candidate can receive the majority of the popular vote, but still fail to become president. This also happened in 1875 when Samuel Tilden won the 'popular vote', but lost out to Rutherford Hayes and again in 1888 when Grover Cleveland received a majority vote, but Benjamin Harrison become president. Some also believe that this happened in 1960 when, amidst rumours of voting fraud, Richard Nixon may have received a higher popular vote than John F Kennedy.

Taking this debate one step further, the president's cabinet is not elected by the voters; its members are appointed by the president. This is not usually the case in Britain, where the majority of the cabinet members are democratically elected Members of Parliament. It is, however, the case that the US cabinet members have to be approved by Congress.

The EU Commission is as close the EU has to an executive. The president of the Commission is agreed by democratically elected governments of the members states (in effect we could compare this to the US electoral college). The Commission president-elect is then ratified by a democratically elected European Parliament. The president of the Commission then appoints a cabinet, rather like the US system. However, the president of the Commission has little say regarding which commissioners can be chosen, as candidates are nominated by individual governments of the member states. All the president of the Commission can do is to allocate those nominated individuals to particular posts.

In the US, no such system exists. If it did, it would mean that each US state would nominate its representative to the US cabinet and the president would then have to choose from among these candidates to appoint them to key roles. It would be a more democratic system, but it would just mean that the cabinet would comprise of a number of individuals appointed by the states (presumably with the most powerful states' appointees getting the most important posts) as opposed to the present system where the president can pick and choose from their own bank of friends, supporters and others.

The House of Representatives

Congress was originally envisaged as being a major institution in the federal government. It was through Congress that the electorate would have control over policy. Congress was also designed to create and pass laws; the president would simply implement them. The House of Representatives would control the purse strings and together with the Senate they would be at the centre of America's constitutional system. It never really worked in the way that it was designed and as America developed firstly the president was elected and then ultimately the Senate.

Originally there was one representative for every 30,000 citizens. This quickly leapt from 65 to 106 and had the same formula been maintained there would be 7000 representatives today. There is a ten-year national census and redistribution of seats and the ratio is now around 1:600,000. Some of the smaller states have just one representative (each state is constitutionally guaranteed at least one). Some of the more populus states have over 20, with California for example having 52 representatives. This gives a current total of 435 representatives.

Members of the House serve two-year terms and thus the life of a Congress is two years. Sessions are held in the Capitol Building in Washington DC. Effectively Congress remains in session from 3 January each year until its members vote to adjourn.

The House of Representatives is considered to be the lower house in the bicameral system, with the Senate as the upper house. As we will see when we look at the organisation of the House of Representatives, one of the key members is the Speaker of the House of Representatives. This individual is elected by the entire House membership at the beginning of each new Congress. The speaker for the 111th Congress (3 January 2009 to 3 January 2011) is California's Nancy Pelosi, the first ever female speaker. Usually the nominee for the post comes from the majority party in the House and although the Constitution does not require the speaker to be a member of the House, all speakers to date have been members. Theoretically, this individual is third in line after the president and the vice-president (less significant after the 25th Amendment).

The role of the speaker is somewhat different from that of the Speaker of the House of Commons. The Speaker of the House of Representatives is not neutral and is the leader of the majority party, a spokesperson for that party and in cases where the president is of a different party, they are in effect the leader of the opposition. The speaker chairs debates and their responsibilities are to:

- act as presiding officer
- decide on points of order and to interpret and enforce House rules
- refer bills to committees
- appoint select committee and conference committee chairs
- appoint members to the House Rules Committee
- influence the flow of legislation.

There are also majority and minority leaders. These are elected by their party groups. The majority leader acts as a support for the Speaker of the House and the minority leader acts as leader of the party in opposition. They both direct the operations of their party during the day, hold press briefings, liaise with the White House and other groups and, as we will see, these leaders in the Senate will make unanimous consent agreements in order to bring bills up for debate.

Learning objectives

- The House of Representatives
- The Senate

The US House of Representatives is housed in the Capitol Building in Washington DC

The Senate

The Constitution requires that US senators are at least 30 years old and that they have been US citizens for nine years, along with being a resident of the state that they represent. Each state is entitled to two senators, therefore there are 100. The state legislature will divide the state into two districts, largely equal in terms of population, and every two years the voters from each district choose their representative.

Senators' terms are six years and every two years a third of the Senate will be standing for election. This means that two-thirds of the senators are always those that have some legislative experience.

The Senate has some special powers that are reserved to it, which include the ability to confirm presidential appointments and ratify treaties. Although senators are elected by one half of the state, they represent the entire state. Senators are more likely to chair committees due to the small numbers of them. They are generally better known and in many cases former members of the House of Representatives will eventually become senators. Many presidential candidates come from the Senate, such as John Kerry (2004), Barack Obama (2008), who was a junior senator from Illinois, and John McCain (2008), a senior senator from Arizona.

Unlike the House of Commons and the House of Lords, there is far more equality between the Senate and the House of Representatives. Bills go through all stages in both houses, but neither can overturn the decision of the other. Both have standing committees and at conference committee stage both houses are represented. This means that both houses have to agree to compromises reached at this stage. Also, both houses need to return a two-thirds majority to override a presidential veto.

The following table looks at the similarities and differences between the Senate and the House of Representatives.

	House of Representatives	Senate
Number of members	435	100
Members per state	In proportion to population	2
Term of office	2	6
Age qualification	25	30
Citizenship qualification	7	9
Average member age	55.9 (110th Congress)	61.7 (110th Congress)
Presiding officer	Speaker	Vice-President
Number of women	74	16
Number of African-Americans/Hispanics	41/27	1/3
Exclusive powers	Initiate money bills, impeachment and election of president if there is a deadlock in the electoral college	Treaty ratification, confirmation of appointments, tries cases of impeachment, election of vice-president if there is deadlock in the electoral college
Joint powers	Legislation, declaration of war, constitutional amendments, confirm the appointment of vice-president	

INTERNET RESEARCH

To access the official sites of the US Senate and House of Representatives, go to www.heinemann.co.uk/hotlinks, insert the express code 1825P and click on the relevant link.

Membership, Leadership and Committees

Learning objectives

- Membership of Congress
- How Congress is organised
- How committees work

Membership of Congress

Compared to the 109th Congress, the average age of senators is two years older in the 110th and a year older in the House of Representatives. The average age for both houses is 57. The youngest member of the House of Representatives was Patrick McHenry at 32, and the oldest was Ralph Hall at 85.

The overwhelming majority of members of the House and the Senate (2008) were former state legislators, with a combined total of 272. Over 100 were former congressional staff, 37 were mayors, 9 were state governors, 13 doctors, 6 ministers and a range of other occupations, ranging from sheriffs, FBI agents, chemists, talk show hosts, professional musicians and carpenters. The vast majority of members in both houses have degrees (498) and the average length of service as a member of the House was 10 years, or just over five terms. For the Senate, the average was 12.8 years, although one member, Senator Robert C. Byrd, served for 48 years.

There is a broad religious representation, although the majority describe themselves as Protestant. There are, however, smaller groups of Quakers, Mormons, Buddhists and two Muslims.

The vast majority of the women in the House of Representatives are Democrats (54 of 74). Six out of 11 serving in the Senate are Democrats. There are 13 African-American women in the House and Senator Barack Obama was the first African-American male Democrat to serve in the Senate.

All the Hispanic senators are male and of the 27 who serve in the House 7 are women. There are 8 members of Asian/Hawaiian Pacific Islands heritage, one Native American and 11 individuals who were born outside of the USA. A large number (127) have served in the US military; this element has been in decline for many years; for example, in the 93rd Congress (1973–75) there were 390 former military personnel.

How Congress is organised

As we have seen, Congress aims to provide representation, along with a legislative function, and to have oversight and veto of the powers of the executive branch. This has meant that committees have become the centre of legislative business in Congress and this is where power lies, coupled with party leadership. There are enormous numbers of committees and sub-committees.

Individual legislators tend to specialise in particular subjects (often linked to their constituents' needs). Congress has its own bureaucracy, which has to match and mirror those in the executive branch, and this means that as federal departments and agencies have increased in both number and complexity Congress has had to respond.

It is important to also appreciate that there are many policy committees that are concerned with general policy, while there are other committees that focus on serving constituencies. The committees that focus on money issues are often referred to as prestige committees. In the committees the tasks of actually framing, amending and rejecting legislation is undertaken. Some of the committees will authorise legislation and other committees will deliberate before providing funds to finance programmes.

Not all of the committees are of equal status or power. The finance committees tend to be the most influential, such as the House Appropriations Committee. The Senate Foreign

Relations Committee is extremely important for foreign policy. There is also a hierarchy in the subcommittees, for example the House Appropriations Subcommittee on Defense is far more influential and prestigious than one that focuses on transport or infrastructure.

Membership of committees is of vital importance to both representatives and to senators. It is the way that they gauge their status and their influence. Understandably, the ways in which members are selected for these committees (and indeed the chairpersons) are always a source of dispute, debate and controversy.

In theory, the party with the majority in a particular chamber will automatically have a majority on committees. The minority party is represented broadly in relation to the number of members it has in that chamber. The majority party also provides the chairperson. Representatives and senators can only sit on two committees (the representatives who are in the Rules, Ways and Means and Appropriations Committee tend not to sit on other committees).

A meeting of party members in each house will choose members of standing committees and the members chosen are usually on the basis of seniority, reputation, connections and experience. In the Senate, in order to initiate new senators, the 'Johnson Rule' ensures that the new senators are assigned to at least one major committee.

How committees work

Broadly there are three different types of committee.

- Standing committees – these have legislative jurisdiction and consider bills and issues, they have oversight responsibilities and, most importantly, they recommend and authorise funding levels for government operations and programmes.
- Select or special committees – these are established by the chamber to carry out investigations and studies. They will often look at issues that do not match the work of an existing standing committee, or perhaps cut across the work of standing committees. Sometimes these committees will be permanent or temporary.
- Joint committees – these have members from both chambers and usually carry out housekeeping tasks, such as looking at printing procedures or working out draft compromises before being submitted to the chambers.

As of the 110th Congress, there were 21 permanent committees in the House of Representatives and 20 in the Senate. There were also 4 joint committees.

The House Rules Committee, although it is a standing committee, has a different set of functions.

- It timetables bills for consideration.
- It deals with bills as they move from the committee stage to second reading.
- It prioritises bills by making sure that important ones are given priority.
- It establishes the rules of debate for each bill, such as suggesting what amendments could be made.

INTERNET RESEARCH

For a full listing of committees and sub-committees in both houses, go to www.heinemann.co.uk/hotlinks, insert the express code 1825P and click on the relevant link. Then select 'Committees and subcommittees'.

2.12 Political Parties

Learning objectives

- The two-party system
- Third parties

The two-party system

The two major US political parties are the Democrats and the Republicans and each has national committees, which are effectively their national party organisation. The party chairperson acts as a spokesperson and is responsible for the day-to-day operations of the party. The national committees tend to meet only twice a year and they have a national convention every four years.

The bulk of the party organisation tends to be at state level, where there are party conventions and committees, county and district committees, city committees, wards and precinct committees. Unlike the British system, where there is a clearly defined leader of a party, the closest the US has is the president, but not even that means that the White House controls the party. In effect both of the major political parties do not have a leader and only at the national conventions is there any indication of real central leadership.

Democrats are considered to be the more liberal of the two parties, but there are different versions; some are liberal, moderate, new or conservative. In the Republican Party there are Christians, moderates, compassionates and right wing. George W. Bush considered himself to be a compassionate conservative. The exact colour of a Democrat or a Republican tends to be reflected by their geographical location in the country. In the south both tend to be conservative, in the northeast Democrats will be liberal and Republicans moderate.

The 1920 Republican Party convention

The two parties dominate the presidency and both houses of Congress. Since 1856 every president has either been a Democrat or a Republican. Since 1916 the two parties have commanded at least 80 per cent of the popular vote. In the last 20 or more election campaigns for the presidency the two parties have polled at least 90 per cent of the votes. In many cases all members of the Senate and the bulk of the members of the House of Representatives are either Democrats or Republicans, as are all state governors.

As we will see when we look at the election system, the US has a first past-the-post, or winner-takes-all system. But the reasons for the dominance of the two parties are far deeper. Arguably in Britain there is a distinct political divide between the two leading parties, if not in policy then certainly in spirit. This is not necessarily the case in the US. Each of the parties is diverse and

The 1920 Democratic Party convention

INTERNET RESEARCH

For more on the current standing of public opinion on parties and their dominance of Congress, go to www.heinemann.co.uk/hotlinks, insert express code 1825P and click on the relevant link. Under 'Politics and government' select 'US poll topics'.

there is a broad range of views that are tolerated within the parties. This does not leave a great deal of scope for a third party.

Some commentators contend, however, that there is not a two-party system but a fifty-party system, with each state having its own peculiar party system. Others would suggest that it is a one-party system, where for periods of time either the Republicans or the Democrats dominate politics. A further view is that the US has no party system at all and that membership of, or identification with, a particular party is of no real consequence, as individuals are primarily elected on the basis of personality and connection with the electorate.

Within the legislature there is often a great difficulty in a party trying to pursue a particular policy agenda, particularly one that would cause certain members difficulty in supporting. Often the parties will have narrow majorities. This means that minority concerns nearly always have to be taken into account. Traditionally parties have found it difficult to impose any degree of control over the legislators. Unlike many parties in Europe the enforcement of party discipline is slack.

Members tend to be judged on their performance and particularly how well they have served their own state or district, rather than how they are perceived by the party. As a result, rather than claiming that the US is a two-party system, it may in fact have a conditional party system. This implies that party cohesiveness and solidarity is retained only to the point where the first legislator identifies an element of a policy in which they find it impossible to agree; at that point the legislator will break ranks with the party and demand concessions. Since the bulk of the legislative work is carried out in committees, there have been attempts to impose some kind of discipline over party members.

Often deals are cut within the majority party in a committee before the committee even meets. This allows a smoother passage of the bill through the committee stage, while at the same time the inbuilt majority within the committee allows it to ignore minority views. In periods when Republicans were in the majority in the House of Representatives, Democrats had constantly complained that a committee chairperson ignored their views, or that legislation was approved and sent to the House without any meaningful Democrat input.

In the Senate, the Republicans in particular in recent years have tried to control troublesome committees and members. This is largely achieved by handpicking members for prestigious committees, as insurance that they will to an extent toe the party line.

Third parties

In the November 2006 election for the House of Representatives, third parties collectively mustered just 2.6 per cent of the popular vote. There are two independents in the US Senate, with the two major parties having 49 seats each. Once again, the election results saw the vast majority of electors opting for Democrat or Republican candidates.

When we examine the electoral system it will become apparent that the odds are heavily stacked against third parties from ever achieving widespread support. In the 2006 election for the House of Representatives no party other than the Democrats or the Republicans managed to secure more than 700,000 votes out of a total vote of nearly 81 million.

There is, however, a broad range of third parties, which we will examine when we look at political parties and pressure groups. These range from right-wingers through to libertarians, greens, peace and freedom supporters, borderline communists and those that believe that the political system would be far more effective if it practised transcendental meditation.

Bernie Sanders

Sanders was the sole independent in the House of Representatives in the lead up to the November 2006 election. Sanders (Vermont At Large seat) left the House to run for the Senate seat vacated by Jim Jeffords (who had retired). Sanders won the Vermont Senate election with 65 per cent of the vote.

Methods and results of presidential persuasion

The president will aim to persuade citizens, the political elite and public servants using a wide range of different techniques. Usually this will mean going public and in effect confiding with the public as a means of persuasion. The president may also try to send private messages to individual Congress members. They will use minor and major speeches.

Persuasion is vital in a political system where there is no direct hierarchy. It is vital in order to ensure effective leadership, and despite the fact that the constitution provides checks and balances to ensure that no single individual or branch dominates the system, powerful presidents have increased influence over all government actions by use of persuasion. Voters will undoubtedly call presidents to account for government actions that actually take place outside their constitutional jurisdiction.

For the vast majority of presidents public attempts at persuasion rely on the strength of their speech-writers. In opportunities to speak directly to the American people or to key decision-makers and power-brokers a well-crafted speech, expertly delivered, is an enormous advantage in forwarding particular points of view. Despite employing experienced speech-writers, many were dismayed by George W. Bush's inability to take advantage of public relations opportunities by failing to deliver a persuasive speech. This was certainly not the case with Ronald Reagan or Bill Clinton and, arguably, Barack Obama had a better delivery than John McCain.

Since most Americans experience democracy and their leaders through the medium of television, the verbal styles of candidates or those in office is vital. From the 1980s, R. P. Hart investigated the style adopted by presidents in literally hundreds of speeches. He identified activity, certainty, optimism and realism as characteristics used by presidents to persuade. Recurrent themes in effective persuasion were 'calling for change', 'taking the offensive on issues', 'emphasising accomplishments' and 'certainty'.

In September 2008 President George W. Bush attempted to use presidential persuasion to convince the US Congress to authorise a massive rescue package for the US financial industry. One of his most persuasive arguments was that the bail out would 'help keep the crisis in our financial system from spreading throughout our economy'. The first attempt failed and it was rejected by the House of Representatives. More Democrats than Republicans actually voted in favour of the rescue plan, perhaps due to the persuasive skills of Barack Obama, who was confident that the package would pass through Congress. Nonetheless, Republican presidential nominee, McCain, blamed Obama for failing to use his persuasive skills to support the package in a forthright enough manner. In its amended form, with much coaxing and persuasion, the rescue measures were finally approved.

Various presidents have used different techniques of persuasion; many rely on personal contacts with key legislators. Presidents have used the threat that they might oppose pet bills of key legislators, or withhold spending projects in their district or state. On other occasions persuasion has centred round the concept of loyalty, where support is seen as being for the good of the party. Presidents will make direct appeals to the public to put pressure on Congress and will certainly use the media to their advantage, because anything said by the president is newsworthy.

The other key persuasive technique is that a popular president may well improve the election or re-election prospects of other members of the same party. This is known as the coat-tail effect.

Learning objectives

- Methods and results of presidential persuasion
- Limits on presidential power

Bully pulpit

This was a term credited to President Theodore Roosevelt when he referred to the office of president as being an ideal platform to push forward an agenda. It now has a broader meaning in that individuals can bring up issues that were not initially in a debate because of their position and the opportunity for publicity.

Limits on presidential power

In early 2007 President George W. Bush and Congress were at loggerheads about his intention to send more US troops to Iraq. Publicly Bush admitted that Congress would vote against the additional troops, but simply said: 'I've made my decision and we're going forward.'

Bush and his vice-president, Dick Cheney, justified their right to ignore Congress by stating that the constitution justified their actions. Cheney said: 'The Constitution is very clear that the president is, in fact, under Article II, commander-in-chief.'

This was at a time when around 70 per cent of Americans were opposed to the way the war was being handled. There was fear that there would be a constitutional clash, as Congress would try to enforce its own war powers. Many believed that the president was reading powers into the Constitution that were never in fact there, such as using signing statements. The Constitution was designed to balance power with checks and balances that in this instance divided war power between the president and Congress. However, the Constitution allows for the president to be the commander-in-chief and therefore at the head of the military chain of command. Congress would be in breach of the Constitution if it required military commanders to answer to them.

Congress has the power to declare war, raise and support armies and 'make rules concerning captures on land and water'.

James Madison wrote:

> *The Constitution supposes, what the history of all governments demonstrates, that the executive is the branch of power most interested in war, and most prone to it. It has accordingly with studied care, vested the question of war in the legislature.*

The Supreme Court has also made it clear that Congress could limit the war powers of the president. In 1799 the Supreme Court decided in favour of the owner of a ship that had been seized on the instructions of President John Adams. The president had acted beyond what was lawful. In 1952 the Supreme Court ruled that President Truman could not take control of steel mills to avert a strike during the Korean War.

A summary of the key limits on presidential power are outlined in the following table.

Limits	Explanation
Removed or impeached	A president can be impeached if convicted of treason, bribery, high crimes or other misdemeanours.
Presidents veto not absolute	The president can veto a bill, but Congress can override the veto.
Term limit	The 22nd Amendment restricts an individual to a two-term limit as president.
Signing bills	If a president does not sign a bill or veto it within 10 days then it is automatically passed, so a president cannot hold a bill up indefinitely.
Treaty-making	The treaty-making process is shared with the Senate.
Members of presidential cabinet and Supreme Court nominations	These have to be approved by the Senate.

INTERNET RESEARCH

To find a useful set of lists of presidential powers and limitations, go to www.heinemann.co.uk/hotlinks, insert the express code 1825P and click on the relevant link. Select 'Powers and limitations'.

The legislative process

Unlike the British system, the House of Representatives and the Senate have equal powers when dealing with legislation. The other major difference is that bills pass through both houses at the same time. It is also important to remember that during any Congress up to 9000 bills may be considered. In fact due to time constraints and opposition only around 400 of these will be passed. If a bill does not make it through all of the phases in one Congress it has to start again at the beginning of the next Congress.

In order for a bill to be passed into law the supporters must win every single stage. The opponents only have to block it once for it to fail. As there is very little party discipline this makes the passing of bills even more complicated, added to which it is unlikely that one party has a majority in both houses. In the majority of cases one party has a majority in both houses, although the same party has not had control of the White House, which leads to divided government.

Legislation comes from a number of different sources, including members of Congress, individuals, citizen groups, organisations, state legislatures, the president or a member of the president's cabinet and independent agencies.

Learning objectives

- The legislative process
- First reading
- Committee stage and timetabling
- Second and third reading
- Conference committee
- Presidential actions

First reading

The first reading of a bill is just a formality. Money bills are introduced to the House of Representatives first. At this stage there is no debate or vote and in the Senate just the title of the bill is read out. The bill is then sent on to committee stage.

Committee stage and timetabling

Before the second reading of the bill it is referred to one of the permanent standing committees. The committee can make any amendments it sees fit but because there are so many bills to be considered many are what is known as pigeonholed, which means they are set aside and never considered.

If a bill is to be considered a hearing will be called and witnesses will be summoned to provide testimony to the committee (sometimes the full committee or a subcommittee). The hearings can be very time-consuming, lasting just a matter of hours or as long as several months. It is very dependent upon the complexity of the bill or whether it is controversial.

After the hearings the committee holds a mark-up session, in which changes are made to the bill before it is sent on to the next stage (known as reporting out). For many bills the committee stage is as far as it gets as many fail at this stage.

Once Congress is in full swing bills will start to stack up to be brought to the floor of the House of Representatives and the Senate. Each of the committees and subcommittees will be generating work for Congress and inevitably there is a traffic jam. Bills start to queue up to be discussed. The House Rules Committee aims to deal with timetabling for the House of Representatives and the Senate uses a Unanimous Consent Agreement, in which the order of the bills to be debated is agreed between the Senate majority and minority leaders.

Filibuster

This is a technique in which a senator or series of senators will attempt to talk out and indefinitely extend the debate to prevent a bill from being voted on. The debate can be brought to an end by 60 senators voting for a closure, or a cloture, which brings the debate to an end.

Second and third reading

This is the first chance to really debate the bill. In the House of Representatives most bills are debated in the Committee of the Whole House. Both houses can make further amendments to the bills and a simple majority is required to pass each amendment. In the Senate opponents can use a **filibuster**. At the end of the debate the vote is taken, with a simple majority required to pass the bill. Non-controversial bills use a voice vote (those in favour say 'yeah' and those against say 'nay'). For other bills a recorded vote is required.

The third reading represents Congress's final opportunity to debate the bill. This may happen some weeks or months after the second reading. In many cases the third reading is a relatively brief one and at the end of the debate another vote is taken.

Conference committee

This is an optional stage in the procedure. Conference committee members come from either house. It only tends to occur when the House of Representatives version of the bill is different from the Senate version of the bill. The idea is to amicably agree to deal with the differences in the two bills. When there are substantial differences that cannot be sorted out then a conference committee is necessary.

Presidential actions

Once the Senate and the House of Representatives have finally agreed a single version of the bill it can then be passed on to the president. The president has three ways of dealing with the bill, as outlined in the following table.

Presidential option	Implications
Sign the bill	If the president supports the bill and wishes to gain some credit for it he will sign it and it will become law. He needs to sign the bill within 10 congressional working days.
Leave the bill	The president may choose to do this if he does not fully support the bill, or is not particularly concerned about it. In some cases it is a sign that the president may have wished to veto the bill but has decided against it. Those left on his desk automatically become law within 10 congressional working days, with or without his signature.
Veto the bill	The president will do this when he opposes the bill. He must veto it within 10 congressional working days and send it back to either house, explaining the objections. In order to override this veto both houses must support the bill by a two-thirds majority.

If the bill appears at the end of a congressional session the president has, in fact, a fourth option. He can use the pocket veto on the bill. If the bill is waiting for the president's action and the Congress session ends then the bill is lost and a pocket veto cannot be overridden by Congress.

It is important to remember that during President Clinton's term of office he had a fifth option, known as the line-item veto. It meant that Clinton could sign parts of a bill into law while vetoing other parts that related to spending. The Supreme Court declared this unconstitutional in 1998.

INTERNET RESEARCH

For a comprehensive, if complicated, explanation of how laws are made in the US, go to heinemann.co.uk/hotlinks, insert the express code 1825P and click on the relevant link.

Oversight of the executive

One of the key roles of Congress is oversight. This means making sure that laws are faithfully executed and that both military and diplomatic activities carried out by the executive are vetted. The idea is to keep mistakes from happening, draw out lessons and stop situations from spiralling out of control. Oversight should cut waste, uncover fraud and scandal and ensure that policymakers are held accountable. It is a time-consuming occupation, looking at the work of agencies or departments, and on many occasions investigations have been undermined by partisan attitudes and sensationalism.

Until the end of last century oversight was common. For example, a special committee criticised Truman's handling of the Korean War. In the 1970s committee investigations looked at intelligence failures and illegal surveillance. In the 1980s they investigated the Iran-Contra Affair.

Oversight began to decline during Clinton's administration and, excluding appropriations committees, the House of Representatives carried out just 287 in the first six months of 1997 compared to treble that in the first half of 1983. Similar falls were seen in the Senate.

Since George W. Bush became president oversight has virtually disappeared. In 2003 to 2004 there were just 37. The allegations of torture at the Abu Ghraib facility amounted to just 12 hours of testimony. In the mid-1990s a Republican-dominated Congress took 140 hours of testimony to decide whether President Clinton had used his Christmas mailing list to find campaign donors.

Oversight has tended to shift to front-page stories in the media. Congress has shown little appetite to carry out oversight. Ruth Marcus of the *Washington Post* believed that the Bush administration did not take congressional oversight very seriously but that they reluctantly allowed it to happen and wanted the process to be over and done with as soon as possible. She also suggested that the Bush administration ignored congressional oversight on the basis that it intruded on the power of the executive branch.

The reason may be that Republicans in Congress have shied away from criticising their own president. The call for oversight, however, is renewed with greater Democrat representation in the House of Representatives.

Relations with the executive and judicial branches

According to the Constitution the executive should administer policies agreed by Congress, direct foreign policy and the president should act as commander-in-chief. But the role of president has developed beyond the original intentions and he is now a legislative leader, recommending legislation to Congress. It is the executive that tends to devise policy, initiate legislation and implement policy, and then carry it out.

The legislature was originally envisaged to initiate, consider, amend and improve legislation, while being a representative of the people and overseeing the work of the executive branch.

The Constitution defines the areas of policy for which the president and Congress are responsible. They have to cooperate, as they are seen as separate institutions that share power. However, the growth in the power of the president has altered the balance and has undermined Congress.

Nonetheless, Articles I and II of the Constitution give Congress all legislative powers and the ability to override a presidential veto. The House of Representatives can impeach the president and the Senate can try him. Most presidential appointments have to be approved. The Senate has

Learning objectives

- Oversight of the executive
- Relations with the executive and judicial branches

The US vs Lopez (1995)

The first case since the 1930s to set limits to Congress's power under the commerce clause of the constitution.

Reno vs ACLU (1997)

The Supreme Court struck down an anti-obscenity provision in the Communications Decency Act, as it violated freedom of speech provisions in the 1st Amendment.

INTERNET RESEARCH

For more on the work and deliberations of the Supreme Court, go to www.heinemann.co.uk/hotlinks, insert the express code 1825P and click on the relevant link.

to approve treaties and all of Congress has to approve a declaration of war, to raise and support armies and to provide and maintain a navy.

Congress can and will block appointments and has moved to impeach presidents. But the president can still veto legislation and convene extraordinary sessions of Congress to discuss matters that he believes to be important. He can influence Congress but the president's role is often difficult due to lack of party loyalty, his ability to persuade and the fact that US voters seem to prefer a divided government, where the president and the houses of Congress are dominated by different parties.

Congress also has relations with the judiciary. The Senate approves federal judicial appointments (Article II). They can impeach and remove a judge (Article I) and they have the power to set up the federal court system (Article IV). Congress has certainly used these powers, refusing to approve appointments of senior judges, impeaching office holders and reorganising the courts, their jurisdiction and procedures.

On the other hand, the judiciary is there to interpret Acts of Congress, which obviously affects their application and their impact. They also have the power of judicial review, which can declare legislation unconstitutional. In excess of 150 federal laws have been declared unconstitutional.

The following table outlines the key struggles between Congress, the executive and the judiciary.

Congress vs The executive	Congress vs The judiciary
Case Act on Executive Agreements 1972 Before 1972 the president could make international agreements by executive agreement. Treaties required the advice and consent of the Senate. In 1942 the Supreme Court held that these international executive agreements, even though they had the same legal status as treaties, did not require Senate approval. A number of executive agreements were made with South Vietnam during the 1950s and 1960s. Congress was not told until 1969. The Case Act required the president to inform the Senate within 60 days of any executive agreement. This affected the president's role as chief diplomat.	Nixon vs United States 1993 It was claimed that Senate committees appointed to gather evidence at an impeachment trial were unconstitutional. This was rejected because impeachment was considered to be a political question.
War Powers Act 1973 (unconstitutional after INS vs Chadha 1983) This was a law that required the president to notify Congress within 48 hours of committing armed forces into action and forbade them from remaining for more than 60 days without use of military force or a declaration of war. This was extended by the Boland Amendments (1982–84), which prohibited military aid for the contra rebels opposing the Marxist Nicaraguan government. This affected the president's role as commander-in-chief.	Regents of University of California vs Bakke 1978 The court held that affirmative action systems are constitutional, but a quota system based on race is unconstitutional.
Budget and Impoundment Control Act 1974 This prevents the president from taking the decision not to spend funds on programmes that Congress has already approved, but that he does not feel is necessary. This affected the president's role as chief executive.	Marbury vs Madison 1803 This was the landmark case that established the US Supreme Court's power to judicial review.
Immigration and Naturalization Service vs Chadha 1983 Six immigrants were given permission by the US Attorney General to stay in America. The House of Representatives used a veto. In the Supreme Court it was held that because the House was the only one that took action they had taken a power of the executive branch and replaced it with a legislative act. They had overruled the executive illegally.	Brown vs Board of Education 1954 This held that racially segregated schools violated the 14th Amendment.

Learning objectives

- Legislature's representation, accountability, sovereignty and effectiveness
- Executive role, power, authority and accountability
- Factors influencing voting

Legislature's representation, accountability, sovereignty and effectiveness

It is always a matter of argument whether an electoral system is able to produce individuals who reflect the wishes of the voter as a delegate, or whether they are simply broader representatives. These are all issues that will be discussed in the question topics. There is also the question as to who the individuals really represent: their constituency, special interests, party, conscience, the nation or their deity?

Members of Congress can be held accountable in general elections, just as in Britain, by losing their seat. However, it is more difficult than in Britain because it is often impossible to find out how a local representative has performed from the performance of the party, because parties are not that important. However, electors tend to elect individuals rather than party members, and voters are not electing a government as such. The electorate has blamed parties in the past for government problems and blamed individuals because they supported that party.

There is a lack of accountability on the following basis.

- The senators serve long terms.
- There are safe seats and no limit to the number of terms served.
- The sitting representatives or members of the Senate have an inbuilt advantage.
- The money for campaigning is a key factor.
- There is no significant choice between candidates in a two-party system.
- It is difficult to blame individuals for a party's performance.
- The electors tend to blame Congress and not their local representative.
- It is difficult to hold Congress to account between elections.

National sovereignty is not as important in the US as it is in Britain, but internal sovereignty is more important. The country has a federal system, dividing sovereignty between the national and state governments and there are constant debates about the balance of sovereignty between the two. State rights are at the centre of sovereignty issues and federal government is strictly limited by the constitution.

Executive role, power, authority and accountability

As we have seen, on paper the US president appears to be less powerful compared to the other branches of government than the British prime minister is compared to the judiciary and the legislature. Yet in practice the power of the president can be paramount, particularly if that president enjoys overwhelming electoral support. The president is able to initiate legislation and to push it through using a balance of persuasion and threats, particularly given that Congress appears far less able and willing to use its oversight and at times its veto.

The president has innumerable opportunities to suggest, outline or announce new policy initiatives, which can then be transformed from policy to legislation. But this requires the support of Congress and ultimately the willingness of the Supreme Court to agree that the measures are not in breach of the Constitution.

Over the years it does appear that the US system is beginning to adopt features of the British parliamentary system, just as the British system appears to be gravitating towards a version of the US system. The president, theoretically using the constitutional checks and balances, is far more constrained and Congress reserves the right to override any vetoes that the president may attempt and, if necessary, to remove that president through impeachment if he is deemed to have acted in a criminal way in prosecuting his policy.

Factors influencing voting

There are a number of theories that have been put forward to explain why members of the US Congress vote in particular ways, which simply cannot be explained in the same way as the overwhelming majority of voting behaviour in the British House of Commons. The following table summarises the key factors that are considered to be the determinants of voting in US Congress.

Voting determinant	Explanation
Political party	This may not be the most important determinant, as political parties are less centralised and ideologically cohesive in the US than in Britain, for example. It is far more likely that members of the House and the Senate are concerned with how their constituents view voting behaviour than how the party views that behaviour. This means they are reliant on their constituents and when party votes are mentioned in US politics it often means that the majority of one party votes one way and the majority of the other party the other way. This is regardless of the numbers of either party that broke with their party majorities.
Constituents ('the folks back home')	Because House of Representatives and Senate members are resident of the state that they represent, there is a direct connection between the individual and their electorate. Some states require members of the House to live in the actual district they represent. Many of the members of Congress were brought up and educated in their home state and they have to be aware that they come up for re-election every two years. Members will canvas for opinion and hold meetings, surgeries, appear on phone-ins, address groups and visit local schools and businesses. This does not necessarily mean that the member will find all of his or her constituents of a similar opinion.
Administration	The term administration means the executive branch. Members of Congress will have been contacted by representatives of the administration to persuade them to vote in a particular way. The administration will keep up regular contact and find individuals who are prepared to cooperate on the basis of mutual benefit. An administration will talk not just to members of their own party, but also to the opposition.
Pressure groups	An enormous number of pressure groups will try to exert influence on members, visiting, calling, and organising rallies, demonstrations and petitions. Pressure groups are also important in fundraising for politicians and those that support a pressure group's cause can expect help and financial aid in return.
Colleagues and staff	Politicians will rely on the advice of legislative staff, other members of their own party, friends, colleagues and members of standing committees to receive advice, as they are unlikely to appreciate the complexities of every single bill or amendment that they will be required to vote on during a Congress term.
Personal beliefs	Many politicians hold fundamental views on issues such as federal government, defence, tax, abortion and capital punishment. Personal beliefs may preclude them from voting along party lines due to closely held views.

F853 Question Topics 1:

2.17 Representation in Congress and the System of standing Committees

Learning objectives

- Is Congress representative?
- What is the importance of standing committees?

Is Congress representative?

Congress was originally envisioned as being representative of the mass of people, even more so when the Senate was also elected directly by the people. As legislatures, it is vital that they represent or reflect the wishes of the people, as they are elected representatives of the voters. In the US, this representative function is perhaps more important than in many other countries; members of Congress give the highest priority to the attitudes, views and concerns of those that elected them, often to the exclusion of the demands of their own party.

However, most senators and members of the House of Representatives are professionals: there are lawyers, business people, journalists, doctors, university professors and accountants. There are many lawyers, although there are considerably less than in the 1970s. In the 107th Congress 40 per cent were lawyers. There are relatively few former blue-collar workers and certainly the under-classes are unrepresented. However, this does not mean that the members of Congress are unable to represent their interests.

Senator Edward Kennedy, for example, an extremely rich individual, has been active in seeking the protection of underprivileged citizens and is a strong advocate for them.

Question topic material

Note that these topics are not written in essay format, but they do include ideas, concepts and information and practices that you would need to think about if similar questions came up in an exam.

Under-representation

African-Americans and Hispanics are significantly unrepresented in both the House of Representatives and the Senate. Ethnic minorities, along with women, would be correct in claiming that equality of opportunity to become members of Congress does not yet exist. Members of religious groups, such as Catholics and Jews, are also under-represented. The bulk of senators and representatives are older than the American average age. Senators tend to be older than representatives, partly due to the minimum age qualification, but mainly because senators will have had to build up a reputation over a period of years in order to defeat an experienced sitting senator. Many senators are able to stay in their post for decades.

It is unlikely that any assembly in which potential candidates are chosen by the electorate will ever be truly a cross-section of that electorate. The choice of candidates is the responsibility of the voters and not a system or mechanic that tries to engineer a more representative group of individuals. However, there are huge discrepancies in representation.

Under-representation tends to be primarily the concern of those who are unrecognised. The way in which this can be offset is to elect members who can show an empathy with those who are not like themselves. They need to be able to express the views of the disadvantaged and to strongly support their causes.

Members of Congress need to either have been taught or to have acquired education and skills in order to be effective in their role. In effect these individuals are volunteers, so it is unlikely that less educated, poorer individuals would risk their lifestyle and their job opportunities for the chance to become a member of Congress.

Senate Committee on the Judiciary

Among the various jobs of the committee is that of conducting hearings prior to a Senate vote on whether to confirm or not confirm judges and justices nominated by the president.

Departmental select committees

In Britain there are 19 of these committees, each with 11 members. Their role is to examine the expenditure, administration and policy of a particular department and any associated regulators and **quangos**.

Quango

This is a quasi-autonomous non-governmental organisation, to which a government has transferred certain powers. Britain is one of the countries that use them.

What is the importance of standing committees?

Range of powers

Standing committees have a fixed jurisdiction, often from one session of Congress to another. These are the most important type of committee and are the focus of much of the work that is performed by the legislature. The Rules Committee, for example, has the power to delay or stop legislation, the Appropriations Committee handles how government spends the finances and the Ways and Means Committee deals with the raising of finance. The House Budget Committee members are usually drawn from these two committees, with one member from each of the other standing committees.

In the Senate, the appropriations, budget, finance and foreign affairs committees are all very powerful.

The power to delay or halt legislation

The importance of the standing committees within the legislative process is also clear in the positioning of the committee stage of the legislative process, compared to the committee stage in the House of Commons in Britain. In Britain the first formal reading of a bill is followed by a second reading debate. There is a vote at the end of that debate, which tests whether the house has accepted the bill. The function of the committee in Britain is to make the bill an effective and unambiguous piece of legislation. General committees (formerly standing committees) in the House of Commons do not have the power to question the principles of the legislation or to propose significant amendments. The vote at the end of the second debate has already shown that the principles of the bill have been accepted.

In the US the system is different. After the bill has been formally introduced and before it is considered by the chamber, it enters the committee stage. In this way the committee is not restrained in any way as to how it approaches the bill. It has the power to change almost everything, from amendments to the basic character of the bill or even to strike out everything and substitute a completely new bill. It can then pass on the bill to the House or to the Senate, with or without amendments, or simply hang onto it and take no action. Most bills suffer this fate, largely because more legislation is introduced than can possibly be enacted. Some of the bills are often introduced at the behest of an interest group by a member of Congress, however that member knows that it will never proceed past committee stage.

Important legislation can also suffer the same fate. A committee can be discharged from further consideration of the bill if it refuses to act on it, but the discharge procedure is difficult.

The standing committees are very expert in their fields of interest and they tend to build up a team spirit, which is often stronger than party loyalties. Committees are where compromises take place and, regardless of their own party, they will be reluctant to have compromises upset by their own leadership or amendments from the floor.

The chairperson of the standing committee has considerable influence over legislation. They have control over the calling of the committee and its agenda. They are chosen on the basis of seniority and usually have safe seats. The chairperson's influence does not end when the committee has reported out a bill. A floor manager is appointed for each bill to make sure that the bill gets through to the final vote. The Rules Committee in the House will have allocated time for the bill and members of the committee will dominate the debate on the floor, and greatly influence just how much the bill is amended.

2.18 The Legislative Process and Checks and Balances

Learning objectives

- Why does Congress reject more legislation than it passes?
- Congressional checks on the president

Why does Congress reject more legislation than it passes?

The need for compromise

In order for a bill to pass into law 218 members of the House of Representatives and at least 51 members of the Senate have to agree with it. The legislative process is dominated by compromise and there are certain members of Congress who have core beliefs which they will not compromise. It is difficult in an assembly at any time to arrive at a consensus and over the past decade or so there has been growing partisanship in Congress, partly due to the fact that the media is quick to jump on a member of Congress who is perceived to be inconsistent in their position.

In the US system legislating is a shared responsibility and there is always a need to find a solution that both sides can claim some degree of ownership for and to accommodate rival interests. There would be little legislation passed at all if there was not compromise.

The US historian Bernard Bailyn wrote: 'If every compromise is taken as a defeat that must be overturned and if no healing generosity is shown to defeated rivals, the best contrived constitution in the world would not succeed.'

Complexity of drafting law

Drafting legislation is extremely complex and it must relate to an appropriate section of the United States Code, which is the compilation and codification of general and permanent federal law. It will inevitably change some existing law and it needs to address each law that it will change. This means that any deletions, additions or changes to existing law have to be detailed.

There are many legislative experts who spend their time writing bills. Writing legislation can be a long and involved process and while this is happening agreements and understandings need to be created. More often than not bills have to be written so that there is room for interpretation. The vaguer the language the more votes the bill is likely to receive. The trade-off is that bureaucrats and judges can interpret it in a variety of different ways.

The passage from bill to law

Although there appears to be a clear legislative process there is a far more complex series of steps from a bill to legislation. The fate of a legislative proposal is also influenced by the president and the bureaucracy of the executive branch. A member of Congress nursing a bill through will not only need to constantly count up supporters and opposition in both houses, but also try to gauge whether the president is likely to veto it or sign it into law.

Most bills that are passed by Congress need to have a broad bipartisan support. Most are intensely debated and there are external factors at work, reflecting regional and business interests, political philosophies, religious beliefs, and other approaches to policy that are brought to bear on members of the House and the Senate.

Congress was originally set up for differences to be aired and, as with any democratic assembly, conflict is built into the system. The intense debates do not necessarily mean that conflicts cannot be resolved, but this slows down the system and makes it less likely for bills to pass into law. It is a deliberative process, involving careful scrutiny, the accommodation of different interests and the reduction of friction. Before a vote members of Congress can be overwhelmed by differing opinions; sometimes they literally receive thousands of letters, emails and telephone calls. They also receive material from think tanks and special interest groups, aiming to sway their opinion. A member of Congress is likely to cast at least 400 votes a year. They will not have knowledge of every bill and they can easily be swayed by well-reasoned opinion.

The following table shows the main barriers to the passage of legislation.

Barrier	Implication
Congress not a coherent policymaking body	The power is dispersed to committees and subcommittees and Congress is more of a forum.
Potential veto points	There are several potential stumbling blocks for a bill and only 10 per cent of bills are actually reported out of committee stage.
Senate filibuster	This is a debating device that has ended the life of several controversial bills in the Senate.
House Rules Committee	This can stop bills but tends to act in accordance with the general wishes of the House.
Floor activity and floor votes	Members of Congress can attach riders and amendments to bills, which can make them more difficult to pass.
Non-starters	Most bills simply lack the support of key members and are only initiated to attract public attention.
Amendment and delay	The heavy workload means that delaying a bill is often the easiest course of action.
Log rolling	This means an exchange of favours, where items are added or deleted from bills to reflect deals done.
Obstruction and confusion	The complex bills are assigned to multiple committees and it is difficult to reconcile differing views on the bill.
Congressional independence	The Congress needs to appear to be responsive to the demands of voters, so sometimes they are openly resistant to the executive.
Inefficiency	The different centres of power make decision-making slow, confused and clumsy.

Congressional checks on the president

There are many checks and balances built into the US Constitution. Others have been developed as a matter of convention. Most presidential appointments need to be confirmed by a majority in the Senate. The president's budget and appropriations for the executive departments need to be approved by Congress. Any legislation the president puts forward has to be passed by Congress. Congress has also inserted in legislation the provision that any executive action can be reviewed and approved by the legislature. This is known as the congressional veto. This means that officials operating on behalf of the president are expected to explain and defend their policies before congressional committees. Most importantly, Congress can also impeach and remove the president from office for 'high crimes and misdemeanours'.

Congress can also force a president's resignation by the threat of impeachment (as in the case of Richard Nixon in August 1974). The Senate also has to ratify any foreign treaties that have been made by the president (by a two-thirds majority).

Ratification of treaties

In September 2007 the Senate approved an amendment to the Convention on the Physical Protection of Nuclear Material and in June 2008 ratified the Protocol on Explosive Remnants of War.

Congress also has the power to override presidential vetoes on legislation (again by a two-thirds majority, but in both houses). In practice, the power of Congress to override a presidential veto is actually a weak check on the president. In recent years the mere threat of a veto from the president has been enough to convince Congress not to proceed with provisions that the president does not like.

Perhaps the most significant check on the power of the executive is Congress's oversight role. It aims to oversee and hold the president, executive departments and agencies accountable for their actions.

Congress has investigative powers, either carried out by standing committees or special or select committees, created for a specific purpose. Standing committee investigations are public hearings into either wrongdoing or inefficiency. A prime example of the select committees was in 1987 when one was set up in each house to investigate the Iran-Contra Affair during the Reagan administration. The investigation led to a series of indictments and prosecutions, including that of Caspar Weinberger, the former Defense Secretary (pardoned by George H. W. Bush in 1992). Congress also investigated the so-called Whitewater Scandal and the property dealings of President Clinton and his wife Hillary Clinton in 1994.

The problem is that Congress has often found it difficult to carry out oversight because it has limited access to information from the executive. Information is carefully guarded by presidents and their bureaucrats. Presidents can refuse or be reluctant to hand over information, claiming executive privilege. This has no clear constitutional status. Richard Nixon, for example, withheld information at least 19 times in the Watergate investigation.

The executive holds the balance of power, largely because an overworked committee may not actually know what to ask for and much of the documentation is huge and complex.

Iran-Contra affair

This scandal surfaced in 1986. It was an attempt by members of the US executive to sell weapons to moderate Iranians via the Israelis in exchange for the release of US hostages. Proceeds from weapon sales were also diverted to fund anti-communist rebels, or Contras, in Nicaragua. President Ronald Reagan had not authorised any of these arrangements. He clearly had little control over the executive office of the president.

The power of the purse and war powers

The power of the purse is used to describe the tool by which Congress can limit executive powers. In effect it can withhold funding or put conditions on the use of funds. Recent examples eliminated military funding for the South Vietnamese government and threatened budget limitations by those in Congress who opposed the war in Iraq. The War Powers Act (1973) requires Congress to authorise sending US forces into action abroad (not if the US is already under attack or serious threat). The president has to notify Congress within 48 hours of committing troops and he cannot deploy them for more than 60 days without authorisation or a declaration of war.

2.19 Members of the Legislature

Learning objectives

- Are members of the legislature delegates, representatives or trustees?

Are members of the legislature delegates, representatives or trustees?

There are three key models to describe those who are elected to a legislature: delegate, representative (or trustee) and mandate. However, always bear in mind that the resemblance model refers directly to the notion that those in the legislature should be typical and represent a cross-section of the electorate.

The US system

According to David McKay, in *American Politics and Society,* members of Congress were not delegates, they were not forced to follow a party programme and they had not been mandated by constituents to follow specific policies.

In fact it is rare to find delegates in legislatures; this is because they represent so many constituents that it would be impossible for those constituents to derive a consensus of opinion on an issue and then for the 'delegate' to consult. Even if a Congress member knew precisely what the electorate wanted, it is unlikely whether that single member would have any meaningful influence in Congress.

Consequently, members of Congress are more likely to be trustees. In seeking election trustees will make a series of promises to their constituents, including supporting their constituents' interests. They will promise to defend and promote their constituents' interests and if they fail to do so, then the constituents will punish them at the next election by voting for an alternative candidate.

In the US the party system is weak, so the link between the legislator, constituent and party is different from that in Britain. Constituency pressures in the US are far more important.

As for the resemblance model, Congress tends to be dominated by white, middle-aged, middle-class males. There are increasing numbers of Hispanic, African-American, American-Asian and female members of Congress, however they are still in a minority. If anything the Senate is even less representative of the population; members tend to be older and have had a previous career, either in politics or as a professional.

The British system

In Britain members of the House of Commons claim to be trustee representatives. This implies that they are elected on the basis of a series of promises made to their constituents who trust them and their judgement. They claim they are not delegates. This is despite maybe having run as a candidate under a party manifesto. Of course an MP may not follow a manifesto to the letter, and so retain their discretion. Nonetheless, most would agree that members of parliament are party delegates rather than trustees.

Members of parliament have to represent their party and their constituency. The key difference between British MPs and US members of the House of Representatives is that the MPs are almost entirely reliant on maintaining the endorsement of their party to improve their chances of re-election. When we consider political parties we will again see how much more control the British party system has compared to the US one.

If we accept that British MPs are representatives of a group then who precisely do they represent? Some would claim that they represent their local party or parliamentary party; others would suggest that they represent their constituents or their local area; while others would grandly claim that they represent the national interest. Through associations with pressure groups and private businesses they can also represent other groups. Some MPs also have close associations with certain professions, such as the armed services, the law or teaching.

British MPs are also accountable to a variety of different groups, to whom they owe allegiance and from whom they receive support. These include the local party, given it chose them as a candidate and campaigned for them, or the electorate, which voted for them. They are also accountable to a national party, as it approved them as candidates, and to the parliamentary party, to which they are expected to show allegiance.

In contrast to the US system, the British one has far more party discipline. To be effective a government needs its MPs to support it and a system to reward or punish them. This would imply that MPs are 'lobby fodder', being herded into lines to vote according to the wishes of the government. That the electorate tends to vote for a party rather than an individual goes some way to support this, although in many cases this is clearly not true. A case in point is that of Oona King, a Labour MP representing Bethnal Green and Bow between 1997 and 2005, who supported the invasion of Iraq in 2003. George Galloway of the Respect Coalition and Stop the War Coalition stood against her in the general election of 2005 and defeated her.

A key point about British MPs is that they have to perform various competing functions which are at odds with one another in terms of giving enough time to each, and so have difficulty in reconciling them.

The House of Lords is a more complex issue because they are neither delegates nor representatives, although some have clear party allegiances. They actually do not represent anyone in particular because they have not been elected and they are not, therefore, responsible to any one group. For the most part members of the House of Lords never claim to speak on behalf of anyone other than themselves. Perhaps the term 'virtual representation', a concept used for several centuries in Britain, is appropriate to describe the House of Lords and, to a lesser extent, MPs. No one has elected members of the House of Lords and it is rare that the majority of potential voters in a constituency have actually cast their vote for the winning MP. Therefore the MP was elected by similar voters.

As with the US system, the bulk of the British parliament is white, middle-aged, middle-class males, although a series of initiatives were launched to select more women and members of ethnic minorities. After the 2005 general election 20 per cent of the 646 MPs were female.

Role of the Legislature

Learning objectives

- Is the most important role of the legislature to check the power of the executive?

Is the most important role of the legislature to check the power of the executive?

Alexander Hamilton wrote: 'Here, sir, the people govern.'

He was referring to the House of Representatives. Congress itself has the power to make laws, levy taxes and decide how the US government will spend money. Congress is also there to reconcile different points of view on policy, to compromise, to persuade through argument, to build consensus and arrive at a solution.

John Adams wrote in 1790:

> *The numbers of men in all ages have preferred ease, slumber, and good cheer to liberty, when they have been in competition. We must not then depend alone upon the love of liberty in the soul of man for its preservation. Some political institutions must be prepared, to assist this love against its enemies.*

This implies that the primary role of the legislature is to guarantee liberty.

The balance of power

The writers of the Constitution went to enormous lengths to try to balance the powers of the three branches of government and to balance the powers between the House of Representatives and the Senate. They also tried to balance the power between federal government and the states, the government and the citizens and interest groups and regions across the country. The idea is that no one part of government should dominate the other, so elaborate checks and balances to prevent abuse and the concentration of power were built into the constitution. In order for a bill to pass into law both houses of Congress have to approve it and the president has to sign it.

While the president can nominate judges to the Supreme Court, the nominations have to be approved by the Senate. The courts can also declare laws passed by Congress (or through executive action) to be unconstitutional. Congress creates and funds the branches of the executive. It also has power over the courts.

This is a complicated system that has adapted to changes over the past 200 years or more. The Constitution is a framework of core principles, incorporating representative democracy, the rule of law, and majority rule with a respect for minority rights and the balance of power.

The system of checks and balances has proved, by and large, to be robust and despite criticisms of policy, politics, politicians or bureaucrats, the overwhelming majority of US citizens and those involved in government have an unshakeable faith in the Constitution.

Checking the power of the executive

Congress's role as a check on executive power is a key part of the system, though it has not always worked or been top of the priorities. Congress and the executive branch, in theory, are equals and together they determine the course of the United States. Many claim that Congress has been timid in recent years and that the initiative has moved to the White House and to the executive agencies. Robert Kaiser, an editor of the *Washington Post,* wrote: 'In fundamental ways that have gone largely unrecognised, Congress has become less vigilant, less proud and protective of its own prerogatives, and less important to the conduct of American government than at any time in decades.'

Members of Congress may either disagree with this view or seek to excuse themselves. Many claim that time spent dealing with their constituents leaves them with only two or three days a week to deal with national affairs. Others claim to be less inclined to collaborate with the opposition party. Kaiser suggested: 'Few members put loyalty to the House or Senate ahead of their political loyalty to a Democrat or Republican team.'

One example of Congress's failure to check the power of the executive relates to the second war against Iraq in 2003. The justification for the invasion was partly based on faulty intelligence. The accusation that the White House and the intelligence community deliberately misled Congress regarding weapons of mass destruction and the Iraqi regime's ties to terrorism now seems clear. However, at the time Congress passively accepted the White House's justifications for launching the war and in effect carrying out a pre-emptive strike against another sovereign state.

That members of Congress are more preoccupied by tending to their constituents' issues rather than the checks and balances of executive power isn't hard to understand. Their constituents vote for them! These two issues are often referred to as 'folks back home' and '**pork barrel politics**'.

Pork barrel politics

This is a derogatory term used to describe actions or support for legislation by a member of Congress in order to primarily benefit their own constituents, particularly if it is a marginal seat.

Congress has played a crucial role in checking the abuse of executive power since 1792. At that time it launched an enquiry into the government's conduct in the wars against Native Americans. Later the government was culpable in the scandals of Watergate and the Iran-Contra Affair. The system of oversight protects the country from a president who assumes imperial tendencies of power and from bureaucrats who view themselves as above the law. It exposes and prevents misconduct and is one way that those representing the citizens can control a president.

Checks on the executive are essential to ensure democracy. Members of Congress involved in oversight rank the protection of democracy alongside the demands of their constituents and their party. In other words, Congress needs to operate as both a partner and a critic of the White House.

However, recent changes in Congress have weakened oversight. Power is now concentrated in the hands of the leadership. The authorising committees which once looked into the activities of executive branch agencies, have been meeting less frequently and have become less influential. Congress has tended to choose to fund federal government through either huge appropriations bills or continuing resolutions. This means that the routine reauthorisation process, which was a powerful way of investigating federal agencies, has almost disappeared.

The priority of Congress is checking the power of the executive. It's most crucial role is probably still the 'power of the purse'. Congress sets spending and taxation policies and approves federal treasury spending. Setting the budget is critical as the government depends on it as the principal means by which it sets its priorities. This is a function that goes back to the framing of the Constitution, with the idea that the power to tax and spend should be in the hands of an elected, legislative branch and not the executive branch.

2.21 The Effectiveness of Congress

Learning objectives

- To what extent is the effectiveness of the legislature down to its organisation?

To what extent is the effectiveness of the legislature down to its organisation?

The late Congressman Clem Miller wrote: 'Congress is a collection of committees that come together periodically to approve one another's actions.'

Many observers believe that political parties in the United States are far weaker than those in Europe. There is much less cohesion and their influence over legislation is weaker, and they only control a small fraction of campaign money. They also exercise very little control over nominations. The common feeling is that parties influence legislators in the US far less than pressure groups, committees or constituents.

If parties are so weak then how is the legislature organised and where does the power lie? In elections it resides with the candidates who have the most powerful organisations; those that can collect the most money and define the course of the campaign. In the legislative arena it is the standing committees and their subcommittees that are the cornerstone of the organisation. To a large extent Congress is an example of committee government, or subcommittee government.

Rather than parties driving the organisation, from time to time groups will coalesce, perhaps around party lines or around interest, to seize temporary power over the structure and process of legislation. With the committee system power is stacked in favour of majority party interests. Those members of majority parties have structural advantages. The key organisers are the members of that majority party and their leadership.

The status of subcommittees was greatly increased in the 1970s. Essentially these were designed as decentralising reforms, aiming to counterbalance the powers of party leaders. In effect they transformed Congress from a committee form of government to a subcommittee form. By the 1990s party government was alive in the form of active coalitions, where there was widespread agreement. This model, known as the conditional party government, saw majority party leadership more consolidated, with its members in broad agreement over key issues.Before then parties had declined in importance, but they were not ignored.

How Congress works

Congress essentially works in three ways.

- Parties had a loose control over members during the committee stages and party leaders tended to exert influence on the floor of the House during debate and voting. Parties did not rely on the structure of the committee system but rather on their ability to muster votes.
- Writing in 1964 (*Party and Policymaking: The House Republican Policy Committee),* Charles O. Jones suggested that political parties exist to organise a resolution to conflict. They assume the responsibility for organising the process. The party provides leaders, individuals, rules and committees without actually assuming responsibility for the results of these groups or the power to control them.

  In other words, any organisations that parties managed to achieve were temporary and only for specific votes. They broke up once the bill had been dealt with.

- The third view is that of conditional party government. David W. Rohde (*Parties and Leaders in the Post-Reform House*, 1991) suggested that unlike in a parliamentary system the party would not be dominant across all issues. Leadership would not be able to make policy decisions that would automatically be supported by the rest of the party. There would be party responsibility only if policy agreement existed across the members. The leadership would use any tools available to them in order to advance a cause that was important to all party members.

  This suggests that the support of the party membership for a particular bill was only on a case-by-case basis.

Organisationally the most influential work takes place in the committees. The decline and weakness of parties has gone hand in hand with the concentration of power in committees and subcommittees.

Richard F. Fenno (*Congressmen in Committees,* 1973) pointed to the fact that committees dominate congressional decision-making. This suggested that committees were autonomous and that they operated on an independent basis. That independence included freedom from the party leaders, the majorities in the chamber and the president. Each committee had a number of legislative experts and, as a result of this, committee decisions tended to be accepted and ratified by the chamber. This meant that committee chairpersons had enormous power, especially to influence the committees.

At least in theory Congress is organised on the basis of three key overlapping principles.

- It is organised on the basis of political parties.
- It is functionally organised on the types of legislation enacted.
- It also has its own leadership organisation.

However both the leadership organisation and the committee organisation is linked to the party organisation. The following table outlines the key considerations in the organisational structure.

Organisation type	Implications
Party	Nearly all Congress members have a party affiliation. Third party candidates are rarely elected. Members of Congress will affiliate themselves with either the Republican conference or the Democrat caucus. Both political parties have policy committees to make strategic and tactical decisions. The parties maintain campaign committees to help members gain re-election. There are distinct committees for both the House and the Senate.
Leadership	Each political party elects its own leaders; they become the leaders of the Congress. The party with the majority in the House or the Senate has the majority leadership positions and the minority party has the minority positions. The pecking order for House leadership is for the majority party speaker, majority leader, assistant majority leader and majority whip. For the minority party it is the minority leader, assistant minority leader and minority whip. A similar system applies to the Senate, but at the top is the president of the Senate (the vice-president of the US), then the president pro tempore, the senator of the majority party with seniority, then the majority leadership and the minority leadership.
Committee	The bulk of the work of Congress is in the committees and there are four different types: standing committees, functionally organised to reflect the organisation of the executive departments; select committees to cover issues not being handled by a regular standing committee; joint committees dealing with either important or very mundane issues with members from both houses; and conference committees, which are created each time a bill is passed in different versions by the House and the Senate; they iron out the differences.

2.22 Power and Decline of the Legislature

Learning objectives

- Is the power and influence of the legislatures on the decline?

Cooperation and co-decision procedures

In the Single European Act (1987) a cooperation procedure was introduced to strengthen the European Parliament. The commission makes a proposal, parliament offers an opinion and then the council adopts a common position. Parliament can then amend or reject it.

Co-decision procedure was introduced in the Treaty of the EU (1992), giving the European Parliament and the Council equal legislative powers when co-decision procedures are applied.

Is the power and influence of the legislatures on the decline?

In the majority of both written and unwritten constitutions around the world a parliament or congress is described as being the major decision-making body in that form of government. At the very least it will have an equal status with the executive branch. In practice, however, the situation may be entirely different and many commentators have mourned the decline of legislatures, the loss of parliamentary control or the dominance of the executive.

In many western liberal democracies legislatures still retain their role in the decision-making process, but many others have found themselves dominated by the executive. In some, authoritarian governments have manipulated them and in a handful they have even been abolished or suspended.

The high point of legislatures and their political significance was in the 19th century, often referred to as the 'golden age of the private member'. By the 20th century there had been a general decline and the power of the executive and of bureaucracies had increased. When looking for evidence as to whether legislatures are comparatively weak, the following points are usually identified.

- Legislatures have transformed into reactive bodies rather than proactive ones. They deal with policy initiatives derived from the executive rather than creating their own policies.
- The executives have significant budgets, human resources and other facilities to support them, which in many cases legislatures lack.
- Executives can draw in technical expertise, knowledge and information from a wide variety of sources, which is not necessarily available to the legislatures.
- The executive, or at least the majority government, tends to monopolise parliamentary time, using a range of procedural devices to force bills through into law.
- In the past many improvements in society were derived from the ideas and the energies of private members in the legislature. There is less opportunity for this and the bulk of initiatives are originated from the executive and from their bureaucracy.

It would be wrong to assume that all legislatures are in decline. Certain legislatures have less comparative power and they have transformed from policymaking and shaping to a way in which policy and ideas are communicated. The televising of legislatures has helped this process and has raised the profile of chambers, as a forum for debate.

To try to offset the overwhelming resources of the executive, many assemblies have now authorised increased staffing levels and access to resources, along with creating committees that focus on oversight of the executive.

Tradition also plays a vital role in actually measuring whether the power and influence of legislatures is in decline. Traditionally powerful legislatures include the United States, Japan, Italy and Sweden. The European Parliament began as a weak legislature but has become significantly more powerful, with the direct election of MEPs.

If nothing else legislatures still have a considerable influence, as they enact legislation, have oversight of the executive and are seen to be representative of the electorate. Even in cases when a government may have a huge majority there will still be dissenting voices in the legislature. In Britain in recent years, with a large Labour majority in both houses, individuals have questioned operations in Iraq, tuition fees, super casinos, ministerial authority, detention without charge and foundation hospitals.

R. Hague and M. Harrop (*Comparative Government and Politics,* 2001) argued that it was premature to consider that assemblies were in decline, even in an era of big government. They suggested that in many ways assemblies were becoming more important. They were involved in raising grievances, in oversight and in the transition from one form of political order to another. They also suggested that the growing trend towards televised proceedings in assemblies was making them more publicly visible and important in political life. Finally they also suggested that particularly in western Europe backbenchers were far more prepared to assert themselves and that party leaders were finding it more and more difficult to control them, as the backbenchers were no longer deferential to them.

Impact of mid-term elections 2006

The mid-term congressional elections in 2006 showed that voters were unhappy with Republican control of Congress and with President Bush. Voters supported the Democrats to ensure greater scrutiny, investigations and enquiries into White House policy.

In the US and in assemblies in Latin America that have presidential systems the concept of decline is even less relevant. Congress is immensely powerful in the US. It can block and delay presidential policies and initiatives; it can cause enormous damage to an administration in its role of scrutinising executive performance even though it may be less influential in determining policy.

In Latin America legislatures have sometimes caused serious conflict in the countries and in some cases have had to be removed by force in a military coup. Governments have tried to control their legislatures and sometimes they have managed to temporarily do so. But legislatures are not without influence. They still play an enormous role in debate and they still have the power to control the executive if they choose to use it.

In Britain the executive does dominate the legislature, particularly the House of Commons. Power is especially strong when there is a large majority. It is far trickier when there is a small majority.

Legislatures tend to be reactive in modern society, although this does not mean that they cannot significantly modify legislation. The use of committees is extremely important, as is support for members to ensure their independence, along with ensuring that the second chamber remains assertive. Even with this level of support and commitment it is still difficult, but not impossible, to challenge a dominant executive.

In the US the constitution was based on the idea of the separation of powers. Each component checked the influence of the other two. The intention was that Congress would dominate the federal government. Congress, being a bicameral legislature, also has the advantage in that both law-making chambers are directly elected. They are broadly equal in power. The Senate is the most powerful second chamber in the world. Throughout the 19th century Congress was dominant and only three presidents, Jefferson, Jackson and Lincoln, had the majority support of their own party in Congress. Even that was no guarantee they would be supported.

Woodrow Wilson wrote: 'In the practical conduct of the federal government, unquestionably the predominant and controling force, the center and source of all motive and of all regulative power, is Congress.'

However, since 1933, when Roosevelt extended federal power to implement the New Deal proposals, the US has had a far stronger executive branch. By the 1960s presidents were acting independently of Congress and the federal bureaucracy had expanded. In the 1970s Congress reasserted itself and during President Clinton's administration his political opponents in Congress undermined him. Congress was resurgent and, arguably, has retained this position to the present day.

2.23 Reform of Legislation

Learning objectives

- Is there a need for institutional reform in the legislatures?

Is there a need for institutional reform in the legislatures?

There are differing views as to whether there is a need for institutional reform in legislatures, not only when we compare the US and Britain, but also in the priorities and the degree to which reforms should impact upon the institutions and their processes.

In the US the three key issues are gridlock, the rules of the House and the Senate and the congressional budget process. All are seen as being areas where reforms would improve the system, but it is unclear how they could be enacted and whether they would even work. As the US population has grown and its society has become more complex the role of Congress has transformed. In the past Congress would have directed an executive department to award a contract to a business that could supply the goods or services required. Nowadays it has to be the lowest bid, with the right mix of minorities and women, which complies with a range of regulations and is not involved in contract fraud. Congress has had to become involved in micromanagement, making it more difficult for it to focus on policy. Less than 20 per cent of the US population now believes that Congress does a good job.

Reform in the US

Yet there are differing views as to how to repair Congress, if indeed it does need attention. Term limits for elected members, a balanced budget amendment to the constitution and the public financing of congressional campaigns are all examples. Few, however, would actually bring about any fundamental changes. Others focus on internal reforms, looking at the rules and processes that govern the way in which Congress operates. The fundamental questions are: 'Would Congress be able to pass more legislation?', 'Would it be less partisan?', 'Would Congressmen be more ethical? and 'Would the public approve?'

Some believe that radical overhaul is all that is needed to achieve the desired results. Members of Congress want to be more responsive, but they are wary of small incremental reforms. Congress has become in many commentators' eyes responsive to the districts that they represent, but not responsive as a whole. When Congress tries to operate as a whole it is often inefficient and when legislation arrives on the president's desk for signature it has gone through ideological, partisan and factional arguments. Congress has become better known for its inability to pass legislation than the passing of it. Gridlock is the common explanation; a White House dominated by one party and a Congress by another, with no incentive to cooperate.

Even when Clinton was elected in 1992 and an era of gridlock was thought to have come to an end, there was no end to the gridlock. David Brady, of the Hoover Institution, said: 'What really drives policy is not party voting but members' preferences.'

Conservative Democrats and moderates in the Republican Party held the balance of power. The key problem was outlined by Morris Fiorina of Harvard University: 'You can't blame divided government if [the public] elects a president who says he'll cut taxes and a Congress that says it will raise spending.'

This is an example of what has been called 'gridlocked electorate' and 'divided government'.

There are definitely tensions between the executive and the legislature no matter who is president and which party dominates Congress. This is a permanent feature of American politics, where there is a presidential veto and a Senate filibuster that means that one part of government can always block the other if that is the intention. Some, however, believe that gridlock is a good thing and is a sign of political health, that politicians are doing something because they believe it to be right and that it represents a clash of values.

Some also believe that Congress has moved away from its original purpose. These views were outlined by a former attorney general, Edwin Meese III.

- Congress does not deal with national issues 'Congress is consumed by benefits and regulations.' In other words they are dealing with what were state issues.
- There is the view that federalism is disappearing and that the 17th Amendment to the Constitution that stripped state legislatures of the power to elect their federal senators has broken the link.
- Nothing alienates Congress from the public more than the way in which they operate and the language that they use.

There is also the view that in order to restore confidence in Congress it should concentrate on legislating. Congress's preoccupation seems to be servicing its constituents and regulatory oversight. There are also calls to make Congress more deliberative, as the system does not allow a great deal of time for serious consideration of issues. The committee system does not help deliberation. Members of Congress have too many committee responsibilities. There should be changes in the floor rules to reduce partisanship and to allow more amendments to be made on the floor.

There is, however, a lack of enthusiasm for reform in Congress. Reform should begin by considering what it is that is wanted from Congress and then to make the necessary changes to ensure that this is the case, while learning from what actually works.

Reform in Britain

In Britain, with the growth of executive power at the expense of the legislature, there are differing approaches to the issue of parliament's main role. For some it is the way in which public opinion can be mobilised, or the way in which opposition parties can criticise government policy. There are others who believe that parliament needs to wield power and influence and should be strong; it should be holding government to account. In Britain reform tends to focus around the following solutions.

- The creation of more powerful select committees, with bigger budgets, stronger powers and access to expertise.
- There should be better pay and conditions for MPs, with secretarial and research support.
- They should be genuinely full-time MPs, effectively preventing MPs from continuing their previous occupations and ensuring they focus on their parliamentary duties.
- There should be a reduction in the number of MPs, to enable better resourced, full-time MPs to provide a more professional House of Commons.
- There should be more free votes so that MPs can vote as they please and not purely along party lines, and therefore a reduction in the use of party whips to ensure that elements of a government's legislative programme is passed.
- There needs to be changes to working hours – this was introduced in 2002 but amended in 2005 to do away with antiquated sitting hours.
- There needs to be improvements in the legislative process – this was introduced after the 1997 election to bring in more consultation on draft bills and the better use of select and standing committees.

2.24 The Bicameral System

Learning objectives

- What is the value of the second chamber?

What is the value of the second chamber?

Abbé Sieyès, a writer during the time of the French Revolution, posed the following dilemma regarding a bicameral legislature: 'If the second chamber agrees with the first it is superfluous [useless]; if it disagrees it is pernicious [dangerous].'

Roles of the legislature

Not all legislatures are bicameral, but where they do exist they can play a variety of different roles.

- They can share the work of the first chamber – in the US each of the chambers are considered equal and are able to propose and amend legislation. They also have oversight functions.
- They can immeasurably add to the work of the first chamber – in the US it is the role of the House of Representatives to impeach a president, but it is the Senate's right to try the president.
- They can take the burden from the first chamber – in Britain the House of Lords tends to be a revising chamber. It usually has more time to consider proposed legislation and it also looks at non-controversial bills first. This allows the House of Commons to concentrate on more politically contentious issues.
- They can act as a check and a balance on the first chamber – again in Britain, when one party has a considerable majority in the House of Commons, without the House of Lords it could push through legislation very quickly with minimal disruption. The House of Lords slows the process down and demands an opportunity to fully discuss the proposal.
- They can be used to make the legislature more representative – in some countries the second chamber comprises of individuals who represent regions (e.g. France), specific groups (e.g. Republic of Ireland) or points of view (e.g. the Church of England in the House of Lords).
- They can provide greater experience – in Britain the House of Lords comprises individuals who have made their mark in society in one way or another, and therefore may have expertise and knowledge that members of the first chamber have not gained.
- They may have additional functions – in its various forms the House of Lords represents the highest court of appeal in Britain.

Role of the Senate

In the US the Senate has a number of formal roles that are derived from the US Constitution.

- They are representative – they represent a whole state or part of a state and are charged with representing the needs of their constituents.
- They are an integral part of the legislature – they can generate, discuss, amend and approve their own legislation. They also consider, amend and approve legislation that has been generated in the House of Representatives. They also discuss, amend and approve legislation that has been proposed by the president.
- They have an oversight function – primarily they have oversight of the executive branch. They have the responsibility of confirming presidential appointments and treaties that have been

negotiated by the president. They can carry out public investigations into executive branch activities, they can use the legislative veto and if the House of Representatives charges an individual in the executive with malpractice it is the Senate that handles the impeachment trial.

The Senate also chooses the vice-president if there is deadlock in the electoral college vote. They have the power to approve, along with the House of Representatives, any proposals for amendments to the constitution and also generally act as a check and a balance on the other branches of the government.

The Senate protects minority rights. A senator will have the right to be consulted regarding executive appointments in their own state and to make recommendations to the president about appointments.

The Senate does share some powers with the House of Representatives. In legislation it is a full partner, but cannot originate bills that raise revenue. Like the House of Representatives it can also override a presidential veto by a two-thirds majority, as it can approve the change in the Constitution by the same majority. It has full powers under Section 8 of Article I of the Constitution.

The Senate alone carries out impeachment trials, chooses the vice-president (in the event of a tie in the electoral college), approves the appointment of presidential nominations and approves presidential treaties, again by a two-thirds majority.

As we will see, the Senate is actually more powerful than the House of Lords. It is an integral part of Congress and unlike the House of Lords it can initiate legislation. In its present guise the House of Lords is considered to be less representative and legitimate because its members are not elected; those in the Senate are elected. The Senate is also willing to use its powers and has at times refused to approve appointments or treaties.

Because of the US separation of powers other branches of government must cooperate with the Senate. However, there are limits to the Senate's powers. The constitution clearly defines its role. As the US has a federal government it also has limited areas of influence. The Supreme Court's ability to carry out judicial reviews enables it to declare legislation proposed and approved by the Senate to be unconstitutional. It also has to share power due to the separation of powers and in the US system the president is the chief legislator.

Role of the House of Lords

In Britain, the power of the House of Lords has undoubtedly ebbed away over the years, but it is still important. It still revises bills from the House of Commons, slowing the process down to give ministers an opportunity to consider the legislation. It can initiate non-controversial legislation and consider delegated legislation. It will debate matters of current interest and scrutinise government policy, implementation and can initiate investigations. In the British system it effectively represents the only constitutional block on a potential elective dictatorship in the House of Commons. Constitutionally, the Lords can reject bills to extend the life of parliament and any private bill or delegated legislation. It can also reject public bills (although not money bills), although in effect this often only delays the bill. It can delay a money bill for only a month. In Britain the Lords acts as a revising chamber, a place where the government and the EU can be scrutinised and a place where issues can be discussed that have been avoided or ignored by government or by the House of Commons.

2.25 Different Forms of Government

Learning objectives

- Are prime ministerial and presidential forms of government similar?

Are prime ministerial and presidential forms of government similar?

A British prime minister has more power within government than the US president. In the US the president's power is restricted by the Constitution. This is to ensure that the executive never becomes more powerful or independent than the legislature.

The following table identifies the key differences and similarities between parliamentary government led by a prime minister and a presidential-style government.

Feature	Parliamentary government	Presidential government
History	This is usually an evolutionary form of government, with an assembly challenging a monarchy and then assuming control and responsibility for government. Britain also has an unwritten constitution.	This form of government is usually derived out of a major upheaval in the country, such as a revolution or the gaining of independence. The political system, such as the US, was designed to make the assembly separate from government. The US has a written constitution.
Division of power	There is a fusion of the executive and legislative branches.	There are clear separations between the executive and the legislative branches.
Post-election	The assembly becomes the parliament and it comprises an executive, which is the government and the assembly, dominated by the majority party.	The assembly remains just that and the executive is considered to be a separate institution that has been separately elected, often at different points in time.
Nature of the executive	The executive is usually divided into two parts: the prime minister, or chancellor, is the head of the government and there is either a monarch or ceremonial president operating as the head of state.	There is no division in the executive. In the US the head of government is the president and the president is also the head of state.
Selection of the executive	Symbolically the prime minister is usually appointed by the head of state, although in practical terms the prime minister is always the leader of the majority party in the assembly.	The president and the vice-president are elected by the people for a set period of time.
Cabinet or government selection	It is the prime minister's role to appoint ministers. They are usually leading figures within the same party, or individuals representing certain wings or interests in the party. In some cases they are members of other parties in order to achieve a coalition government.	The president will appoint heads of department. These will be close allies, personal friends and advisers, but in the US the assembly must give approval to the appointments.
Nature of cabinet	The cabinet is a collective body and ministers exert considerable influence. The prime minister is considered to be 'the first amongst equals'.	The president is the sole decision-maker in the executive. All of the heads of department of the executive branch are subordinate to the president. This means that the cabinet is very different from one in a parliamentary system.
Ministers and the assembly	Ministers are usually members of parliament and continue to represent their constituencies, even though they are members of the cabinet. They are therefore accountable to both the parliament or legislature and to their constituency.	There is strict separation between cabinet and the assembly. Members of the assembly cannot be cabinet members and members of the government cannot be part of the assembly.

Feature	Parliamentary government	Presidential government
Executive responsibility	The cabinet is responsible to the assembly. Without the assembly or parliament's support the government could be forced to resign and this would mean that the head of state would have to appoint a new government, or an election would have to be called.	Ultimately the executive is responsible to the Constitution and the way in which the terms of the Constitution are interpreted. Presidents are required to follow constitutional rules, procedures and precedents.
Executive dominance over the assembly	The head of government, or prime minister, has the right to dissolve parliament and can use this as a threat to control the assembly.	The president cannot dissolve or coerce the assembly, as they are constitutionally separate and have no direct linkage, as they were elected at different times and by different methods.
Assembly dominance over the executive	In theory the executive does not dominate the assembly, nor does the assembly dominate government. It is parliament as a whole that is dominant.	The separation of powers, checks and balances in the system, judicial independence and the importance of the rule of law mean that no one part of government dominates another. Power is separated, but the assembly has more options open to it, including the ability to impeach the president.
Responsibility to the electorate	Government is only indirectly responsible to the electorate. Ministers who become part of government are selected from elected representatives who have stood to represent their own constituencies. Voters do not vote for a government as such, but for a party or an individual.	The assembly and the president have both been elected by popular vote. The president in particular is the only individual in the system who has faced the vote of the entire electorate of the country. As such this means that the president is directly responsible to the electorate. It is less clear for members of the assembly.
Focus of power in the system	Parliament is the focus because there is a fusion of power between the executive and the legislative branches.	There is no specific focus of power. There is no concentration of power or unity. There is division of power and fragmentation of power.

There are some other key differences.

- In the British system the prime minister, chancellor and foreign secretary deal with spending and foreign policy issues, but in the US the Congress has greater control.
- In Britain the chancellor has the greatest influence in manipulating the economy, whereas to a large extent a US president lacks that power.
- Crucially, the House of Commons tends to be dominated by MPs who belong to the same party as the prime minister, giving the prime minister an inbuilt advantage in the legislature. In the US this is more often not the case, as Congress may be dominated by the opposition party. This makes it difficult (even if members of Congress follow the party line) to push through partisan legislation.

F855 Question Topics 8:

2.26 Comparisons of US and British Systems of Government

Learning objectives

- What are the merits of presidential government over prime ministerial government?

What are the merits of presidential government over prime ministerial government?

The legislature and executive

In a presidential system the executive is elected separately by voters and is in theory equal in power to the legislature. In a parliamentary system a prime minister is the leader of the majority party and has the power to create his or her own cabinet around them.

Andrew Heywood (*Politics,* 1997*)* believed that the key differences were that a parliamentary system of government had a fused legislature and executive, as the government governed through the assembly. In the parliamentary system the assembly and the executive were bound together and this violated the doctrine of the separation of powers, thereby setting parliamentary systems apart from presidential systems.

While in the US the president and the legislature have at times dominated one another, in Britain historically the legislature has tended to dominate the executive. However, in recent years the executive has dominated the legislature, largely due to the strong majority governments that have been produced as a result of the party system and the electoral system used in Britain. Lord Hailsham described this as 'an elective dictatorship'.

In a parliamentary system government and the prime minister have their powers checked by parliament. It can examine, criticise and check on their activities. Each minister is individually and collectively responsible to parliament and if the administration as a whole is defeated in a vote of confidence it should resign. On a daily basis scrutiny takes place at question time and through select committees.

In comparison, in a presidential system there is both a constitutional and political separation of power between the executive and the legislature. Crucially the president is chosen by the electorate and not by the legislative branch. The president also acts as the head of government and as ceremonial head of state. The president directs the government and makes its appointments. Neither the president nor those appointed by the president are part of the legislature. The key difference between the presidential and prime ministerial system is a separation of powers, rather than a fusion of powers.

The president serves for a fixed term and unless impeachment proceedings are brought the president cannot be defeated by the legislature or forced to resign by losing a vote. A presidential system has a single executive, with all power and responsibility in the hands of an individual. In a parliamentary system, although the prime minister is dominant over cabinet colleagues, there is a collegial or plural executive.

Ceremonial and political roles

One of the more obvious differences between Britain and the US is that in Britain the ceremonial and political roles are separated. The monarch is the head of state, while the prime minister is the chief executive and political head of government. In the US the roles are combined in the office of the president and while this may be an onerous task, it gives the president the opportunity to receive a great deal of press and media coverage. The prime minister, on the other hand, can concentrate on matters in hand and politics in the general sense of the term. The president, however, has the additional prestige and it is often the view that the president is both in and above any political infighting and is there to represent the national interests.

Cabinet and party system

Both prime minister and president direct the work of executive departments of government, but in the US the cabinet is far less significant. Cabinet colleagues tend to be drawn from business, the professions or are academics and return to their former roles once the president's term of office comes to an end. Cabinet members in Britain have their own distinct political identity and in time may well become prime minister themselves.

A British prime minister will control a disciplined party but the president does not have this support. Consequently it is the president who finds it more difficult to obtain a majority in transforming proposals into law. This could be due to state rights, views of Congress or even the Supreme Court. M. Walles (*British and American Systems of Government,* 1988) explained that the prime minister has party support and can therefore take more authoritative action. The president, on the other hand, often lacks party support and this means the president is at a disadvantage in being able to create working programmes out of policies.

Policymaking and scope of powers

A British prime minister can declare the direction of foreign policy, as can the president, but treaties have to be approved by the Senate. Administration policy differs and prime ministers tend to put their views before the cabinet whereas a president may only consult the Secretary of State. Prime ministers have foreign secretaries, with whom they are in broad agreement and are used as a primary vehicle for policy.

Prime ministers can be defeated in the House of Commons and may not necessarily see out their term of office. Such was the case with Margaret Thatcher. A president, unless impeached, will see out their fixed term in office.

The other key consideration is that an individual who has served as a president for two terms cannot be re-elected for a third term. A prime minister has no such impediment and may, in theory at least, be prime minister on a number of occasions. Winston Churchill served as coalition prime minister during the Second World War and as a Conservative prime minister in the early 1950s.

In terms of domestic policy, again the prime minister has the edge. There is a centralised party, which supports party government, giving the prime minister freedom of action. A president's powers are far more constrained.

However, it is perhaps important to point out that the most striking difference is the scope and power of the two comparative offices. In the past the British prime minister may have had the ability to stride the world stage with considerable power and influence. This is no longer the case, but it is certainly true of a US president. Comparatively, in global terms and in terms of world leadership, a US president has unsurpassed powers. The president is the leader of the most significant country in international terms and therefore any real debate about the relative powers has to be put into this perspective.

Speed of decision-making

A presidential government has the advantage in terms of speed of decision-making compared to prime ministerial government, which relies far more on collective decision-making. In theory using executive powers a president should be able to respond decisively and quickly compared to a prime minister.

2.27 Executive Power and Policy

Learning objectives

- Is a strong executive essential for the effective formulating of policy and its delivery?

Is a strong executive essential for the effective formulating of policy and its delivery?

Scope of presidential power

In the US President George W. Bush relied heavily on his role as commander-in-chief as the constitutional basis for a number of policies and delivery of those policies. In the past few years the Supreme Court has attempted to limit presidential powers and reassert the role of Congress.

The US Constitution defined the scope of the president in a rather open-ended way. The Constitution gives the president a range of powers and was granted a considerable amount of discretion, which successive presidents have used to expand their authority. The constitutional set-up requires the president to negotiate in a system that has shared powers. Many presidents have found this system to be frustrating and there has been an increasing demand for strong political direction and the assumption that only a president can provide this. The president has a national mandate, an obligation to provide effective leadership and the right to pursue policies in the national interest. Nonetheless the president has to operate in a system with checks and balances and in order to fulfil goals has to use persuasion.

Some see the presidency as the dominant institution in the US and that presidents have used ambiguities in the Constitution to strengthen their position and to follow policies that have effectively centralised and politicised the whole of the governing process.

There was a period of presidential weakness after the Watergate scandal, where the concept of the imperial president fell into disrepute. Congress was strengthened and presidents found it difficult to mobilise support due to well-organised interest groups, diverse opinion and a more proactive Congress. Presidents had to come up with new ways of governing; they had to be able to use the executive branch in such a way as to offset its dependence on the legislature. They also tended to go public on strategy issues to gain public support, rather than having to spend time and effort trying to pressurise their rivals in Congress.

Use of presidential power

Nixon and Reagan both used presidential powers and prerogatives to sidestep Congress, particularly in the appointments powers, the use of executive orders and making signing statements. Reagan was also very good with the media and was a popular president. George W. Bush built on this strategy.

Newly inaugurated presidents will often claim that they want a clean slate, but there is always a legacy of previous presidents and how business has been done in the past. Undoubtedly, the catastrophic events in 2001 focusing on the terrorist attacks on the US propelled President Bush into a situation where he needed to show clear, decisive, effective leadership that would have a long-lasting impact on the political landscape. Bush broadened his powers to withhold documents; he used his executive privileges, powers and prerogatives. Some simply see it as an extension of Nixon or Reagan's strategy, but others view it as a means by which Bush avoided accountability.

The events of 2001 certainly enhanced Bush's presidency, made him a national leader, created legitimacy and he acted and was accepted as being presidential. The crisis allowed him to take the initiative at a time when Congress was unwilling to challenge him. But ultimately his decision-making flaws were open to criticism, which eventually deflected him from the rest of his policy agenda. A prime example was his hopeless handling of a devastated New Orleans in the aftermath of Hurricane Katrina. Bush was keen to exert his executive privilege and just as Clinton had done he used executive orders, proclamations, signing statements, memoranda and national security directives as a means by which he could forge a strong presidency. Time after time he acted unilaterally and seized the policy initiative.

Although many of Bush's actions were later challenged by Congress and by the Supreme Court, he proved that authority alone was a strong enough resource to push through policy and to bypass Congress, which could have provided legislation, albeit very slowly. Bush used executive orders and national security directives to freeze suspected terrorist assets, reduce the impact of industrial and environmental regulations and to create military tribunals. All of this was done without recourse to Congress. Bush even used a recess appointment to secure the appointment of John Bolton as Ambassador to the United Nations after the Senate had blocked his appointment.

Nonetheless, Bush had to make compromises, just as other presidents were forced to do before him. He made compromises on the 'No Child Left Behind' initiative and on a host of other issues. However, from a point of relative weakness when he was first elected in 2000, the 2004 election was seen as an endorsement of his policies. Republicans gained control of Congress and they set on a road together to reform social security and the legal system.

The power of the British prime minister

As for Britain, that the executive has become increasingly powerful and, arguably, increasingly essential since the Second World War has been the subject of continued analysis. Tony Benn, the former MP and government minister, writing in 1985 in A. King's *The British Prime Minister,* contended that the British prime minister's powers were now so great that they impinged on the legitimate rights of the electorate, the role of parliament and the functions of collective cabinet decision-making. Benn believed that this centralisation of powers into the hands of one individual amounted to personal rule at the heart of a parliamentary democracy.

It is difficult to measure the power of the prime minister, but a prime minister can appoint or dismiss members of the cabinet or other ministers. They can determine the structure and membership of any cabinet committee, they have a central, non-departmental function, which can oversee all policy areas and become involved in. They are also leader of the party and enjoy a high media profile.

Nonetheless, the relationship between the prime minister and members of the cabinet is complex, as was obvious in the relationship between Tony Blair and Gordon Brown. It is also the case that the comparative power across the cabinet has fluctuated and will continue to change with individuals and roles gaining and losing ascendency.

Decisive versus consensual policymaking

A president who wishes to act unilaterally can use executive orders and agreements, which do not need congressional approval unless they require congressional appropriations. A British prime minister is essentially a 'coordinator-in-chief'. They can exercise tight control over government but need the cooperation of key cabinet members and the guarantee of support from the House of Commons.

2.28 Presidential Appointments

Learning objectives

- What are the factors influencing the chief executive when making appointments?

What are the factors influencing the chief executive when making appointments?

The confirmation process

Presidential appointments can be extremely significant especially to the federal judiciary, as it is the role of these judges to interpret the Constitution. They may be in post for 20 or 30 years, so many groups take an interest in the confirmation process.

Two prime examples show how pressure groups, for example, spent considerable time and money in trying to influence presidential appointments to the Supreme Court. In 1986 a number of liberal pressure groups spent over $15 million on a successful campaign in order to oppose the nomination of Robert Bork to the Supreme Court. In 2005 President George W. Bush was forced to withdraw his nomination of Harriet Miers to the Supreme Court after a series of concerted attacks by right-wing activists who were suspicious of her supposed conservative leanings.

Harriet Miers nomination and withdrawal

Harriet Miers had never served as a judge, her intellect was in question, and she had close ties to Bush and an unclear record on a number of issues. She was seen as ill-prepared and uninformed, with no experience of constitutional law. The Senate Judiciary Committee had grave misgivings and found many errors in her answers about constitutional and equal protection issues.

There are around 1000 presidential appointments that require Senate confirmation, including all those in the executive departments, some in independent executive agencies, the 150 or so ambassadors, 200 US attorneys and marshals, 130 regulatory positions in agencies and 160 part-time presidential appointees, such as members of the broadcasting board of governors.

The Senate's power is vested in Article III, Section 2 of the US Constitution. Although there are many who believe that the Senate should confirm anyone who has been nominated by the president, this is a vital check and balance. Stephen Carter (*The Confirmation Mess: Cleaning Up the Federal Appointment Process,* 1995) considered that the tradition of the Senate being deferential to the cabinet choices made by the president was never as historically or constitutionally established as many believed. It was not the intention of the founders of the Constitution for the Senate's confirmation of cabinet officers to be simply a rubber stamp. It was intended to perform a vital check on the president's selection of his own team and therefore part of the check on the president's policymaking.

Alexander Hamilton in the *Federalist Papers* No. 77 wrote: 'If by influencing the president be meant restraining him, this is precisely what must have been intended.'

Hamilton also wrote in the *Federalist Papers* No. 76: 'It would be an excellent check on a spirit of favouritism in the president, and would tend greatly to prevent the appointment of unfit characters from state prejudice, from family connection, or from a view to popularity.'

Stephen Carter's research into the confirmation process seemed to indicate that many different groups actively searched for reasons to question nominees, rather than trying to find a way in which to streamline the process. The suggestion was that the president should have to demonstrate that the nominee is qualified and worthy of the post. He suggested that the Senate should then be able to 'reject a nominee on no other ground than that the affirmation case has not been made'. Otherwise the continued practice of trying to smear candidates by looking for any mistakes they may have made, ethically or legally, in the past would continue. One of the issues also suggested was that in order to avoid nominees who may have made errors in the past, less qualified nominees who lack a contentious past are chosen.

Political appointments

J. Jacobstein and Roy Mersky (*The Rejected: Sketches of the 26 Men Nominated for the Supreme Court but Not Confirmed by the Senate*, 1993) felt that politics rather than qualifications were now the basis of presidential appointments. The character of nominees was brought into question, but this was no recent trend; it had begun during the term of the second president of the United States, John Adams, and had continued unabated ever since.

It seems that the authors were correct, as in the cases of 16 presidents out of the 40 from George Washington to Ronald Reagan had at least one or more of their nominees for the Supreme Court alone rejected.

The influence does not just extend to interest groups, the media and views of senators. During the administrations of Ronald Reagan and George H. W. Bush, not a single pro-abortion member of the judiciary was appointed, due to the influence of the Roman Catholic Church.

The often murky world of lobbying against presidential nominees came to a head in 2001 when John Ashcroft was nominated as US Attorney General. Several civil rights groups and other organisations were accused of violating their tax exempt status by getting involved in lobbying against his nomination.

Until relatively recently some 97 per cent of presidential cabinet appointments had been approved by the Senate. Typically a president will make 3000 appointments. During the Clinton administration the Republican Senate refused to hold hearings in the case of over 140 federal judges nominated by Clinton. George W. Bush had far better success.

Patronage is also a key influence and invariably influences appointments. Posts have to be filled and this process revolves primarily around placing individuals who are in many cases rewarded for their support and hard work in securing the election or re-election of the president.

Sympathetic pressure groups that have established insider status within a president's camp or the White House can have enormous influence on key appointments. Typically (in the case of federal judicial appointments) these interest groups will:

- compile detailed dossiers on the nominees' judgements and private lives
- ensure that their membership knows about the group's views on the nominees and encourage them to contact their own members of Congress
- mount demonstrations during the confirmation hearings
- pay for TV advertisements and features in newspapers, explaining why or why not the nomination should be confirmed
- contact their allies in the Senate and brief them on the most damaging questions to ask the nominee.

It is at this Senate confirmation hearing stage that the president will be notified whether their nominee has been confirmed or rejected. The Senate has three options: confirm, reject or take no action. Clearly the greatest influence is brought to bear at this point by interest groups, in order to derail undesirable presidential nominees.

Political legacy

Given the fact that Supreme Court justices can only be replaced by appointment if a sitting judge retires or dies, then the likelihood is that Supreme Court judges' careers will be far longer than a presidential term. The president's power to nominate judges is one of his most powerful tools and will leave a legacy far longer than any policy initiative.

Experience and character as appointment factors

President George W. Bush believed that the success of the Bush-Cheney administration was dependent on the quality of the appointees that they had chosen. As far as Bush was concerned, the most important quality was that they would work tirelessly for the nation, take decisions based on the facts only and not make decisions or frame policy merely to appeal to public opinion and support. Bush claimed that he would not rule out any suitable individual, regardless of their background or allegiances.

As G. Calvin Mackenzie suggested in *Innocent until Nominated* (2001), working for the president as an appointee is an ordeal. Americans are cynical about the appointment process and any new president faces a daunting challenge. Trust, honesty, integrity, but not necessarily impartiality, are key requirements in addition to any political or bureaucratic qualities.

2.29 The Presidential and the Legislative Process

Learning objectives

- What tactics are used by the executive to secure the passage of legislation?

What tactics are used by the executive to secure the passage of legislation?

Persuasion and bargaining

Many presidents found it difficult to advance their policy agenda through the legislative process without relying on persuasion. But other techniques are certainly necessary and across all of the presidential administrations less than 5 per cent of public bills have been vetoed by the president. Yet it is this technique, as a means of persuasion, which can be a useful weapon in a president's armoury. President George W. Bush, during his first term, did not issue a single veto. He said: 'The best tool I have beside persuasion is to veto.'

What he meant by this was that using the threat of a veto as a bargaining tool and the fact that the threat of the veto is often more important than actually following through with it. Congress is perfectly well aware of just how difficult it is to override a presidential veto and would seek to avoid it. Congress is therefore pragmatic and often of the view that passing some legislation on an issue is better than nothing, largely because nothing is often the outcome of a legislative process. Therefore Congress is more likely to pass a bill that will avoid a veto, even if it means making significant compromises with the president. Occasionally a majority in the Congress may actually want to provoke a veto and will willingly sacrifice the bill in order to turn it into a campaign issue.

Richard Neustadt, (*Presidential Power*, 1960) focused on the fact that the president had shared authority and did not have the power to command the obedience of Congress. He had to be able to have effective persuasive techniques. A president had to be able to convince members of Congress that they should follow what the White House wants them to do and that they should do it for their own sake and on their own authority.

The president will therefore use both formal and informal persuasive techniques, trying to match the self-interests of members of the Congress with their own presidential goals. Neustadt saw the president as a bargainer and that bargaining was key to a president's influence over policy. It also meant that legislators should anticipate that the president should be successful as a part of the game of bargaining; otherwise the president would not enter into the negotiations.

In order for the president to be able to use bargaining techniques they would deploy informal party ties, links with committee leaders, along with deference shown to the president by members of Congress and the promise of advancement in return for support.

Interest groups and coalitions

In recent years the president has faced a different set of circumstances with the US subcommittee system, which has effectively fragmented power in Congress and made every single member of Congress an independent, free-thinking target. This has meant that traditional bargaining and persuasion is more time-consuming and less predictable. Presidents have therefore switched from bargaining to going public as a means by which they can get their points of view across and use as leverage on Congress. Presidents will directly target key interest groups and coalitions in order to gather support for policy initiatives.

The president will use various methods of persuasion, either directly or indirectly, as can be seen in the following table.

Persuasion through people	Persuasion through promises
The vice-president is the presiding officer in the Senate and therefore can directly talk to other senators and members of the House of Representatives in the course of their work.	The president may make personal phone calls to individual members of Congress.
Many former vice-presidents were members of Congress, including Al Gore and Dan Quayle.	The president may promise to assist with legislation that would directly be to the advantage of the Congress members' constituents.
Congressional liaison staff, who are members of the White House, are in effect the president's full-time lobbyists to Congress.	The president can offer to make an appointment that is in the interests of a member's constituents.
The president's cabinet officers are expert in their own policy areas and are used to persuade contacts.	The member can be invited to a meeting at the White House.
Party leaders in Congress, whether they are the House Speaker or the majority or minority leaders, are used in order to help persuade other members of Congress.	The president can go to Capitol Hill to personally address a number of members of Congress.
Whips, committee chairs and other individuals whose position is often reliant on the president, or well-placed party officials can also be used.	The president can offer to make a personal appearance during a re-election campaign for a member of his own party.

As David Mervin wrote, *George Bush and the Guardianship Presidency*, (1996), the US president is the 'bargainer-in-chief'. The president needs to ensure that favoured legislation is passed, appointments are confirmed and treaties are ratified.

In order to judge the relative persuasive techniques a presidential support score is created, which measures how many votes a president has won in the House and in the Senate on which the president took a clear position. It is not a measure of how important any of the bills were; simply what the president got out of it. Of course the president can manipulate the score by not taking a position on a vote that he is likely to lose.

F855 Question Topics 12:

2.30 Cabinet Government vs Presidential Government

Learning objectives

- Examine the claim that cabinet government is more effective than presidential government.

Collective responsibility

This is a cabinet convention that requires members to fully support a decision made by the cabinet, regardless of whether they have argued against it. They are required to back the decision otherwise they should resign. The purpose of this is to ensure unity of the government and that the prime minister can be assured of the support of cabinet members. In effect they cannot break ranks.

Examine the claim that cabinet government is more effective than presidential government

It is important to remember that it is the executive branch of a government that implements legislation and that the legislative branch of government approves the legislation.

In the vast majority of liberal democracies, where there is a president or a prime minister, there has been a tendency for authority to become concentrated in a single individual.

Although there are cabinets in both the British and US systems their functions are entirely different. In the US system, and although all presidents have had one, the cabinet has a lower level of influence and is there effectively in an advisory role. The British system, however, based on a parliamentary system, is a more collective executive and has shared decision-making in the form of a cabinet. This is despite the fact that in the past 40 years or more there has been a drift towards the dominance of that executive by the prime minister.

Cabinet government in Britain

In Britain it has become increasingly more difficult for cabinet government to operate for a number of reasons.

- Government of the country is far more complex than ever before, which has led to ministerial overload.
- The prime minister has become far more than the first among equals and effectively dominates the executive branch of government.
- The public interest in the functioning of government has become overwhelming, particularly because the media has placed such an important focus on its operations.

In the US it has never been particularly a question of whether their cabinet system has declined in influence or importance; simply it has never developed. Bill Clinton, for example, tried to integrate departmental heads and White House officials by creating committees of cabinet and sub-cabinet members, such as the National Economic Council.

In parliamentary systems the average cabinet membership is around 20 and in Britain it is up to around 25. George W. Bush's cabinet in his second term was 19, consisting of the president, vice-president, 14 departmental heads, ambassador to the UN, director of the Office of Management and director of the Office of the Budget.

In Britain and in Germany, for example, the cabinet is at the centre of decision-making. In Britain it is based on the concept of collective responsibility. This means that all ministers are involved in the decision-making and are expected to publicly defend those decisions. This helps ensure ministerial accountability and it also means that ministers are subject to parliamentary, media and electorate scrutiny. It takes a brave minister to break ranks with cabinet and publicly state their disapproval of policy, as this usually signals an end of their cabinet career.

Cabinet government and, to a large extent, the European Commission, operates as a forum where discussions can take place, agreements can be reached and then the ministers present a cohesive front and a unified approach. This is usually only achievable if all the cabinet members belong to a single party; hence there are difficulties in countries such as Germany that have coalition governments.

Cabinet government does have weaknesses in times of crisis and where there are significant divisions in cabinet the process is slowed down. Where there is a weak cabinet system, such as in the US, individuals can break ranks and go public. The arguments between Donald Rumsfeld and Colin Powell over foreign policy were kept from the public at the time.

Cabinet government, however, is under threat. In Germany the chancellor is becoming increasingly more powerful, in Europe the European Commission is under threat from proposals to increase the power of the president of the commission and certainly during the terms of office of Margaret Thatcher, Tony Blair and to a lesser extent Gordon Brown, there was what has been described as a British presidency. This form of leadership has advantages in terms of quick decision-making, but flaws in terms of accountability. It was ultimately accountability that brought about the fall of Margaret Thatcher.

A prime minister, in order to claim enhanced leadership, needs to have a mandate, real or implied, from the electorate and undoubtedly have well-placed supporters who can silence critics and dissenting voices.

Presidential government – the US

In the US the president is often seen as a unifying force during times of emergency. This has been seen on numerous occasions during the administrations of Roosevelt, Johnson, Kennedy and George W. Bush. Sometimes this leading role has hopelessly backfired on a president, as in the case of Jimmy Carter, who was held to blame for a number of policy failures.

A president has a direct mandate from the people, which enforces or at least reinforces their leadership credentials. Nonetheless the sets of checks and balances in the US system mean that a president cannot run away with power and totally override the role of Congress and of the judiciary. In fact many presidents have remarked that they would far rather have the powers of a British prime minister than the limited powers they have as a US president.

As we have seen, the US and British cabinets are very different. The US contribution is far less than the British one, as the political writer M. Walles noted in 1988: 'No party pressures to induce a sense of collectivity and no electoral demands to impose an outward unity'.

This sums up the position of the US cabinet. President Carter allowed it to meet on numerous occasions during his first two years as president. He was convinced that he wanted a strong cabinet system. Ultimately he became disillusioned with it and in 1979 he invited his cabinet secretaries to resign.

The British executive is very much based on cabinet government. In a parliamentary system there tends not to be the same focus on who leads the team. More use is made of cabinet committees and the cabinet itself is bypassed in many situations. The cabinet retains its position as the forum in which key decisions are taken, and it ratifies decisions.

In a presidential system departmental heads tend to follow their own agendas and, as R. Hague of the University of Newcastle wrote in 2001: '[Cabinet meetings are often] little more than a presidential photo opportunity.'

Exam Café

Relax, refresh, result!

Relax and prepare

Questions for the exam are likely to be drawn from the following topic areas or similar. Use these to help focus on what areas of the subject you should be revising.

- The functions of legislatures and how well these are performed.
- The factors influencing the voting of elected representatives.
- The relations between the executives and legislatures.
- The powers of executives and institutional organisations and arrangements therein.
- Having a clear understanding of the constitutional arrangements in the UK and the US and the implications for the relative powers of the executives and legislatures therein.
- The preparation of arguments which explain why the executive in the US cannot effectively dominate the legislature as in the UK.
- These arguments should be based upon the central principles of the separation of powers and checks and balances in contrast to the consequences of having a parliamentary system of government.

Refresh your memory

As a help in revising for your exam try to do the following exercises. They will help you structure your notes and give you a guide as what you need to know. Remember to work through unit F853 first as this will provide the base you will need for F855.

The Congress

- Create a table which identifies the functions of Congress and include a column which comments on how well it fulfils these functions, with contemporary examples for each function. For example, Function – scrutiny and oversight: Armed Services Committee and the Iraq war; General Petraeus reports. Function – check executive power: Confirmation of appointments by the Senate.
- Examine the reasons why legislation is so difficult to pass through the Congress.
- Consider the role of party and other key influences on voting in Congress. This may be related to the legislative problems of Congress mentioned above. Examine key policy debates and assess the impact of the 'folks back home', forthcoming elections, pressure groups and the media, presidential efforts and personal conscience on moral and ethical issues such as abortion rights.

- Prepare a table of the constitutional checks the Congress has over the presidency and provide up-to-date examples for each check, for example confirmation of appointments; the withdrawal of Miers and narrow confirmation of Alito by the full Senate 58–42 and rejection by the Senate Judiciary Committee 10–8.

The presidency

- Prepare a table which outlines the powers of the presidency in one column and provide up-to-date examples of how these powers have been used recently. For example Function – commander-in-chief. Comment – the Bush doctrine of unilateral pre-emptive retaliation, the Afghan and Iraq wars.
- Create another table which details changes in presidential power over time. Focus on the creation of the *modern presidency* under FDR, the rise of the *imperial presidency* after the Second World War, the *imperilled presidency* after Watergate, the *resurgent presidency* during the Reagan era.
- While the above is fundamental to the study of the presidency, avoid too much historical detail in an exam unless the question specifically demands it. The Bush administration and the contrast between his first and second terms (*imperial* to *imperilled*) provides an excellent insight into the factors which influence presidential power.
- Create a table which outlines the arguments for and against the cabinet and EXOP providing useful support for the president. Examine the presidential style of the new president (2009) and the significance of appointments made to each of these institutions.

Exam tips

These are some reasons why students do badly in exams. They provide a guide to what you need to avoid and by implication what you need to do to perform well in the exam.

- They do not have a clear understanding of contemporary developments and of the recent relations between the executive and the legislature.
- They do not always focus on the question set.
- Students frequently possess lots of knowledge about the president and Congress but if this is not focused on the actual question, they can write a great deal of irrelevant material.

Get the result!

These are some ideas to help you in your revision and to keep up to date with the latest developments in US politics.

- Keep a scrap book of newspaper cuttings and articles from journals such as the *Economist* of occasions where the Congress and president have been working together or at odds with each other. Issues such as the Iraq war, the budget and taxes, and health–care reform are all likely to be contentious in the near future.
- Use the House and Senate websites to get up-to-date examples of committee work and details of their composition.
- Use case studies such as health-care reform to inform discussion of the work of the Congress and the relationship between the executive and the legislature.
- Look out for assessments of the Bush presidency and the first 100 days of the Obama presidency.
- Regularly read the websites of the *New York Times*, the *Washington Post* and CNN for in-depth coverage of the most recent developments and incorporate these into your notes and essays. This will give you a real edge in the exam.
- At A2 more emphasis is placed on analysis and evaluation and therefore you must provide an answer to the question set. Outlining the powers of the president alone for a question such as 'The most important power of the president is the power to persuade' will not score you the AO2 marks for analysis and evaluation.
- A simple technique to employ is to use the words in the question frequently as you write. A direct attempt to answer the question head on need not wait until the conclusion. It could be used at the start or end of a paragraph in the main body of the essay. Thus a paragraph could begin ***'The power to persuade'*** *is central to any presidency as party discipline is weak in the Congress and Bush has encountered greater problems since the 2006 mid-terms when the Democrats were returned with majorities in both House and Senate.'*
- Remember most questions ask you to discuss both the case for and against, and you should use this to structure your essays accordingly.

In Focus – F855

The following will help you in revising and in developing your knowledge at this level in order to gain a higher mark. These are the key areas to focus on.

- Contrast the governmental arrangements in the UK and US and assess the extent to which each system assists the formulation and delivery of policy as well as serving democratic purposes.
- Keep an eye out for backbench rebellions and government defeats in the House of Lords, such as over proposals to allow detention without trial for 42 days.
- Consider the varying fortunes of the British prime minister. Assess the factors which weaken or strengthen his position. Consider the extent to which the prime minister is able to dominate the cabinet.
- Try and incorporate discussion of the EU into your answers even if only briefly. Recognition of the relative impotence of the European Parliament and the dominance of the Council of Ministers and Commission will get you extra marks.
- Similarly, you may undertake a case study of another country, such as France or Germany, which if used in the exam will also gain you marks.
- Create a table to outline the functions of a second chamber and consider how well the functions are performed by the Senate and House of Lords. It is worth stating that the Senate is a co-equal (if not more prestigious) chamber.
- Students can often get bogged down in debates about the composition of the House of Lords. While important, the role and functions of the second chamber need to be separated from this debate.
- Consider the advantages and disadvantages of a singular (presidential) as opposed to a plural executive (as in the UK model of cabinet government).
- Draw parallels between the notion of presidential government in the US and prime ministerial government in the UK.
- By way of contrast mention how notions of a British presidency fall short due to the constraints of the British Constitution and the nature of the office. This may lead you to conclude that while British politics has become more presidential, due to media attention particularly, and prime ministerial power may have increased over time, it would be incorrect to assume that the UK has reformed the organisation of its executive and its relationship with the legislature completely.

3 Political Parties and Pressure Groups

US politics is dominated by two political parties, the Democrats and the Republicans. Rarely have independent or third parties had any long-lasting impact. US political parties tend to be far less well organised and disciplined than the major parties in Britain. Individual members of Congress are far more independent and prone to being overly concerned with their constituents and open to influence from pressure groups.

There are tens of thousands of pressure groups operating in the US at national, state or local level. They have an enormous influence, as the US system has multiple access points to decision-makers.

There are many other marked differences between the political parties in the US when compared to parties that you may be more familiar with in Britain and Europe. They have different ideologies, sets of policies and differing agendas and priorities. Nonetheless, the philosophy, ideology and policies of the two major parties have gone through a series of changes or phases over the years, which have helped develop the Democrats and the Republicans into the types of parties that we now see operating in the US.

There are nine key themes in this chapter.

- Role, functions and power in political parties
- Party systems and ideology
- Ideology and policy (1)
- Ideology and policy (2)
- The Republicans
- The Democrats
- Third parties and renewal and decline
- Issue-centred politics and current issues
- Pressure groups

These are represented by the first nine topics, which are supported by five question topics for F853, looking at the most common essay titles, and six F855 question topics, which again look at popular essay themes in the examination.

This chapter contains 20 spreads in total, representing the following.

The chapter is rounded off with an exam café feature on page 164.

Learning objectives

- Political parties and the constitution
- Role and function of political parties

Centrist

A view that in terms of policy a party can neither be described as being left or rightward leaning; it can even be non-doctrinaire.

Political parties and the constitution

When the US Constitution was written the separation of powers and, in particular, the indirect election of the president using an electoral college aimed to protect the country from political parties and factions. In the US the development of political parties is closely linked to the broadening of voting rights. As the electorate expanded political parties grew to mobilise those voters, in order to gain political control. The parties became institutionalised and by the 1830s were firmly established and very powerful.

The current party system is dominated by the Republicans and the Democrats. They provide the vast majority of presidents, members of Congress, governors and members of state legislators. It is rare for an independent or third party representative to win an election.

The two parties dominate government at all levels. But they are perhaps less ideologically cohesive than the parties in Britain or in many other European countries, although there have been signs of increased partisanship in the Congress. As we will see, the US has essentially a two-party system, which has held sway since at least the 1860s. Both parties seek broad-based support, drawing voters from various classes and demographic groups. The parties show flexibility in terms of policy and could be broadly described as being **centrist**. This is often seen as reflecting the dominant ideology of liberal capitalism in the US.

As the parties are not ideologically driven there is enormous diversity within the ranks of each party. This has effectively absorbed third parties and protest movements. If anything the Republicans can be seen to be the more conservative, focusing on private wealth and property rights, whereas the Democrats are at best liberals. However, both parties, when they gain power, tend to be pragmatic in policy terms.

Role and function of political parties

Political parties, although they are often accused of putting themselves before the needs of their country or the people, provide a series of vital functions in all political systems where there is a democratic tradition. As we have seen, in the US parties tend to be non-ideological, weak in terms of organisation and constantly in a situation where they are either in financial or policy crises. The following list looks at 13 key functions of political parties. Clearly some political parties in different political systems are more or less successful in fulfilling these roles.

- Promoting ideas – parties provide a forum in which individuals with similar ideas or values can join together to take concerted action.
- Providing a programme – the parties, after due deliberation and perhaps through an internal democratic process, adopt a series of policy options and then create a single coherent programme of action, which provides the focus of their offering to the electorate.
- Recruiting people – parties will seek out talented individuals who have a desire to become involved in politics.
- Providing leaders – parties will identify, select and develop potential leaders from their membership, who can take senior positions within the party and ultimately in politics itself.

- Encouraging voting – parties will encourage their members, supporters and the broader population to cast their votes in elections. Party members will also be of assistance to the party in the administration and promotion of elections.
- Educating the public – parties aim to inform and educate the general voting public about issues and they will suggest policy solutions to those issues. They will highlight key concerns, which may have been overlooked by an opposition party in power.
- Reinforcing allegiances – parties will encourage individuals to show clear loyalty and allegiance to the party and to the broader democratic process.
- Filling political office – parties will groom and support candidates who will ultimately take a place in government at some level.
- Representing the broader public – parties will aim to articulate the views and opinions of their members and the voters in line with the party's broader ideological or policy beliefs, highlighting key concerns and offering solutions.
- Formulating goals – parties will set out clear objectives for a region or the country and present workable programmes that will achieve these objectives.
- Defending interests – parties will aim to protect or to promote the interests of their members and of their core supporters (either financial or voters).
- Socialising and mobilising – parties will aim to involve individuals in the political process and extol the virtues of the democratic process and to encourage participation and interest, not only in elections but also in the broader political field.
- Organising government – parties, in developing individuals who will become acknowledged experts or spokespersons in a particular field of interest, will be creating a pool of individuals who understand issues and can cope with the demands of a government position. They can also provide a platform of criticism and opposition to an opposing party's government or policy programme.

In the US political party committees need to register with the Federal Election Commission (FEC) once they reach certain thresholds for spending or contributions. For third parties with less financial support this is often an impossible hurdle and it penalises them financially. According to the FEC: 'The commission determines whether committees meet the criteria for state or national party committee status through the advisory opinion process.'

To gain national committee status a party would usually have to have:

- nominated qualified candidates for president or for Congress in a number of states
- engaged in voter registration or other voting drives on an ongoing basis
- publicised the party and primary issues
- held a national convention
- set up a national office
- established state affiliates.

In the 2008 presidential election there were six candidates from the tiny Reform Party (Ted Weill) with just over 42,000 registered members, to the massive Republican Party (John McCain) with 30.59 million registered members and the Democratic Party (the winner, Barack Obama) with 39.3 million registered members.

INTERNET RESEARCH

For a useful summary of the main platforms and policies of the parties and a number of useful articles about the role and functions of political parties in the US, go to www.heinemann.co.uk/hotlinks, insert the express code 1825P and click on the relevant link.

Learning objectives

- Two-party, multi-party and dominant party systems
- The role of ideology in political parties

Two-party, multi-party and dominant party systems

With the exception of certain African countries and communist countries, including China, Cuba and North Korea, that have single-party political systems, the majority of countries have a range of political parties. They are often typified not by how many parties there are, but by how many have a reasonable expectation of playing a part in government. There are, of course, some countries that do not permit any political parties. These are countries that tend to be run by authoritarian military regimes.

In a country with a two-party system the two main parties dominate politics and tend to form most of the governments. Examples are Britain, the United States and the Republic of Ireland. There are clear political divides in all of these cases: New Labour and Conservative, Democrat and Republican and Fianna Fáil and Fine Gael.

Andrew Heywood defines the two-party system in the following way.

- Two parties have significant electoral and legislative strength and are the only parties, even though a number of minority parties exist that have a reasonable expectation of achieving government power.
- On the basis of a legislative majority, the largest party is able to rule alone and the biggest minority party serves as the opposition.
- Both of the major parties are electable and the opposition party serves as a 'government in the wings'.

Although Britain, the US and the Republic of Ireland have two-party systems it is often difficult to ideologically place parties to the left or to the right. In these cases the countries are said to have indistinct two-party systems (US and the Republic of Ireland). Where there is a clearer divide, such as in Britain, it is said to have a distinct two-party system.

In countries that have three or more parties that receive a reasonable share of the vote and hence a reasonable number of seats in the legislature there is a multi-party system. This is relatively common on mainland Europe, such as Germany and Italy, where proportional representation systems reward parties in relation to the number of votes cast in their favour. In these systems it is unlikely that one single party could gain sufficient seats to form a single-party government. As a result governments tend to be coalitions.

There are other countries whose voters seem to consistently return the same party to power time after time. There may be a number of different parties, but only one of them has a reasonable expectation of forming a government. In a 43-year period, from 1932, Fianna Fáil was in office for 37 years. In Britain the Conservative victories from 1979 to 1992 led many to believe that the country had become a dominant-party system. The landslide New Labour victory in 1997 saw the Conservatives routed after 18 years in office.

The US system is far more complicated, as one party can dominate the legislature and another the presidency. In some US states the opposition party or parties is so weak that there is, in effect, almost a single-party system, with no real prospect of the dominant party ever being ousted. As M. Vile wrote in *Politics in the USA*: 'Politics operate in a framework of fifty systems, for much decentralisation has occurred.'

The following are some of the important reasons why both Britain and the US have two-party systems.

- Issues are expressed in terms of for and against.
- One party favours retaining the status quo while the other seeks change.
- Major parties are the only ones that have the resources available to them to launch the necessary campaign to win an election.
- Both countries have a first-past-the-post electoral system, with no prizes for second place.
- Parties will adopt ideas that have been developed by the other, making the parties flexible enough to provide solutions for current preoccupations.
- In both countries many voters are led to believe that casting their vote for a third party that cannot form a government is a wasted one.
- In both countries there is a largely homogenous population and no major parties are based on regions, race or religion, unlike the situation in Spain.

The role of ideology in political parties

As we will see when we investigate the ideologies in rather more detail, there is often very little to choose in terms of philosophy and ideology between the two major parties in the US. Beyond stating that the Democrats tend to be more liberal and the Republicans more conservative, it is undoubtedly true that there are many different variations of Democrat and Republican within the parties.

Democrats can be described as being liberal, moderate, new or conservative; Republicans as right-wing, Christian, moderate or compassionate. The two leading lights of the Democrat Party in the past fifty years have been John F. Kennedy and Barack Obama, both liberal Democrats with a focus on civil rights.

For the Republicans, George W. Bush coined the phrase 'compassionate conservative' in his 2000 election campaign. Arguably, the 2008 Republican candidate, John McCain, would also fall into this category.

Ideology also tends to be geographical in the US. In the northeast and on the west coast the Democrats tend to be liberal and the Republicans moderate. In the south of the country both parties tend to attract conservatives.

The most important aspect about the two major political parties is that they are fully prepared to accept individuals and indeed promote candidates from the broadest possible range of beliefs.

Even though each of the two major US political parties may be broad churches, this does not mean that they are not antagonistic towards one another. They have ideological differences, moralities and methods of operating within Congress. Perhaps the parties are even more ideologically distinct than before. Republicans now tend to be towards the conservative end of the spectrum, while Democrats are at the liberal end.

The important battlegrounds in the 2008 election showed the key differences on economy, the environment, defence, law and order, and foreign policy. Republicans, believing in traditional values, tend to be anti-abortion, pro-death penalty and pro-prayers in schools. Democrats focus on tolerance, self-expression, harmony and choice.

INTERNET RESEARCH

To access the Republican National Committee and the Democratic Party websites, go to www.heinemann.co.uk/hotlinks, insert the express code 1825P and click on the relevant link.

Learning objectives

- Social democracy and New Deal Democrats
- Liberalism, Reagan and Republican revolutions
- Party divisions

Social democracy and New Deal Democrats

While there are major reservations about the divide between liberals and conservatives, American liberalism is often described as being a dynamic movement and that classical liberalism is now a thing of the past. Liberalism is largely associated with protecting the individual by regulatory action. Most accept wealth inequalities as being inevitable and sometimes desirable, but that everyone should have a fair deal. It was out of this model to steer the US out of depression that Franklin D. Roosevelt engineered the New Deal.

The period of the New Deal Democrats is generally taken to be 1933 to 1945. It was spearheaded by the progressive governments led by Franklin D. Roosevelt. New Deal Democrats favoured economic regulation and insurance against hardship.

The first New Deal was launched in 1933 and was followed by a sweeping legislative programme, which imposed regulation on business and banking, created jobs through huge public works projects and set up a social security system. Roosevelt was considered something of a liberal and faced major opposition within his own party. Under him the Democratic Party became more and more associated with liberal ideologies, including civil rights, business regulation, the creation of labour unions and the promotion of social welfare. By this stage his opponents, who favoured lower taxes and entrepreneurialism, were describing themselves as conservatives.

Liberalism, Reagan and Republican revolutions

Roosevelt-style liberalism largely went out of fashion and neo-liberalism, with more commonalities with classical liberalism, or *laissez-faire* approaches, stressed a minimal state and a strong commitment to economic freedom. In the US, liberalism can be a term of abuse used by the political right. In the context of their times Jefferson, Jackson, Lincoln, Theodore Roosevelt, Harry Truman and John F. Kennedy were all liberals.

Ronald Reagan, 40th president of the United States, who was re-elected in 1984 in a landslide victory

During the 1980s within the Republican Party there were clear divisions between the old-fashioned conservatives, the new far right and the centre of the party. Ronald Reagan began to frame a revolutionary social movement that aimed to bring about sweeping political and ideological change. It was conservative in nature and pulled together a wide variety of different ideas.

The anti-environmentalist, Ron Arnold, explained how the movement came about after having read Luther Gurlich's *People, Power, Change* (1970). Arnold saw in Gurlich's analysis that in an activist society like the US the only way that social movement could be defeated was by another social movement.

The social movements that they wished to sweep aside incorporated the New Deal and various forms of social and environmental activism that had grown up in the 1960s and 1970s. The conservatives captured the social movement field so completely that they replaced it with their own future-orientated vision, which would seek to arrest the long decline that the US had suffered since the 1970s. It was to place the US firmly back at the centre of global politics, deal with oil crises, inflation and near bankruptcy.

Ronald Reagan's ideologies were based on anti-governmentalism, the lowering of taxes, small not big government, individualism, private enterprise and self-reliance.

As we will see, Democrats have generally taken a broadly liberal position, whereas Republicans have tended to take a more conservative stance. It would also be fair to say that generally American politics has shifted slightly to the right. However, as the following table suggests, there are still likely differences between liberals and conservatives in terms of approach and policy.

Issue	Liberals	Conservatives
Role of government	Important to regulate a free market	Only if it is in the public interest should government be involved
Spending	More focus on the disadvantaged	As low as possible
Taxation	Higher taxation for the rich	As low as possible
Abortion	Freedom of choice	Right to life
Affirmative action	In favour	Reluctant
Victims of crime	Focus on causes of crime	Tough on criminals, focus on rights of victims
School prayers	Opposed	In favour

Party divisions

As we will see, each party has its own character. It is too much of a generalisation to suggest what a typical Democrat or a Republican may or may not be. While we may believe that a Democrat believes in social welfare, regulation of business, fairer distribution of wealth and the supporting of a free world, this is as inaccurate as picturing a Republican as strong on law and order, limited government, pro-big business and essentially isolationist.

Where the parties diverge is on contentious matters, which could be pictured as being beyond ideology, including abortion, civil rights, affirmative action, federal government and education, poverty and welfare, medical care, urban renewal, defence spending and the role of America in the world. Within each party there are conflicting sets of values.

Republicans tend to have traditional values, aiming to uphold the family and individual discipline. They see these as vital for social stability and therefore government should intervene. Democrats view morality as a private concern. They promote free choice, self-expression, tolerance, diversity and harmony. If they are expressed as moral absolutes or ideologies they can preclude compromise. But often policies revolve around compromise, or the sharing of benefits and burdens. Where there are absolutes there is no middle ground, and it is where absolutes are concerned or true ideologies are involved that there is hostility between the parties. It is a feature of US government and politics that fierce antagonisms often hinder constructive policymaking and this is counter-productive when intense bargaining and exchanges of favours are necessary, in order for bills to pass into law.

Broadly, the Democrats have been supported by those with low incomes, particularly the urban working class, including the bulk of ethnic minorities. US voters seem to be able to tell the parties apart; business owners and professionals and larger farmers support the Republicans and see the Democrats as 'the party of the little man'. Voters see the Republicans as not wanting to expand the role of government, especially not Washington.

The support of interest groups also reinforces the differences. Many members of organised labour and smaller farmers from the National Farmers' Union support the Democrats, whereas the National Association of Manufacturers and the American Medical Association are associated with the Republicans.

INTERNET RESEARCH

For an in-depth look at the views and administration of Ronald Reagan, go to www.heinemann.co.uk/hotlinks, insert express code 1825P and click on the relevant link.

Learning objectives

- The New Right and neo-conservatism
- Third Way and New Democrats
- Compassionate conservatism
- Dominant ideology and the end of history theses

The New Right and neo-conservatism

The New Right is most closely associated with the policies of both Margaret Thatcher and Ronald Reagan, which coalesced into an ideology towards the end of the 1970s. The ideology focused on creating an environment in which private enterprise should be encouraged and rewarded for effort. This was linked with lower taxation, ensuring that those who generated wealth were not penalised. There was a belief in a strong state, yet a focus on the individual. The freedom of the individual, particularly in business, was a key. Radical change was seen as a necessary step and there was strong opposition to the welfare state.

The New Right wanted to sweep away what was known as the 'culture of dependency', based on the idea that the poor needed to take more responsibility for themselves as dependency created poverty and unemployment. There would be a marketisation of education, a view that ill-health was due to unhealthy lifestyles. To some extent it was reflected in fundamentalist views of the new Christian right. Single-parent families were seen as a cause of crime and soft sentencing was blamed for lack of crime prevention and deterrence. Huge cuts were made in welfare provision, and society was seen as individuals who should be free to make their own choices. There was also a belief that the approach would take society back to a golden age that focused on family, religion, quality education and a pro-life stance on abortion.

Neo-conservative ideology is closely aligned to traditional conservative views of the free market, limited welfare and traditional values. Significantly, however, it is their interventionist approach to international affairs that sets them apart from mainstream conservatism. They believe that interventionism defends national interests.

Central theorists were Irving Crystal and his son William. Their views were particularly relevant at a time when the US postured itself as the leading democratic nation in the world, facing the Soviet Union and the perils of the Cold War. Neo-conservatives wished to spread democracy throughout the world. Michael Lind ('A Tragedy of Errors', *The Nation*, 2004) explained that neo-conservatism began in the 1970s. Essentially it was a movement of anti-Soviet liberals and social democrats. Many of them preferred to call themselves paleoliberals following the traditions of US political leaders such as Humphrey, Henry Jackson, Johnson, Kennedy and Truman. What now remains of the neo-conservatives is just a fragment of a far broader coalition. Lind argued that they are still ideologically left of centre but see religion as a means of promoting morality.

After the September 11 attacks in 2001 Gerald Baker, writing in the *Times* in April 2007, suggested that after the attacks and the election of George W. Bush in 2001 neo-conservatism became a dominant ideology. Bush believed that the US should be instrumental in promoting liberal democracy across the world. This was a key reason for the US involvement in Iraq. As far as Bush's critics were concerned neo-conservatism now stood for military adventurism, state-sanctioned torture and the support of expansionist Zionism.

The Republican candidate for the 2008 presidential election, John McCain, was also closely associated with the neo-conservatives. A number of his prominent advisers were neo-conservatives and certainly his views on foreign policy combined neo-conservative ideologies.

Moral majority

The moral majority was a conservative Christian Political Action Committee (PAC) with literally millions of members. It was credited with delivering two-thirds of the white evangelical vote for Ronald Reagan in the 1980 presidential election. They wanted to outlaw abortion, oppose homosexuality, oppose equal rights, enforce traditional family values and impose strict censorship on the media.

Neocons

President George W. Bush's state of the union speech in January 2002 was written by neo-conservative David Frum. It suggested pre-emptive war against dangerous regimes. This became known as the Bush Doctrine and in September 2002 it was described as being the willingness to deter and defend against any perceived threat, even before the exact nature and timing of that threat had been determined. In other words, the Bush Doctrine called for pre-emptive strikes against perceived threats, a proactive rather than a reactive stance.

Third Way and New Democrats

The Third Way was seen as a means of blending liberal and social democrat ideas, with the emphasis on community and citizenship. Tony Blair in Britain and Bill Clinton in the US were seen as the two main supporters of the Third Way.

In the US the Democrats had been involved in internal fighting and had appeared to be out of touch and elitist. In 1992 Clinton's team had effectively reinvented the party, as New Democrats, as reflected in the concepts of the Third Way. As Tony Blair explained:

> *The Third Way stands for a modernised social democracy, passionate in its commitment to social justice and the goals of the centre left, but flexible, innovative and forward looking in the means to achieve them. It is a third way because it moves decisively between an old left preoccupied by state control, high taxation and producer interests; and a new right treating public investment, and often the very notions of society and collective endeavour, as evils to be undone.*

The key considerations were:

- making the state more flexible, proactive, a regulator rather than a provider
- combining social justice with economic efficiency
- ensuring opportunity for self-fulfillment and access to the requirements of a decent life
- a reciprocal relationship between the individual and the institutions
- government expenditure would no longer be public spending but an investment.

Compassionate conservatism

It was George W. Bush who put forward the idea of compassionate conservatism; a concern for the disadvantaged that a free market tends to ignore. It incorporates care, inclusivity and fostering positive notions of government. While Reaganite conservatives would cut back government, 'comcons' would use government to assist citizens. But it was only really achievable if there were a budget surplus.

The approach aimed to foster a relationship between government, charities and churches, allowing the latter to use government funds. Low-income families were promised tax relief, education vouchers to choose private schools and other measures to enable individuals and families to improve themselves.

Despite this the underlying conservative ideologies had not disappeared. The death penalty, anti-abortion, anti-gun control and anti-gay rights still were embedded in this approach.

No Child Left Behind Act (2001)

This controversial law reauthorised federal programmes that aimed to improve the performance of US schools, increase accountability and provide parents with more school choice.

Dominant ideology and the end of history theses

In 1960 Harvard University's Daniel Bell made the influential suggestion that there was an end of ideology. To Bell this meant that there was broad agreement among political parties and there seemed to be no significant ideological division or debate. The extremes of communism and fascism were no longer popular.

Francis Fukuyama on the triumph of liberal democracy

In his first major work, *The End of History and the Last Man* (1992), Fukuyama suggested that western-style liberal democracy had been the winner of the Cold War and it marked the last ideological change. After the September 11 attacks in 2001 critics suggested that Islamic fundamentalism threatened the power of the west, but Fukuyama described them as being 'a series of rearguard actions' against the prevailing political philosophy of new globalism. Although Fukuyama was considered to be a major neo-conservative figure, he has in recent years distanced himself from this. He became an opponent of the allied invasion of Iraq and criticised neo-conservatives.

INTERNET RESEARCH

There is a good summary of the views of Francis Fukuyama at www.heinemann.co.uk/hotlinks, insert the express code 1825P and click on the relevant link. From the opening page select 'Library' and then using the menu find 'Fukuyama' in the list of authors.

His views were given a broader perspective by Francis Fukuyama (who would later endorse Barack Obama in the 2008 presidential election). Fukuyama believed that with the collapse of communism in Europe in 1989, Marxist-Leninism as an ideology had lost its significance, as had fascism with the fall of Italy in 1943 and Germany in 1945. He suggested that liberal democracies, with market economies and open competitive political systems, were, in effect, the norm.

Fukuyama argued that the success of liberal democracy was based upon the three key elements of:

- dynamic capitalism
- support for liberal individualism
- the appeal of political pluralism giving real electoral alternatives.

It is important to remember the context in which he was writing – when Soviet-led communism was collapsing in Eastern Europe. Fukuyama's views have been extended by writers such as Philip Bobbitt (2002). He believed that liberalism had finally won what he called 'the long war' that had raged between 1914 and 1990 between liberal parliamentarianism, fascism and communism. He illustrated his point by suggesting that market reforms and democratic government had spread into Africa, Asia and South America. Indeed by 2000 around 60 per cent of states across the globe had major liberal democratic characteristics.

But as with any theory, new ideologies emerge and render it inaccurate. Political Islam, the continued success of Communist China and the various revivals of nationalism, racialism and religious fundamentalism across the world does not necessarily point to liberal democracy as being the final winner in the ideological debate.

3.5 The Republicans

Party history and development

The Republican Party is often referred to as the Grand Old Party (GOP). It was founded in 1854, essentially as an anti-slavery and modernising party. Abraham Lincoln was their first president and steered the Union to victory during the American Civil War (1861–65).

The Republicans played a key role in securing the vote for women, adopting it as a policy in 1896. The first female to be elected to Congress was also a Republican, Jeanette Rankin, in 1917. Notable Republican presidents have included Theodore Roosevelt, Dwight D. Eisenhower, Richard Nixon, Gerald Ford, Ronald Reagan and George Bush senior and junior.

Although the Republican Party began as a third party (at that stage the principal opposition to the Democratic Party was the Whig Party) support steadily grew and by the mid-2000s they were the second largest party in the US, with 55 million registered voters, or around a third of the electorate.

Learning objectives

- Party history and development
- Contemporary policies and leadership

Republican delegates arriving for their convention in 1868

Contemporary policies and leadership

George W. Bush was the 19th Republican to hold the office of president. He and his vice-president, Dick Cheney, were seen to be national leaders of the party. However, Mike Duncan, as chairman of the Republican National Committee, and Jo Ann Davidson, the co-chairperson, were effectively party leaders in that their role was to encourage the continued growth of the party and support the political organisation.

The following table outlines the key elements of the Republican platform as they went into the 2008 election campaign, which of course encompassed not only the presidential election but also congressional elections and other state posts.

Policy area	Brief explanation
Separation and balance of power	Republicans are firmly of the opinion that the Supreme Court should not legislate from the bench and that this is the preserve of the legislature. They have blocked activist judges and preferred those who showed judicial restraint. They have attempted to limit judicial review. They have focused on limiting federal power, giving a bigger role to the states. They are in favour of a unitary executive.
Economy	The focus is on corporate and personal decision-making, ensuring economic prosperity. They are in favour of a free market, economical liberalism and are fiscally conservative. They believe that reduced tax increases GDP growth (essentially Reaganomics) and that private spending is more efficient than government spending. They are against a universal health-care system, preferring to opt for Medicare and Medicaid, but primarily health insurance. They are opposed to labour unions, minimum wages and abuses of the welfare system.
Environment	They are sceptical of global warming and have refused to sign agreements to reduce greenhouse gases. The Republican platform at the GOP National Convention on 12 August 2000 adopted market-based solutions to the environment: 'Economic prosperity and environmental protection must advance together, environmental regulations should be based on science, the government's role should be to provide market-based incentives, to develop technologies to meet environmental standards'. They support increased oil drilling and what is known as 'cap and trade' policy, setting a limit on the amount of a pollutant that can be emitted and if a company exceeds this allowance they must buy credit from a less polluting business.

The Republican elephant, which is the symbol of the Republican Party, probably first appeared in 1874

Policy area	Brief explanation
Social	They are pro-life, pro-faith, anti-affirmative action, pro-gun ownership, anti-gay marriages, in favour of broad school choice, greater school accountability and against stem cell research.
Defence and military	They are in favour of a strong military, unilateralism, and pre-emptive attacks against perceived threats. Although inherently against interventionism this view has certainly changed since the 1990s.
International policy	They actively seek democratisation across the globe, they are pro-free trade, they are divided on immigration and in 2006 they supported immigration reform that would allow millions of illegal immigrants to become US citizens, but this was rejected by the House of Representatives.

In running for president in 2008 John McCain and Sarah Palin outlined several key policy areas.

Policy area	Description
Economy	Workplace flexibility, relief for families, more efficient federal government, support for small business, support for renewal energy, better health care, simplified taxation and lower barriers to trade
Energy	Expansion of oil and gas exploration and production, breaking the dependency on foreign oil, search for alternative energy sources, environmental protection, energy efficiency and prevention of oil price speculation
National security	Strong military, improved intelligence system, effective missile defence, modernisation of the armed forces and targeted defence spending
Health care	Improving Medicare through reform and an employer-based health-care system
Iraq	Support for the counter-insurgency strategy, search for political reconciliation, focus on the Iraqi economy, pressurise Syria and Iran and pulling out troops from Iraq as soon as is feasible
Home ownership	Purchase more mortgages from home owners and mortgage providers and replace them with flat rate mortgages and stabilise the housing market
Veterans	Tax relief to deployed service members, expand retirement benefits for reservists, improve their health care, care for disabled veterans, assist them to transform to civilian life and create a national monument
Immigration	Secure the border, provide additional funding and training to border states, prosecute businesses that employ illegal immigrants and encourage high-skilled worker immigration
Education	Support of the 'No Child Left Behind' strategy, allow schools to compete for the best teachers, improve accountability and responsibility and allow greater choice of school for parents
2nd Amendment	Fundamentally against any form of gun control that would undermine the 2nd Amendment, but longer sentences for criminals who use firearms
Judicial philosophy	In November 2006 John McCain had noted that a US citizen's freedom is as vulnerable to arbitrary judicial power as it is to an arbitrary act by the executive, the legislative or a state power. In McCain's view, judges needed to make decisions that were based on more than just their subjective views, or the fact that they felt that they were right or wanted to deal with a social ill. McCain and Palin favoured judges who applied the law and did not impose opinions. They were against judicial activism and would only appoint judges who were faithful to the Constitution.

Policy area	Description
Homeland security	Favour intelligence sharing, greater oversight of homeland security, international cooperation, cooperation between federal and local authorities, improved border security, including screening at airports and ports, improve the country's ability to deal with catastrophes and protecting the infrastructure
Crime	Pro-federal law enforcement and child protection and targeted funding
Agriculture	Support for rural America through changes in taxation and regulation, drive to sustainability and investment in infrastructure
Sanctity of life	Promote adoption and marriage and child protection
Climate change	Cap and trade policy, international solutions based on scientifically sound targets
Ethics reform	End pork barrel politics, check the influence of lobbyists and improve transparency
National service	Launch programme to attract volunteers, create better opportunities, make better use of former servicemen and assist with education
Technology	Encourage innovation, skill acquisition, fair trade, improve intellectual property protection, keep the Internet free of regulation and improve Internet access

The Grand Banner of the Radical Democracy was the banner of radical Republicans who advocated the abolition of slavery and opposed Abraham Lincoln's nomination as the party's candidate of the 1864 presidential election.

Learning objectives

- The Democratic Party history and development
- Contemporary policies and leadership

The Democratic Party history and development

The Democratic Party can trace its origins back to the Democratic-Republican Party founded in 1792 by Thomas Jefferson and James Madison. As leader of the Democratic-Republican Party Thomas Jefferson won the 1800 presidential election, the first of his party to do so. For many years its principal opponent was the Whig Party. It effectively became the Democratic Party in the 1830s under the leadership Andrew Jackson. For the remainder of the 19th century there were a series of splits within the party, primarily along northern and southern lines.

By the 20th century, the party had become more politically competitive. Woodrow Wilson was president from 1912 to 1916; Franklin D. Roosevelt served four terms in office, from 1933 to 1945, the only president to have served more than two terms; John F. Kennedy was elected in 1961; Lyndon B. Johnson was in office from 1963 to 1969; and in recent years Bill Clinton served from 1992 to 1996 and Barack Obama began his presidency in 2008.

War and peace Democrats

During the American Civil War northern Democrats were divided into war Democrats and peace Democrats. The war Democrats supported the Republican president Abraham Lincoln.

Contemporary policies and leadership

From the 1890s to the late 1960s the Democratic Party could be broadly described as being liberal; since the 1970s it has adopted a more centrist or socially progressive stance. Democrats tend to be supported by well-educated and more conservative members of the working class. They are broadly in favour of a mixed economy, affirmative action, balanced budgets, social freedoms, and are anti-poverty and anti-social injustice. They are also in favour of progressive taxation.

By the middle of the 2000s the Democratic Party had around 72 million registered voters, by far the largest party in the US. Within the party, however, there is a broad spectrum.

- Social liberals or progressives – this is probably the largest part of the party. They prefer diplomacy over war, stricter gun control, environmental protection, abortion rights; they are in favour of immigration and cultural diversity, and support stem-cell research and same-sex marriages.
- Civil libertarians – they focus primarily on civil rights and a separation of church and state. They oppose gun control, protectionism, debt and interventionism.
- Conservatives – around 15 per cent of the party are social conservatives or moderates, mainly from the South. Some are pro-life (anti-abortionists).
- Centrists – they support the use of military force, welfare reform and tax cuts. Essentially they are Third Way politicians and were strong supporters of Bill Clinton.

Blue dogs

Blue dog Democrats are a block of moderate and conservative Democratic Party members of the House of Representatives. They have southern roots and favour fiscal conservatism, pro-gun rights, pro-life and immigration reduction.

As with the Republicans, it is often difficult to positively identify common issues and viewpoints that are generally accepted across the whole of the party. The following table seeks to identify key generally-held Democratic Party views:

Issue	Broad consensus
Economic	Higher minimum wage, renewable energy, progressive taxation, oppose cuts to social services, in favour of affordable and quality health care, environmental regulation and there is concern regarding global warming. They are also in favour of publicly-funded education and concerned with inequalities between nations.
Social	They are in favour of equal opportunity, divided on same-sex marriages, in favour of access to birth control and stem-cell research.
Foreign policy	They are in favour of authorising use of military force against terrorists, therefore pro-involvement in Afghanistan but less certain about the continued involvement in Iraq. Democrats tend to oppose unilateralism and believe that action should only be taken when there is international support.
Legal	They are in favour of the right to privacy and consumer protection, some gun control measures and against the use of torture.

INTERNET RESEARCH

For Barack Obama's website, go to www.heinemann.co.uk/hotlinks, insert the express code 1825P and click on the relevant link. Find 'Issues' for more information.

The current (as of November 2008) Democrat congressional leaders are Nancy Pelosi in the House and Harry Reid in the Senate. The chairman of the Democrat National Committee is Tim Kaine.

During the 2008 presidential election campaign Barack Obama outlined several key policy areas, as shown in the following table.

Policy area	Brief explanation
Civil rights	Combat employment discrimination, strengthen civil rights and expand hate crime legislation
Defence	Rebuild the military, improve national guard and reserves, act in cooperation with allies
Disabilities	Provide education, end workplace discrimination, support independent living
Economy	Tax cuts for working families, small businesses and business startups
Education	Reform 'No Child Left Behind', invest in early school education and make college affordable to all
Energy and environment	Support private businesses to produce clean energy, save oil, support hybrid cars, use a cap and trade programme to reduce greenhouse gases
Ethics	Centralise ethics and lobbying information, require independent monitoring, stop political appointees lobbying the executive after leaving government service
Faith	Believes that faith plays an important role in American life and should be used for its values rather its religion-specific content
Family	Tax cuts for working families, strengthening fatherhood, restoring work–family balance
Fiscal	Review the budget and eliminate programmes that do not work, tax cuts for poor and middle-class families, reverse the Bush cuts for the wealthiest, close corporate tax loopholes
Foreign policy	Stop production of new nuclear weapons material, enter into diplomatic talks with Iran, rebuild alliances across the world
Health care	Make health care affordable and accessible, lower health care costs and promote public health
Homeland security	Continue war against al Qaeda, prevent nuclear terrorism, strengthen American biosecurity
Immigration	Secure borders, improve the immigration bureaucracy
Iraq	Phased withdrawal, encourage Iraq to spend their oil revenue on reconstruction, concentrate on the stability of the region
Poverty	Expand access to jobs, increase benefits for working parents, raise minimum wage, invest in rural and urban businesses, schools and infrastructure
Rural	Support small farmers and small business development and improve health care and infrastructure in rural areas
Service	Expand the AmeriCorps and the Peace Corps, have all middle and high school students do 50 hours community service and invest in the not-for-profit sector
Seniors and social security	Protect social security, provide cheaper prescription drugs and strengthen Medicare
Taxes	Cut taxes to most, eliminate capital gains tax for small businesses and simplify the taxation system
Technology	Protect the openness of the Internet, invest in communications infrastructure, support the export of US technology abroad
Urban	Target depressed urban areas with federal funds, job creation, training and make housing more affordable
Veterans	Provide care and benefits including health care and homelessness
Women	Support research into women's health, in favour of stem-cell research, abortion, combat domestic violence, support pay and conditions equality

Learning objectives

- Third parties, their role and impact
- Renewal and decline of parties in the US

Third parties, their role and impact

In the US the third parties have traditionally been vehicles for protest in elections, particularly when a body of individuals believes that the two major parties are unresponsive to their needs. However, third parties have tended to be absorbed into one of the two major parties.

The US system is definitely stacked against third parties and independent candidates. Campaign finance laws and restrictions on ballot access make it difficult for third parties to develop. There has only ever been one third party that has ever transformed itself into a major party and has produced a president, and that was the Republicans back in 1860.

There is a broad range of third party types in the US. They can be typified in the following ways.

- National parties – including reform, green, libertarian and natural law parties.
- Regional parties – such as George Wallace's American Independent Party in 1968.
- State parties – such as the New York Conservative Party.
- Permanent – in the sense that they retain an existence beyond that of an election campaign and have a permanent infrastructure, such as the Greens and the Libertarians.
- Temporary – a party which comprises of a number of previously disparate groups that join together to fight an election campaign, such as the Reform Party or the American Independent Party.
- Issues-based – those whose predominant focus is on single issues, such as the Greens.
- Ideological – those parties that have split or have never been part of one of the two major parties due to fundamental policy differences, including the Socialists, Constitution Party and the Peace and Freedom Party.

In the 2008 presidential election, beyond the Democratic and Republican parties, there were a number of third party and independent candidates.

- Boston Tea Party/Personal Choice Party – this is a libertarian US political party that was formed in 2006. They finished 14th in the 2008 election, with their presidential candidate Charles Jay.
- Constitution Party – founded in 1992 it aims to reflect the fundamental principles of the Declaration of Independence, the Constitution and the Bill of Rights. Their presidential candidate was Chuck Baldwin. The party received almost 173,000 votes in 2008.
- Green Party – their presidential candidate was Cynthia McKinney in 2008. Overall they attracted 0.1 per cent of the vote.
- Independent/America's Independence Party/American Independent Party – featured Alan Keyes as their presidential candidate in 2008.
- Independent Ecological Party/Peace and Freedom Party/Natural Law Party – their presidential candidate in 2008 was Ralph Nader. This was Nader's fifth presidential campaign.
- Libertarian Party – the presidential candidate was Bob Barr in 2008. He was seen as a conservative alternative to John McCain.

- Party of Socialism and Liberation – presidential candidate was Gloria Lariva in 2008, an anti-war, pro-immigrant rights activist.
- Prohibition Party – this was fronted by a temperance minister, Gene Amondson, in 2008.
- Reform Party – the presidential candidate was Ted Weill in 2008.
- Socialist Party USA – an anti-war party with Brian Moore as their presidential candidate.
- Socialist Workers' Party – Roger Calero was their presidential candidate.

As mentioned, third parties have an enormous number of problems facing them to break into the political system. The following list outlines the key considerations.

- The electoral system, being first past the post, makes it almost impossible for third parties to gain any representation.
- Funding is problematic due to the fact that major parties can acquire matching funds if they can raise at least $5000 in contributions of $250 or less in at least 20 different states.
- Third party candidates need to get at least 5 per cent of the votes to qualify for matching funds.
- Ballot access laws make it difficult for them to get their names on the ballot papers. Third party candidates need a petition with a certain number of registered voters' signatures on it to be included on the ballot (each state has different requirements).
- Fund-raising is very difficult, as potential supporters are unwilling to give funds to candidates who will undoubtedly lose.
- Media coverage is slanted towards the major parties.
- Third parties are portrayed as being too ideological or extreme.
- The two major parties will quickly move in to steal support by adopting some third party policies if the third party begins to gain support.

Renewal and decline of parties in the US

Due to the electoral system and the ability of the two major parties to incorporate third party ideas, the US is undoubtedly dominated by the Republicans and the Democrats. Over the years there have been suggestions that the two-party system and parties in general in the US are in decline. The following reasons have been suggested.

- It is presidential primaries rather than parties that now tend to choose potential presidential candidates.
- Matching funds that were introduced in the 1970s are given to candidates and not to parties.
- The media is the principal way in which a candidate interacts with potential voters, rather than the party being the primary vehicle through which candidates and party ideas are transmitted.
- Election campaigns tend to be issue- or candidate-centred rather than encompassing a broad range of party policies.

Despite this many commentators believe that the view that parties are in decline is premature and, indeed, that they are enjoying something of a renewal.

George Wallace

George Wallace was a **Dixiecrat** who ran for president four times; once as a Democrat and three times for the American Independence Party. He survived an assassination attempt in 1972.

George Wallace of the American Independent Party (seated left) with President Gerald Ford in 1976

Dixiecrat

Segregationist conservative from the southern US state who aimed to protect the Southern way of life from the federal government.

INTERNET RESEARCH

There is useful information about super delegates and other information about the parties on the Council on Foreign Relations' website. To see this, go to www.heinemann.co.uk/hotlinks, insert the express code 1825P and click on the relevant links. Choose 'Publication type' to find the material.

Super delegate

They are elected officials, such as members of Congress or party officials. They can support whoever they wish to at the convention.

- The bulk of members of Congress, state governors and state legislators are still members of either the Democratic or Republican parties.
- Parties have taken steps to try to regain control over the presidential selection process. The Democrats introduced the concept of **super delegates** in the 1980s. In the 2008 Democratic National Convention super delegates made up 20 per cent of the number of delegates.
- The parties have tried to strengthen their internal structures, creating permanent headquarters and making greater use of information technology.
- They have tended to nationalise campaigns, including mid-term elections, to gain voter interest and specifically voter registration.
- There appears to be an increased sense of partisanship in Congress, where increasing numbers, particularly in the House of Representatives, are voting along party lines.

The US has had a number of third parties. In recent years they have tended to be the Libertarian Party, the Green Party and the Reform Party. For many US citizens and commentators there is no viable third party, particularly a third party presidential candidate.

Third party efforts tend to fall into one of two categories.

- Grassroots parties – this occurs where the third party has been able to mobilise general voter dissatisfaction with the two-party system. This may be true of the Libertarian Party and the Green Party in recent years, although this has rarely meant more than 3 per cent of the popular vote. Prime examples include Teddy Roosevelt and Ross Perot, who were able to win a significant number of votes and tap into popular sentiment.
- Cult of personality – these are parties that are primarily driven by a single individual who has a high public profile. Again we could suggest Roosevelt and Perot as examples of this. Their simple forceful personalities and access to media coverage made them for a time credible candidates.

Whether a third party will ever emerge as a powerful force in US politics depends on their ability to overcome a number of obstacles.

- It is difficult for them to gain the necessary media attention.
- It is difficult for them to get onto the ballot in each state.
- There is no consensus on one third party.
- Existing third parties show little willingness to merge, such as the Green and Libertarian parties.
- Centrist parties only tend to split off some votes from the Democrats and the Republicans and have no meaningful power base of their own.
- Third parties lack strong grassroots organisation.
- The US political system works against third parties largely because it does not have a parliamentary form of government.
- The costs of running a national campaign prohibits most third parties from breaking through.
- The third parties are often seen as simply publicising a single issue, which is often snapped up by one of the two major parties thus nullifying the third party's unique appeal.

Do parties still matter?

The founders of the US Constitution were of the opinion that parties and factions would only promote conflict. This is often seen as the first of criticisms of political parties in the US, but the criticisms have continued. In the past 30 or 40 years polls, consultants, new media and a host of other issues have transformed the way in which campaigning is carried out, and there have been countless examples of candidates not really needing a party apparatus behind them in order to promote their policy ideas and attract voters.

The political columnist David Broder, writing in the 1970s, was firmly of the opinion that voters were no longer receiving the bulk of their information about candidates from parties. They were receiving it through television and campaigning, and political ideas were actually coming from pressure groups.

Although he was writing about politics in New Zealand, Geoff Mulgan, in 1997, added to the debate by claiming that parties were not capable of adapting to changing political environments. He thought this was a good thing because the newer social movements that emerged were more likely to draw people into an interest in politics.

Clearly political parties, among others, have grave concerns about these views of the apparent decline in importance of parties and the fact that politics has become increasingly candidate-centred. They mourn the dumbing down of politics, reducing political ideas to sound bites and superficiality. They believe that the electorate are more inclined to base their voting choice on personality and that they can be easily swayed by slick campaigning and overt or covert media pressure.

As far as party membership is concerned, many countries have seen marked declines. Supporters have either permanently left mainstream politics or have been drawn to more extreme parties on the left and on the right. There have been marked pockets of support for extreme parties, such as the Freedom Party in Austria or the Front National in France. But the pattern of decline of parties is patchy and dependent upon different sets of circumstances.

- In many countries in Europe traditional parties have tended to lose ground against newer ones and there has been a development in the actual number of significant parties.
- In Britain, however, the first-past-the-post system has still ensured that the two major parties dominate British politics despite clear gains by the third party, the Liberal Democrats.
- In the US, according to J. Blondel (1995), the parties, being more symbolic than those in Europe, have had a different experience. US political parties do not propose programmes and neither do they select candidates (candidates are chosen in the primaries and therefore not controlled by party leaders). Blondel suggested that parties only continue to exist because it is the general consensus of opinion that democracies need parties.

In Britain, for example, every election since 1945 has produced a single-party government and in the past 50 years the two main parties have achieved over 70 per cent of the vote consistently, even though at the beginning of this period it was hovering around 97 per cent.

In the US, with its historically weak parties, it does appear that the party grip on politics has eroded. Mass media, personal electioneering, issues that divide members of the party, increased importance of pressure groups and changes in voting behaviour and party loyalty have all impacted on the parties. Nonetheless, they remain a reference point for voters and for members of Congress. They have become more organised and they are better funded, wealthier and more stable. They have also been able to draw in expert staff to sustain them and help them flourish.

Learning objectives

- Do parties still matter?
- Contemporary issues of parties

Social movements

American historian Charles Tilly defined social movements as a series of displays or campaigns by ordinary people to make collective claims on others. He saw them as a major vehicle for citizen participation in public politics.

Sidney Tarrow, a political science professor, in *Power in Movement: Collective Action, Social Movements and Politics* (1994) defined social movements as collective challenges involving people who had common purposes and solidarity. They were a challenge to elites, authorities, other groups and cultural codes, and were involved in sustained interaction with authorities, elites and opponents.

Contemporary issues of parties

Britain and the US still have, to a large extent, a two-party system. Britain, however, given devolution, has developed into a party system that differs from region to region. The country as a whole could be classed as a two-and-a-half party system (with Liberal Democrats). Scotland and Wales could arguably have a three- or four-party system, adding in the nationalist parties.

In the US a third party has yet to penetrate the two-party system. The two parties in any case are ideologically closer. The Democrats are considered to occupy the progressive, or left wing, side of politics, while the Republicans hold the more traditional or conservative edge. With the electorate's deep-rooted suspicion of the left, a socialist party or anything that equates to it has never developed in the US.

Parties still retain an important role, recruiting talented individuals, educating the electorate, profiling issues and policies, and offering a way in which ordinary voters can become involved in the political process.

The following table briefly outlines the key areas of similarity and difference in Britain and the US.

Similarities	Differences
In Britain, Labour is considered progressive and the Conservatives more traditional. In the US the Democrats are progressive and the Republicans more conservative.	The Liberal Democrats are a significant third party nationwide and the nationalists represent a fourth party. In the US no third party has made inroads and there is either a two-party or a 50-party system.
In Britain both parties draw support from a wide range of views and have distinct wings, with the Conservatives having more difficulty in balancing influence. In the US there is again wide appeal and different wings but moderates in the Republican Party have tended to be pushed out by the Christian New Right.	Parties choose all of their candidates in Britain and support them in elections. In the US it is the electorate that chooses the president and parties provide a supportive role.
The two main parties still dominate in Britain, particularly in the House of Commons, but the Liberal Democrats have broad countrywide support. In the US the two parties dominate presidential elections but state by state there is almost one-party domination.	British parties are far more ideological than US ones, but religion plays a larger role in US party ideology.
	There tends to be strong party loyalty and unity in Britain in the House of Commons. In the US discipline is looser and there is less loyalty in voting in Congress.
	The policymaking and organisation in Britain are centralised. In the US parties are largely decentralised, with weak national party organisation.

INTERNET RESEARCH

On the University of Keele website there is a very useful set of links to political parties around the world, allowing you to keep abreast of their activities, including a full set of US parties. To see this, go to www.heinemann.co.uk/hotlinks, insert express code 1825P and click on the relevant link.

Function and power

Pluralism is often used to describe the way in which political power is distributed. Classical pluralists believe that power is equally and widely spread and not concentrated in the hands of the elite. Pluralists assume that:

- citizens belong to groups and that many citizens belong to a number of groups
- groups are roughly equal and each group has access to government and none of the groups has a dominant position in their access to government
- there is internal responsiveness within groups and the leaders are accountable to the members
- the state itself is neutral and the government is fragmented and thus allows a number of different groups to access it
- groups have competing interests, but groups in general support the political system and value its openness and competitive nature.

How far this is true is open to debate. But we can identify three key groups operating: parties, pressure groups and the media. Free societies and democracies are those best described as being pluralist. In these countries the power of the state is limited and, as such, pressure or interest groups can operate. Governments tend to be responsive to group interests.

Theoretically, none of these groups, which include political parties, has an absolute monopoly of power and the ability to manipulate the system. In countries such as Britain, the US and France there are thousands of pressure and interest groups that attempt to influence the conduct of power and publicise their views. In many cases the most powerful are those that represent business interests.

Not all the groups are necessarily democratic in the way they have been created or structured. Some are controlled by an elite, others have a more democratic nature, some are large and operate nationally or internationally, while others are relatively small and operate on a regional or local basis. Some cover issues that have a broad appeal, while others focus on minority interests. There are some that have operated for a considerable period of time and have made slow but significant progress, while others are short-lived and have comparatively little effect on the political process.

Broadly, there are five significant functions of pressure groups.

- They represent the interests of a particular group in society, perhaps a trade union comprising workers in similar or allied occupations. Others are professional groups, representing a fairly close-knit occupational group, such as doctors or lawyers. Some groups represent a single issue or have a single issue focus, such as road safety or pro/anti-abortion. Others are ideologically based, such as the American Conservative Union. Some groups also represent broader collections of individuals, such as the National Association for the Advancement of Colored People (NAACP) in the US, while others have a broader public interest focus, such as Friends of the Earth or Greenpeace.
- They encourage citizen participation, which gives ordinary individuals the opportunity to make an impact on the decision-making processes of government at its various levels between elections.
- They attempt to educate and mould public opinion by raising issues and encouraging debate.

Learning objectives

- Function and power
- Contemporary issues associated with pressure groups

Madison and Dahl

James Madison noted that there were countless different groups and interests all competing with one another. He believed that unless they all had a political voice, there was a danger to the stability and order of society.

Robert Dahl recognised that although some politically privileged and economically powerful groups had more influence than others, there was no permanent elite that dominated the political process.

Revolving doors and cosy iron triangles

Revolving doors refers to situations where individuals cycle between roles in industry and roles in government that influence that industry.

An iron triangle refers to a close relationship between the legislature, the executive (or agency) and interest groups, one of the cosiest being the House and Senate committees on armed forces, the US Department of Defense and defence contractors.

- They attempt to encourage political parties to incorporate solutions to specific issues in their political agendas. They also try to influence key bureaucrats and legislators to give their issue priority.
- They will monitor, investigate and comment on government and government institutions in related areas of activity, particularly if promises have been made or deadlines and deals agreed.

Due to the nature of the US system, pressure groups can focus on Congress (the legislature), the federal bureaucracy (the executive) and the courts (the judiciary), giving the groups more options to access government. There are more access points to government in the US than in Britain, and given the relative weakness of political parties in the US pressure groups tend to have rather more impact. The following table briefly outlines the influences that pressure groups can have on the three elements of the US political system.

Legislature	Executive	Judiciary
They can make direct contact with either members of Congress and their staff, or committee members and their staff.	They can attempt to build up a network of contacts with executive agencies, regulatory commissions and government agencies.	They can submit an *amicus curiae* (friend of the court) brief, which provides information and argument revolving around a case. It outlines their views in writing before any argument in court.
They can mobilise constituents of particular members of Congress, in order to apply pressure on them.	They can offer their expert opinions on specific aspects of the regulatory work carried out by federal government.	They can sponsor cases that come before the court, such as the NAACP in the Brown vs Board of Education (1954).
They can highlight the voting records of particular members of Congress, in order to indicate those that oppose or support particular issues.	They will specifically target the executive through daily contact and develop a cooperative relationship, trading expertise for favourable decisions.	They can bring cases to court themselves, such as the Reno vs American Civil Liberties Union (1997).
They can give overt support to members of Congress during re-election campaigns, or campaign against those who do not support the issue.	They will directly recruit former members of the bureaucracy, using their contacts and influence to further their cause.	They can lobby the Supreme Court to launch a judicial review, to overrule a decision of the executive or establish the meaning of legislation.
They can carry out fundraising and campaigning on behalf of Congress members and pay for publicity.	They can form 'iron triangles', with committee chairmen and government departments, based on interdependent self-interest.	They can fund their own lawyers to research implications of statutes and regulations, to either bring the case themselves or to support one already in progress.

Contemporary issues associated with pressure groups

Undoubtedly, from a pluralist democratic perspective, the proliferation of pressure groups has tended to undermine the power of many of the larger pressure groups that had enormous political influence in the past. Coalitions of smaller pressure groups and groups that have focused at a regional or local level have found ways in which to further their causes, despite their lack of access to central government.

The NAACP Convention in 1951

The following table briefly outlines some of the other key contemporary issues and provides some examples.

Issue	Explanation	Example
More pressure groups	There are huge numbers of single issue, local or campaign-based organisations, vastly increasing the number of pressure groups operating.	Green issues have spawned hundreds of groups, some focusing on broad issues and others on limited single issues.
Losses and gains	In the US, business, agriculture and labour were the three key interests that had influence. As consolidated groups they have certainly lost influence.	In the US, the American Medical Association is no longer the dominant force in health and medical issues. Insurance companies and a host of other groups compete.
New targets	In the US, groups target states and localities and in Britain the EU is a new target.	Many key pressure groups have established permanent headquarters in Brussels.
Changes in approach	Major pressure groups have their own specialist lobby departments or employ professionals and agencies that trade their knowledge and expertise.	The lobbying industry has been imported into Britain from the US. It is still viewed with suspicion, but not so in the US where it is acceptable practice.
Acceptability of direct action	Mass protests, demonstrations and a host of other media-worthy actions are more than the norm.	In the US, Operation Rescue launched direct action against abortion clinics in the 1988–91 period.

INTERNET RESEARCH

There is a useful guide about lobbying the House of Commons and the House of Lords. To see this, go to www.heinemann.co.uk/hotlinks, insert express code 1825P and click on the relevant link.

3.10 Political Parties

Learning objectives

- What are the functions of political parties?
- Are political parties indistinguishable?

Question topic material

Note that these topics are not written in essay format, but they do include ideas, concepts and information and practices that you would need to think about if similar questions came up in an exam.

What are the functions of political parties?

Political parties are vital to the smooth running of a political system and democratic society. The key functions of political parties are outlined in the following table.

Function	Explanation
Forming a government	A party that wins an election will provide the prime minister and ministers to look after various departments of state. The policies expressed in the manifestos are designed for translation into government programmes.
Being the official opposition	If a party does not win a general election and providing it has the second largest number of seats, it becomes the official opposition, or the alternative government in waiting. It is their role to keep the ruling government in check by questioning decisions.
Organising opinions	The manifesto represents a list of policy proposals. The parties by publishing their proposed policies give the electorate a clear choice and a means of measuring the likely party successes or failures.
Linking the individual to the political system	Political parties act as a vehicle by which individuals can attain power. However, individuals or small groups of the electorate with specific interests may find it very difficult for those interests to be represented, as parties take a broader view of interests and devise policies in the national interest rather than that of small groups or individuals.
Mobilising and recruiting	Political parties provide opportunities for activists to work for a party and for some to train to become politicians. Over time an individual who has joined a particular party, can represent it at various levels and perhaps become an MP and maybe even a minister.
Representing views	Ideally, the policies of a party represent various views. Parties select and mould ideas and turn them into clear policies and proposals that can be presented to the electorate. This is known as an aggregation of interests. Only when this has been achieved can the policies be presented to the electorate as clear ideas and proposals. This may also involve prioritising policies in the order of support and importance.
Encouraging participation	Active individuals can become involved with political parties at a number of different levels. Some will deliver leaflets or canvas on behalf of the party. Some will attend conferences and others will stand as representatives of the party at various tiers of government. To an individual the party they choose represents their preference for a particular kind of society. This should be irrespective of the differences in ideology, class and ethnicity.
Communicating and providing choice	The manifesto and the key representatives of a political party are the means by which the party's ideas can be communicated to its membership and to the electorate at large. Parties are a link between the government and individuals and groups in the country. Policies are publicly aired and debated between competing ideologies, so that the electorate has clear choices between the different approaches.

Are political parties indistinguishable?

In the US the range of political parties is as broad as anywhere else. Each party has its own distinctive range of policies and ideas. However, only the Democrats and the Republicans have any realistic prospect of forming a government.

It is integral to the US political system and the way in which the major political parties operate that it is able to incorporate the very best in political talent, even though some of these individuals may at times have held more extreme views. It is widely held that the new Democrats of the Clinton era and, to some extent, the new Obama administration, have much in common with George W. Bush's compassionate conservatism. It appears that they have moved closer together.

However, between 1995 and in 2006 when incumbent presidents faced a Congress dominated by the opposition party, it was impossible for them to reach compromises, which suggests that there are still key differences between the parties.

The Democratic Party has been associated with the policies of tax and spend since Roosevelt's New Deal. So, Democrat governments tended to increase federal spending in an attempt to redistribute income to the population. They have also been more committed than the Republicans to civil rights and civil liberties (such as the Civil Rights Act 1964, Medicare and Medicaid).

The Republicans on the other hand favour lower taxes and less government. They follow a more aggressive foreign policy, favour the pro-life movement, support the family and are more anti-drugs. Ronald Reagan stated: 'The era of big government is over.'

When Bill Clinton came to power he chose key policies from the Republican agenda to fit alongside more identifiably Democrat views. The Republican Party in turn moved closer to the centre under George W. Bush and might have moved even closer had McCain won the 2008 presidential election. In a move away from traditional Republican policies, the Bush administration authorised vast federal spending, particularly to support the No Child Left Behind Act and Medicare.

However, there are still key differences between the parties. Republicans tend to be more faith-based, pro-life and support constitutional amendments to outlaw same-sex marriages. President Obama has pledged to reverse Bush tax cuts for the more wealthy; he favours a gradual withdrawal from Iraq and a far more collaborative approach to foreign policy, working with the United Nations and NATO.

Both the major parties have a very broad range of views. Of course there is always a range of views within the parties, encompassing the moderates and extremists. This has been a strength and weakness and sometimes it is difficult to distinguish between the extremes of each party. Neither party has a single figure, not even the president, who can speak for the party as a whole. The president also cannot speak for the congressional or state parties. There is no 'party line' as such, as you find in Britain. There are also considerable differences within the parties based on the geographical location of the membership and key figures. In both parties, southern representatives tend to be conservative, while on the west coast and in the northeast Democrats are liberal and Republicans are moderate. Both support liberal capitalism and their similarities outweigh their differences. This is said to be a key factor in party decline, which appears to be reflected in the election votes cast for an individual rather than a party in both presidential and congressional elections.

New Labour and One Nation Conservatism

David Cameron has distanced himself from the right-wing Conservative policies of the past. Conservatives now have very similar aspirations to New Labour. They realised that Labour had moved to the centre ground while they had moved to the right. Now they focus values and principles that distinguishes them from New Labour.

Role of Political Parties

Learning objectives

- What is the role of parties in the organisation and function of legislatures?
- What are the consequences of the presidency and Congress being controlled by different parties?

What is the role of parties in the organisation and function of legislatures?

Political parties act as what is known as linkage institutions, which means that they translate ideas and needs from the public into outputs in the form of policy. In other words they are channels through which the public's concerns become political issues on a government's political agenda. In addition they pick candidates, run campaigns, highlight key issues and solutions to voters, articulate policies and coordinate policymaking.

They also provide individuals with a sense of party identification, allowing them to have a preference for one party or another. There are, however, key differences between the US and the British political systems, as can be seen in the following table.

US	British
The parties can represent the views of constituents and groups.	The political parties are of vital importance in the House of Commons and, to a lesser extent, the House of Lords.
They organise the work of Congress.	The party, through manifesto pledges, is there to translate electoral wishes into choice of government.
They provide vital scrutiny and accountability.	The parties represent the views of groups in society that have common beliefs.
They assist in the formulation of policy.	Parties provide a full legislative programme.
They do NOT translate electoral wishes into choice of government or provide a legislative programme.	Parties provide the prime minister and the bulk of the cabinet members.
They do NOT provide ministers or sustain the government in power.	Parties are a focus for scrutiny and accountability.
There is a broad range of beliefs within each party, which not only makes it difficult to enforce party discipline, but also for the party to agree on anything other than key issues.	They can choose to sustain or withdraw support from a government.
Representatives tend to focus on the importance of local issues rather than national ones.	It is the activities of parties that ensures that the majority party can govern through supporting legislation and policy.
There is low party loyalty. Party members may or may not vote with the opposition.	The minority or opposition party represents an alternative government in waiting should the current government fail.
In the majority of cases it is rare for both parties to control the legislature and the executive at the same time, making coordination difficult.	Parties and their views dominate parliament.
There is a general acceptance that the bulk of legislation comes from the executive rather than parties in the legislature.	Although parliament is not the policymaking body, the majority party within it generates policy.
The changing role of the president has also impacted on the role parties play in the legislature.	Minority or opposition parties may choose to either support or oppose legislation sponsored by the governing party.

What are the consequences of the presidency and Congress being controlled by different parties?

The two key branches of US government are Congress and the White House. Only five times since 1945 have there been instances when the House and the Senate have been controlled by different parties; only 10 times in the same period have both branches of Congress, as well as the presidency, been controlled by both parties. Inevitably this puts the White House and Congress on a potential collision course. In truth, however, this is an essential part of the balance of power and separation of power originally envisioned by the Founding Fathers who wrote the US Constitution.

Use of blocking tactics

There have been a number of studies that have looked at instances when at least one chamber of Congress has been controlled by a party in opposition to the party of the president. This gives that House the opportunity to block the most divisive of measures proposed by the other party. William Niskanen, a former member of President Reagan's Council of Economic Advisers, identified three key characteristics of such sets of circumstances.

- When divided government exists the rate of growth in federal spending is much lower. During the first George W. Bush administration it was 4.4 per cent even though the country was at war.
- If major reforms are proposed they will usually last longer because they have bipartisan support. Both parties are more likely to protect the reform against subsequent change by a majority party. A primary example is Medicare.
- The prospect of a major war is higher with a united government. Each of the four major wars in which the US became involved during the 20th century were initiated by a Democrat president with the approval of a Democrat-dominated Congress. This was also the case in Iraq, with a Republican president and a Republican Congress.

Although in theory a party in opposition to the president in Congress could conceivably block each and every legislative proposal, the government does not need to win on every issue, as even losing a major vote does not endanger the executive's term in office, as it would do in a parliamentary system such as Britain's. The executive can draft laws, but only the legislature has the authority to introduce those laws onto the floor of Congress. The president has the right to veto legislation from Congress, which in turn is difficult to overturn, as a two-thirds majority is needed to accomplish this in both houses and party discipline is weak.

Budget shutdown

In 1995 a Republican-dominated Congress refused to approve budgetary spending and for a time there was a budget shutdown, when the then Speaker, Newt Gingrich, tried to force the shutdown of four federal agencies, balance the federal budget and turn power over to the states and reform welfare. In the end it was solved by negotiation.

Gridlock

The US system can inevitably produce opposing parallel power structures, which could create undesirable gridlock. If neither side budges it will be impossible for any legislative programme to be pursued while there is divided government. Therefore there has to be a degree of compromise between the executive and the legislature in order to ensure that the important decisions that need to be taken by government can be made. However, due to the weak party structure and discipline in the US system individual members of Congress have considerable freedom of action. While this can also cause gridlock in its own right, it can give the president or the legislature room for manoeuvre in ensuring that vital legislation is not blocked by partisan opposition without regard to the legislation's positive benefits.

3.12 The Party System

Learning objectives

- Does the US have a two-party system?
- What is the importance of third parties and independent candidates?

Does the US have a two-party system?

The US Constitution sets no limit on the number of parties; in fact nothing is said about political parties. The US political system has reformists, greens, libertarians, pacifists and even socialists. Yet virtually every single office in the US is held by either a Democrat or a Republican, with the exception of a handful of independents.

In the 1950s the French sociologist Maurice Duverger looked at a number of political systems and came to the opinion that a system like that of the US or Britain inevitably drifts towards a two-party system. It was largely down to the way in which the political system works; both the US and Britain share the 'whoever gets the most votes wins' and 'winner takes all' combination (although this is clearly not the case when alternate electoral systems are used, such as in the London Assembly). Candidates just need enough votes to beat the nearest runner-up. The loser gets nothing. As a result, third party successes are few and far between and tend to be temporary. The two-party system retains its dominance.

Both the Republicans and the Democrats are not just a union of individuals devoted to the same policies and principles. Each is a political organisation devoted to gaining power. They have a strong incentive to absorb any minority parties or views on their fringes. Inevitably this means that they become more inclusive and more vague and indistinguishable. Consequently, neither of the main US parties has any real incentive to have a definite position on anything contentious. The safest course, as both parties have discovered, is to become the least unattractive alternative to one another. At election time both of the major parties appear to be almost indistinguishable. Voters may swing to the left or to the right, but the two main political parties have never created this shift; they have merely reflected it.

Wallace's Dixiecrats

In 1968 Alabama's Democrat former governor, George C. Wallace, ran for president on the American Independent Party ticket. The party captured a huge number of electoral votes in the Deep South. This was the high point of the so-called Dixiecrats.

Ross Perot came closest to a breakthrough since the American Civil War when he gathered 19 per cent of the vote in 1992. Back in 1912 Teddy Roosevelt's Progressive Party (known as the Bull Moose Party) pulled ahead of the Republicans but it lost the election and by 1916 had been absorbed into the Democratic Party.

The fundamental problem in breaking any two-party system is for a third party to prove that it can deliver. The only way it can prove its competence is to have power and the only way to get power is to obtain the votes. In other words, for a party to win an election it must have already won some elections in the past. Third parties can therefore go through cycles, where they come close but then fade away.

Going back to Duverger, he believed that a successful third party would not eliminate a two-party system but merely amend it. A third party can only succeed in one of two ways. It can take enough votes from one of the two dominant parties to replace it, which means the country is back to a two-party system, or it can drain votes from both parties, in which case they would consolidate, become one party and the country would still be back to a two-party system.

Many claim that the only way to break the two-party system is to change the mechanics of the electoral system. Workable alternative systems exist in Europe and other parts of the world, such as proportional voting or fusion voting. Fusion voting is an arrangement between two or more political parties to support a common candidate. In the US this arrangement was banned in 18 states by 1907. Elements of electoral fusion still take place in New York and Oregon.

What is the importance of third parties and independent candidates?

There are upwards of 50 different political parties in the US and nearly 40 that have put up candidates to run for president. The political process itself, however, despite the fact that the other parties have contributed ideas and policies that will become mainstays of political life and law, relegates them to the sidelines.

A prime example is Ralph Nader. He stood as an independent candidate in the 2004 presidential race, having made his name as a consumer advocate. He had run on two occasions for the Green Party, as their presidential nominee, and in 2000 he came third behind Al Gore and George W. Bush. Democrats roundly blamed Nader for being responsible for Gore's defeat by siphoning off the votes that Gore would have received had Nader not stood. Equally, Ross Perot, who stood for president in 1992, siphoned off votes from George H. W. Bush, allowing Clinton to win.

The Libertarians are the third largest US political party and the oldest. They believe that government should only act as a form of protection for citizens and while some of its members have offices in state and local government they have singly failed to make any headway as presidential election candidates.

The Constitution Party (formerly American Taxpayers Party) stands for a stricter interpretation of the Constitution and a reduction in federal power. Even so, their most popular candidate, Howard Phillips, received less than 1 per cent of the vote in 1992.

Arguably one of the most influential third parties was the Reform Party. Ross Perot was their presidential candidate in 1992. He focused on reducing the federal budget deficit and this has been an issue that has been part of every presidential campaign since. Perot received 19 per cent of the vote. According to the historian Michael Beschloss, speaking in February 2004, Perot was the first candidate to suggest that a budget deficit was a bad thing. When Bill Clinton was elected in 1992 he could not ignore the deficit and had to do something about it. Ross Perot had highlighted this as a concern for immediate action.

Perot's support came from across the political spectrum. He had drawn 38 per cent of his vote from Bush and 38 per cent from Clinton. Even so, he only managed to finish second in two states.

In the early 1900s socialists were in favour of women's suffrage and child labour laws. Their influence undoubtedly led to the Fair Labour Standards Act of 1938, creating a 40-hour working week. According to Sean Wilentz of Princeton University in a radio broadcast in 2004, third parties often highlight neglected issues or policy areas that are often ignored by the major parties from the political debate because they are contentious and would polarise the voting public. Wilentz suggested that slavery was one such issue. Third parties often raise these issues that no one else will raise. They can direct the political debate and sometimes the policy but then they burn out as a political force, as their key policies are absorbed by the larger parties.

This phenomenon is often referred to as 'sting and die'. The third party raises a key issue, such as Perot and the tax budget, fail to achieve power in the elections and then solutions to the problem are implemented by one of the main parties.

John Bibby of the University of Wisconsin, speaking in 2004, suggested that Americans tend to ignore the extremes of political beliefs and that the majority of them are moderates. They are happy to operate in a system where the two key political parties are just to the right or to the left of the centre. As a result they do not see any particular need for any alternatives to the two main parties.

This may help to explain why there is an absence of any party based on race, or region or, for that matter, a socialist party in the US.

3.13 Pressure Groups

Learning objectives

- What is the value and influence of pressure groups in US politics?
- How do pressure groups gain success?

What is the value and influence of pressure groups in US politics?

In order to influence the outcome of the 2008 US presidential election trade unions, political action committees and other special interest groups spent upwards of $100 million. These groups spent almost twice as much as national party committees on independent advertising, canvassing and other campaigns. They spent $22 million during the primaries. Once the contest was between the two candidates, between June and November the various groups spent $48 million backing Obama and $28 million to support McCain. They also played a role in the congressional elections, targeting some $41 million towards this.

Positive impact of pressure groups

Interest groups have always featured in US politics and understanding them is central to understanding how the politics work. Their roles and the power they have has changed over the years; many writers and political thinkers, including de Tocqueville (*Democracy in America,* reprinted 2002), argued that interest groups make a positive contribution to democracy. From the 1950s and 1960s pluralists also maintained that these groups played a key role in democratic politics. Such groups represent the right to 'petition government', which is enshrined in the US Constitution. They ensure that minority interests are not ignored for the sake of the majority. They remind politicians about the interests of the people; they contribute to public policy by providing quality sourced information and ideas on which to form policy. Below are some of the key democratic arguments in favour of pressure groups.

- Pressure groups are a product of freedom of association and are essential to the effective functioning of the liberal democracy.
- Democratic societies are open; competing groups can freely form.
- Politics should not be dominated by one group but by conflicting and cooperating groups.
- Political power should be fragmented because resources are widely dispersed.
- Politics should be about bargaining and group action can help ensure this.
- Political parties should not be the only way in which interests and opinions are articulated and presented.
- Pressure groups are there to help governments develop and implement policies.
- They improve surveillance of the government.
- They pressure for social progress and give citizens opportunities to influence public policy.
- The countervailing or opposing groups check and control one another.
- They provide political victories for Davids versus Goliaths, such as the victory of the Civil Rights Movement and the 30 years of campaigning against the tobacco industry.

Negative impact of pressure groups

Negative impacts of pressure groups include the following.

- As it costs money to operate and maintain these groups their relative strength reflects inequalities in the US.
- Some interest groups may be aware that they will benefit from a particular policy and will rally to support it, whereas those who are not aware of this may lose out by not counteracting this pressure.
- Interest groups are fragmented and competitive and actually contribute very little to solving government problems.

In a highly competitive political system support for a particular policy by an interest group can lead to disaster. The Chamber of Commerce supported President Clinton's solutions to the health-care system. But they lost members to the National Federation of Independent Business, who were opposed to reforms.

In Britain the situation is different; there is less competition and environmental groups, for example, have worked with financial institutions and industry to come up with solutions. Had this happened in the US, the groups would have been accused of collaboration and betraying the environmental cause.

The key advantages and disadvantages of pressure groups are shown in the following table.

Advantages	Disadvantages
They can provide detailed and valuable information to assist government decision-making.	Leadership and membership tend to be unrepresentative of the population.
They can raise and explain issues and therefore play an educative role.	They are controlled by self-perpetuating elites that can be out of touch with public opinion.
They keep issues in the spotlight between elections.	They have undesirable behind the scenes influence in government.
They defend the interests of minorities, particularly those who do not have representation.	They do not represent the community equally; it depends on the pressure group's resources and relationships with government.
They encourage participation among those who are not involved in conventional politics.	They represent a sectional interest; some groups are less well organised and have no room to bargain.
They provide a forum to discuss policy issues outside the focus of political parties.	The use of money to influence elected representatives by using campaigners is not healthy; some activists without access to representatives may choose illegal direct action.
They help to disperse power and decentralise it.	The numbers of interest groups undermine government because they generate a great deal of work and make it difficult for government to make decisions.

How do pressure groups gain success?

Interest group tactics are as varied as the groups themselves. Some, such as Greenpeace, will seek to generate media or government attention whenever possible; others avoid media attention while maintaining contact with government. In general, interest groups can only use the tactics they can afford to use; many cannot afford opinion polls, focus groups or advertising.

The following table briefly outlines some key tactics used by pressure groups.

Tactic	Explanation and example
Lobbying	There is a constitutional right to lobby, although some laws restrict this right and require more extensive and accurate reporting by pressure groups on how much they spend on lobbying.
Campaign contribution	The actual effectiveness of this is debatable; some interest groups give contributions to politicians who have been refused contributions by another group. Other politicians receive funds because they have similar ideological viewpoints. Other interest groups give funds to the powerful, rather than the friendly, and other interest groups are involved in behind-the-scenes deals that are difficult to identify.
Campaigning for candidates	In order to avoid limits on campaign contributions interest groups launch campaigns themselves, separating themselves from a friendly candidate. For example, they may support a candidate's position and criticise an opponent if they did not explicitly say who to vote for or against. The Bipartisan Campaign Reform Act (2002) sought to regulate issue ads, prohibiting them from running close to primaries, corpuses or general elections.
Relations with the executive	Much policy comes from executive agencies in the US. It was common for interest groups to establish a relationship with the executive branch and the relevant congressional committee that oversaw that agency. The triangle would exist beyond political parties and from one administration to another.
Court action	Interest groups can argue that acts of Congress have been ignored by executive agencies, or that their action violates the Constitution. Interest groups have become involved in issues from abortion rights to affirmative action, and businesses in particular challenge regulations that adversely affect them.

The following table compares pressure group action in the US and Britain, linking it to the nature of the political system.

Feature	US	Britain
Size and character of country	Diverse with regional variations, a pluralist society with influential ethnic groups	Small and homogeneous, growing ethnic groups
Constitution	Written with secure group rights, secured by 1st Amendment	Rights of groups are not guaranteed
Degree of centralisation	Federal system gives prominence to state capitals, where key decisions are made but federal government is still important, so there are many access points	Power is in Whitehall and Westminster, although some lobby local councils and increasingly the EU and the devolved parliaments and assemblies
Access points	Separation of powers means targeting the three areas, as well as the public	Insiders concentrate on the executive; others target parliament, the EU and other pressure groups
Party system	Activists form groups rather than parties, due to two-party system, but looser party discipline gives opportunities for persuasion	Two parties dominate, but other key parties offer opportunities. Party discipline discourages Westminster influence
Election funding	Through PACs with strong political and financial power	Funding mainly through parties. Unions have backed Labour and industry associated with Conservatives
Open or closed government	Open government, access to documentation, pressure groups involved in public examination of government activities	Powerful insider groups work behind closed doors. There is generally a closed system of government

For more on the success of pressure groups, see Topics 3.14 to 3.19, pages 149–60.

3.14 The Power and influence of pressure groups

Are the wealthiest pressure groups the most successful?

Pressure groups use different ways to gain political influence or power. The most commonly used strategies are cultivating access, lobbying, using the courts, going public with issues and using electoral tactics. To influence Congress or any other part of government, interest groups need to cultivate their access to decision-makers. They do this by lobbying, in other words communicating directly with the government in order to influence the passage of legislation, as in the following cases.

- Pressure groups engage successful lobbyists who have access to government officials.
- Interest groups and law-makers assist one another within the boundaries of the law.
- Wealthy companies, such as Microsoft, Exxon and Wal-Mart, have successfully lobbied Congress to gain favourable treatment or to have specific modifications made to a bill.

Some lobbyists have access to the president, such as Tom Kuhn, who managed to convince President George W. Bush to weaken the limits of power plant emissions. Wealthy groups can use the courts to influence policy through lawsuits, filing ***amicus curiae*** briefs, sponsoring litigation or providing attorneys to others fighting mutual-interest causes. Wealthy pressure groups sometimes form political action committees (PACs) to contribute money to candidates and the campaigns of politicians who support their objectives.

- Many politicians are dependent on interest group PAC money.
- PAC money from wealthy interest groups assists candidates who support those wealthy interests.
- The Bipartisan Campaign Reform Act (2002) limits soft money to parties, but did not reduce the influence of PACs. Actually it strengthened interest groups and weakened parties by making candidates more reliant on PAC money.

A new tactic used by interest groups is sponsoring ballot initiatives at both state and local level. They also sponsor the expensive initiative process in an attempt to circumvent legislative opposition.

Do pressure groups damage democracy?

A question often asked is whether pressure groups have a positive or negative impact on democracy. This depends very much on an individual's view of what democracy actually is. The following table seeks to identify the positive and the negative impacts that pressure groups may have on the democratic process.

Learning objectives

- Are the wealthiest pressure groups the most successful?
- Do pressure groups damage democracy?

Amicus Curiae

Latin phrase that literally means 'friend of the court'. William H. Rehnquist defined the term as referring to someone (or a group) who is not a party to the litigation, but who believes that the court's decision may affect its interest. According the rules of the Supreme Court, an *amicus curiae* brief that brings to the attention of the Court relevant matter not already brought to its attention by the parties may be of considerable help to the Court.

Abramoff affair

Lobbyist Jack Abramoff siphoned off lobbying funds provided by Native American tribes and directed the funds to Michael Scanlon, a Republican political publicist. In return Abramoff received kickbacks amounting to $19 million.

527 groups

These are tax exempt organisations named after part of the US tax code. They seek to influence the nomination, election and appointment of sympathetic candidates to public office or to defeat unsympathetic ones. They are not regulated by the Federal Election Commission or by state election commissions and are therefore not subject to the same financial contribution limits as PACs.

Positive impacts	Negative impacts
Pressure groups are seen to be essential as they ensure that decision-makers are kept up to date with public opinion. By organising people with similar views the pressure groups ensure that views are more likely to be heard than would be the case for a series of individuals.	Only rich pressure groups, supported by rich and powerful individuals or interest groups, have any real possibility of success, for example the CBI. The poor and the weak have to rely on poorly financed groups, for example Education for Choice.
With power becoming increasing centralised by government, pressure groups help provide a means by which powerful executives and legislatures can be controlled, or at least checked, before making a decision.	Much pressure group activity is essentially undemocratic. Information, views and influence are traded and applied behind closed doors. This favours rich insider groups and marginalises weaker outsider groups.
Pressure groups provide assistance in representing the views of minorities. Decision-makers often overlook minorities.	Pressure groups tend not to represent the views of the majority. They are run by well-organised and active minorities, which may not represent the views of the public at large.
Pressure groups provide alternative points of view and can highlight issues within a particular cause.	Pressure groups are not representative of their membership, (the membership does not directly control them).
Pressure groups can provide valuable advice and information to the government during the development and implementation of policy.	If policies are created as a result of negotiations with pressure groups then it is felt that the power of parliament or Congress is reduced, as un-elected pressure groups have exerted power.
Pressure groups provide a safety valve for aggrieved individuals who can channel their energies through the pressure group.	Pressure groups can often encourage some of their members to be deliberately disruptive, and at times act unlawfully, by using direct action.

There are four theoretical approaches to analysing pressure groups. These can help us understand the impact of these groups on the democratic process.

Theoretical approach	Explanation
Corporatism	Some pressure groups are backed by private businesses and have a considerable influence in policymaking. This is a corporatist approach to explaining pressure groups. Governments have often allowed private businesses to exert this influence, as in the case of the British Conservative Party reducing government interference in business matters.
Elitism	The elite model of pressure groups recognises that not all interest groups are equal in status: some are more powerful, better organised and better financed, making it more likely that their causes and points of view have a greater likelihood of influencing government policies. There will always be inequality and exploitation while elite groups control both the decision-making and the key economic assets of a country, that is, some pressure groups will always fail while others will succeed.
Pluralism	Pluralists argue that good democracy means that power is shared and decisions are made through negotiation between competing groups. Pressure groups compete to gain the attention of decision-makers and play an important part in policymaking.
Marxism	Marxists reject that there is a pluralist democracy and see pressure groups' power as linked to their economic strength and whether or not they are part of an elite. This naturally makes organisations such as the trade unions far less likely to influence government. Marxists argue that many pressure groups are doomed to failure, as decision-makers are also part of the same elites and have no interest in adopting causes and issues, changing policies or laws, which could adversely affect their own position.
New Right public choice approach	This is the view is that government should be allowed to govern and therefore should have little contact with pressure groups that may unduly influence them or hinder their operations.

3.15 Relevance and Ideology of Political Parties

Learning objectives

- What is the relevance of political parties?
- Are political parties ideological?

What is the relevance of political parties?

Traditionally, US political parties had a clear political function: Republicans and Democrats controlled elections, organised Congress and had government offices allocated to them. However as the 20th century progressed their power at a national level waned.

Campaigns and discipline

Political parties now use professionals to run their election campaigns and party activists, who are considered to be amateurs, no longer play a leading role, as the stakes are often considered to be too high to risk their input. The concept of party does still exist, but often it will be referred to as '50 parties' – one in each state, with its own distinctive approach and flavour.

US political parties tend to be very broad-based coalitions. They are decentralised and lack internal discipline. This is largely due to the fact that they have to operate within a federal system and cater for a wide variety of potential supporters. Traditionally, US political parties have lacked strong central authority. Many commentators believe that US politics is far more based on political personalities, rather than policies or party unity.

Candidates and leaders

Parties, however, still have key functions within the political system. They provide most of the leaders in government. The political elite tends to operate within the party systems, having built up powerful party connections in order to become a candidate and a leading figure in that party. Nonetheless, national parties play a much lesser role in national politics, particularly electoral politics, as campaigning is much more candidate-orientated than it is in Britain.

In the past parties used to control elections and candidates were nominated through the party apparatus. There was high voter loyalty and the focus of the parties was aimed at convincing their supporters to turn out and vote. Activists now work for individual candidates and are preoccupied with single victories, rather than the overall picture of party success or failure. Some party activists at state or local level will even distance themselves from presidential candidates who have proved to have been unpopular in their own state. Direct primaries have strengthened local parties, but at the same time have weakened national parties.

Candidates use their own organisations to gain nomination, rather than working through the party. Parties have now in effect lost direct control over the nomination process.

In the US there are no hard-line party controls in the legislature, or at least they are not strong enough to prevent individual members of Congress from following their allegiance to supporters, or their local constituents, rather than the party itself.

Policies and Finance

Parties have very little control over the policies adopted by a presidential candidate. The candidate will have had to acquire the support of the majority of party members, but once they have been nominated as the presidential candidate it is they and not the party who determine the policies upon which the candidate will fight the election.

The two major political parties have considerable financial muscle, largely due to having virtual monopoly of government power and because financial backers are reluctant to support third parties, or candidates who have little chance of success. The two main political parties have stifled the development of other political parties. Individuals are often loyal to their own state party, but little else, and need careful persuasion to support presidential candidates.

Are political parties ideological?

In the 1968 presidential campaign George Wallace said: 'There isn't a dime's worth of difference between the two parties.' Admittedly Wallace was an independent candidate and he had a very good reason, therefore, for claiming that the Democrats and the Republicans could not be split ideologically.

Professor John Gerring from Boston University carried out a systematic investigation into the ideological themes of the Republican and Democratic parties based on a period of 170 years. While most US citizens would suggest that the Republican and Democratic parties have differing ideologies, many have suggested that this is not the case. It was Gerring's belief that American political parties were more ideological than many believed and that overseas parties were actually less ideological.

Parties in Europe are viewed as being more ideological, as there is a major distinction between the left and the right. There is no serious organised left-wing party in US politics and right-wing extremists are fragmented. US politics is often accused of being interest-driven rather than being ideological.

Gerring also suggests that parties that have strong internal divisions fail to qualify as being fully ideological. There is certainly factionalism in Italy, France and Japan. Gerring also describes the British Liberal Democrat Party as being ideologically schizophrenic. He also describes many European parties as ranging from 'moderate, pure liberal, pure radical, advanced socialistic, radical and social, advanced radical, convinced collectivist, economist, imperialist and individualistic'. As far as US politics is concerned, Gerring believes that self-interests have been converted into ideologies.

Alexis-Charles-Henri Clérel de Tocqueville (1805–1859)

A French political writer best known for his 1835 book *Democracy in America*, which he wrote after extensive travel in the United States.

Louis Hartz (1919–1986)

A US award-winning political scientist whose book *The Liberal Tradition in America* (1955) is still a key text for political science graduates studying US politics.

Alexis de Tocqueville wrote: 'The parties by which the union is menaced do not rest on principles, but on material interests.' E. E. Schattschneider (*Party Government*, 2003), the late American political scientist, believed that it was a waste of time to even consider whether or not an individual was politically stimulated by interests or by ideas because individuals have ideas about interests. Louis Hartz believed that liberalism existed in the US on both the left and the right, but there was no socialism or conservatism in the sense that we understand it in Britain. He believed that there was conflict but there was no ideology. Gerring outlined four periods in which he identified the ideological basis behind the two dominant parties, as can be seen in the following table.

Period	Brief explanation
Neo-liberal 1928–92	Republicans believed in equal opportunities and individual freedom. They wanted to remove restrictions on free trade and blamed excessive interference of government for problems.
Jeffersonian 1828–92	Gerring believed that the Democratic Party was pro free trade, free market, *laissez-faire,* for the development of industry, philosophically individualistic and in favour of protecting civil liberties and rights. Democrats were anti-state and opposed to Republican protectionism.
Populist 1896–1948	The Democrats were increasingly in favour of government intervention. They targeted big business and monopolies. They preferred a liberal interpretation of the Constitution; they were concerned with social welfare (New Deal), human rights and redistribution of wealth.
Universalist 1951–92	The Democrats instituted great society reforms, were pro-private sector and embraced Keynesian economics.

Are modern political parties failing to perform their traditional functions?

Political parties still perform vital functions in each and every political system. In countries that have democratic traditions they are a key part of the democratic process.

In the US context, for example, there are five major functions, as can be seen in the following table.

Functions	Explanation and example
Aggregation of demands	Groups in society need a means by which their demands can be articulated in government and traditionally political parties have performed this function. Initially Democrats represented southern interests, then by the 1930s they represented northern industrial workers. Republicans were originally northern anti-slavers. However, US parties are not exclusively associated with one class, group or region; they are coalitions of interests, aggregating the demands of a number of different groups.
Conciliation of groups	Inevitably there are groups with conflicting or competing interests. Political parties try to conciliate between them and provide a platform that can articulate their diverse interests. Until 1964 the Democrats reconciled the interests of the urban industrial north with rural segregationalist southerners. John F. Kennedy, in 1960, managed to appeal to the Catholics of the north and to the southern Protestants. In 1980 the Republicans brought together the religious or moral Christian right and those who supported a demand for free enterprise. This won Ronald Reagan the presidency. Clinton revived parts of the old New Deal coalition, appealing to the middle classes, minorities, women and industrial workers.
Staffing the government	Parties are a link in the relationship between the people and the government and if governments are seen to fail then voters replace them with an alternative at elections. Parties provide a focus for accountability, so when judging the performance of a government the electorate looks at their record as a party, even though many decisions may have been made by unelected, non-party officials. Staffing the government through a party ensures a link between policy and public preference. In the US when party organisation becomes the vehicle for promoting a particular candidate rather than actually reflecting the interests of social groups, then there is a problem.
Coordinating government institutions	US government is fragmented by the legislature being separated from the executive. States have considerable independence. This is very different from countries such as Britain where there are powerful party orqanisations that nominate candidates, fight elections and form the government out of a majority. British parties can generally ensure the obedience of MPs; because party government is dominant a party can coordinate the members in supporting policies and actions. In the US there is no such coordination; Congress and the president have different constituencies and agendas; only a common party label can provide coordination. A Democrat mayor, for example, would have more in common with a Democrat president than with a Republican one. Some presidents, such as Lyndon Johnson, used party ties to improve their relationship with Congress. Issues arise when there is divided government. Generally the US is divided and fragmented both institutionally and politically. Political parties can fill this void but only when there is the will for compromise.

Learning objectives

- Are modern political parties failing to perform their traditional functions?
- To what extent is the number of political parties determined by the country's electoral system?

Functions	Explanation and example
Promoting political stability	Parties do not always promote political stability; some desire regime change. Multiparty systems tend to undermine stability (Italy has had nearly 30 governments since 1970). In the US the two-party system is resilient; although there are numerous political parties most are marginalised. The two main parties have adapted and incorporated third parties, activists and protestors. US political parties absorb potentially destabilising social movements, but this may be because there have been few deep divisions in the US in recent years. If the US were more divided the two parties would not be able to cope.

To what extent is the number of political parties determined by the country's electoral system?

In the US the Republican and Democratic parties have a stranglehold on the political process. Over 60 per cent of the US electorate describe themselves as either being Republicans or Democrats. In the five presidential elections between 1980 and 1996, 75 per cent of independent voters who leaned towards either the Democrats or the Republicans voted for their preferred party's presidential candidate. In 2000 79 per cent of Republicans voted for George W. Bush and 72 per cent of Democrats voted for Al Gore.

After the 2002 congressional and local elections there was only one independent senator and two members of the House. In each of the elections since the Second World War the two major parties have shared an average of 94.8 per cent of the vote.

At state level all 50 governors are either Republicans or Democrats and only 0.003 per cent of state legislators are members of a party other than the two main parties.

There are several reasons for the domination of US politics by two parties.

- The standard arrangement for electing national and state legislators is the single-member district system. Whoever receives the greatest number of votes is elected. There are therefore incentives to form broad-based parties, while minor and third parties are almost doomed to defeat.
- The electoral college system favours two-partyism. Technically US voters do not vote for a candidate; they vote for a slate of electors who pledge themselves to one or other of the presidential candidates. The president requires a majority of votes in the electoral college system. This also makes it very difficult for third parties because it is under a winner-takes-all, first-past-the-post system.
- With Democrats and Republicans in control of government machinery the electoral rules work to their advantage. Even getting a party's name onto a ballot is difficult and expensive. In North Carolina a petition with nearly 60,000 voters' signatures is needed for a new party to appear on a presidential ballot.
- The Federal Election Campaign Act gives special benefits to major parties, principally public funding.
- The nominating process is a barrier to third parties. The US relies on primary elections to nominate partisan candidates and under this system voters select their party's nominee. These partisan nominations are controlled by the party and their leadership, but in the US the voters determine who the Republican and Democrat nominees will be.
- The primary nomination process channels dissenting voices into the two major parties, making it difficult to form a third party. The two parties are adaptable and accept outsider-type candidates (e.g. Sarah Palin) or fringe social movements.

3.17 Candidates, Leaders and Political Parties

Is there a need for leadership and internal discipline in political parties?

US political parties are far more loosely organised than those in many other countries. Neither the Democrats nor the Republicans have a formal organisation at national level. At this level is the Democratic National Committee and the Republican National Committee. These are made up from representatives from state parties, affiliated groups and organisations, and other individuals. While they are involved in campaigning and fundraising they cannot direct the activities of individual members. When a particular party controls the White House the president is the party leader and it is he who controls the National Committee. When not in power the leadership is defuse. There are state parties in each state with different rules and different structures.

In Britain the situation is entirely different. Broadly, each ordinary member of the Conservative, Labour and Liberal Democrat parties has an equal say in the election of their party leader. The Labour Party, for example, allocates a third of the vote to ordinary party members, a third to affiliated trade union members and a third to MPs and MEPs. A party leadership election is triggered by a two-thirds majority at a party conference.

In Britain party discipline is also important in parliament; losing party discipline could be disastrous for a government. It is widely believed that the open fighting and divisions within the Conservative Party, in and out of parliament, were primarily responsible for the defeat of John Major's government in 1997. The Labour Party under Blair and Brown has maintained strong party discipline in an attempt to appear to be a united group. There have been some cracks in discipline, as in 2005 when 34 Labour MPs voted against the government's terrorism bill.

A whipping system is used in Britain to keep control of MPs. It is used to maximise turnout for major votes in parliament.

- Whips are appointed by political parties and consist of a Chief Whip, Deputy Chief Whip and a number of junior whips. The government Chief Whip is also known as the Parliamentary Secretary to the Treasury.
- Whips keep MPs and members of the House of Lords fully informed about parliamentary business. They ensure that members attend votes and follow the party line in divisions.
- They feed backbencher opinions to the party leadership.

Failure to comply to the party whip may result in disciplinary action.

In the US there is no such formal system of control. Members of Congress are technically free to vote in whichever way they choose, although there are informal pressures placed upon them to support key party policies.

Outline the importance of parties in selecting potential candidates and party leaders

In the US party organisations have some control over nominations. At presidential level the vast majority of Democrat and Republican delegates to national conventions are chosen or bound by primary elections. Caucuses are also used. This is a meeting of supporters or members of the political parties. A caucus is the way in which the two major parties in the US select their

Learning objectives

- Is there a need for leadership and internal discipline in political parties?
- Outline the importance of parties in selecting potential candidates and party leaders

presidential nominees. Primaries are also used in order to whittle down the number of potential candidates.

Presidential candidates

In order to win the presidential nomination an individual needs over 50 per cent of the delegates at the party national convention. This is achieved by gaining delegates through primaries, caucuses and the support of unpledged delegates. The primaries allow registered party members to vote to determine how many delegates each candidate takes to the convention. The Democrats use a proportional representation system and the Republicans use a combination of different methods. This explains why the battle between Hillary Clinton and Barack Obama for the Democrat nomination for president was drawn out, while John McCain won the Republican nomination far earlier.

Caucuses are not run by all states; delegates are selected for a state or county convention to select delegates to go to the national convention. There are also unpledged delegates or super delegates (as they are known in the Democratic Party). They are automatically allowed to go to the national convention and support whoever they wish.

Each state has a different number of delegates, based on the number of congressional districts. Some states also have extra delegates, as they may have elected officials.

Congressional candidates

For members of Congress the choice of candidates is made locally; there is no central review and no approved lists and neither is there the power of veto. Registered party members make their decisions in primary elections. If individuals seeking office can gain a sufficient number of signatures then their names will appear on the party ballot.

In Britain, choice is made by a selection committee of the constituency organisation. In the Labour Party approval of party headquarters is required.

The general elections

In the US ordinary voters take part in the choice and candidates need to convince a larger proportion of the electorate. The turnout in primaries is often low, giving an advantage to those who are well organised and well funded. In having a more open system more of the electorate is politically involved. They offer a choice of person and policy and they eliminate the power of cliques that can dominate local parties. The problem is that the candidates end up fighting two elections; one to get onto the ballot and the election itself. This makes money far more important. In the US there is also considerable emphasis on personality and the appeal of candidates and not necessarily on their policies. Once primary elections and conventions are concluded general elections are used to determine who will be elected to office.

For US presidential nominees it is a long and involved process; state primaries and caucuses usually take place between January and June and the national conventions in the late summer or early autumn. In many cases the eventual nominees are known before the conventions and, as a result, the conventions have become little more than ceremonial.

3.18 Pressure or Interest Groups in Politics

What is the role of interest groups in modern politics?

Interest groups are valuable ways in which US citizens make their views, needs and ideas known. The structure and informality of US politics makes it possible for interest groups to have considerable influence. US political parties are weak, partly due to the separation of powers between the executive and the legislature. Each US legislator needs to create a coalition in order to successfully win an election and weak party loyalty can mean that interest-group influence during elections (through financial support) and afterwards (by influencing policymaking) can be considerable.

The decentralisation of political power through federalism also encourages interest groups and a strong independent judiciary enhances the power of interest groups. They can utilise litigation to achieve policy objectives that cannot be achieved through legislative action.

The virtually unlimited freedom of the press, speech and assembly also means that any pressure group, regardless of their radical nature, will be heard.

In the past three key categories of interest groups seemed to hold sway in the US political system: business, labour and agriculture. Agricultural groups have certainly lost a great deal of influence and there have been many new groups that do not fit readily into the remaining two categories. The following table outlines the main types of interest groups and their role in US politics.

Interest group category	Role
Business	Through their importance to the US economy they can have direct influence, as elected officials are held accountable for the economic performance of the country and fear passing anti-business legislation. Some businesses are members of trade associations, representing whole industries, or umbrella groups that speak for a broader business community. Businesses funnel literally millions of dollars in campaign contributions to candidates that they support.
Labour unions	Although their influence has declined since the 1960s, in terms of financial support and in terms of membership, they are still significant in that they represent the views and interests of a sizeable number of the working population.
Professional associations	They can provide valuable insights into the values and interests of particular professions; they can testify before Congress and organise their members to speak with representatives at state or district level.
Intergovernmental groups	These include organisers such as the National Conference of State Legislators or the National Governors Association. The latter has direct administrative and political responsibility for carrying out programmes mandated by the federal government. They have been influential in helping Congress to draft legislation. They have no official role in the federal system, but they make their views known to Congress and to the administration.
Public interest groups	These support specific goals that are not necessarily of direct benefit to its members, but relate to broader society values. These groups would include civil and women's rights and the environmental movement. Many have been advocates of programmes to benefit the poor, prevention of child abuse or championing the rights of the disabled. While they lack financial resources they can use their expertise and information gathering to raise issues that many other groups fail to address.

Learning objectives

- What is the role of interest groups in modern politics?
- Assess the view that pressure groups make the US more or less democratic

Assess the view that pressure groups make the US more or less democratic

Senator Edward Kennedy once said: 'We have the best Congress money can buy.'

The implication of this is that pressure groups can undoubtedly hinder US democracy. The power of pressure groups was brought into sharp focus in January 2006 when Jack Abramoff, a former lobbyist, was found guilty on three counts of fraud. Two-and-a-half years later he was also found guilty of trading gifts, meals and holidays in exchange for political favours. The corruption investigation later led to the conviction of two White House officials, a Republican member of the House of Representatives and nine other lobbyists and congressional aids. At various times, Abramoff had had direct contact with the George W. Bush administration, although Bush and other key officials denied all knowledge of him.

As far as pluralists such as Robert Dahl are concerned, pressure groups, as long as they have equal power and influence, would enhance democracy. C. Wright Mills, on the other hand, would claim that wealthy pressure groups are likely to have too great an influence.

Negative effects of pressure groups

It would appear that the US certainly has an elitist model as far as interest groups are concerned. Wealthy and powerful interest groups have an enormous impact on candidate success in congressional, presidential and state elections. They also have many points of access to the political system. Many of the groups are unelected and unaccountable and any influence they may have that furthers their own cause in the minds and the policies of elected representatives of the people must be considered to be undemocratic. Small, elite and wealthy pressure groups have a disproportionate influence on government policy. This is compounded by the fact that over the years many of the well-established pressure groups have created strong and resilient relationships with government departments and congressional committees. These are known as policy networks, or iron triangles. The American Farm Bureau, for example, has strong links in both the House and the Senate with the Agriculture Department and congressional committees. For many years there have been farming subsidies and trade tariffs on cheap imported food to the US.

Also many former politicians from the bureaucracy, the executive and from Congress become well-paid lobbyists, due to their connections in Washington. Pressure groups have undoubtedly played a role in preventing gun control, blocking health-care reforms and convincing the Bush administration to reject the Kyoto Agreement. In the latter case oil companies, popularly known as 'big oil' or 'the energy lobby', used their considerable resources.

Positive effects of pressure groups

Some interest groups represent many individuals. The Christian Coalition of America had a huge influence in the 1990s, probably out of proportion to its real membership that has been variously claimed to have as many as 40 million members. Interest groups have also been instrumental in pushing through democratic change, such as the NAACP, the American Civil Liberties Union and the National Council of La Raza.

There is always a tension between the principles of majority rule and the protection of individual and minority rights. Democratic government aims to protect the rights of minorities, but key pressure groups have often played a vital role in ensuring that minority rights are not inadvertently infringed or ignored by government action and legislation.

That pressure groups are opposed by other pressure groups in pursuing their interests and influencing those with political power to some extent mitigates their effect on Congress and beyond. However the financial muscle they possess to those in power can have a less than positive impact on American democracy.

Government and Pressure Groups

Should governments resist interest groups?

According to pluralist theories pressure groups, or interest groups, can organise and compete freely in a system where no one group dominates. The US system is open to influence from a wide range of interest groups and their influence varies from state to state. This is the predominant form of political influence that interest groups have in the US, although some would suggest that it is closer to the elitist model. However, in the case of **neo-corporatism** governments actively involve a group in the process of governing, which again has parallels in the US.

Corporatism suggests that government operates as a mediator between various organised interests. A prime example would be in wage negotiations between employers' associations and labour unions. The approach also suggests that government should only become involved to problem-solve and to deal with situations that cannot be resolved between two competing groups. In the US Dahl and Lindblom called this 'polyarchy', which is a democracy in which 'non-leaders exercise a high control over governmental leaders'. The writers also warned against the dangers of bargaining on behalf of huge organisations, as this would jeopardise the sovereignty of the people.

There are institutionalised interactions that take place between organisations and government in the US. The main difference between European corporatism and American pluralism is that in Europe representatives of these groups are invited to participate in policy and decision-making, which is often referred to as 'legitimate interaction'. In this respect, governments work as mediators rather than initiators. Dahl and Lindblom also warned that interest groups are likely to pursue manipulative purposes, as in a federal system there are many ways in which interest groups can target parts of the government apparatus at different levels and that government is far more open.

On the one hand, therefore, some governments will actively seek the participation of interest groups to assist with policy and decision-making. These could be described as being insider groups that have direct access to the government apparatus. On the other hand, other political systems portray governments that are either willing or unwilling mediators between two or more groups.

In theory, in resisting the influence of interest groups a government is able to maintain democratic accountability. It is, however, extremely difficult to show that members of Congress vote on the basis of interest group influence. There are many other factors, such as constituent interest. Party and committee membership has an impact. Congress members may vote according to the outcome of opinion polls, meetings, or communications with constituents. Ultimately, whether they are influenced by interest groups or not, their ability to reflect the views of their constituents may well determine whether they are re-elected. If, for example, constituents lost jobs as a result of a pro-business vote then it would be hard for the member of Congress to justify that decision.

What factors determine the effectiveness of interest groups?

Political action, campaigning, lobbying and court action

In the US persuasion is accomplished through the creation of politician action committees, grassroots campaigns, and lobbying and court action. Interest groups know that important legislative work in congress takes place in committees. Lobbyists will therefore testify at

Learning objectives

- Should governments resist interest groups?
- What factors determine the effectiveness of interest groups?

Neo-corporatism

This is the idea of special interest groups, such as large corporations, bargaining with government to gain favour for their particular interest.

hearings, provide information and, in some cases, even write the legislation. This seems to be an exceptionally cosy set of circumstances; certainly many lobbyists have close personal relationships with Congress members and the executive branch. The reality is that many of them actually worked with those who they are now lobbying, as they once served in the government themselves.

There are certainly ties between congressional committees, administrative agencies and lobbyists. At the grassroots level interest groups can influence policy by urging their members to write to members of Congress. They use direct mail to secure popular backing and funds. Demonstrations are also used to gain media attention and groups will also provide campaign workers for candidates, public endorsement and donations. Political action committees are also highly effective. In effect they are the campaign financing wing of a larger lobbying effort.

Studies suggest that it is actually doubtful whether financial support in campaigns has a direct impact on the way in which a member of Congress votes once they have won an election. Nonetheless, the inference is there and a clear relationship between the member of Congress and the interest group has already been established.

In cases when Congress or the executive branch remains unresponsive to the interest group, they are prepared to turn to the courts. They can file suits, seek injunctions, provide attorneys, pay for the costs of legal teams or provide *amicus curiae* briefs to support one side or another in a court case.

Access and influence

Undoubtedly the key factors that determine the success or failure of an interest group in the US are access and influence. In its simplest form access can be broken down into three clear steps:

- locating the point of the decision
- establishing contact with those involved in that decision
- persuading those involved in that decision.

It is not as clear cut as it first may appear. An agency may in fact just ratify a recommendation made by others, so lobbyists need to have long-term social and political relationships in order to know precisely where decisions are being made. Lobbying is undoubtedly worthwhile and effective. Some attempts at influence are subtle, while others are more blatant. The National Rifle Association is extremely effective; it rates candidates at election time and can mobilise avalanches of constituent mail. On the other hand, the pro-Israel lobby is more subtle and aims to create a sympathetic approach.

Undoubtedly there is differential access; some have an enormous advantage. For example, a Democrat president is more likely to be sympathetic to organised labour.

Influence is the other key consideration. Interest groups are most effective in a supportive role, giving assistance to candidates or even providing aid to candidates from both parties. Influence in Congress and the executive is usually down to money, expertise and labour, along with creating long-lasting relationships that are of mutual benefit. These are variously known as iron or cosy triangles or sub-governments.

How Interest Groups affect Government

Learning objectives

- Do interest groups help or hinder representative government?
- Discuss the view that pressure groups have too much influence in Congress
- What are the different types of pressure group?

Do interest groups help or hinder representative government?

Interference in policymaking

The government's role is to arbitrate between competing interests. Operating in the public interest, or equilibrium, is achieved by balancing various different interests. The key problem is that no policy is ever likely to either completely work against or be in favour of one interest group. But governments try to modify policy so that it does not adversely affect a key interest group and, indeed, powerful interest groups would try to prevent this from happening.

If we accept this approach of representative government then all governments merely act as a mechanism in which real power is held by competing interest groups. However there is no guarantee that the groups have equal power and influence. If the interests of a particular group are thought to be in danger then they would organise and attempt to access representative institutions to pressurise them into redressing the balance.

David Truman, in *The Governmental Process* (1951), recognised, however, that not all groups, regardless of their size, could actually gain access to representative government. He cited African-Americans in the 1950s as being a prime example; they simply had no access to the policymaking process.

In stark contrast has been the continuing battle between the National Rifle Association and attempts to ban handguns and heavier weapons. In DC vs Heller (2008) the Supreme Court upheld an individual's right to possess a firearm for private use under the 2nd Amendment. The Supreme Court agreed with the Court of Appeal that they should strike down provisions of the Firearms Control Regulations Act (1975).

Balancing competing interests

The problem for representative government is that if they give each interest group equal access and influence then at best government policy will be fragmented and at worst they will spend an enormous amount of money in an inefficient way, handing out benefits to too many competing interest groups. Even reducing the scope of government is not a solution, as pressure groups have a vested interest in maintaining the way in which the political system works and how expenditure is distributed. The main problem is that pressure groups are enormously unequal; there is an inbuilt bias toward advantaged groups, while other groups, notably the poor and minorities, are disadvantaged. This needs to be rebalanced by representative government that carefully weighs up the impact of accepting the views of particular interest groups.

The US system in particular, but equally any political system that does not wholly fund political parties and electioneering, is prone to external influence through the availability of money used to fund political activity. While pressure groups may make legal contributions to candidates, undoubtedly democracy has been undermined by covert financial deals.

If representative government were truly free from the influence of interest groups then disadvantaged groups that were in that position decades before would not still be in that position. They would have voted for representatives who could not be swayed by more powerful interest groups or held to a particular course in policy by their party and supporters. On numerous occasions in the US, and notably during the Clinton administration, balancing the budget without increasing taxation derailed any attempts to redistribute income.

As interest groups have increased in number and there is a broader availability of support and funds, government representatives have become less tied and reliant upon a handful of highly influential pressure groups. This has given them greater freedom of choice.

Discuss the view that pressure groups have too much influence in Congress

Disproportionate influence

Cash-rich interest groups undoubtedly have enormous political influence in Congress. There is a two-year election cycle in the House of Representatives, which means that members of Congress need to start raising funds almost immediately after winning an election. It has been estimated that a House of Representatives candidate needs around $1 million to win a seat and that a senator needs over $5 million.

There have been attempts to limit donations to candidates and parties, notably the Federal Election Campaign Finance Act (1971) and the Bipartisan Campaign Finance Act (2002).

In the 2004 presidential election the top ten political action committees each spent between $9.5 million and $22.7 million each. These are private groups that are organised to elect political candidates. They receive and raise money and make donations to political campaigns. This has been seen as a way in which interest groups can circumvent legislation and the donations are always made with strings attached.

Positive role of pressure groups

Although it may appear that interest groups have a disproportionate influence over Congress by virtue of the money that they can provide, this does not necessarily mean that they have power over Congress. They are probably far more powerful in that they can mobilise voters for or against particular candidates. Members of Congress can be deluged with mail and phone calls on particular issues, prompted by an interest group. An interest group can also fund campaigning against a particular candidate if they are opposed to the views of the interest group.

The American Association of Retired Persons has a large membership of around 33 million. It would therefore be undemocratic for members of Congress not to listen to their views. There has also been a process of partisan de-alignment over the past 40 to 50 years. While voter turnout has fallen, as has party membership, membership of pressure groups has increased. Therefore including pressure groups in the democratic process should enhance democracy and not adversely affect it.

Members of Congress also actively court the views and expertise of particular pressure groups, such as Greenpeace, on highly specialised issues, helping them formulate a broader and more informed view. Congress will, if it feels that there is a groundswell of opposition, act against the wishes of pressure groups. Many members of Congress will still vote along party lines and in favour of their local constituents, as well as their own personal beliefs.

Although pressure groups can undoubtedly exert disproportionate influence to either their size or relevance to the general needs of the country, they do have a positive role to play in supporting the work of Congress. This of course assumes that the relationship between Congress and those interest groups is a transparent one and that there are processes and procedures in place to avoid any misunderstandings. Therefore scrutiny is vital to ensure fairness.

What are the different types of pressure groups?

Over the years groups have developed to try to promote or defend interests that could be affected by government policy. In many cases governments actually view pressure groups as being very valuable, both as a source of support and of information. Membership is usually restricted to those who have a particular interest in the work or cause championed by the pressure group.

There are four key types of pressure group, although it is notoriously difficult to actually categorise some pressure groups, as they appear to have the characteristics of more than one type. The following table identifies the four main types of pressure group.

Type	Explanation	Advantages and disadvantages
Sectional	This type of group aims to look after the interests of a particular section of society. Membership is usually closed and only open to those in a particular occupation. Membership within an occupation is usually very high as a percentage.	The pressure group is often seen to represent a particular occupation, making it more likely for the government and the media to take their point of view seriously. They can be seen as being blinkered and only concerned with their own sectional interests.
Cause	These can be either single cause or broader cause groups. A single cause group may have a limited objective, such as the building of a new supermarket, or it may have broader objectives that are longer-term, such as Greenpeace's campaigns to protect the environment.	The group may be able to raise significant funds from sympathetic individuals and may be able to put direct pressure on central or local government and departments. The cause may be seen as being of little importance to many people, particularly if it is perceived as extreme.
Insider	These have a status and position in the political system and use their methods to gain influence. They are often consulted by parties and by government in the framing of policy.	As they have expertise in a particular area and providing their aims are realistic and reasonable, they are able to exert considerable influence in furthering their aims. Because of the close relationship between government and some of these groups it is sometimes believed that the insider groups benefit to the exclusion of the more general public interest.
Outsider	These groups are either unable to gain recognition from the government or do not wish to be closely associated with it. Policymakers often view their ideas to be unrealistic or unreasonable.	These groups do not feel constrained by their relationship with the government or parties. Their views are often seen as extreme, their cause not important to policymakers, and they sometimes find it difficult to present clear proposals. Often they are not seen as representative of the group they are campaigning for.

In the US there are also other ways of typifying pressure groups.

- Economic pressure groups – these include businesses and trade union groups as well as individual companies. Large private corporations have their own full-time officers and staff in Washington.
- Public pressure groups – these are groups that represent a section of the public and are seen as representing particular issues. They are often referred to as sectional as they may represent the specific interests of a small group.
- Attitude pressure groups – these are the fastest growing pressure groups and some of the most powerful. They represent individuals with common beliefs and objectives on single issues. This group includes Christian Fundamentalist groups and the National Rifle Association.
- Intergovernmental groups – due to the growth in federal programmes intergovernmental lobbying has increased. These are groups that aim to influence federal government on behalf of specific states and cities in bidding for extra resources.

Exam Café

Relax, refresh, result!

Relax and prepare

Questions for the exam are likely to be drawn from the following topic areas or similar. Use these to help focus on what areas of the subject you should be revising.

- The functions of parties and how well these are performed.
- The ideologies of the parties and issues such as convergence.
- Party decline and renewal.
- The party systems.
- The methods of pressure groups and their effectiveness.
- Issues concerning the democratic worth of pressure groups.

Refresh your memory

When revising this topic, try the following exercises. They will help you structure your notes and will provide a guide as to what you will need to know for the different papers. Remember to work through unit F853 first as this will provide the base you will need for F855.

Political parties

- Use mnemonics (see page 165 for example) and similar methods in order to ensure that you can remember the key parts to a topic.
- Identify the functions of political parties. You can develop the following mnemonic to assist you in this purpose.

	Party functions	Comment
P	Participation	Participation is a central pillar of democracy. Parties are a medium of participation which is vital in an indirect democracy. Since the decline of the New Deal coalition in the 1960s party membership has fallen despite the attempts of people like Karl Rove to revive the 'base'. Thus parties are failing in this function.
A	Aggregation of interests	
R	Representation	

	Party functions	Comment
T	Training and recruitment	
I	Ideological choice	
E	Education	
S	Supplying a government and opposition	

- Comment on how well parties perform each of these functions and link this to party decline.
- Set up a two-columned table with the arguments in favour of party decline and renewal.
- Ensure contemporary examples are used as much as possible in the above.
- Use a sheet of A3 paper to list the main ideological characteristics of the following: traditional Republican and Democrat ideologies, Reagan's New Right conservatism, Clinton's New Democrats/Third Way, the Republican Revolution/Contract with America, Bush's compassionate conservatism and the policy positions of Obama and McCain.
- Separation of policy into economic, social and foreign policy will provide a good basis for comparative analysis.
- Consider the role and significance of Third Parties and Independents with particular reference to the most recent presidential and congressional elections.

Pressure groups

- Identify the functions of pressure groups and contrast these with political parties.
- Create a table which identifies and ranks in order of importance the factors which can bring a pressure group success.
- Ensure you have a recent example to support each argument. For example, reference to the role of the ACLU in the Boumediene vs Bush case of 2007 will be a more impressive illustration of the use of the courts than that of the NAACP in Brown vs Board of Education 1954.
- Create a table to contrast the arguments for and against pressure group activity in the US today. The following mnemonic might be useful in this regard.

Arguments for pressure groups in a democracy

P Participation, for example AARP 33m members, NRA 3m members
R Representation
E Education
S Scrutiny
S Safety valve
U Pressure groups are not umbrella groups and allow a focus on a single issue
R Minority rights protection
E Expertise

Arguments against pressure groups in a democracy

U Unequal resources
S Selfish
C Congress may be bypassed
L Laws may be broken

- Develop the arguments and use contemporary examples to illustrate each argument.
- Divide a page into four quarters and identify the main characteristics of the following models of pressure group activity: pluralism, corporatism, New Right/public choice and elitism.
- Consider which model the US comes closest to. This will help you answer the question as to their democratic worth.
- In a conclusion it might be worth referring to the might of the military–industrial complex and linking this to US foreign policy. Read up on the views of Chomsky in this regard.

Exam tips

These are some reasons why students do badly in exams. They provide a guide to what you need to avoid and by implication what you need to do to perform well in the exam.

✦ They do not focus on the question and provide detail that is not relevant.
✦ They do not use enough examples from the US on questions on pressure groups.
✦ They are not aware of the contemporary developments.

Get the result!

- Look at the websites of the Republican and Democrat national committees, individual candidates, and television and newspapers such as the *New York Times* and the *Washington Post*, the BBC and the *Guardian* in order to get up-to-date examples.
- Ensure your answer focuses on the question set. There is no need to provide a history of the parties or to outline the various types of pressure groups that exist if the question does not ask for this. You will merely be wasting precious time before you start scoring exam marks.
- Identify the key words in the question before writing and ensure they are addressed as you write. Avoid the temptation of merely identifying the topic area and writing an answer that you had already prepared on that topic. A question on party decline is markedly different from one that asks you to consider ideological similarities between the parties.
- Consider both the case for and against if the question asks you to 'discuss, assess, evaluate' or 'analyse'.
- Separate each argument by the use of a new paragraph and try and support the argument with a contemporary example.
- If identifying a range of factors as in a question on pressure group effectiveness, try to avoid writing a list by ranking the factors in order of importance and discussing how their importance may have changed over time.

In Focus – F855

The following will help you in revising and in developing your knowledge at this level in order to gain a higher mark. These are the key areas to focus on.

- Identify similarities and differences between the parties and pressure groups in the US and UK. Recognition of the 'new politics' would be worthwhile. Consider the decline in party membership, the rise of pressure groups and new social movements, the use of the Internet, the decline in voting and alignment when considering the respective functions and roles of parties and pressure groups in a democracy.
- Consider ideological convergence in the UK with the advent of New Labour and Cameron's compassionate conservatism and the parallels that might be drawn with Bush, Obama and McCain.
- Recognise the dominance of party in the UK in contrast to the weak system in the US.
- Assess the impact of the first-past-the-post electoral system and the electoral college on third parties and independents in both the UK and the US. This will invite a consideration of the impact of other systems on party systems such as in the AMS in the Scottish Parliament and Welsh Assembly, STV in Northern Ireland and regional lists for the European Parliament. Other countries may also be brought into play, such as Israel and the Netherlands, if these have been studied.
- Consideration should be given to fhe nature of society with regard to party systems. Heterogeneous societies such as the UK tend not to have a multi-party system, whereas pluralistic societies such as Spain have a greater range of regional parties represented at national and local level. The impact of devolution on the UK is worthy of consideration in this regard.
- You should recognise how the different political systems in the US and the UK have a great impact upon the effectiveness of pressure groups. In the UK, 'insider status' has been described as the holy grail of pressure groups as close relations with the government are the key to success given executive dominance over the legislature and judiciary. In the US the separation of powers and the federal system means that power is not as concentrated in one sole branch of government and thus a different analysis needs to be applied. Ultimately it is difficult to avoid the conclusion that 'money talks' and that the system is far more elitist than in the UK. This latter point is of course key to arguments relating to pressure groups and their role in a democracy.
- Reference to the EU is a quick way to gain synoptic marks. Similar elitist arguments may be levelled with regard to the ability of a pressure group to maintain offices in Brussels, and the NFU's decision to relocate from London to be closer to the Commission tells its own story.

4 Elections

The US electoral system, while it shares some common features with the British system, in as much as it has a first-past-the-post electoral system and elections at various levels at set times, it is markedly different.

The key functions of elections, representation, participation, accountability and legitimacy are delivered in slightly different ways according to the particular type of election in question. Perhaps the most striking difference between the US and the British system is the way in which presidential candidates are nominated and how the presidential campaign is run, and consequently the votes counted. Britain has a prime minister who is the leader of the majority party, and the electorate does not have the opportunity to vote directly for the leader of the executive. In the US, elections for the legislatures and for the executive are separate. The presidential election is a long and involved campaign, requiring candidates to secure state-by-state support to become the nominated candidate for their political party. On election day voters cast their ballots for their preferred candidate. A candidate by winning the majority vote in a state will receive all of that state's votes.

Rather like Britain, where there are calls for changes in the electoral system, specifically to adopt a form of proportional representation, there are constant demands in the US for changes that would more accurately represent the wishes of the people. This is for local or state elections, for Congress or for the presidency itself.

There are five key themes in this chapter.

- Functions of elections
- Democratic elections
- Electoral systems
- Presidential elections
- House and Senate elections

These are represented by the first eleven topics, and in turn these are supported by three question topics for F853, looking at the most common essay titles, and three F855 question topics, which again look at popular essay themes in the examination.

This chapter contains 17 topics in total, representing the following.

The chapter is rounded off with an exam café feature on page 212.

4.1 Functions of Elections

Learning objectives

- Representation and accountability
- Making government
- Recruiting politicians
- Influencing policy
- Educating citizens
- Building legitimacy

Representation and accountability

Voting is one of the primary principles of democracy. Elections aim to be fair and free. However, with large populations most citizens never have the opportunity of direct decision-making in society and instead they elect representatives to act on their behalf. Citizens' demands are channelled from the public to politicians via elections. Politicians require the consent of the citizens in order to govern on their behalf. This means that they have to be elected and this is usually only possible if they have been in the past, or make pledges to respond and prove themselves as far as the citizens are concerned.

Elections take place at a number of different levels. In Britain, for example, there are local, regional (county or metropolitan), national (House of Commons) and international (Members of the European Parliament) elections. Many representatives of elected assemblies are tied to specific geographical areas or constituencies. In Britain there are currently 646 constituencies, each with one member of parliament.

In the US each state directly elects two state senators, meaning that each state is equally represented. There are also 435 members of the House of Representatives, each representing nearly 700,000 constituents, which means that more populous states have more senators than others. Elections in the US are staggered; members of the House must face election every two years and senators serve six years, with around a third of each of the seats up for election every two years. Members of Congress are considered as local representatives and they are expected to defend the interests of their constituents. Individual MPs in Britain also represent their own constituents and effectively operate as local ombudsmen. In a large number of democracies voters will also elect local council representatives, or they will vote for regional assemblies, such as state governors and assemblies in the US states or the Scottish Parliament in Britain.

Assemblies should be representative in the sense that they reflect the relative support for different political parties. As we will see, some systems are rather more precise about achieving this aim. In Britain the first-past-the-post system does not provide an accurate reflection of support, but those that use a form of proportional representation, such as the Republic of Ireland, more accurately mirror public opinion.

The other key issue is that of accountability. If an individual or a party effectively loses the support of the voters then they are forced from office. In Britain this impacted on the Labour government in 1979 and the Conservatives under John Major in 1997. Also, if a party fails to connect with public opinion it has very little chance of gaining power. The Labour politician Gerald Kaufman once said that the party's 1983 manifesto was 'the longest suicide note in history'.

Making government

In the US the executive, or rather more precisely the single most important individual in the executive, the president, is directly elected by the citizens following a long and difficult election process. As we will see, the election begins even before the primary votes are cast and culminates in a national election based on an electoral college system.

In Britain, where there is a parliamentary system of election, the executive is the leadership of the party that has won the majority of the seats in the House of Commons, the elected chamber.

The general election is fought under a first-past-the-post system, and it usually produces a majority party. However, the system distorts the number of seats won compared to the actual number of votes cast. Other countries, such as Belgium, Holland and Italy, have parliamentary systems but their electoral process rarely produces a majority government and, therefore, many of the governments are formed out of coalitions.

Recruiting politicians

In democratic countries elections are a primary means by which the politicians and decision-makers can be recruited into politics. Potential candidates and existing politicians have to face the public's criticism, hostility and the media. All of this ensures that politicians stay as much in touch with the voters as possible. Each MP, although supported by a party, stands or falls on their own ability to win an individual election contest.

In the US the House of Representatives, being elected every two years, makes politicians very aware of current constituency opinions. For the US president the long election process involves mass participation of supporters and politicians at various levels.

Influencing policy

In Britain, political parties fight elections on the basis of the policies that they have published in their manifestos. In effect an election victory gives them legitimacy to pursue those policies and most governments do attempt to implement them. It cannot necessarily be said that the voters approve of all of the policies; just the majority of them.

In the US a presidential candidate would make fewer concrete promises, mainly because due to the system they are often not able to deliver them. Where voters feel that they do not have a connection with the policymakers turnout tends to be low. Local elections and European Parliament turnouts are low in Britain, as are state election turnouts in the US.

Educating citizens

Theoretically, an election should provide citizens with a huge amount of information upon which to base their decisions, and, more generally, on important policies, party records, personalities and political parties. The problem is that media coverage is often overwhelming and also parties resort to negative campaigning, which alienates voters. In the US many of the campaigns revolve around TV advertisements and sound bites and also with a focus on personality. With the exception of the last presidential election, recent turnouts in the US have been relatively low.

Building legitimacy

With elections being at the centre of democratic **legitimacy**, it is the voting process that gives a party the right to govern. Even in countries such as China, which is a one-party state, and where the campaign is non-competitive, elections are still held to impart legitimacy. This is why the legitimacy of national or regional assemblies is important. They need high turnouts to justify their existence and establish their own identity. It is equally true in the US, as each state has its own set of powers, with a governor and an elected assembly, which needs legitimacy to make decisions.

Barack Obama's infomercial

On 29 October 2008 Barack Obama featured in a 30-minute infomercial (paid for advertisement), conservatively costing $4 million. It was shown on CBS, NBC, Fox and other cable channels. It is a prime example of how an enormous campaign fighting fund can severely imbalance the exposure a candidate can receive in the media.

Legitimacy

Derived from a Latin word that means to declare lawful, this is the process that effectively transforms power into authority. Legitimacy implies some kind of respect and acknowledgement that obedience is a duty.

INTERNET RESEARCH

There is a comprehensive link site on elections and their functions at the University of Keele, To see this, go to www.heinemann.co.uk/hotlinks, insert express code 1825P and click on relevant link.

Learning objectives

- Direct democracy
- Representative democracy
- Models of representation
- Similarities and differences

Direct democracy

Direct democracy is a system of government where decisions are made by the collective choice of citizens rather than representatives.

Ancient Greece was not a single country, but a patchwork of independent city states. Around 600 BC the Athenian statesman Solon put forward a constitutional reform package, laying out the bare bones of a democratic system. A hundred years later it was taken up by Cleisthenes. He championed political reform, which in 508 BC brought in the Athenian Democratic Constitution.

This form of democracy differed from what we now understand to be democracy. It was smaller in scale, participation was limited and individuals had to be eligible. The Athenians totalled no more than 250,000. Only around 30,000 of these were citizens, defined as adult males of Athenian birth with full citizen status. Only 5000 of these would regularly attend the assembly (ecclesia), which met forty times a year on a hill called the Pynx overlooking the city.

The assembly made decisions on questions submitted by the Council of 500 (boule). After discussion voting was conducted by a show of hands, with a majority determining the result.

- Six thousand citizens were selected to be jurymen to staff the jury courts, with the average jury size of 501.
- To make participation fair most officials and jurymen were selected by lot; elections were believed to be flawed, favouring the rich, famous and powerful.
- Only adult males having both an Athenian mother and father could involve themselves in democratic government, making the citizen body a closed political elite.

Aristotle defined the democratic citizen as a man 'who has a share in [legal] judgement and office'.

Serious threats to democracy were dealt with by a form of reverse election. A citizen who presented a threat could be ostracised, meaning they were exiled for ten years. Citizens would scratch or paint the name of the individual on a piece of pottery. Six thousand citizens had to vote in favour of the ostracism for it to be valid. This system was later replaced by a legal procedure delegated to the jurors of the peoples' courts.

Administrative officials were selected by lot in boards of ten and covered ceremonial issues, military affairs and management of the treasury. The enormous numbers of offices and official duties were taken very seriously. Experienced orators, such as Demosthenes, fundamentally influenced the voting of the assemblies in a way that has never quite been replicated, even in today's mass media communications world. Comments on the Athenian system are shown in the following table.

INTERNET RESEARCH

For articles and discussions on democracy around the world, go to www.heinemann.co.uk/hotlinks, insert express code 1825P and click on the relevant link.

Criticism	Explanation
Not all men were equal.	Slaves, women and foreigners were excluded and those with time and expertise had more influence.
Protecting traditional customs and values of society against temporary majorities would be difficult.	The system can be seen as undemocratic, as only a small proportion of adults could vote, however the ultimate right of all citizens to vote would protect traditions.

Criticism	Explanation
The rule of law could not be protected.	Athenians did not see the rule of law in the same way. They focused on ad hoc discretionary decision-making, as opposed to what we would call the rule of law.
Democracy encourages the emergence of factionalism, losing sight of the national interest.	Factions were a reality and in one extreme case in 411 BC the democratic assembly was replaced by the Council of 400. Political enemies were executed or forced into exile.

Representative democracy

Representative democracies are political systems in which voters elect representatives, rather than engage in direct democracy. Modern-day democracy bears little relation to the Athenian model. Government and decision-making is in the hands of professional politicians who have the responsibility to make decisions on behalf of the people.

Representative democracy can be described as being a limited and indirect form of democracy. It is limited in the sense that citizens' actual involvement in the democratic process is restricted to a handful of voting opportunities in elections throughout their lives. It is indirect in the sense that the citizens only choose who should govern and do not exercise power themselves. However, the ability of citizens to radically change their voting habits if unhappy with the present government does ensure public accountability.

In 1863 US President Abraham Lincoln used the phrase 'government of the people, by the people, and for the people'. This is a classic definition of democracy that has two different notions. 'By the people' means that the citizens participate in government and govern themselves; that is, self-government. 'For the people' suggests that government benefits the people even if this means that citizens do not rule themselves.

Thomas Paine and the rights of man

Paine believed that the concept of society is so embedded that government is barely necessary to maintain it. Paine was a radical democrat. He did recognise the need for representation. He proposed that regular elections were needed to ensure a frequent change of views between representatives and their constituents. This was to ensure that 'the elected might never form to themselves an interest separate from the electors'.

Thomas Paine supported the call for the American colonies' independence from Britain in his highly influential pamphlet *Common Sense* (1776)

Models of representation

There is debate around the four key models of representation and the role of elected representatives to which the models apply, as shown in the following table.

Representation model	Explanation
Trustee	This model suggests that a representative should be in a position to exercise their judgement on matters of importance. The problem is that the representative may only represent their own interests and not the interests of the electorate.
Delegate	This is a representative who acts on behalf of the voters on the basis of receiving clear instructions from them. A delegate should not exercise their own judgement; just perform as they have been instructed. The representative acts for their constituents primarily and not necessarily for the good of the nation.
Resemblance	This assumes that a representative should be representative of the group that they represent. While on an individual basis this may be difficult, across an assembly there should be a fair gender split and ethnic minority representation. This system does assume that only those who have a resemblance to a group can represent their interests.

Representation model	Explanation
Mandate	This model suggests that individuals are elected on the basis of the party that they represent, rather than on their own personal abilities. It assumes that representatives should ensure that they implement their manifesto promises. It does not take into account the fact that voters may not necessarily agree with the full range of policies.

Similarities and differences

High levels of participation as typified in direct democracy are only workable in small communities. Mass meetings involving millions of citizens is unworkable. Equally, if citizens are consulted on every single issue and given the opportunity to be involved in the debate the country would become ungovernable and decision-making impossible. Most citizens lack the time, knowledge and willingness to become more directly involved.

Representative democracy, therefore, provides an alternative, producing a group of individuals who can devote time to government and do a better job than the average citizen.

However, government needs to be responsive and not bureaucratic; otherwise citizens become disengaged from the democratic process, as evidenced by falling levels of voting in elections. Voting is seen as a meaningless ritual and little to do with democracy.

Redistricting

It is a requirement of the US Constitution that election districts have approximately equal populations. If the federal census indicates a population change then state and local government need to determine whether the existing districts satisfy this requirement. If they do not, then the district needs to be rebalanced by having the boundaries redrawn.

A deviation of less than 10 per cent in population change will not require redistricting. If it does exceed 10 per cent, then if redistricting does not take place it could be challenged as being unconstitutional. This 10 per cent is rather more complex than would first appear, as it is a comparison between the district in the area with the greatest population and the district in the area with the least population. In other words, none of the districts should have a more than 10 per cent variation. The other important aspect is that the redistricting should not of course create any districts that fall outside the 10 per cent deviation rule.

Referendums and initiatives

Referendums are valuable additions to elections. Elections tend to imply that voters are endorsing every aspect of a party's programme, but referendums can ask specific questions on single issues and do not unduly affect representative democracy.

Initiatives are in effect petitions requiring a number of registered voters to force a public vote on a specific issue. In the US a number of uses have been made of initiatives, a prime example being Proposition 13, a ballot initiative to amend the constitution of the state of California in 1978.

Gerrymandering

This is a form of redistricting, in which the boundaries are changed either to help or to hinder a particular political group, racial group, religious group or class. The term is believed to be attributed to the governor of Massachusetts, Elbridge Gerry (1744–1814). In 1812 he signed a bill into law that redistricted Massachusetts to benefit his Democratic Republican Party.

There have been a number of examples of gerrymandering in the US over the years. Some state legislatures, such as Alabama, for virtually 60 years in the 20th century refused to redistrict, favouring the predominant rural to urban split in the state despite mass migration to the cities. They feared redistricting would undermine traditionally conservative dominance of the state.

As late as 2002 there have still been examples of gerrymandering. In Ohio Republicans redistricted in order to remove Democratic voters from areas, so that their own Republican candidates could get a clearer run to the House of Representatives.

Candidate selection

Britain

In Britain, anyone over eighteen with a deposit of £500, but excluding clergy, judges, civil servants, non-discharged bankrupts and those guilty of electoral malpractice, can stand in an election. In practice, most candidate selection is controlled by political parties, as independents have very little chance of success. It is important to remember that it is the local party that chooses the candidate and not the electorate. This has given rise to the term 'the selectorate', indicating the disproportionate amount of power of local party members.

Considerable power is also retained by the party leadership. Labour Party nominees have to be approved by the National Executive Committee (NEC). Each constituency Labour Party (CLP) then draws up a shortlist and the local party makes their choice of candidate. The Labour Party system is far more democratic than it had been in the past, with a one member, one vote system. Primary losers have been the trade unions and affiliated organisations and, to a lesser extent, the CLP. In practice the actual number of individuals selecting a candidate can be small and they are rarely representative of the electorate.

Some constituencies are considered to be safe seats, those with enormous majorities, and are much coveted by aspiring party leaders. This was an accusation levelled at the adoption of David Milliband and Ed Balls; they were both given safe seats when the sitting MPs were encouraged to retire and given peerages.

In the Conservative Party candidates have to be approved by Central Office (CO). Candidates can be proposed to a constituency via the National Union's Standing Advisory Committee. The constituency party then draws up a shortlist and each member of the party can vote.

There have been moves to increase the number of women and representatives from ethnic minorities as election candidates, but still the majority of MPs are white males. These initiatives have been launched under David Cameron's leadership of the party.

United States

In the US, primaries are used for presidential, congressional and local elections. To some extent they can be considered more democratic than the British model. The primary season begins in January and runs through to April. Candidates need considerable financial support to succeed.

In order to win, nomination presidential candidates, for example, have to win the primary vote in enough states to give them the majority of delegates at the convention. The whole process is long and involved. While a British party leadership fight may take a month the presidential primaries are eight weeks, and there may be a year of campaigning before that period.

In effect a primary and a caucus perform the same function. In a primary, such as New Hampshire, registered voters will cast their ballot for their preferred candidate. In a caucus, such as Iowa, a number of small meetings, or caucuses, are held across the state, sometimes in individuals' homes, or in schools, or even in fire stations. The attendees indicate their support for each candidate by a show of hands, or by using a signing sheet, or by splitting into groups. This system is used by the Democratic Party, but in Republican caucuses each voter in attendance casts a secret ballot. The primaries and caucuses are still in effect a selectorate. The voters are not necessarily representative and, in any case, the party members may favour a candidate's policy but not recognise that the candidate does not have broader appeal to the electorate.

Learning objectives

- Candidate selection
- Conduct of election campaigns

Invisible primaries

This was a term first coined by Arthur T. Hadley. He defined it as 'that period of political time between the election of one president and the start of the first state primary to determine the next political candidates'. In other words, this is the period before the primaries in which the potential candidates try to become the front runner for their party's nomination and also try to attract funds. For more discussion on this see 4.12 page 196.

INTERNET RESEARCH

The online edition of *Newsweek* has an excellent seven-part series called *The Road to the Inauguration,* detailing the conduct of the US 2008 presidential campaign. To see this, go to www.heinemann.co.uk/hotlinks, insert express code 1825P and click on relevant link. Then click on the 'Politics' section.

US elections

The US is unusual in many ways because there are an enormous number of elections for political offices. Routinely, voting takes place for school boards and town councils, county treasurers, district attorneys, sheriffs, as well as more recognisable positions, such as senators, members of the House of Representatives and of course the president.

US election campaigns tend to be drawn-out affairs. Unlike Britain, where the period between the calling of an election and election day may only be a matter of a few weeks, some US election campaigns can last literally years.

Some lower level offices are not partisan in the sense that the candidates do not necessarily associate themselves with specific political parties. They may, however, be supported by a political party, an interest group or a professional association. Money, organisation and public image are the key focuses to run a successful election campaign. An individual will make a public announcement that they intend to run. In practice this means that campaigns will often begin months before the real campaign and confirmation of those that are running has been made.

Candidates will tour the areas in which they are running to meet voters, to gain media coverage and to rally supporters (both organisational and financial). Volunteers will try to identify supporters and ensure that they are registered to vote. Routinely, candidates will use television, radio and direct mail to get their messages across.

Above all, to secure nomination a candidate needs money and organisation. William Brock, the head of the Republican Advisory Committee on presidential nominations, in his report stated that he believed that a front-loaded nomination system effectively ruled out all but the very best connected and funded candidates. In effect the nomination system is almost over at the beginning and does not allow voters the time to look at the qualities of the different candidates and their views.

Conduct of election campaigns

In Britain performing well during the election campaign is vital. This is because many traditional party voters have become disconnected from the parties, creating a significant numbers of floating voters and because the media places the campaign in sharp focus. British political parties spend an enormous amount of money and invest a lot of time in the last few weeks and days before an election. In many cases political parties will focus their attentions on marginal seats, assuming that they will retain their safe seats. As a result only a handful of seats usually change hands.

Parties' conduct in the campaign can have a massive impact in terms of persuading undecided electors, but as we will see, their record in office or in opposition over the preceding months or years can also determine voting intentions. Philip Gould, an adviser to Tony Blair, wrote in 1992: 'You can't win campaigns in four weeks, but only in four years.'

This certainly suggests that voting intentions can be more deeply entrenched than parties hope in certain circumstances.

In the 2008 presidential contest between Obama and McCain, Obama ran the largest, best-financed campaign to get minorities and the young out to vote. In the past the Democrats had relied on volunteers and labour unions to get the vote out. This time they had 1400 neighbourhood teams in Illinois alone and the party had spent months recruiting, training and managing them. Millions of dollars were spent on TV campaigns and 35 million had watched a half-an-hour infomercial on Obama.

Republican campaign strategist and public relations advisor, Steve Schmidt, spoke about the McCain campaign on election day: 'I think we did our absolute best in really difficult circumstances. It's highly doubtful that anyone will have to run in a worse political climate than the one John McCain had to run in this year.'

The campaign had run for 23 months, full of stage-managed events, focus-group-tested sound bites, massive TV advertising, cable news showcases and actually less spin than in previous campaigns. There was hard news reporting, with the candidates clashing in stage-managed 'arguetainment' head to heads on national television in the presidential debates. At times the campaign had been very personal, not least between Obama and Clinton in the run up to the Democrat presidential nomination and then, perhaps less so, between Obama and McCain.

Media and campaign finance

In a study of 2412 campaign stories from 48 different news outlets the Project for Excellence in Journalism concluded that it was not so much that Barack Obama was cast in a favourable light by media coverage, but that John McCain had been cast in a negative light. Most of the McCain coverage was unfavourable and became more and more so towards the end of the campaign.

The study found that some 35 per cent of the stories on Obama were positive, 35 per cent were neutral or mixed and the remaining 30 per cent were negative. For McCain 57 per cent were largely negative and only 14 per cent were positive. Although McCain's running mate, Sarah Palin, received three times the coverage of Obama's running mate, Joe Biden, the media's approach to her was very mixed, but more positive than McCain's. The key findings suggested that:

- initially Obama coverage was negative
- McCain's coverage began positively but turned sharply negative
- Palin was slightly more negative than positive
- Biden was almost invisible.

The financial crisis in the US during the election campaign proved to be an enormous bonus for Obama. His reaction was seen as being far more positive and decisive. It proved to be the turning point as far as media coverage was concerned.

As far as the voting public was concerned, the massive coverage of the campaign was criticised for a number of reasons, such as:

- unconfirmed rumours were aired
- much of it was superficial, overly opinionated or trivial
- too much time was spent on personalities of the candidates and not enough on policy.

While the US media was somewhat partisan during the 2008 election, the British experience is slightly different. Broadcast media is required to be politically impartial, but not so the newspapers, magazines and other news outlets.

Understandably the media and political parties in Britain view one another with suspicion. The media is uncomfortable with parties using spin doctors and they feel that parties are deliberately obstructive and uncooperative if a negative story emerges. Much of the media may have its own agenda and political bias, but politicians need them and their cooperation to distort news stories in their favour.

As in the US, broadcast media focuses on sound bites, extracts, personality and other superficial issues. The print media, as far as some are concerned, merely reflects the views of their readership; others maintain that they shape it. The editorial position of key newspapers can reinforce perceptions, directly influence voting behaviour and effectively shape the agenda. In the 2005 general election only three newspapers remained in support of the Conservatives (*Daily Mail, Daily Express, Daily Telegraph*). This compared to Labour's last general election defeat in 1992 when they could muster the support of just two newspapers (*Daily Mirror* and *Guardian*).

Total party spending in the British 2005 general election was £42 million, 84 per cent of which was spent by Labour and the Conservatives. Both of these parties spend around £20 million a year each just to run their parties. In the run-up to the general election Labour received

Learning objectives

- Media and campaign finance
- Policies and personalities

Fox or Faux News

The Fox news channel was accused of being blatantly anti-Obama during the presidential campaign, featuring a number of stories that either criticised Obama or questioned his lead in the polls. One such story was a rumour that Obama had already written his inaugural address before election day. The host suggested: 'Can this potentially give McCain an opening in this last leg of the race?'

£9.1 million, Conservatives £8.1 million and the Liberal Democrats £4.2 million in donations. Once again it rekindled the argument for state funding of political parties, due to the fear that wealthy individuals and organisations can exert an undue influence.

Undeclared loans and cash for peerages

In Britain it has been argued that parties, in trying to bypass the Political Parties, Elections and Referendums Act (2000), have succumbed to awarding honours in return for cash donations. In other cases cash donations have been described as loans to the party.

In the US Barack Obama raised a staggering $116.4 million in September 2008 alone. McCain raised $5.3 million in the same period. It has been estimated that Barack Obama spent $573 million and John McCain spent nearly $260 million.

Policies and personalities

In each and every election it is clear to see that policies and personalities are interwoven. In the US often less tangible questions of leadership, strength and trustworthiness come to the fore. Initially McCain was perceived as being honest and trustworthy, as well as being a strong and decisive leader.

Obama's chief strategist, David Axelrod, recognised these qualities as being a threat. He believed that voters made multidimensional choices. Personal qualities were extremely important to voters. The voters would be seeing the winning candidate virtually every day for four years and the winner would be making important decisions on their behalf. Consequently voters would choose a candidate who they felt comfortable with and showed self-confidence.

In the 2000 presidential election George W. Bush won because he was able to connect with the voters, just as Ronald Reagan had done in the past. In the 2008 presidential election Obama explicitly made the point: 'You know, this whole résumé contest is not what the American people are looking for. I have to make it clear what is at stake in this election.'

In the US perhaps the greatest triumph for personality politics in which policies, ideologies and programmes were swept aside was the election of Arnold Schwarzenegger as Governor of California.

Boris Johnson, the Mayor of London, is another example of personality politics at work. It is difficult to know what he stands for politically. His appeal seems to transcend party loyalties; he openly courts the attention of the media and is a prime example of the 'presidentialisation' of British politics. He once stated that he is: 'Free market, tolerant, broadly libertarian, inclined to see the merit of traditions, anti-regulation, pro-immigrant, pro-standing on your own two feet, pro-alcohol, pro-hunting, pro-motorist.'

In Britain it seems that many politicians focus less on their differences with the electorate than on their similarities. Tony Blair portrayed himself as an ordinary father, as has Gordon Brown. Many believe that Gordon Brown is one of the only genuine political personalities in British politics. He appears determined, intense and obsessive; he does not pretend to do politics. Others have tried to project a strong public image, such as Iain Duncan Smith, but many wrote off his attempts as being plastic. Henry James, the American-born British author, once wrote: 'Ideas are, in truth, forces. Infinite, too, is the power of personality. A union of the two always makes history.'

INTERNET RESEARCH

The Hoover Institution has a comprehensive collection of campaign finance information. To see this, go to www.heinemann.co.uk/hotlinks, insert express code 1825P and click on the relevant link.

One of the most dominant political personalities of recent years was Margaret Thatcher; she had a strong inner conviction that she was right. She was a strong believer in that people were individuals, with their own individual life, and individualism was at the core of her personality, which led to disastrous consequences for many.

Theories of voting behaviour

Models seek to explain the reasons why people display certain behaviours at different times. A person may vote normally, according to their class (social structure model) but because of specific issues at the time of the election, such as being fundamentally against the war in Iraq, they may vote differently (voting context model). The following table outlines the key theories of voting behaviour and suggests reasons why they may or may not be appropriate. (For more on voting behaviour see also 4.13, page 199.)

Learning objectives

- Theories of voting behaviour
- Theories in practice

Model	Explantion	Complications
Social structure	This is based on the assumption that you can categorise voters who have shared common characteristics that reflect divisions in society, such as wealth and occupation, age, gender or ethnicity.	This has become less significant over recent years, particularly in Britain. It no longer fully explains why people vote for a particular party. A major factor is known as class de-alignment, which means the long-term decline and consistent voting for a particular party on the basis of social factors. Key reasons can be changing patterns of employment, mixed-class households and neighbourhoods, home ownership and more fluid family structures.
Party identification	For many years it was believed that voters retained a loyalty to a political party from election to election. It is actually difficult to define party loyalty or how strong this is as a factor.	Less than half the electorate would consider themselves to have a fairly strong party identification. Consequently there are large numbers who show what is known as 'partisan de-alignment'. In effect they are no longer loyal to a party that either they or their family have traditionally supported. They are detached from them, sometimes indifferent or at worst hostile. The reasons are greater political awareness, influence of the media, disillusionment with politics and the decline in ideology.
Rational choice	This is an economic model, which suggests that voters will make their choice on the basis that they will support whoever will fulfil their personal self-interests. In essence voters are like consumers, choosing the party (brand) that offers the best range of policy products to suit them.	There is much evidence to suggest that voters make up their minds before parties even publicise their policies and, in any case, parties cannot possibly provide a range of policies that would suit everyone's tastes. It also makes the assumption that voters can be bothered to investigate what is on offer and then come up with a reasoned decision.
Dominant ideology	This suggests that powerful groups in society directly influence voting behaviour, such as businesses, the media and rich interest groups. It suggests that behaviour of individual voters is shaped, controlled and manipulated. Even the agenda for political parties are set by these groups.	The model ignores individual interests and personal freedom. Democracies have a secret ballot, so there is no guarantee that an influenced voter will cast their vote in the way in which the powerful group intends. It suggests that all voters are socially conditioned to obey.
Voting context	This model suggests that voters weigh up the consequences of their vote and look at the different options. Differing levels of party support in general elections compared to by-elections, local elections or European Parliament elections are thus explained, where protest or tactical votes can be cast.	Whether prevailing views on key contemporary issues are that influential is in dispute. However, voters may cast their votes according to how they think political parties will handle specific issues. Voters may in any case have preconceived ideas of what a party's policies are, which may be at variance with the actual party line.

Theories in practice

De-alignment is a key issue in both Britain and in the US. The following table outlines some of the major features.

Britain	US
Class is still a main determinant of voting. Seventy per cent of the working class tends to vote Labour and 80 per cent of the middle class Conservative. However, the number of working-class Conservatives was a vital factor in the string of Conservative victories from 1979.	There was strong alignment for the Democrats from the 1930s to the 1960s, known as the New Deal Coalition. This declined in the 1960s with greater de-alignment but again this has stabilised since the 1970s.
Class de-alignment has occurred as a result of increased standards of living, the fact that the working class has become more middle class, a switch from manufacturing to service employment, coupled with a switch from public to private sector employment, as well as trade union decline and increased numbers of women in the workforce.	Approximately 46% of adults identify with the Democrats and 37% with the Republicans. However, de-alignment has led to split ticket voting, where voters cast their vote for one party's candidate as president and another in congressional elections.
An individual who would vote for a political party regardless of any circumstances is said to have a strong party identification, or strong partisan alignment. It suggests that British politics is tribal, like football.	The split ticket voting factor has led to divided government and political gridlock, where one party controls the presidency and the other Congress.
Partisan de-alignment began in the 1970s when there was an appalling economic situation following a long period of growth. People challenged orthodox views and were more prepared to look for a solution elsewhere. This adversely affected loyal Labour voters in particular who switched to Conservative allegiances.	Class plays a lesser role in the US than it does in Britain. The two main parties have broad national appeal.
There has been an increased number of floating voters and voting has become more volatile or unpredictable. This has meant that Labour has become less dependent on its working-class support while all parties try to draw support from all classes.	Due to de-alignment the personality of the candidate has become far more important and the US certainly has candidate-centred elections.
Assuming the electorate is not aligned then free choice based on the best policies for issues that concern them is a reasonable suggestion. Issue voting often revolves around education, employment, health and more latterly the economy.	Of the 140 million US citizens who voted in the 2008 election, Barack Obama won 95% of the black vote, 55% of the white vote, 66% of the Hispanic vote and 56% of the women's vote.
Judgemental voting has also been suggested, in which policies, ideologies, leadership, past performance and party competence are key factors in determining voting behaviour. A weak leader with a divided party, such as John Major in 1997, was a key factor that sealed his fate.	Obama also managed to secure 71% of of first-time voters. He had worked particularly hard to secure their interest and their allegiance.

INTERNET RESEARCH

The British Election Study at the University of Essex has an enormous amount of data and analysis of surveys and results. To see this, go to www.heinemann.co.uk/hotlinks, insert express code 1825P and click on the relevant link.

4.6 Electoral Systems (4)

Learning objectives

- Representation
- Participation
- Democracy

Representation

Elections should form the basis of a strong democratic society. British elections are, in general, fair and meet many of the ideals of what elections should achieve. British parties tend to stand or fall on their manifesto promises and are reasonably inclined to translate these into policies should they win. There are still clear differences between the bulk of the electorate and the MPs who represent them. In terms of background, education, social class and income there is quite a gap between a typical MP and the voters they represent.

In the US members of Congress are not delegates because they are neither tied to a party programme nor mandated by their constituents to carry out specific policies. Perhaps they are trustees, as they promise to exercise their judgement on behalf of their constituents' interests. If members of Congress are not delegates or representatives, then they cannot be considered to be representatives using other measures, such as class, education, ethnicity, gender and age. Most are actually white, college educated, middle class, middle-aged and male. Only a handful are female and there are even fewer from ethnic minorities.

Congress was always intended to be a representative body; on the one hand it is criticised as being too responsive to constituents and organised interests, but on the other it is too insulated from the public. However, once elected voters have little control over their selected representative, nevertheless Congress does respond to the public when voters provide clear direction.

Participation

Low turnout is a major problem in British elections: the lower the turnout the less likely the result will reflect the wishes of the electorate. On average since 1945 the turnout has been 78.3 per cent. In 2001 it was just 59.4 per cent. This meant that five million fewer people voted than in 1997. The 2005 turnout was marginally up at 61.3 per cent, still well below the post-war average. Why is this? Does low turnout really threaten a government's right to govern? The major reasons put forward for low turnout are hotly debated.

- Practicality – there are voters who do not have the time to visit the poll station to vote. Of course they may believe that the result is a foregone conclusion, as in 2001, and decide that their vote is of no consequence. Turnout does tend to be higher in seats where the outcome is in the balance (known as a marginal seat), or when the outcome is close, as in 1992.
- Party alignment – those with strong ties to a party are more likely to vote. However there are now far fewer people who have strong links to a party. Non-voters often feel that 'their' party has let them down. Disillusioned Labour voters refrained from voting in vast numbers in the 2001 and 2005 elections, as they felt let down by Tony Blair.
- Disinterest – those who are apathetic about politics are unlikely to vote. Elections do not excite them or the parties have failed to convince them to participate. People are broadly interested in politics, but often find that direct support of pressure groups and campaigns are more fulfilling. Many of the unemployed also do not vote or have no interest out of a sense of being left out.
- Social groups – there is evidence that the working class and the young are far less likely to vote. However, those over 65 are twice as likely to vote. Targeting low-voting social groups needs to be a priority.

HAVA

In 2002, Congress passed the Help America Vote Act (HAVA), which includes several notable elements. The federal government offered payments to states and localities to replace outdated punch-card and lever-voting machines. It also established an Election Assistance Commission to provide technical assistance to local election administration officials and establish standards for voting devices. The commission is involved in studying voting machine and ballot design, methods of registration, methods for provisional voting and for deterring fraud, procedures for recruiting and training poll workers, and education programmes for voters, among other matters.

Making voting easier and offering voters alternative ways of casting their vote could be a solution. Extending the postal voting system or allowing people to vote online are ways this could be done. People failing to vote is not the factor undermining the electoral system. Parties tend to focus on winning elections rather than debating issues. They tend to simplify and to misrepresent opposing views. The media is preoccupied with political celebrities and oversimplify debates and fail to provide sufficient analysis.

Participation in US elections has been steady but flat since the 1980s, but there was a surge of interest in 2008. The average voting turnout in the US has been just over 50 per cent in recent times, reflecting a drop since the 1960s. Many voters have turned to getting involved in specific campaigns, by joining civic groups and protests, and undertaking community actions or signing petitions. This reflects an increase in direct political participation as an alternative to voting, which essentially produces an indirect result.

Political participation and its future depends on how effective it is in influencing matters in the short or medium term. Elections are important in selecting political elites and as a source of democratic legitimacy, but they appear less effective in energising the public to participate in the democratic process.

Participation is, therefore, very much linked to influence and it can be seen that rather than putting democracy at risk it actually represents an opportunity to expand and enrich democratic participation. To some extent this can be achieved through referendums, town meetings and tele-democracy. Town meetings have been held in six states in New England for generations. Tele-democracy has been used for some years in North Carolina, with citizens interacting with panels during a phone-in programme. This has been extended to enable voters to call in and cast votes. Hopefully this can be extended to direct voting via computers or digital television.

INTERNET RESEARCH

There is a comprehensive look at democracy in the US in the American Studies part of the University of Virginia website. There is particularly useful material in the Hypertext Project, including the full works of Alexis de Tocqueville on democracy in America. To see this, go to www.heinemann.co.uk/hot links, insert express code 1825P and click on the relevant link.

Democracy

In 1999 Kenneth Dolbeare believed that American democracy was in decline and that the size and power of the Washington government meant that it was 'increasingly connected only to a steadily shrinking proportion of its affluent citizens'. Dolbeare singled out a number of reasons for the decay of American democracy. These are:

- political parties were in decline
- the media had too great an influence
- money distorted results in electioneering
- political action committees were too influential
- it was increasingly difficult to beat a sitting member of Congress in an election
- opinion polls drove government responses to issues.

Dolbeare also believed that political participation was declining in the US. His criticisms also applied to some extent to British democracy, notably that strong majority governments represent a dwindling majority of the electorate. This occurs because it is possible when using the first-past-the-post system to achieve a majority with a minority vote. There is also a lack of opportunities for minority and independent candidates to enter parliament.

Learning objectives

- The nominating process
- Primaries, caucuses and national party conventions
- The role of parties

The nominating process

Presidential elections illustrate the complexity of the election process. As far as the general public is concerned the process starts at least a year before the elections when states hold primaries or caucuses. But in reality the process is started far earlier than this, even as much as four to eight years before the election day. Two years before the election hopefuls aim to raise millions of dollars to help them run their campaigns; this is all part of the so-called invisible primary process. Eighteen months before the date they announce that they are actively campaigning to become president.

Candidates need to win the support and endorsement of key political figures if they are to have any chance. They need to be endorsed from established sections of their party. An incumbent president obviously has a distinct advantage and on no occasion in recent years has a president who chooses to stand for a second term failed to secure nomination. Incumbent vice-presidents actually rarely become elected presidents. George H. W. Bush was an exception, having, while he was serving in Reagan's second term, secured the support of many leading Republicans to being nominated as the presidential candidate.

The key is whether a candidate can secure enough party support at the forthcoming primaries and caucuses, which are held throughout January and June in the election year.

Primaries, caucuses and national party conventions

Primaries are electoral contests held to determine each political party's candidate for a particular office. Primaries can take place for all levels of government, including for mayor, governor, senator, House of Representatives and the president.

The primaries for the president are held at state level. Depending on state law, voters cast ballots directly for their preferred presidential candidate or for delegates who are pledged to support that candidate at the convention. There are closed primaries, where only registered members of the party can vote, or open primaries, where voters of one party (known as crossover voters) can vote in another party's primary. The idea, as with caucuses, is to choose delegates to attend the national party conventions and to demonstrate the popularity of candidates.

The caucus literally means a gathering of each party's local political activists to select delegates to county meetings, who then in turn select delegates to the state meetings. The state-level conventions then select the delegates to the convention. The caucus system indicates who the preferred presidential candidate is, and is a way of democratising presidential nominations.

These are the key issues regarding the primary and caucus system.

- A primary is an election among supporters of the same party to choose that party's candidates to run in the general election.
- The caucus process allows partisans living in a small geographical area to meet and select delegates pledged to specific candidates.
- The actual size of a state's delegation to the convention is calculated on a formula established by the party.
- The US Constitution allows states to make their own election laws.
- The Democrats have imposed a set of national rules, but the Republican Party has not.

- More states have moved their primaries and caucuses to the beginning of the process, to have a greater influence. This has led to a front loading and regionalising trend in the nomination process that benefits nationally recognised candidates.

Super delegates

Super delegates, or unpledged delegates, are individuals who can have massive influence on the nomination process in both the Democrat and the Republican parties. In the 2008 Democratic National Convention super delegates cast 823.5 votes and the Republican National Convention cast 123.

The national conventions are run in July or August for four days prior to the presidential election. They need to choose the presidential candidate, the vice-president and the party platform (i.e. the policies or manifesto).

Invariably the winners of the primaries and the caucuses are virtually assured that they will be nominated by their party. Once the necessary number of committed delegates has been determined, the convention is more ceremonial than a contest. The convention confirms rather than chooses the presidential candidate.

The Democrat National Convention took place at the end of August 2008, giving Obama 3188.5 votes and Hilary Clinton 1010.5. The Republican Party National Convention took place in the first four days of September. John McCain received 98.45 per cent of the vote, or 2343 votes, well in excess of the 1191 he needed.

For additional information on primaries and caucuses see also 4.12, page 196.

INTERNET RESEARCH

The official sites of the Democratic Party and Republican Party conventions can be found by going to www.heinemann.co.uk/hotlinks, insert the express code 1825P and click on the relevant link.

The role of parties

The presidential nomination process has become considerably more democratic. Prior to the 1970s ordinary party members played very little part in selecting the delegates to attend the conventions and choose the presidential candidates. It was state and local party leaders who dominated the process. In those times to win a presidential nomination all a candidate needed to do was to win the approval of the party leaders. Now they need to win the support of the party membership.

The old system was clearly open to abuse and corruption, but reforms have opened up the process to allow tens of millions of people a vote in primary elections. Democrats have also instituted the rule that half of convention delegates must be women.

The Great Presidential Puzzle. This was a cartoon drawn by James Albert Wales in 1880. The blocks in the puzzle are the heads of potential Republican presidential candidates, including Ulysses S. Grant and James S. Sherman

However, the way in which primaries and caucuses are now structured means that the nominating conventions are something of an anti-climax as the nominees can be known months before the convention takes place. As a result convention news coverage has fallen, as has public interest.

Primaries are sometimes said to be the death knell of political parties in the US. This is because candidates seek nomination as individuals with their own set of policies. They need not have much political experience. George W. Bush had very little, and comparatively speaking neither does Barack Obama. The selection process now rests firmly on campaign skills and not on the ability to govern.

National conventions, however, are an opportunity to promote party unity. They are the only time in four years that a party meets as a cohesive unit. Otherwise they are just 50 separate state parties. This is an opportunity for the winning candidate to win the support of the whole party and for the defeated candidates to pledge their allegiance, healing any wounds caused during the primaries. Sometimes it appears as a mere charade, something often highlighted by the media. But it can serve to enthuse the party faithful for the coming presidential election battle and is a means of communicating the party's enthusiasm to the voting public.

Factors influencing the presidential campaign

Without doubt, the media focuses strongly on the presidential campaign, they highlight the strategies and tactics of the candidates and pinpoint their mistakes, but is this really an influencing factor at all?

Many commentators have argued whether the campaigns actually matter at all. However it is often not a question of whether they matter, but for whom and under which conditions do the campaigns matter and how are they influenced and what influence do they have on the voters.

Are all voters equally likely to change their vote choices in response to campaign efforts? Are some campaign activities more effective than others? Voters bring prior beliefs to the campaign and are therefore more or less susceptible to influence, they also have important affiliations and interests and these have a direct impact on whether they are influenced by the campaign or not. In effect, the influence of a campaign may well depend on the three key criteria of:

- the stored political information of the voter
- their long-term partisan predisposition
- the existing candidate support.

Voter decision-making is a dynamic process as is the actual running of the campaign. The 2000 campaign suggested that nearly 45 per cent of the electorate changed their minds at least once. Obviously, the voters who are more likely to do this are:

- undecided voters
- independents
- mismatched partisans (partisans supporting the candidate of the opposing party)
- third party supporters.

If a candidate can identify the characteristics of these voters and then target them (all of which have practical implications), then using persuasive tactics the candidate can capture a considerable number of supporters.

The key battleground issues that shaped the 2008 campaign were:

- the state of the economy
- fuel and oil prices
- stem-cell research
- Iraq
- health-care reform
- gay marriages.

Many commentators believe that it was as much the case that McCain lost the election as Obama actually won. The key arguments that shaped the campaign and ultimately led to McCain's defeat are shown on the next page.

Learning objectives

- Factors influencing the presidential campaign
- Voting behaviour 2000–2008

Issue	Implications
Lack of finances	McCain could not compete with Barack Obama's $650 million (£403 million) campaign fund. By accepting federal funding (which Obama declined) he capped his general election campaign spending at $85 million (£53 million).
Loss of the airwaves	McCain could not compete with Obama's newsworthiness and dominance of television.
Competing in the wrong states	Obama always had the initiative and forced McCain to spend time and money in the wrong battlegrounds.
Bush factor	McCain as a Republican was tarnished by Bush's poor reputation, Obama kept on reminding people that McCain had supported Bush's policies.
Maverick	To cut himself from the Bush label, McCain had to appear different on issues, but this alienated elements in the party.
Conservative Republicans	Right-wing, evangelical Republicans who had got Mr Bush elected were unhappy about McCain, and they forced him to select a vice-presidential candidate who would reassure them.
Palin	She failed to impress in interviews, was tainted with corruption allegations and other problems, and proved to be a disaster.
Negative advertising	McCain ran only 10% more purely negative adverts than his rival, according to monitoring groups, but they were more deeply personal attacks.
Changing voice and image	McCain went from war hero, to the voice of experience, to maverick, to tax-cutter.
Town hall disaster	In the town hall televised debate setting, McCain wandered around and forgot that what may work in a real town hall does not work with a TV audience.
Lost debates	Obama was cool and unshakable in the presidential debates, McCain seemed barely able to compete, and when he confronted Obama on issues he seemed to lose his temper. However, most of the TV debates were considered a draw.
Economy	The Republican economic policies McCain had supported were in tatters during the campaign.
Past came to haunt him	All of his quotes from the past that contradicted what he was saying now were highlighted.
Man of the past, not the future	Even McCain's experience was against him as he was seen by many as too old and yesterday's man.
Taxation	McCain's tax plans seemed to favour the rich not the poor.
Suspended campaign	McCain's abrupt suspension of his campaign to return to Washington and 'fix the problem' (the growing financial crisis) seemed erratic and ineffectual.
Off message and poor appeal	McCain simply could not get his message across to the electorate and could not project the right kind of image in the face of a younger and more engaging opponent. Consistently Obama was compared to John F. Kennedy and certainly was the best campaigner since Bill Clinton.

Facebook

With the help of Facebook founder Chris Hughes – who devised an innovative internet fundraising system – the Obama campaign eventually attracted more than three million donors. They donated about $650 million (£403 million) – more than both presidential contenders in 2004 combined.

TV Advertising

TV advertising is the life-blood of a campaign which has to span some 3.5 million square miles (9 million sq km) and 300 million people, and Obama had no problem buying airtime.

Presidential campaigns

In the 2008 presidential election both Obama and McCain poured the majority of their resources into a handful of states that would ultimately decide the election. These are often referred to as Triple A states; that is, the traditional swing states, such as Pennsylvania, Florida and Ohio. Both candidates subjected themselves to crippling schedules, touring up and down the swing states. In Florida, for example, in the area around Orlando and Tampa there were 159,000 recorded Republicans and 157,000 recorded Democrats, showing just how tight the potential vote and the importance of campaigning.

Voting behaviour 2000–2008

The pattern in recent years was that most of the states on the east and west coasts voted Democrat and most of the others voted Republican. There were a number of states that could have gone either way, including Florida, Ohio and Pennsylvania (each with 20 or more electoral college votes); other swing states included Colorado, Indiana, Missouri, Nevada, New Mexico, North Carolina, North Dakota, Virginia and West Virginia. Interestingly, neither Virginia nor North Dakota had voted for a Democrat presidential candidate since 1964.

The first table below shows the results in the 2000 presidential election and the second in 2004.

Candidates	Votes	Vote (%)	States won	EV
Gore	50,996,116	48	21	266
Bush	50,456,169	48	30	271
Other	3,874,040	4	0	0

Candidates	Votes	Vote (%)	States won	EV
Bush (incumbent)	62,040,606	51	31	286
Kerry	59,028,109	48	19	252
Nader	411,304	1	0	0

These diagrams show voting behaviour by gender and political party in the 2004 presidential election.

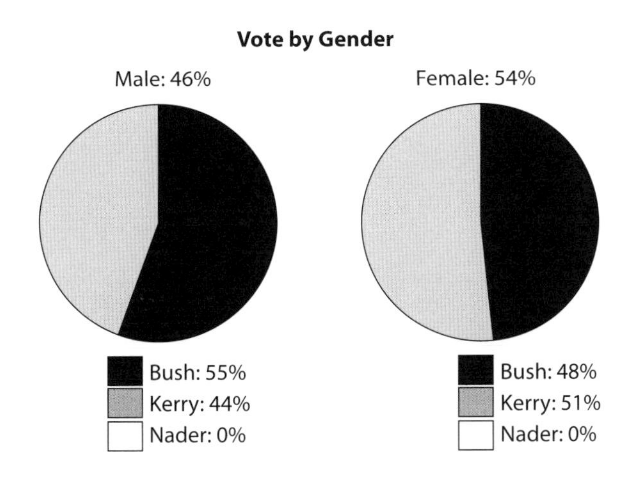

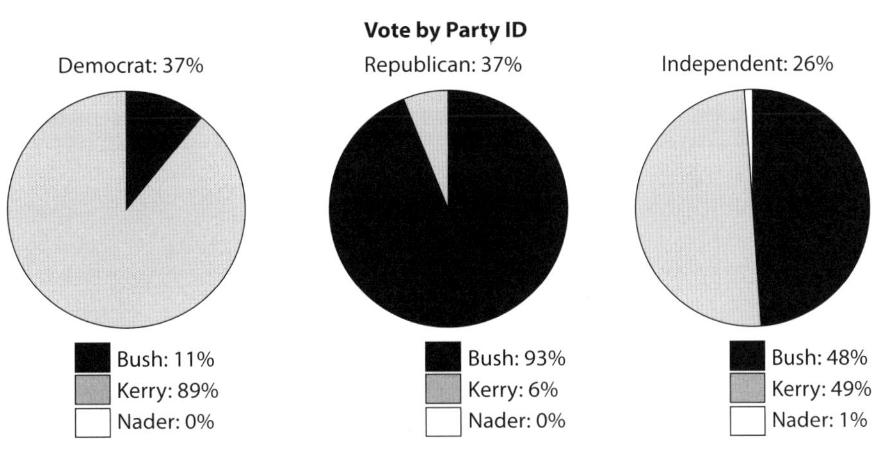

INTERNET RESEARCH

One of the best link and information portals on US politics can be found by going to www.heinemann.co.uk/hotlinks, inserting the express code 1825P and clicking on the relevant link.

The following table shows the results for the 2008 presidential election.

Candidates	Votes	Vote (%)	States won	EV
Obama	66,882,230	53	30	365
McCain	58,343,671	46	22	173
Nader	698,798	1	0	0

4.9 Presidential Elections (3)

Learning objectives

- The electoral college
- Distribution of 2004 and 2008 electoral votes
- Deciding the winner, results and controversies

The electoral college

The campaign to become president begins in earnest at the beginning of September and the voting takes place at the beginning of November. Strictly speaking, the US citizens do not actually vote for the president, but for lists of electors who will then decide who will become president. This has been the system used since the very beginning of an independent America.

Duncan Watts (*Understanding US/UK Government and Politics,* 2003) wrote:

> *The Founding Fathers wanted a method of choosing their president which would shun 'mob politics'. Democracy was then not yet in fashion, and as they were creating an elected office they wanted to ensure that they were not handing power to demagogues who could manipulate popular opinion. As Hamilton put it in the* Federalist Papers: *'The immediate election [of the president] should be made by men most capable of analysing the qualities needed for the office.'*

Each state was left to decide how these electors were chosen; some of the states decided to leave it to their own state assemblies to choose some of their own members as electors. In the early years, the electors actually met to discuss the relative qualities of the candidates and then elected a president by ballot with the runner-up becoming the vice-president. It was not until 1820 that the electors were directly chosen by the citizens. Today, electors are symbolic in a sense; they are usually party activists who have the privilege of casting their personal votes for the president at the beginning of December. However, because each of the states is separately represented, this means that there are still implications today.

Citizens cast their votes for their preferred presidential candidate, but not in a national election, rather in a state-wide election. Each state and Washington DC, has a number of electoral college votes allocated on the basis of the population. This is equal to the number of members the state has in the House of Representatives, plus two senators that they have in the Senate. As a result, California, for example, has 55 votes, smaller states may only have three.

The public votes directly for presidential candidates, not in one national election but through votes counted separately in the 50 states (plus Washington DC) rather than by a national majority.

There are 538 electoral college votes in total and to win a presidential candidate must win a minimum of 270. This means that there are 51 separate contests, each under the first-past-the-post system, with the winner claiming all of the electoral college votes in a state if they have a simple majority, even if this means that they have polled less than 50 per cent of the vote.

Congressional district method

Maine and Nebraska use a different method of distributing their electoral votes. It is known as the Congressional District Method. The states are divided into districts and one of its state-wide electoral votes is allocated to each district. The winner of the district is awarded that district's electoral vote. The winner of the state-wide vote is then given the state's two remaining electoral votes. Maine has used this method since 1972 and Nebraska since 1996.

Distribution of 2004 and 2008 electoral votes

The total electoral vote is 538 and the majority needed to elect a president is 270. The table on page 190 lists the allocation of votes in the 2004 and 2008 presidential election.

Deciding the winner, results and controversies

In the election each elector has one vote; a state with five electors will get five votes. If none of the candidates obtains 270 electoral votes, the 12th Amendment means that the election is then decided by the House of Representatives. The combined representatives of each state get one vote and a simple majority of states is required to win. This has only happened twice, when presidents Thomas Jefferson in 1801 and John Quincy Adams in 1825 were elected in this way.

For more consideration of the electoral college system see also 4.14, page 201.

State	2004 and 2008
Alabama	9
Alaska	3
Arizona	10
Arkansas	6
California	55
Colorado	9
Connecticut	7
Delaware	3
Washington DC	3
Florida	27
Georgia	15
Hawaii	4
Idaho	4
Illinois	21
Indiana	11
Iowa	7
Kansas	6
Kentucky	8
Louisiana	9
Maine	4
Maryland	10
Massachusetts	12
Michigan	17
Minnesota	10
Mississippi	6
Missouri	11
Montana	3
Nebraska	5
Nevada	5
New Hampshire	4
New Jersey	15
New Mexico	5
New York	31
North Carolina	15
North Dakota	3
Ohio	20
Oklahoma	7
Oregon	7
Pennsylvania	21
Rhode Island	4
South Carolina	8
South Dakota	3
Tennessee	11
Texas	34
Utah	5
Vermont	3
Virginia	13
Washington	11
West Virginia	5
Wisconsin	10
Wyoming	3

Even though the state electors are pledged to vote for the candidate of the party that chose them, there is nothing written in the Constitution that requires them to do so. In very rare cases, an elector will defect and not vote for their party's candidate. Such faithless votes rarely change the outcome of the election and the laws of some states prohibit electors from casting them.

By midnight on election day, one of the candidates will have almost certainly claimed victory and some will have conceded defeat. It is not until the first Monday after the second Wednesday in December, when the electors of the electoral college meet in their state capitals and cast their votes, does the US officially acquire a new president and vice-president elect.

Rogue electors

Also known as a 'faithless elector', a rogue elector is a member of an electoral college who does not cast his or her electoral vote for the person whom they have pledged to elect. On 158 occasions electors have cast their vote either for the president or vice-president contrary to their pledged vote.

It is perfectly possible for a candidate to fail to win a single vote in 39 of the states or in DC, yet they can still become president by winning the popular vote in 11 of the following 12 key states.

- California
- Florida
- Ohio
- North Carolina
- New York
- Pennsylvania
- Michigan
- Georgia
- Texas
- Illinois
- New Jersey
- Virginia

On three occasions, a presidential candidate has lost the nationwide popular vote, but has achieved a majority in the electoral college and has been confirmed as president. These occasions are shown in the following table.

Date	What happened?	Outcome
1876	There were a total of 369 electoral votes available with 185 needed to win. Republican Rutherford B. Hayes, with 4,036,298 popular votes, won 185 electoral votes. His main opponent, Democrat Samuel J. Tilden, won the popular vote with 4,300,590 votes, but won only 184 electoral votes.	Hayes was elected president.
1888	There were a total of 401 electoral votes available with 201 needed to win. Republican Benjamin Harrison, with 5,439,853 popular votes, won 233 electoral votes. His main opponent, Democrat Grover Cleveland, won the popular vote with 5,540,309 votes, but won only 168 electoral votes.	Harrison was elected president.
2000	There were a total of 538 electoral votes available with 270 needed to win. Republican George W. Bush, with 50,456,002 popular votes, won 271 electoral votes. His Democrat opponent, Al Gore, won the popular vote with 50,999,897 votes, but won only 266 electoral votes.	Bush was elected president.

INTERNET RESEARCH

The US National Archives has a superb resource centre on the electoral college system. To see this, go to www.heinemann.co.uk/hotlinks, insert express code 1825P and click on the relevant link.

The 2008 presidential election – the front runners, a comparison

For the first time in presidential election history both the candidates were sitting senators, Obama for Illinois and McCain for Arizona. It would therefore be the first time, regardless of the result, that a sitting senator had become president since John F. Kennedy in 1960, and in fact only the third time in US political history. Biden was also a sitting senator and had been for 36 years.

The following table outlines the key characteristics of the two candidates.

Barack Obama	John McCain
Graduate of Columbia University and Harvard Law School and first black president of the Harvard Law Review	Prisoner of war after capture in the Vietnam War
Worked as a community organiser and practised as a civil rights attorney	Entered politics in 1981
Served three terms from 1997 to 2004 in the Illinois Senate	Elected to the House of Representatives in 1982, serving two terms
Taught constitutional law at University of Chicago (1992–2004)	Became a senator in 1986, re-elected in 1992, 1998 and 2004
Failed to gain a seat in the House of Representatives in 2000	Considered a maverick
Elected to the Senate in November 2004	Championed campaign finance reform
In 109th Congress focused on legislation to control weapons and financial accountability	Chaired Senate Commerce Committee
In 110th Congress involved in the created of legislation related to lobbying and electoral fraud, climate change, nuclear terrorism, and care for military personnel returning from Iraq and Afghanistan	Sought nomination for the Republicans in 2000 and failed
Announced his candidacy for president on 10 February 2008	Nominated in 2008 and chose Sarah Palin (Governor of Alaska) as running mate
Became nominee for president on 3 June 2008	Attracted 59.2 million votes, the second highest total in US presidential history (after Obama)
Won the presidency race with 53% of the vote in November 2008	

Learning objectives

- The 2008 presidential election – the front runners, a comparison
- Why did Obama win?

The table below lists the presidential results after the 2008 election. It shows the electoral college rolls for the presidential, Senate and House of Representatives election, and for each of the states and Washington DC as the results were recorded in US eastern time.

Barack Obama 365 (53%)	**PRESIDENT**	**John McCain 173 (46%)**
Democrats 58* (+7)	**SENATE**	**Republicans 40 (-7)**
Democrats 256 (+20)	**HOUSE**	**Republicans 175 (-20)**

7:00 ET	**Obama**	**McCain**		**Obama**	**McCain**
Georgia (15)	**47%**	**52%**	South Carolina (8)	**45%**	**54%**
Indiana (11)	50%	49%	Vermont (3)	67%	32%
Kentucky (8)	**41%**	**58%**	Virginia (13)	53%	46%
7:30 ET	**Obama**	**McCain**		**Obama**	**McCain**
North Carolina (15)	50%	49%	Ohio (20)	51%	47%
West Virginia (5)	**43%**	**56%**			
8:00 ET	**Obama**	**McCain**		**Obama**	**McCain**
Alabama (9)	**39%**	**60%**	Massachusetts (12)	62%	36%
Connecticut (7)	61%	38%	Mississippi (6)	**43%**	**56%**
Delaware (3)	62%	37%	Missouri (11)	**49%**	**50%**
DC (3)	93%	7%	New Hampshire (4)	54%	45%
Florida (27)	51%	48%	New Jersey (15)	57%	42%
Illinois (21)	62%	37%	Oklahoma (7)	**34%**	**66%**
Maine (4)	58%	41%	Pennsylvania (21)	55%	44%
Maryland (10)	62%	37%	Tennessee (11)	**42%**	**57%**
8:30 ET	**Obama**	**McCain**		**Obama**	**McCain**
Arkansas (6)	**39%**	**59%**			
9:00 ET	**Obama**	**McCain**		**Obama**	**McCain**
Arizona (10)	**45%**	**54%**	New York (31)	62%	37%
Colorado (9)	53%	45%	North Dakota (3)	**45%**	**53%**
Kansas (6)	**41%**	**57%**	Rhode Island (4)	63%	35%
Louisiana (9)	**40%**	**59%**	South Dakota (3)	**45%**	**53%**
Michigan (17)	57%	41%	Texas (34)	**44%**	**56%**
Minnesota (10)	54%	44%	Wisconsin (10)	56%	42%
Nebraska (5)	**42%**	**57%**	Wyoming (3)	**33%**	**65%**
New Mexico (5)	57%	42%			
10:00 ET	**Obama**	**McCain**		**Obama**	**McCain**
Iowa (7)	54%	45%	Nevada (5)	55%	43%
Montana (3)	**47%**	**50%**	Utah (5)	**34%**	**63%**
11:00 ET	**Obama**	**McCain**		**Obama**	**McCain**
California (55)	61%	37%	Oregon (7)	57%	40%
Hawaii (4)	72%	27%	Washington (11)	57%	41%
Idaho (4)	**36%**	**62%**			
1:00 ET	**Obama**	**McCain**		**Obama**	**McCain**
Alaska (3)	**38%**	**60%**			

Why did Obama win?

The following table briefly outlines some of the key issues that propelled Obama to victory in November 2008.

Issue	Explanation
Voter age	Voters in the 18 to 24 age group exceeded 68% for Obama to 30% for John McCain, according to the exit polling. Those in the 25 to 29 age bracket were 69% to 29% in Obama's favour. McCain was only more popular in the 65 and over group, 54% to 44%.
Minorities	Minorities heavily supported Obama. African-Americans were 96% Obama and 3% McCain. Hispanics were 67% Obama and 30% McCain and Asian-Americans 63% Obama and 34% McCain. Hispanics flooded to Obama due to their disapproval of how Bush had been performing (80% said he was poor compared to 72% of all Americans). Race played a slightly less important role than age.
Candidate age	While Obama was to become the first African-American president, McCain would have been the oldest-ever president. Many voters cited this as a key reason for choosing Obama; on these grounds 78% went for Obama and 21% McCain.
Economy	This was the top issue with 62% of the voters.
Iraq war	This was second placed in importance. Those who picked the Iraq war as their top issue mostly voted for Obama in all but two states.
Health care and terrorism	These were tied at 9% as the most important issue, but for those that chose terrorism to be the top issue most voted for McCain.
First-time voters	These overwhelmingly voted for Obama (72%) compared to McCain (27%).
High-income voters	Among these, marginally more voted for Obama with 52% compared to 47% for McCain.
Taxation	Many voters said they expect a post-election tax increase, with 49% predicting their taxes will rise no matter who is elected president. An additional 22% said taxes will go up only if Obama wins and 12% said taxes will go up only if McCain wins. Only 15% thought there would be no change to taxes.
Government intervention and federal involvement	51% of voters thought that government should do more to solve problems. 43% thought it was doing too much. Only 40% supported the financial package to bail out the US financial system (both candidates were in favour of this).
Palin and Biden	The Republican vice-presidential nominee Sarah Palin was not liked. Some 60% of voters indicated that she was not qualified to become president, only 38% thought she was. Over two-thirds thought Biden was adequate and 31% not.
Early decision-making	Many voters had made up their minds early in the campaign season, with 61% claiming that they had made their minds up before September and 13% by the end of October; only 3% had made their minds up in the last three days before the election.
Hillary to Obama	Democrats who supported Hillary Clinton during the primaries voted for Obama in the general election, 84% to 15% for McCain.

Barack Obama, the first African-American presidential candidate, defeated his Republican rival John McCain to win the 2008 presidential election

Sarah Palin, Governor of Alaska, was the surprise choice as vice-presidential running mate to John McCain in the 2008 presidential election

INTERNET RESEARCH

To see current and archived political news stories and documentaries, go to www.heinemann.co.uk/hotlinks, insert express code 1825P and click on the relevant link. You will need Real Player to view them.

Learning objectives

- Congressional elections
- Process and significance
- Results

US Senate campaigns

A third of the 100 Senate seats are up for election every two years. In November 2008, 34 senators faced election. The winners would serve a six-year term until January 2015. When Senate elections coincide with a presidential one the Senate campaign is somewhat overshadowed. However it does not necessarily follow that the presidential results will be reflected in Senate results. In the 2008 election there were 13 key Senate races. Ultimately, the Democrats triumphed and sealed a Senate majority. This makes the fight for the seats as important to both parties as the outcome of the presidency. In many cases the incumbent senator will have something of an advantage, but when senators resign, retire or die there in no incumbent and therefore the race is far more open, as was the case in Nebraska, New Jersey, Nevada, New York and Florida.

Congressional elections

Elections for Congress are often as competitive and important as those for president. Unlike a parliamentary system where the chief executive is drawn from the ranks of the majority party, the US system has a separate electoral system for the legislature and the executive. The congressional election results can be vital to a president for the following reasons.

- The president may propose laws to Congress; they have to be drafted in Congress by his allies within that institution, and must be passed by the Congress before being sent back to the president for his signature.
- The House and Senate are legally and politically independent of the will of the president.
- Party discipline is less strictly observed in Congress in the American system than in the parliamentary system; this makes it easier for members of Congress to vote on policies as they see fit (particularly if they feel it will help their own re-election).
- Congressional leaders and the president must put together a winning coalition one member at a time, rather than count on automatic support from highly disciplined parties, so every single congressional win at election time is vital.

Even though the House and the Senate have virtually equal powers, the methods of election are very different. The House is designed to contain representatives who are closer to the people (in terms of opinions, wishes and ambitions). Consequently, the House is the larger of the two as it is made up of individuals from smaller legislative districts. The representatives must also face election more regularly (every two years). This means that to stay in touch with their electorate, representatives will invariably return to their districts every week to ensure continued contact and support.

Process and significance

Each of the House seats has a unique geographical constituency (just like the British system). Each member is therefore elected as the sole representative of that district by a plurality vote. Each of the states is guaranteed at least one seat, with the rest of the seats available on the basis of the population of that state. Each House seat represents a unique geographic constituency, and, as noted above, every member is elected as sole representative from that district by plurality rule. Each of the 50 states is assured of at least one seat in the House, with the rest allocated to the states according to population.

One study estimates that 14 seats would shift between the states following the April 2010 census.

Gain more than one	Gain one	Lose one		Lose more than one
Texas +4 Arizona +2 Florida +2	Georgia +1 Nevada +1 North Carolina +1 Oregon +1 South Carolina +1 Utah +1	California -1 Illinois -1 Iowa -1 Louisiana -1 Massachusetts -1	Michigan -1 Minnesota -1 Missouri -1 New Jersey -1 Pennsylvania -1	New York -2 Ohio -2

Following each ten-year census, the number of seats allocated to each of the states is recalculated to take into account changes in the population. State legislatures also redesign their congressional district boundaries to reflect the changes in the number of seats that have been allocated to them.

The Senate was originally designed so that its members represented the whole of the state and to provide equal representation for each state regardless of the size of the population. This means that smaller states have precisely the same amount of power and influence in the Senate as the larger ones.

When the 17th Amendment to the Constitution (1913) was made, senators were directly elected by their state's voters. Before that, they were selected by the state legislatures. Each state has two senators, elected for staggered six-year terms; this means that a third of the Senate is up for re-election every two years. Like the House, the senators are chosen by plurality vote.

In the past voters tended to be party-centred in congressional elections and with long-held loyalties, so they tended not to be swayed by individual personality and performance. However, more recently, the tendency is for the views and the personality of candidates to play an important role and the significance of party loyalty has diminished.

Many of the congressional contests over the past 50 years have been candidate-orientated, partly due to the increasing coverage and influence of the media, along with more aggressive fundraising, use of opinion polls and more modern forms of campaigning. Consequently, voters have more opportunity to compare candidates and consider their strengths and weaknesses.

Having said this, being an existing member of Congress is an enormous advantage and re-election rates are in excess of 90 per cent. Most members of Congress, while ignored by the national media, are heavily covered at state level and usually in a positive light by the media. Equally, with ongoing relationships with interest and lobby groups, the incumbents have a greater access to campaign funds.

Results

In the 2008 election, the Democrats registered a clear victory over the Republicans in both houses of Congress. In all, 435 seats in the House were up for election, while 35 of the Senate seats were available. In the House, the Democrats built on the 235 seats they had secured in the 2006 mid-term elections, making a net gain of at least 20 seats.

In the Senate the Democrats won 56 seats compared with 40 for the Republicans. Two other seats were taken by independents, who vote with the Democrats. This means that the Republicans still have blocking power in the Senate, as it requires 60 votes to end a filibuster. In other words, the Republicans can still block legislation.

The following shows the state of the parties in Congress after the 2006 elections.

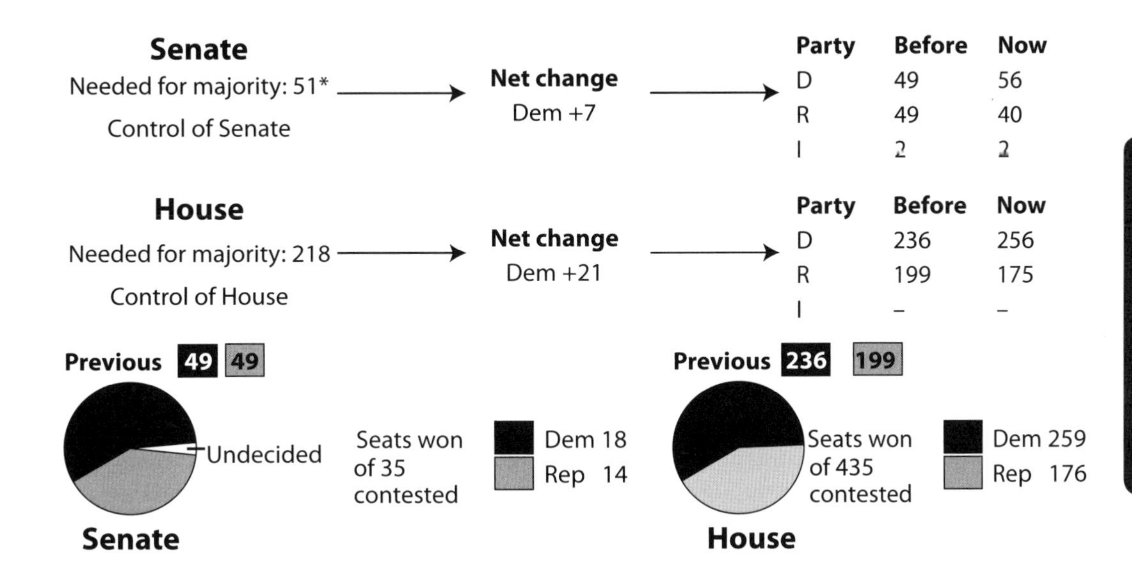

Mid-term elections

In every even numbered year the elections are held for the House of Representatives and either 33 or 34 Senate seats. Mid-term refers to elections that take place for Congress, state legislatures and governors in years when the presidential election does not take place. The next mid-term elections will take place in November 2010.

The last mid-term elections took place in November 2006, where turnout was relatively high and the Democrats won the majority of state governorships and the contested House and Senate seats. It was generally believed that the single, most important issue was the ongoing war in Iraq and specifically George W. Bush's handling of that war. He had only been re-elected in November 2004. Exit polls had suggested that a large number of the electorate had voted against the Republicans because of their personal opposition to Bush. One development that caused problems was the so-called robocalls. These were automated messages that were being sent to selected house districts, sometimes several times an hour and into the night, with negative messages about particular Democratic candidates.

INTERNET RESEARCH

The US Census Bureau has historical data on voting patterns for Congress dating back to the 1960s. To see this, go to www.heinemann.co.uk/hotlinks, insert express code 1825P and click on the relevant link.

4.12 Primaries and Caucuses

Learning objectives

- What happens before the first primaries and caucuses?
- How are candidates chosen in presidential primaries?

Question topic material

Note that these topics are not written in essay format, but they do include ideas, concepts and information and practices that you would need to think about if similar questions came up in an exam.

What happens before the first primaries and caucuses?

The term 'invisible primaries' was first suggested by Arthur T. Hadley in 1976. Hadley defined it as: 'That period of political time between the election of one president and the start of the first state primary to determine the next political candidates.'

This is the preliminary stage of the nomination process before the primaries when candidates aim to become the front runner for their party nominations and, above all, seek funds to bankroll their campaign.

In the 2008 presidential election, the early contenders in the invisible primaries were numerous. It is interesting to see how they were positioning themselves in 2005 well ahead of the primaries and often before they had made any public statement to the effect that they were standing for president. The table on page 197 shows this in more detail.

How are candidates chosen in presidential primaries?

Primaries are seen as the main way in which voters can learn about the candidates. Once the national conventions take place, the focus is usually on two candidates only, one from the Democrats and the other from the Republicans. In the primaries however, the voting public is introduced to a range of different candidates from either party, as well as to the third party candidates. The media also focuses in on the primaries and each of the candidates is likely to receive a fair amount of media attention. The primaries are designed to provide a platform for a free exchange of views and ideas and are seen as one of the main building blocks of US participatory democracy.

The primaries also act as a means by which the main candidates can build their platform of support for the November election. It is often the case that even if a candidate drops out during the last weeks of the primaries, but they proved to be popular in terms of policies and ideas with the electorate, that those still in the running will adopt elements of their ideas.

Primaries also give a large number of US citizens the opportunity to get involved in the process of choosing a potential leader; they galvanise the electorate and encourage first-time voters to participate. Although some states have dropped their primaries due to the costs and other factors, they still remain a vital part of the process.

How the primates and caucuses work

Primaries are held at all levels of government; essentially there are two variants.

- The closed primary in which only registered members of a party can vote.
- The open primary in which voters of one party can vote in another party's primary.

The presidential primaries at state level are there to indicate which candidate that state prefers and depending on state law, the voters will cast their ballots either directly for that candidate or for a delegate who is pledged to support that candidate at convention time.

Invisible primary candidate/party	Early signs	Genuine hopeful?	Actual decision
J. E. Bush/Republican	The twice-elected governor is prohibited by Florida state law from running again for the mansion house, but John Ellis Bush also publicly ruled himself out of the 2008 presidential race.	Despite encouragement from his father, he is adamant that 2012 may be a better option. Conventional wisdom suggests that the US public would not back another Bush. He would also suffer from association with the less popular and less successful policies of his older brother.	Maybe in 2012
Condoleezza Rice/ Republican	As the 66th US Secretary of State, she was well placed and a trusted adviser to the president.	As a black woman it could be a step too far for the US voters, but she would attract levels of black and female support for a Republican. But would she stand?	Never gave a sign that she would stand
Rudolph Giuliani/ Republican	In an interview on 2 October 2005, Giuliani revealed that he is preparing to stand in 2008.	The former mayor of New York and inspirational leader after the terrorist atrocities in the city.	Decided to run
John McCain/ Republican	The Arizona senator, is ex-services and popular in the party.	In October 2005 opinion polls showed the senator only narrowly behind Rice and Giuliani.	Republican candidate for president
Hillary Clinton/ Democrat	The early front runner and retained that position. Although the wife of Bill Clinton, she was successful in her own right.	In late September 2007 polls put her ahead of her Democrat rivals. Some 42% of voters believed she would make the best candidate, followed by John Edwards and John Kerry, both on 14%.	Failed to secure nomination and now Obama's Secretary of State
John Edwards/ Democrat	He failed against Kerry in 2004 due to perceived lack of experience.	He was eager for another attempt.	After a good initial showing was pushed into third place and dropped out in January 2008
John Kerry/Democrat	He failed against Bush in 2004 when his campaign suffered from disorganisation, confusing policy stances and his own negative image.	He was eager for another attempt.	Dropped out in January 2008
Joe Biden/Democrat	Biden is the most senior Democrat on the Foreign Relations Committee and is respected for his straight-talking approach.	He sought nomination in 1987, but perceived Hillary Clinton as too hard to beat on his own.	Became Obama's running mate and vice-president, never achieved good personal support
Barack Obama/ Democrat	He was a long shot, and the only African-American in the Senate.	At 42, Obama can look forward to more realistic challenges for the nomination in 2012 and 2016.	Nominated as Democrat candidate and won the election

To become the Democrat nominee for president, a candidate needs 2026 delegate votes. State primaries and caucuses select pledged delegates, who are obligated to vote for the candidate their state chose. Additional unpledged delegates consisting of party leaders and elected officials are free to vote for any candidate. Daily delegate totals reflect all delegates allotted to the state, even though some may not pledge their vote until a later date. To become the Republican nominee for president, a candidate needs to capture 1191 delegate votes.

Primaries and caucuses give registered voters the chance to influence a political party's nomination process. Each of the states has a certain number of delegates (based upon population). They will attend the national convention and vote to select the party nominee. When voters cast their ballot for a particular candidate, they are actually voting to allocate their state's delegates to each candidate. The Democratic Party system states that delegates are apportioned based upon the percentage of votes a candidate receives.

In addition to the pledged delegates, the Democrats have unpledged 'super delegates' who account for some 15 per cent of the total delegate pool. These individuals tend to be high-ranking party and elected officials, including governors, congressional representatives and DNC members. They have the freedom to nominate any candidate they choose and are not bound by the state's popular vote.

There are distinctions between primaries and caucuses. A primary is simply an election that allows voters to go to the polls and cast their ballot for a candidate. This determines the percentage of the state's delegates to each candidate. A caucus is a state convention or a public place for party members to gather. They will listen to speeches, and then vote for delegates to represent candidates at the national convention. Some states only allow voters to participate in their party's primary, while other states have no party restrictions and allow voters to participate in any one primary they choose.

4.13 The Voters

Learning objectives

- What factors have influenced the voting in recent presidential elections?

What factors have influenced the voting in recent presidential elections?

Political experts maintained in late October and early November 2008 that early voting was changing campaign strategy and voter behaviour like no other presidential race in history. Calculations by news organisations indicated that many, if not most, of the early votes in more than 30 states were cast by registered Democrats. Tucker Bounds, a McCain campaign spokesman, indicated that the Democrats had done a good job of motivating supporters to get to the polls in early voting states. He said: '[McCain] encourages it, but it's not the primary driver of our get-out-the-vote effort. And I think that's in sharp contrast to the Democrats, who have prioritised early voting.'

More broadly, voter turnout in the 2004 and 2008 elections showed a marked increase compared to the 1996 and 2000 figures. Voter registration has increased, while the general trend was for voter turnout to fall. During the period from the 1960s to the 1980s voter registration hovered around 65–70 per cent, from 1996 to 2000 it rose to 75 per cent. Despite this, turnout had not appreciably increased and since 1968 had been between 50–60 per cent; it was under that in 1996, but in 2008 it rose to 64.1 per cent.

A summary of the key factors that could influence voting in the presidential elections is outlined in the following table.

Influence	Explanation and consequences
Gender	Women are more likely to register and to vote than men and increasingly tend to support the Democratic Party.
Gender gap, issue- based	The gender gap is issue-based, and tends to reflect the fact that female voters are more inclined towards Democrat policies on education, abortion, gun control, capital punishment, welfare provision, environment and women's rights.
White voters	Traditionally, white voters have tended to support the Republicans. In 2004 Bush was supported by white voters by a margin of 57–42%. He led 61–38% of white males and 54–45% white females.
African-Americans	They have provided solid support for the Democrats since the passage of civil rights legislation in the 1960s; at least 80% of all African-Americans have voted for a Democrat candidate since 1956.
Hispanic	A growing, but divided group. Cuban-Americans tend to vote Republican, while Puerto Rican and Mexicans vote for the Democrats.
Religious groups	In the 2000 and 2004 elections some 63% of churchgoers supported Bush. Kerry and Gore received 64% of the voters who did not go to church.
Poor/rich households	There is a strong link between household income and partisan support. Lower-income households tend to support the Democrats; higher-income groups are more likely to be Republican (although many actually support Democrat civil liberties policies). While poorer households support federal welfare programmes and are therefore Democrats, a good number vote for the Republicans as they are conservative, isolationists and prefer more aggressive foreign policy approaches.
Age	Until the 2008 election there seemed to be little correlation, but the young and first-time voters support the Democrats (they tend to be more liberal on equality, gender and freedoms), however the turnout of the under-29s is traditionally low.
Independent voters	'Independents' are heavily influenced by the supposed experience, image, style and integrity of the candidates.

Influence	Explanation and consequences
Issues	In good times voters tend to back the incumbent candidate, while in bad times they tend to opt for the challenger. Key issues that can bring out voters are taxes, abortion, gay rights, school prayer, health care and gun control.
Converting vs galvanising	This is not so much about converting the opposing party's supporters, but getting existing supporters to come out and vote. However, it is important to convert independent supporters by squeezing out third party candidates.
Defection and partisan elections	Examples of defection were the landslide victory for the Republicans in 1972, when 33% of Democrat voters failed to vote for McGovern, and in 1984 when 21% failed to vote for Mondale when he ran. The 2000 and 2004 elections were very partisan with party support holding up well, with Bush retaining 91 per cent of Republicans and Gore 86% and Kerry 87% respectively retaining Democrats.
Voters' mood	In 1960 Kennedy won as voters wanted vitality, in 1968 Nixon won as they wanted an orderly government, in 1976 Carter won on the grounds of integrity, Reagan won in 1980 because they wanted strong leadership and in 1992 Clinton beat Bush as he had empathy with the voters.
Poll approval ratings	It is very influential for voters if the incumbent appears to have overwhelming approval in polls, in excess of 50%. Less than this suggests to voters that the incumbent is in trouble.
Wedge issues	The moral and righteous approach has been used as a key influencing feature if the candidate is seen to support 'family, faith and the flag'.
Exit polls	Given the different time zones, early exit polls can be highly influential if the contest appears to be heading in one direction; closer exit polls in the face of overwhelming opinion polls can cause voters to cast their ballots contrary to the predicted results.

Contemporary issues and the candidates' stances on these issues clearly play an important role in influencing voter behaviour as can seen in the following table relating to the situation in the US one month before the presidential election in November 2008.

Issue	McCain	Obama	Implications
Iraq	Voted for the 2003 invasion and has said US forces should remain until Iraq is able to defend itself	Opposed the war in Iraq from the outset and has said there is 'no military solution' to the situation	Fatigue with the war is high in the US, there is fear of another Vietnam
Economy	Put preserving America's economic freedoms at the heart of his campaign	Wants the interests of big business to be set aside and to focus on reforming health care and education	McCain was too closely associated with the failed policies of George G. W. Bush
National security	Backed the Patriot Act in 2001 and 2006	Has urged bipartisan cooperation on the issue, criticised the Patriot Act but voted to re-authorise it in 2006	Obama had clear advantage as he sat on the Senate Committee on Homeland Security and Governmental Affairs
Illegal immigration	Better border security, but was criticised for co-sponsoring a bipartisan bill which opponents claimed offers an amnesty to illegal immigrants	Better policed borders, highlighted the plight of illegal immigrants and wants stiffer penalties against those that employ them	Little difference, but slightly softer touch of Obama assisted in securing Hispanic vote
Health care	Supported reforms in health care	In favour of universal health care for all	Far more sweeping changes in Obama stance largely popular
Social issues	Mixed messages over abortion	Pro-choice for abortions and in favour of civil partnerships	Certainly attracted the female vote

4.14 The Electoral College

Is the electoral college system undemocratic and does the process of electing the president need reform?

Learning objectives

- Is the electoral college system undemocratic and does the process of electing the president need reform?

There are seven key criticisms of the electoral college system.

The winner-take-all system distorts representation.
The senatorial ECVs – electoral college votes – which states have regardless of population, distort representation.
The overall results are distorted, so popular votes do not translate accurately into ECVs.
The chances of a 'misfire' (i.e. the presidential candidate with less overall votes than his main rival actually wins) is a serious possibility.
The votes of citizens in some states are worth more than citizens in others and this has serious political consequences (e.g. politicians concentrate their attention on the biggest states).
The constitutional procedures for dealing with stalemate are unsatisfactory.
There is a potential problem of 'elector' betrayal.

The following table examines each of these issues in more detail.

Criticism	Examples
Electoral distortion	The operation of the winner-take-all system results in effective massive disenfranchisement of voters who support losing candidates. In 1996 there were 18 states where Clinton or Dole won all the EC (electoral college) votes of states with less than 50% of the vote.
Senatorial distortion	Each state has two EC votes to reflect its two senators, regardless of population. All states are not equally represented. An electoral vote in Wyoming corresponds to 151,196, while one in California corresponds to 551,112.
Overall distortion	The disparity between popular votes and electoral college votes can be enormous. The first presidential election of the 1980s produced the greatest disparity between electoral college votes and popular votes in the history of American presidential elections. In a three-way division of popular votes, Ronald Reagan saw his winning popular vote margin of 50.7% swell into a landslide 90.9% of ECVs. The disparity between Reagan's popular vote and electoral vote percentages was 40.2%, a new record for the 43 elections for which popular vote totals are available.
Misfire	A candidate could become president with fewer popular votes than his opponent. Even when one candidate has 1 million to 1.5 million votes more than his challenger, there is a one-in-four chance that the 'losing' candidate will win on ECVs. Until 2000, this had happened three times in American history (1824, 1876, 1888).
Votes worth more	The seven most populous states have 214 ECVs between them, about three-quarters of the total necessary to win the presidency. The political strategies of candidates are shaped by this. The electoral college focuses attention and resources on those large states. The political interests of the large, 'swingable' states are amply looked after; those of the other states are neglected.

Criticism	Examples
Stalemate	Arguably the procedures for dealing with a situation in which no candidate receives an absolute majority of the electoral college vote (i.e. 270) are unrepresentative. If the selection does go to the House of Representatives, under the terms of the constitution, each state has one vote, regardless of the size of its congressional delegation. The candidate with the most popular votes wins the election because his party controls a majority of the state delegations. Or the Republicans with a majority in the House but with the Democrats controlling a majority of the delegations. Or, the House picks a president of one party; the Senate picks a vice-president of the other party. The other possibility is that should the House fail to secure a majority for one of the candidates, the person chosen by the Senate as vice-president would become acting-president.
Electoral betrayal	The individual electoral college 'electors' may cast their vote for a candidate other than the one to whom they were pledged, thus denying the electorate's wishes. These votes are not formally cast until after the election.

There are several potential reform proposals, but the two key options are a direct vote or proportional representation.

Direct vote	Proportional representation
This has received the most attention and support. It is designed to eliminate the college entirely and count the votes on a nationwide basis, and electing the popular vote winner provided the winning candidate received a certain percentage of the total vote.	Keeping the present electoral vote allocation among the states, but those ECVs to be distributed among the candidates according to the proportion of the popular vote received, that is, a candidate receiving 50% of the popular vote in Nevada would receive 50% of the ECVs.
40% of the total vote would be necessary. If no one got the required percentage, a run-off between the top two candidates would be held to determine the winner.	If no candidate received at least 40% of the ECVs (50% plus 1 is currently needed), the members of the House and Senate, in joint sessions, and each with one vote, would select from the leading two candidates.
A direct popular vote would remedy a major problem of the present system – the possibility of electing a non-plurality president.	It would encourage greater two-party activity in one-party dominated states. Any increase in support for a party could be reflected in an increase in the number of ECVs received and encourage voter turnout.
The large competitive states would lose their ability to distort the political focus of the campaign.	It would not rule out the possibility of a candidate being elected with a minority of the popular vote. Given the increased opportunities offered to minority candidates to pick up ECVs there would be a strong possibility that most elections would be decided by Congress.
The provision for the situation in which no one received the required percentage of the popular vote has its drawbacks as well. A run-off election would extend the length of the campaign and add to costs. It would reduce the short transition period for a newly elected president and drain the time and energy of an incumbent seeking re-election.	Operating under a proportional plan would also make the electoral college vote much closer.
Turnout should improve because every vote would count in a direct election.	Had this plan been in effect in 1960, Richard Nixon could have defeated John Kennedy by 266.1 to 265.6.

Direct vote	Proportional representation
It might encourage spoiler candidacies. Third parties and independents seeking the presidency could exercise power in the event of a close contest between the major parties.	
The organised groups geographically concentrated in the large industrial states would have their votes diluted by a direct election.	
Republicans perceive that they benefit from the current arrangement, which provides more safe Republican states than Democrat ones.	

The following are arguments against reform.

Despite 2000, there is no evidence that the system will be changed, simply too many interests would lose by this. The system is based on the federal principle, which would be eroded by change. In the US fundamental reform is difficult to achieve as it requires constitutional amendment and all the alternatives have their own shortcomings. The current system puts stress on the states as units and emphasises the continued importance of the federal principle.

The unitary rule is praised for discouraging the growth of splinter groups, which might lead to more deadlock in the college and subsequent use of the House of Representatives to pick the president. It is claimed that the exaggeration of the winner's popular majority when translated into electoral votes helps to give added legitimacy to the presidency.

4.15 The Voting System

Learning objectives

- Do elections fulfil their functions?
- Are first-past-the-post elections more accurate?

Do elections fulfil their functions?

Elections can change governments or confirm governments in office. In parliamentary systems governments consist of members of political parties (either one party or a coalition of parties) and these parliamentary governments require the support of party majorities in the legislature. In Britain, elections confirmed Labour governments in 2001 and in 2005. In the US the presidential election confirmed the government of George W. Bush in 2004.

In many election campaigns the focus is on the choice of government, where voters are encouraged to vote for a party and a candidate will ask for votes on the basis of party affiliation. In this way elections allow the electorate to deliver a verdict on the policy proposals of competing parties, or on the past record of a government. Victory provides a mandate or a licence to implement policy proposals based on a manifesto.

Elections give legitimacy to governments and to the legislature that supports them. Elections also:

- offer an opportunity for public participation
- offer a means by which activists are recruited for political careers
- contribute to political education of the public.

Are first-past-the-post elections more accurate?

The proportionality of a voting system reflects how accurately it translates votes cast into seats won at an election. The closer the percentage of votes is to the percentage of seats won, the more proportional the system. First-past-the-post scores very badly on proportionality. FPTP fails to produce proportional results because, as candidates do not need to obtain an overall majority of votes cast in their constituencies to be elected (over 50 per cent), a large number of votes are 'wasted' – that is, they do not go towards the election of any candidate.

Other key issues include the following.

- Because of the wasted vote problem, a gulf exists between the popular vote a party receives and the number of seats it receives.
- The 'cost' in votes per seat varies greatly from party to party, election to election.
- FPTP tends to favour the two main parties and makes it difficult for smaller parties to gain representation that reflects their support. The system performs worse than any other voting system in distributing seats according to a party's national share of the vote. Under FPTP, a small party whose votes are evenly spread geographically may receive a significant share of the vote nationwide without winning many seats. Conversely, concentrated support for a party produces results.
- Regional and national imbalance is another consequence of the wasted vote.
- Because the distribution of votes is important, there is no logical connection between votes gained and seats won and it is possible for a party to win less popular votes than it did at a previous election but win more seats. It is even possible for a party gaining less popular votes to win more seats than its main rival.

- The support for both the major parties has declined in Britain, yet this has not been accurately reflected in the percentage of seats the two biggest parties hold – still around 85–90 per cent. This is because both major parties have many safe seats, that is, ones where they have big concentrations of their supporters and win by large margins. The support of the 'third' party, the Liberal Democrats, is much more evenly spread.

The case for and against FPTP is shown in the following table.

For	Against
FPTP is simple to understand both for the voters and for the counting of votes.	It is unfair, unrepresentative and therefore undemocratic.
The central point which defenders of both the political right and left believe is of crucial importance is that FPTP encourages single-party majorities. The electoral system tends to magnify the winning party's victory when popular votes are translated into seats.	Robert Blackburn in *The Electoral System* argued 'Even the former prime minister, Margaret Thatcher, at the height of her political triumph after the 1983 election, with a huge Commons majority of 397 seats to Labour's 209, had, in fact, been rejected by 57.6% of all voters in the country.' Governments can effectively implement policies, however radical and unpopular, against the wishes of the majority of the electorate.
The electoral system encourages, supports and reinforces the concept of a general election as an electoral choice between two alternative teams of political leaders.	Professor Sir William Wade said, 'if it is accepted that a democratic parliament ought to represent so far as possible the preferences of the voters, this system is probably the worst that could be devised'.
The system gives wide-ranging powers even though a government rarely has 50% plus of popular votes. Decisions are taken within a cohesive framework of principle and priorities because of the ideological nature of the political parties.	Because constituency parties choose only one candidate, parties are not choosing female candidates or those from minority ethnic groups to fight 'winnable' seats.
It can be clearly seen who is responsible for government decisions, and the cabinet can be held accountable through parliamentary procedures and, ultimately, at the next election.	FPTP is about confrontation politics and elective dictatorship. The British party system leads to confrontation, limits rational debate, and compromise.
There is normally a clear connection between general elections and government formation in the sense that there is no post-election bargaining between parties for office.	The workings of the House of Commons are dominated by the clash of parties and each issue becomes a 'trial of strength'. This means weakness because the ability to check and scrutinise the executive is limited. Few checks on a government with a majority leads to an 'elective dictatorship'.
A simple transfer of power, that is, the 'Ins and Outs' of government, are regulated by the decision of the electorate even when the popular vote is close and thus there are only rarely constitutional problems in forming governments.	Policies are initiated, justified and opposed on 'party' lines and votes in the House of Commons are almost always occasions at which party 'loyalty' expresses itself.
It produces a mandate that is a grant of authority from the electorate. The winning party claims popular consent for its programme. The twin doctrines of manifesto and mandate are central to the quality of British government.	FPTP does not necessarily deliver stable government. Although governments often have large majorities this is not always true. In 1964–66, 1974–79 and 1992–97 governments had very small or no overall majority.
MPs are a channel through which ordinary people can protect their interests and many MPs make a career of being a good constituency MP.	
Britain's democracy is one of the strongest in the world, it works and since no system is perfect, why should we go through the massive overhaul of changing?	

4.16 Voting Behaviour

Learning objectives

- Is there no single theory of voting behaviour that can explain voting preferences?
- Analyse the view that money and the media play too great a role in elections

Is there no single theory of voting behaviour that can explain voting preferences?

There are many different theories of voting behaviour. None of them by themselves can fully and permanently explain voting preferences; at best they may help us understand a particular phase or episode in voting behaviour. To understand voting behaviour and voting preferences, it is important to appreciate that this involves a combination of different theories. The scientific study of voting behaviour, known as psephology, aims to help in the understanding of voter preferences and in the prediction of election results.

Approach	Explanation
Party identification	This is based on a psychological attachment to a party; it is less significant than in the past in Britain and has never been a major feature in the US.
Political socialisation	Voting along family, neighbourhood or occupation lines (also educational) is less significant as voters are more independent and better informed by the media than ever before. It presumes that early political socialisation occurs within the family and is reinforced by other factors throughout life.
Partisan de-alignment	This aims to explain the fall in party identification and habitual voting processes in recent years.
Sociological models	This suggests that voting behaviour is linked to the economic and social position of a particular group that the voter belongs to, including their social class, gender, ethnicity, religion and region. To some extent this may be a partially viable explanation, it does however ignore the influences of individual and self-interest.
Rational choice	There is empirical evidence to suggest that while the sociological and the party identifications have declined, individuals are tending to cast their votes according to personal self-interest.
Issue voting	Contemporary issues can have a major impact on the voting behaviour of individuals, particularly if they had been undecided or have been radically affected or influenced by current issues. This also applies to personal interests or concerns in certain areas such the environment.
Dominant ideology	In some ways this is similar to the sociological approach, but the focus is on the concept of social conditioning, usually through the media or the influence of key interest groups. It is suggested that the media and the interests dominate and manipulate perceptions and voting behaviour, and have considerable control and influence over the voting patterns, behaviours and preferences.

Analyse the view that money and the media play too great a role in elections

The media and election coverage

Many analysts believe that the mass media has too much influence on the democratic process and the outcome of general elections, by manipulating readers, viewers and listeners. In an election campaign, the media is likely to feature the following.

- Opinion polls – these are commissioned by the media, on which they will comment or report on the results of opinion polls commissioned by other groups.
- Policy articles – these are articles that feature, compare and comment on party policy.
- Personalities – these are features examining the characteristics (positive and negative) of candidates, the leading party figures and influential supporters.
- Opinion pieces – these are written commentaries in the media identifying what they regard as the important issues and priorities, rather than those selected by the parties.

During an election campaign political parties will seek positive media coverage for themselves, regardless of the depth or quality of that coverage, and attempt to minimise or instantly quash any negative comment and views.

The media in shaping voting behaviour

Many politicians, activists and analysts believe the media is biased and manipulative, seeking to shape voting behaviour, rather than reflecting the existing voting preferences of their audiences. Three distinct views of the media have been put forward.

- Manipulative theory – the media is controlled by a small powerful elite of individuals or groups whose interests are in protecting their power, therefore they will use that power to influence voters to vote for a party that better suits their interests.
- Dominant power theory – those in the media have shared views based on their class, age and education. Whether they are aware of it or not, they write or broadcast biased or prejudiced views that support the establishment.
- Pluralist theory – the media only ever reflects public opinion, it does not shape it. There is a broad range of media output, so different parts of the media are impossible to control or manipulate. In any case, voters are rational, educated and adult, and too sophisticated to be manipulated.

Election funding

In the US, campaign funding consists of 'hard money', from political donations that are regulated by law through the Federal Election Commission, and 'soft money', which is donated to political parties in a way that leaves the contribution unregulated. In 1978, the Federal Election Commission issued an administrative ruling stating that the funding rules established by law only applied to political campaigns. They did not apply to 'party building' activities. Parties ignored it until 1988, but then the loophole was used extensively to top up election funds. To limit the wealthy candidates from having an unfair advantage, legislation sets guidelines on how much money candidates can spend. In Buckley vs Valeo (1976) the Supreme Court held that because campaign finance reform was an important safeguard against corruption, it is within the

Constitution to restrict how much money someone can donate to a campaign. Furthermore, it decided that as wealthy candidates cannot bribe themselves by restricting what a candidate can spend it would therefore not prevent corruption and would be an unconstitutional restriction of free speech.

The Bipartisan Campaign Reform Act of 2002 (BCRA) restricts campaign funding and advertising. Effectively it banned soft money and stopped parties using it to back candidates. However, as far as campaign finance reform opponents are concerned this means that there are limits to freedom of speech. Voters will not vote for an unknown politician who needs funds to advertise themselves, so limiting where the funds come from means limiting free speech. Opponents of reform also contend that it makes the media more powerful. The media can say what it wants about candidates, so those who believe that the media influences public opinion are concerned about the effects of media bias during a campaign.

Election expenditure

US election campaigns represent a multi-billion dollar industry. They are often dominated by professional political consultants. These are taken on by the candidates themselves. Parties do play a role in fundraising and drafting individuals in to run campaigns, but the majority of the work is directed by the candidates themselves. The US campaigns have become very reliant on the broadcast media and on direct mail. Smaller, lower cost campaigns use direct mail and what is known as lawn signs, which are literally signs placed in the front gardens of the supporters of the candidates or near to polling stations on election days. Rising costs discourage those without good financial connections. Money that is raised and spent is often derived from political action committees, although increasingly there is what is known as independent expenditure, which is carried out by political party committees, groups and PACs, taking the form of advertising and is made without the cooperation, approval or direct knowledge of specific candidates. There is, however, a feeling that television advertising is not as effective as it has been in the past. The Internet is becoming increasingly important and even text messaging was used in 2008.

Are elections decided by record in office rather than the election campaign?

The influence of performance

Voting behaviour can be influenced by actual performance or record, as it can be by the electorates' perception of a party's policy being the solution to a key issue. A party in power has, depending on the circumstances, a major advantage or disadvantage in terms of their record. The electorate can make the judgement as to how they handled a situation in the recent past. For a party in opposition, proof of a consistent and reliable record is more problematic. Often the electorate will judge them on the distant past (regardless of changes in leadership, direction and personnel), or simply the party's performance as an opposition party.

A political party's record is therefore judged in two different ways.

- Prospectively – the party needs to convince voters that in spite of, or because of, the party's record they can expect a positive future if they vote for them in the election.
- Retrospectively – the party relies on the positives of their past record to convince the electorate that they have the proven qualities to govern the country.

Other factors can undermine any attempt to trade on the record of the party. These factors include:

- policy failures (or radical policy changes)
- weak leadership
- a sense of lack of direction
- party disunity
- trustworthiness.

The British political parties' record and the last three elections reveal the following.

- In 1997 the voters had a negative view of the Conservative Party's performance in government.
- In 2001 voter satisfaction with Labour's performance was in decline, but still sufficiently high to return them to power.
- In 2005 voter satisfaction with Labour continued to decline, and the Conservatives were judged on the their last period in power (eight years before).

Party performance and voter perceptions are short-term factors impacting on voting behaviour. These factors refer to the electorate's opinion on how parties have proved themselves as being able to manage the economy or govern the country.

The influence of policies and competence

Voter opinion on party preference has fluctuated, but so too has the key political topics. There have been divisions between Labour and Conservative on policy areas such as devolution, Europe and asylum seekers, but rarely have they caused large numbers of voters to change their allegiance. In recent elections the major issues have been the economy, health and education. According to opinion polls in the period 1997 to 2005 the Labour Party's competence in key

Learning objectives

- Are elections decided by record in office rather than the election campaign?
- Is the election of modern politicians determined by image?

House of Representatives campaigns

Every two years all 435 seats in the House of Representatives are contested. The winners of the 2008 election will serve from January 2009 until January 2011 and form the 111th US Congress. Money is incredibly important, along with connections, in either achieving election or re-election to the House of Representatives. Political action committees are very important in raising money and galvanising support. Aside from seeking votes from the electorate, each of the candidates must try to raise finances, in order to pay for the sometimes expensive and extravagant electioneering. One of the early races and indications of likely success is how well each candidate does in being able to attract funds.

areas was perceived to be greater than the Conservatives. In their strong traditional policy areas, such as law and order, the Conservatives fell behind Labour. Labour was seen as being competent in running the economy. By 2001 to 2005 the two leading parties had formulated similar policies on major issues. This meant that voters based their choice of party preference not on policy difference, but on their perceptions of how each party would cope with the challenges.

Dramatic events can change voters' views on a party's competence and this can sometimes even have a long-term positive or negative impact on their perceptions of the party (regardless of how long these perceptions were factors in their voting decisions).

Parties are judged on their past record, as well as on their prospective performances in the future and these cross over. A positive performance by a party in the past may influence the electorate's perception of how the party might perform positively in future years and therefore increase the party's prospects of winning future elections. A negative performance could damage a party's prospects of winning a future election.

Is the election of modern politicians determined by image?

Since 1992 the Labour Party and the Conservatives have had five leaders between them, with the Liberal Democrats having three. Party leaders rarely retain their position for long, recent notable exceptions being Margaret Thatcher, who survived for 15 years, and Tony Blair, who lasted 13 years.

Since William Hague replaced John Major, only two of the Conservative Party leaders (Hague and Howard) have tested their popularity in a general election. Iain Duncan Smith was replaced before the 2005 election and David Cameron has yet to fight one. This suggests that failure at a general election is not the only reason why a party leader may be deposed. Voters have their own perceptions of the personality or competence of a party leader; events, the media and personal experiences that are affected by a leader's decision can influence those perceptions.

Changes in the class structure and party de-alignment have raised the question of party leadership to the political foreground. Long-term factors, such as the class structure, are less important in elections, whereas short-term ones, like party leadership, play a significant role.

With the media focusing so much on personalities rather than policies, the question of party leadership has escalated in importance at each election since the 1970s. During the last three elections, the following party leadership issues were clear.

- In 1997 Tony Blair's rating as a leader, in the opinion polls and in positive media coverage, was a factor in ensuring a Labour victory.
- In 2001 an *Observer* pre-election poll reported that 54 per cent of voters believed Tony Blair would make the best prime minister compared to the Conservative Party leader, William Hague, who lagged behind on 18 per cent. Blair was given a 56 per cent approval rating for his ability to do his job and Hague was on 25 per cent.

A recent poll by MORI, looking at the period 1997 to 2007, the time during which Tony Blair was prime minister, revealed certain aspects of party leadership and voter views. These are outlined in the table.

Factor	Explanation and relevance
Comparison with Cameron	Blair's satisfaction rating was two points lower than Cameron's in the month before he resigned. This suggests that a significant number of voters still supported him after 10 years in power.
Approval of electorate	When Margaret Thatcher resigned her satisfaction rating was 46%. When Blair resigned his was 28%, suggesting that Blair's popularity was waning and voters wanted change.
Out of touch?	In October 1997, 6% of the electorate thought Blair was out of touch with ordinary people; by the time he resigned this had risen to 51% (when Thatcher left office it was 63%). This suggests long periods of power lead to this gulf between the leader and the electorate.
Trustworthy?	In October 2000, 46% of the electorate thought they could trust Blair. By September 2006 this had dropped to 29% and was a major factor in the drop in Blair's popularity.
Good at the job?	In September 1997, 54% of Conservative voters thought Blair was doing a good job. By 2007 this had dropped to 12%. The Labour Party was losing potential voters who were defecting back to the Conservatives. In 1997 89% of Labour voters thought he was doing a good job. Ten years later it was 51%. This might explain the gradual fall in the majority enjoyed by the Labour Party between 1997 and 2005.

It is difficult to separate voters' views of a party leader from their overall views of that party. However party image is difficult to assess, as it brings in issues such as policies, history, structure, range of key figures and the influence of the mass media.

It becomes even more difficult to separate them when their policies are not too dissimilar. The image of the party is one of the key determining factors in separating the parties, in seeing them as sufficiently distinct; if the party has a strong, positive image it can give them a major advantage.

Leaders are crucial to 'selling' the party to the electorate. If a leader or the main spokespersons of the party are perceived as inadequate, voters are unlikely to be persuaded to vote for the party. If the key figures are perceived as strong, competent, trustworthy and hard-working, the party's overall image is positive.

Exam Café

Relax, refresh, result!

Relax and prepare

Questions for the exam are likely to be drawn from the following topic areas or similar. Use these to help focus on what areas of the subject you should be revising.

- The nomination process (the invisible primary, primaries and caucuses, the national party conventions), the campaign, voting behaviour and the electoral college.
- The outcome and significance of congressional elections.

The following suggestions will also help.

- Look at past questions in order to identify issues for debate surrounding the above topics.
- Try to focus on the most recent elections as much as possible.

Refresh your memory

When revising this topic, try the following exercises. They will help you structure your notes and give you a guide as to what you will need to know for the different papers. Remember to work through unit F853 first as this will provide the base you will need for F855.

- Consider the differences between US and UK elections. This could centre on the nomination process but also consider issues relating to timing, duration and finance.
- Identify the role played by the invisible or hidden primary before the nomination process starts officially with the Iowa caucus.
- Assess the significance of the Iowa caucus and New Hampshire primary and Super Duper Tuesday.
- Consider whether the system selects good candidates in terms of the qualities needed to be a good president and whether the system should be reformed.
- Outline the key developments during a presidential campaign. This might include references to keynote speeches at the national party convention, the selection of running mates, TV debates, fundraising and advertising, as well key issues during the run up to the election.
- Examine the workings of the electoral college in order to determine whether or not the process is in need of reform.
- Collate data on the most important factors influencing voting behaviour. Consider the extent to which there have been changes since the 2004 and 2006 elections and the degree of volatility in the vote. Examine the rank importance of issues and the significance of short-term factors such as region, race, religion and gender.

- When discussing the impact of the media, consider the debate surrounding its impact, for example the filter and reinforcement effects.
- Contrast the votes in the electoral college with actual voting and consider the role played by large and swing states.

Exam tips

These are some reasons why students do badly in exams. They provide a guide to what you need to avoid and by implication what you need to do to perform well in the exam.

- They do not always realise the difference between the *selection* of a presidential candidate and the *election* of a president.
- They cannot discuss in detail recent elections and developments.
- They do not pay sufficient attention to the wording in the question.

Get the result!

These are some ideas to help you in your revision and to keep up to date with the latest developments in US politics.

- Use the nominations and elections of 2008 as much as possible to inform your discussion.
- Prepare a list of key developments during the 2008 campaign such as the Denver speech of Obama, the selection of Palin and Biden and the reasoning behind it, Obama's fundraising and subsequent advertising boost and organisational advantage and the impact of the 'credit crunch/recession'.
- If discussing the media make sure you provide American examples such as references to *Saturday Night Live* and the Palin impression, appearances on Letterman, Leno and the *Daily Show*, press endorsements from the *New York Times* etc.
- See the candidates' TV advertisements on YouTube and Facebook.
- See the websites of the BBC, *Guardian*, *New York Times* and *Washington Post* for their in-depth election specials.
- See 538.com for details on the election and the electoral college.
- Sites like Wikipedia are useful although a degree of caution needs to be exercised with regard to some of the views expressed and the accuracy of some of the statistics offered. As a general rule, the site is a valuable research tool but should not be quoted for exam purposes.
- At A2, the words in the question are critical and if these are not given sufficient attention a candidate can write an essay that lacks focus. Recently a question asked if the electoral college was 'undemocratic and unnecessary'. Most students offered their standard essay on the merits and faults of the college without paying much attention to the word 'necessary'. This was a vital part of the question which needed to be considered in order to reach the higher mark bands as it invited a discussion of alternatives and possible reforms.

In Focus – F855

The following will help you in revising and in developing your knowledge at this level in order to gain a higher mark. These are the key areas to focus on.

- For the synoptic paper, consideration will need to be given to the arguments surrounding electoral systems. For the sake of contrast, the use of first-past-the-post in the UK and the US will need to be considered against alternatives such as AMS in Scotland, Wales and Germany, the second ballot in French presidential elections and list systems as used for the European Parliament and the Israeli Knesset.
- Keep an eye out for any other elections which occur during the course of your studies with a view to incorporating them into discussion of elections, party systems and relations between executives and legislatures.
- It might be useful to separate the functions of elections in any assessment of their worth. Plurality and majoritarian systems may be lacking in terms of representation and participation but may be regarded as highly efficient in terms of selecting a government and vice versa with regard to proportional systems.
- Parallels can be drawn between British and American voting behaviour. De-alignment in both countries (mention the decline of the New Deal coalition and absence of Republican realignment despite the best efforts of Rove in the Bush era) has meant that short-term factors, such as the media, campaign, personality and issues, have become more important in both countries.
- Note however that in the US, long-term factors, such as race, region, religion and gender, still play a significant role.
- Similarly, income (in the US) and class (in the UK as much as it can be defined) can still be regarded as the best indicator of voting behaviour in both countries.
- However, voting behaviour remains an individual act and what is important to one person may not register with another, for example some may despise Cameron and others admire him. Consequently there are those who question the validity of voting behaviour as an exact science.
- Avoid too much historical discussion of past trends and elections. The role of the media in the 1992 election (*'It's the Sun wot won it!'*) and even class de-alignment is a bit dated now. Similarly the daisy chain advertisement came from the 1964 presidential election.
- Place more emphasis on the most recent trends evident from recent elections such as declining voter turnout in the UK, its causes and solutions.

THE JUICE BAR
LEMON SURPRISE
MANGO MADNESS
THE APPLE

5 Supreme Court and Judiciaries

The US Supreme Court is one of the three key separated powers of US government. It has considerable political influence. It protects the Constitution, the rule of law and is determined to ensure its judicial independence. Its membership, while determined by the president, is subject to approval by the US Senate. The nine justices represent the highest court in the US. Their membership is drawn from experienced individuals who have been involved in the judiciary for many years.

The Supreme Court has been instrumental in the development of the rights of states and of individuals. However, while it is involved in judicial review and in some cases judicial activism, its involvement is largely determined by cases that are referred to it. In this respect it will rule on cases that are believed to be at variance with the constitutional rights of individuals or groups in the US.

In effect, the judiciary as a whole undertakes the role of enforcing the legislation of the US. They are separate from the executive and the legislature, as they are the elements of the government that devise and make the laws. The judiciary does not have the power to create law, but simply to interpret the meaning of existing law.

There are nine key themes in this chapter.

- Functions of the judiciaries and their political influence
- The rule of law and judicial independence
- Membership and appointment
- Courts, democracy and accountability
- Activism and restraint
- Judicial relationships
- Judiciary and rights
- Judiciary and the Constitution
- Contemporary issues

These are represented by the nine topics, and these are supported by one question topic for F853, looking at the most common essay titles, and three F855 question topics, which again look at popular essay themes in the examination.

This chapter contains 13 topics in total, representing the following.

The chapter is rounded off with an exam café feature on page 248.

5.1 Functions of the Judiciaries and their Political Influence

Learning objectives

- The role in theory
- Judges' political influence and significance
- The US system

The role in theory

The judiciary is a branch of the government. It is responsible for the interpretation of law and dealing with disputes between parties (individuals, groups, organisations and parts of the government, etc.).

In theory, their role is:

- to peacefully resolve disputes between individuals, making adjudications (decisions) within the limits of the existing law
- to interpret the law in order to determine what it actually means and how it applies to particular cases
- to uphold the law and the will of the legislature but because of the checks and balances and the separation of powers they do not always carry out the will of the legislature
- to act as guardians of the law, taking the responsibility for applying its rules
- securing the liberties of individuals
- ensuring that governments comply with the spirit of the Constitution
- to carry out judicial review of particular laws
- to occasionally chair enquiries (independent investigations)
- in Britain, to sit in the House of Lords (if they are Law Lords – until the Supreme Court is created in 2009).

The separation of powers means that the judiciary takes the role of enforcing the legislation whereas it is the role of the executive and the legislature to devise and make laws.

The judiciary examines cases when individuals or organisations have been accused of breaking the law. Their role is then to make a judgement as to whether or not this is the case. In theory, the judiciary is independent of the executive and the legislature. In other words, any judgements made should not be under the direction or control of the executive or legislature. In turn, the judiciary does not have the power to create law, but simply to interpret the meaning of existing law.

Judges' political influence and significance

The judiciary in Britain focuses on the interpretation of law, such as whether or not an individual or organisation has actually operated within the law. According to H Davis (1995) the law was a set of general rules. These general rules had been created by the legislature. The laws themselves are then transformed into policies and then enforced by the executive. The laws and the policies apply to general situations, rather than specific cases. This therefore leaves the judiciary with the interpretation of those general laws.

In other words, judges need to apply a particular 'general rule' to a specific case, interpreting the law as it applies to that case. If a senior court makes a particular interpretation the lower courts are bound by that interpretation (called the principle of precedent). Law made by judges is called common law.

Judges are also required to administer the law. This means that if an individual or an organisation has been found to break the law, the judge has to determine the punishment.

Judges can and in fact have a political role in two senses.

- They can be asked to decide whether a prosecution should be made against an individual or an organisation. In 2001 the High Court was asked whether it was legal for Steven Byers (then the Secretary of State for Transport) to sack the head of London Transport (Bob Kiley), as the devolved London Assembly had appointed him to the position. This was a political debate.
- They can also be asked to undertake a judicial review to consider whether central or local government has acted in a lawful manner. This too is seen as a political role as it could affect, very directly, the policies and practices of the executive.

Judges are also involved in the legislature (the Law Lords directly, as they sit in the House of Lords until at least 2008). In any case, according to H Davis (1995), senior judges contribute to debates on controversial government policies through speechmaking or the writing of articles. It is also the case that government will appoint judges to lead enquiries into controversial issues and then to take the judges' conclusions into account when framing future legislation.

Another, newer role for judges, now that Britain has incorporated the European Convention on Human Rights (by passing the Human Rights Act), is making sure that no government legislation is a breach of the convention. The judiciary now rules whether legislation is compatible with the convention, although due to parliamentary sovereignty they cannot stop a government or parliamentary Act, as they do not have the power of judicial review.

One of the major issues over the judiciary's role is the right to interpret legislation. In theory, legislation (or general rules) has been created by democratically elected governments that have been given the mandate to do so by the electorate. What right then do unelected individuals have to interpret these general rules? Does it mean that judges interpreting the rules could place a completely different meaning on the legislation than was intended?

This goes to the heart of the role of the judiciary. Generally there are three ways of looking at it.

- Firstly, according to Lord Devlin, judges should never make interpretations that effectively make new laws; they are not reformers of the law.
- Secondly, according to Lord Denning, the sole purpose of the judiciary is to ensure that justice is done. If this means new interpretations or even overturning laws then this should happen. Judges should take into account what parliament may have intended the law to achieve.
- Thirdly, judges should do what is right, regardless of the consequences.

As we will see, the debate over the role of judges and the influences on them continues, despite considerable attempts to clarify their actual role in practice.

The US system

One of the elements of the US legal system that makes it so complex is that both the federal government and each state has its own judicial system. Each judicial system is marked by differences in function and operation. There is also overlapping jurisdiction and so the fact that any court may hear issues of federal and state law only complicates matters. The court systems in the United States are similar in most fundamental ways; they are courts of general jurisdiction.

Each system is hierarchical in the form of a pyramidal structure, allowing review and if required revision by upper-level courts. A brief view of the court structure can be seen in the table.

Court system	Brief explanation
Federal	The courts are organised in a three-tiered hierarchical structure and along geographic divisions. At the lowest level are the district courts, which are the trial courts. Appeals are taken to the courts of appeals, often referred to as circuit courts. From there, cases may be brought to the Supreme Court.
Special	The federal court system does not create special courts for specific matters (two exceptions are the Court of Federal Claims and the Court of International Trade).
Administrative	With federal agencies playing a large role in developing and carrying out laws, this means that an agency will sit as a fact-finding tribunal in applying federal regulations. When disagreements occur, the parties present their evidence to an administrative law judge (ALJ), who acts as the fact-finder.
State	Each state, as well as the District of Columbia and the Commonwealth of Puerto Rico, has its own independent judicial system.
Local	Each of the 50 states is divided into localities or municipalities called cities, counties, towns or villages. Local governments, like their state counterparts, have their own court systems, which are presided over by local magistrates.

INTERNET RESEARCH

The US Supreme Court is a good place to start your research and has some very useful links. To see these, go to www.heinemann.co.uk/hotlinks, insert express code 1825P and click on the relevant link.

5.2 The Rule of Law and Judicial Independence

The rule of law

The rule of law determines the relationship between the state and its citizens. It ensures that actions by the state are both responsible and limited (to obey the law and recognise citizens' legal rights). All citizens, including the monarch, the executive, judiciary and legislature are under the law. They must all obey the law and everyone is equal under the law. If anyone has acted outside their authority then they can be held accountable for their actions in court.

The rule of law states that the judiciary is independent and is free from interference. Citizens are entitled to a fair trial and should not be imprisoned without regard to legal processes. Citizens have the right to take the government or a local authority to court if they feel they have not been treated properly.

Despite this, the rule of law is under threat. Governments have legislated to limit the rights of asylum seekers, for example, restricting their rights to the legal process or the right to protest, which does not relate to foreigners.

Parliamentary sovereignty, in theory, means that the rule of law is vulnerable, as citizen's rights can be removed by parliament. However, in Britain, due to parliamentary sovereignty, the law is whatever parliament deems it to be and the judiciary must enforce that law. So in this sense the rule of law is not under threat in Britain. With the exception of cases such as asylum seekers, any government that attempted to restrict citizens' rights would find themselves opposed at every turn, and any proposals they made would be considered anti-democratic and illegitimate. Despite this recent anti-terror legislation in Britain has had a dramatic effect on rights and liberties.

In the US, the most famous reference to the rule of law was drafted by John Adams for the Constitution of the Commonwealth of Massachusetts, justifying the principle of separation of powers:

> *In the government of this commonwealth, the legislative department shall never exercise the executive and judicial powers or either of them: the executive shall never exercise the legislative and judicial powers, or either of them: the judicial shall never exercise the legislative and executive powers, or either of them: to the end it may be a government of laws and not of men.*

Thomas Paine in *Common Sense* wrote:

> *... the world may know, that so far as we approve of monarchy, that in America THE LAW IS KING. For as in absolute governments the King is law, so in free countries the law OUGHT to be King; and there ought to be no other.*

Practically this means that the rule of law has the following implications.

Implication	Explanation
Nullum crimen, nulla poena sine praevia lege poenali	A latin phrase, conceived by Paul Johann Anselm Ritter von Feuerbach (1813), meaning 'no crime, no punishment without a previous penal law'.
Presumption of innocence	All are considered to be innocent until their guilt has been proven.
Legal equality	Regardless of class, religion, politics or any other discriminating or identifying factor, all are equal before the law.
Habeas corpus	This is Latin, meaning literally 'you must have the body to be subjected (to examination)'. An individual is entitled to know what they are being accused of doing and to request that they are seen by a member of the judiciary and that the innocent are freed.

Learning objectives

- The rule of law
- Judicial independence

Judicial independence

Judicial independence is the notion that judges are free to make decisions without the influence of the executive or the legislature. As we will see, an independent judiciary is vital for democracy, as well as maintaining the separation of powers. If any other branch of government is able to exert an influence over the appointment or the dismissal of judges then this is a serious concern for judicial independence.

In Britain judicial neutrality is guaranteed in several ways.

- The judges are not expected to take an active role in party politics.
- The Law Lords are not expected to contribute to debates on controversial party political issues.
- In court, judges are expected to stick to the law and restrict their work to the case itself.
- The rules of appeal allow for controversial judgements made by judges to be challenged.
- In certain cases, there is always another court to refer the case to if a citizen feels that they have not had their grievance properly redressed.
- The media and pressure groups keep a close eye on the neutrality of judges, particularly in high profile cases.
- Senior judges can only be removed for serious misconduct and/or by a resolution of both Houses of Parliament.

The recent changes to the post of the Lord Chancellor under the terms of the Constitutional Reform Act (2005) asserted the belief that it was no longer acceptable for a government minister to be involved in the appointment of judges. This has led to the creation of the Judicial Appointments Commission.

- The Lord Chancellor's judicial functions to be transferred to the Lord Chief Justice.
- The launch of a new independent Supreme Court in 2009, separate from the House of Lords.
- The creation of a new Judicial Appointment and Conduct ombudsman, responsible for investigating and making recommendations about complaints on the judicial appointments process and the handling of complaints.
- The creation of the Directorate of Judicial Offices of England and Wales (this provides administrative support for the judiciary).
- The duty of government ministers to ensure the independence of the judiciary.

In the US there are two acknowledged variations of judicial independence.

- Institutional independence – this means that the judicial branch is independent from the executive and legislative branches.
- Decisional independence – this is the notion that judges are able to hear cases and make decisions purely on the basis of the law and the facts.

To support this, all members of the Supreme Court, district courts and appeals courts have lifetime tenures. Other judges have significant tenures (around 15 years). Federal judges can be impeached by Congress if they are suspected of misconduct such as bribery, criminal conviction etc. In effect, this means that most federal judges have lifetime tenures.

The American Bar Association (ABA) advocates the appointment of judges who have been cleared by screening committees. Most state legislatures prefer election. The ABA sees judicial elections as reflecting the political skills of the candidate rather than their judgement as such.

INTERNET RESEARCH

The judiciary of England and Wales has an excellent website. To see this, go to www.heinemann.co.uk/hotlinks, insert express code 1825P and click on the relevant link. Select 'About the judiciary'.

Selection of judges

In Britain, the task of filling judicial posts is the responsibility of the Judicial Appointments Commission (JAC). They find the best candidate for the post, sifting through candidates and checking their qualities and abilities. At the end of the appointments process the commission recommends one candidate to the Lord Chancellor. The Lord Chancellor can either accept or reject the candidate. If the Lord Chancellor rejects the candidate then he must give his reasons to the commission. He cannot select an alternative candidate. The JAC was launched in April 2006, under the terms of the Constitutional Reform Act (2005). The commission will take over responsibility for making selections for the appointment of judicial office holders, with some limited exceptions.

- The Lord Chancellor will temporarily retain responsibility for any appointments that might arise to fill any vacancies among the Heads of Division and members of the Court of Appeal until the new commission begins its work.
- The Lord Chancellor will continue to advise the Queen on the appointment of any High Court vacancies.

Judges can be dismissed. Only the monarch can remove the Heads of Division, Law Lords, Justices of Appeal and High Court judges, after a request from both houses of parliament. This has never actually taken place. The Lord Chief Justice can remove all other judicial office-holders. The reasons are mainly incapacity (inability to do the job) or misbehaviour (an act in competition with the post). Again this is very rare. In the case of full-time judges, this has only ever happened once, in 1983. A circuit judge was removed from his post after being found guilty of several counts of smuggling. Other office-holders, who hold their posts on a five-year contract, may not have their contracts renewed if they are found guilty of misbehaviour.

The procedure for appointing a justice to the Supreme Court is contained within the Appointments Clause (Article II, Section 2, Clause 2) of the US Constitution. It states that the president 'shall nominate, and by and with the Advice and Consent of the Senate, shall appoint Judges of the Supreme Court'.

The process of appointing justices has changed since the Constitution was written, but not markedly so. The Senate Judiciary Committee is now part of the process and is involved after the president has selected a candidate, but before the Senate considers that candidate.

On occasion presidents have been able to make appointments without the consent of the Senate. These are known as recess appointments. In theory these recess appointments are temporary, with the terms of the individual expiring at the end of the Senate's next session. These are controversial appointments as they bypass the Senate's role in the process.

As of 2008, of the 158 nominations, the Senate has confirmed 122. In the majority of these cases, where there has been unsuccessful nominations, the president has either withdrawn the candidate, the nomination has been postponed or the candidate withdrawn before the Senate even voted.

The Senate Judiciary Committee was set up in 1816. Before 1868 over two-thirds of all nominations were referred to the committee. In 1868 the Senate decided that from then on all nominations would automatically be referred to the committee. Since the 1960s the committee's consideration has consisted of three phases.

Learning objectives

- Selection of judges
- Membership of the judiciary
- Judicial neutrality and accountability

- A pre-hearing investigative stage – this is when the committee looks into the nominee's background, FBI reports are sought, the nominee is evaluated by the American Bar Association and questioned on a range of legal and constitutional issues.
- The hearings – the committee questions the nominee on various subject areas. Inconsistencies or queries about their background are focused on, and testimony is heard from public witnesses.
- Reporting the nomination – the committee now makes a recommendation to the Senate, supporting or opposing confirmation. By this stage opposition to confirmation from the committee usually indicates that the nominee has little chance of having their appointment confirmed by the Senate.

In the US, the appointment of US judges involves partisan (party biased) decisions by both the president and the Senate Judiciary Committee, but ratification is by the whole of the Senate. The US Supreme Court is seen as part of the process of government whereas British courts tend to be viewed as 'above' party politics.

Membership of the judiciary

President George W. Bush nominated two justices to the Supreme Court following the death of Chief Justice Rehnquist and the retirement of Sandra Day O'Connor. The current US Supreme Court comprises of nine individuals.

Name	Nominated	Position
John Paul Stevens	1975 by President Ford	Moderate
Antonin Scalia	1986 by President Reagan	Solid conservative
Anthony Kennedy	1987 by President Reagan	Legal conservative
David Souter	1990 by President George W. H. Bush	Legal conservative
Clarence Thomas	1991 by President Bush	Conservative
Ruth Bader Ginsburg	1993 by President Clinton	Moderate liberal
Stephen Breyer	1994 by President Clinton	Middle of the road
John Roberts	2005 by President George W. Bush	Conservative
Samuel Alito	2006 by President George W. Bush	Conservative

In Britain, senior judges are drawn from barristers (lawyers who present cases to judges). Becoming a barrister is a long and expensive business. Many of the barristers need an additional income in their early years, in order to financially survive. This means that most of the population are excluded from becoming barristers, let alone senior judges. As a result, the bulk of senior judges come from very privileged backgrounds. Although there are increasing numbers of women who reach the ranks of the senior judiciary, the numbers of ethnic minorities are still very low. The following table, based on the Annual Diversity Statistics (April 2007), outlines the latest available information.

Post	Total	Female		Ethnic minority	
		Number	%	Number	%
Lords of Appeal in Ordinary	12	1	8.3	0	0
Heads of Division	4	0	0	0	0
Lord Justices of Appeal	37	3	8.1	0	0
High Court Judges	108	10	9.3	1	0.9

As we can see, the judiciary is still predominantly white and male. Equally, the ages of the judges tends to be high (understandable in some respects, as the senior judges have to be established and experienced barristers). Most of them attended public school and the majority went to either Oxford or Cambridge universities. The average age of a senior judge is at least 60 years old, with the most senior judges well above the average.

Judicial neutrality and accountability

British judges are meant to be above politics. They are meant to interpret the law, not make laws. However, as we have seen, the Human Rights Act may have changed this view of the judiciary. British judges are now are more willing to challenge government decisions and have more power to rule against government actions.

Given that judges retain their neutrality, there has always been the problem that when judges interpret the law there have been occasions when some have actually made law by setting a precedent for future rulings. Judiciary neutrality means the absence of any kind of bias among the judges. This is particularly important as a judge is not supposed to show any favour towards a particular political party. This underpins the requirement that the judiciary remains independent. In order to ensure that the judiciary operates in a non-partisan way, judicial neutrality is vital, particularly for retaining the public's confidence in processes, such as judicial reviews, where the judges should be more concerned that the right procedures were followed rather than the conclusions of the process.

There are five major criminal cases of recent times in which both the public and the government (or at least a public body) were involved in wishing to secure a conviction. That these cases led to convictions that were later found to be miscarriages of justice illustrates the importance of the judiciary in maintaining their neutrality in the face of public opinion and political influence. These were the five cases in question.

- In 1991 – the Guildford Four were released. They had been convicted of IRA bombings in 1975.
- In 1991 – the Brighton Six were released. They too had been convicted of IRA bombings in 1974.
- In 1997 – the Bridgewater Three were released. They had been convicted of the murder of Carl Bridgewater (aged 13) in 1978.
- In 2001 – Stephen Downing was released. He had confessed to a murder but later retracted the confession. He had spent 27 years in prison.
- In 2003 – Angela Cannings was given a life sentence for murdering her two sons. It was later found that they had died of cot death.

Learning objectives

- Role of courts in democracies
- Accountability and democratic control

Ultra vires

This means striking down legislation on the grounds that it exceeds the constitutional authority of Congress in the US, and in Britain it can be applied to prerogative powers that are seen to be a threat to the rule of law.

Role of courts in democracies

A constitution will usually requires that the judiciary is independent of the government. This is in order to ensure the rule of law, in other words that the law is enforced impartially and consistently, regardless of which political party is in government.

The separation of powers is a principle of the Constitution that the state has three distinctly separate arms: the executive, the legislature and the judiciary.

The separation of powers and, therefore, judicial independence, is secured in a number of ways in Britain:

- A judge's decisions on their cases are final and authoritative (subject to appeal).
- A judge's decisions must reflect that judge's judgement.
- The judges are difficult to remove, as long as they retain 'good behaviour' (i.e. not found guilty of a criminal offence).
- A judge's pay is set by the Senior Salaries Review body (whose recommendations are rarely rejected by parliament).
- A judge cannot act as a director of a private company.
- A judge is required to remain uninfluenced by any outside individual (including another judge) or organisation.

Nonetheless, judges have been involved in areas that directly conflict with both the separation of powers and their neutrality.

- In 2003 Justice Collins (High Court) criticised the Nationality, Immigration and Asylum Act (2002) on the grounds that it breached the human rights of asylum seekers.
- Even before the Human Rights Act came into effect, judges had openly criticised the then Home Secretary, Michael Howard, on minimum sentencing.

In the US, courts are political actors in the system and their decisions have policy repercussions. This is particularly so with the Supreme Court. Even so, courts operate under legal guidelines, not partisan or overtly political calculations. There is the view, as indicated in the table, that in a democratic society, the judiciary has to be political in some way.

Issue	Explanation
Protecting citizens	Protecting the citizen from an over-powerful state has emphasised the impartiality of the judicial process and the independence of the judiciary.
Ensuring accountability	The principal task for the courts is to ensure that public bodies act in accordance with the powers granted to them by parliament in the UK or the Constitution in the US.
Controlling public bodies	The main conceptual tool used by the judges in performing this task is the ***ultra vires*** doctrine (beyond the powers). This rests on the theory that public bodies only have those legal powers which have been conferred explicitly or implicitly.
Checks and balances	The separation of powers stresses the need to restrain both government and the power of majorities. The non-majoritarian institutions of the courts are vital in providing checks and balances.
Legal accountability	Ministers and public bodies must be held legally accountable through the courts. This argument is at the heart of the concept of judicial review in the United States.

Accountability and democratic control

The Lord Chief Justice of England and Wales, Lord Woolf, speaking in 2005 said:

> *Independence of the judiciary is not only important to the judiciary, it is also important to the public. Judges provide protection by upholding the rule of law. They do so by enforcing laws, which the government provides to protect the public. Justice is provided irrespective of whether the claimant is a prisoner, a powerful business tycoon or an asylum seeker. Rank and gender are of no importance. These qualities of our justice system are as important today as they have ever been.*

The Constitutional Reform Act came as a surprise to many. Lord Woolf said:

> *When one of the roles of the judiciary is to act as a watchdog on behalf of the public in relation to any attempts by public bodies to abuse their power, public bodies and the government should not be in a position to influence the decisions of the judiciary.*

In consultation with the judiciary, the executive had established the following.

- The government should not have control over the appointment of judges (but they could have an input).
- The government should not be able to remove a judge, unless the Lord Chief Justice agrees.
- The government should not be able to pick a judge to hear a particular case.
- The government should have no input over the use of judges and where they sit as a means of disciplining a judge.

Until the changes in the role of the Lord Chancellor, the theoretical separation of powers between the judiciary and the executive were not actual in practice. The appointment of judges was down to an unelected (and unaccountable) individual. Added to this, the Lord Chancellor was a member of cabinet committees that discussed political issues. This was too close a relationship between the judiciary and the executive to ensure that the judiciary remained independent. Despite this, the last three Lord Chancellors were all keen not to be unduly influenced by the executive. Lords MacKay, Irvine and Falconer seemed all to be of the opinion that it was better to change a system that had ensured independence, rather than try to change one that was failing and rush at it, so it was a good time to consider reform.

Just as the apparent separation of powers between the judiciary and the executive existed in theory, but not in practice, so too does the relationship between the judiciary and parliament (legislature).

Ideally, they should be separate so that they can independently check on the actions of one another. In theory, the process should be such that:

- parliament can remove a judge who is seen to be corrupt or has committed a criminal offence
- judges can declare a law passed by parliament if the interpretation is that it violates one of the conventions of the European Convention on Human Rights
- parliament alone makes the laws
- judges implement and enforce the laws
- parliament votes to fund judges
- judges are subject to being dismissed by parliament.

INTERNET RESEARCH

In May 2007 the responsibilities of the Department for Constitutional Affairs was transferred to the new Ministry of Justice. To see the Ministry of Justice's website go to www.heinemann.co.uk/hotlinks, insert express code 1825P and click on the relevant link. It has a very useful archive of publications on legislation, policy, statistics and independent reviews.

Learning objectives

- Judicial activism
- Judicial restraint
- Activism vs restraint

Judicial activism

Judicial activism suggests that judges are more willing to get involved in situations beyond making legal decisions. It also implies that they are willing to influence government policy. Those who believe that judicial activism is positive, believe that the courts should take an active role in cases involving immigration, citizens' rights, asylum and other sensitive issues. Judicial activists are seen to be 'doing the right thing' rather than simply following the exact letter of the law.

Judicial activism has increased in Britain for a number of reasons.

- The tendency of governments to legislate over newer and broader areas, such as restrictive legislation on asylum seekers, which could breach the terms of the Human Rights Act.
- The greater willingness of citizens to use the courts. In the past the courts were seen as protecting the status quo and were also distrusted.
- The development of international agreements and conventions, such as the European Convention on Human Rights. This has encouraged the view that government decisions should be questioned.
- Judges have been seen by the media and pressure groups as having greater confidence to tackle policy issues. The more courts are used the greater the willingness for judges to get involved, thus encouraging more cases to be taken before the courts.

K. Ewing and C. Gearty (*Freedom Under Thatcher*, 1990) posed the question as to whether or not a group of individuals who were selected by the prime minister from a small and unrepresentative group should have the final political decision on an issue. They questioned its legitimacy and suggested that questions that are either ethical, social or politically difficult should be referred to the judiciary.

Central to the legal and political power of the US Supreme Court is judicial review. This gives the court the power to declare that any action or law of a government institution is unconstitutional. In order to do so, the majority of the nine justices have to agree that the law or action violates one or more clauses of the US Constitution. If it is seen as such, then it is considered null and void. The Supreme Court's decision is based on its interpretation of the Constitution and the decision is final, unless the court can be persuaded otherwise.

In the US, judicial review also allows them to look at alleged violations of federal laws and actions by other organisations; this is known as the power of statutory interpretation. The key difference between constitutional interpretation and statutory interpretation is that if the Supreme Court interprets a federal statute in such a way as it goes against the intention of Congress, then the legislators can simply amend the law, making the court decision irrelevant. If the court's decision is based on a constitutional interpretation, then Congress cannot overturn that interpretation.

Under the judicial review system, any government policy can be challenged in the federal courts as being unconstitutional. This means that, theoretically, as the Supreme Court is the final court of appeal then it is superior to both the executive and the legislature in areas of legislation and policy. For this reason critics claim that the dominant political power in the US is neither the executive nor the legislature, but the judiciary. This is perhaps an overreaction; while the court is the authoritative interpreter of the Constitution, it does not drive legislation or policy; it is however a major power that has to be taken into account when framing legislation and policy.

Judicial restraint

Even though the Supreme Court may have considerable political powers, there are key judicial restraints that control its actions. The court does not frame its own agenda; it is reactive in the sense that it can only consider cases and situations that are brought to it. In many cases a major constitutional issue may remain unresolved until a case is brought before it for deliberation. The Justice Department plays a major role in deciding which cases are taken to the court and will have developed a range of political and legal arguments before this happens.

The Supreme Court does not look at hypothetical cases. In other words, the court does not comment on the constitutional implications of proposed legislation. It has to focus on the political issues that actually exist, which limits the scope of the court's impact. It will only look at cases where a party has actually suffered a personal harm. Also, the Supreme Court does not have enforcement powers, so there are limited ways in which it can demand that anyone complies with its decisions.

Also, there are major areas over which the Supreme Court has no jurisdiction whatsoever; these include:

- welfare policy
- foreign policy
- business policy
- fiscal and monetary policy.

Finally, the Supreme Court is wary of contradicting decisions and principles that have been established by it in the past. An example was Roe vs Wade, 410 US 113 (1973), which resulted in a landmark decision regarding abortion. According to the Roe decision, most laws against abortion in the United States violated a constitutional right to privacy under the due process clause of the 14th Amendment. Since then, the court has upheld several related cases.

Stare decisis

This is a legal principle in which judges have an obligation to follow the precedents that have been established in prior decisions. It has not always been followed exclusively by the US Supreme Court, particularly in the years 1946 to 1992, when they reversed decisions in 130 cases. However, it is a key part of the English legal system.

Activism vs restraint

Judicial restraint refers to situations when the Supreme Court is of the opinion that it should not overturn a prior court decision, while judicial activism tends to suggest that the court is prepared to overturn prior decisions on the basis that there have been relevant societal changes. The former Supreme Court Justice Sandra Day O'Connor (now retired) and the serving Justice Anthony M. Kennedy favour judicial restraint, upholding past decisions whether they are in favour of them or not. In comparison, the more liberal justices (including David H. Souter, Stephen Breyer, and Ruth Bader Ginsburg) are more in favour of judicial activism. They base their decisions to overturn past decisions on whether the decisions have any bearing on modern society. William H. Rehnquist, Clarence Thomas and Antonin Scalia are also in favour of limited judicial activism, but their focus is on overturning liberal interpretations of the constitution so that the original meaning and intent of it can be restored. Justice John Paul Stevens tends to fluctuate and is sometimes in favour of restraint and sometimes in favour of activism.

INTERNET RESEARCH

The *New York Times* often has well-reasoned and detailed articles in judicial restraint and activism. To see this, go to www.heinemann.co.uk/hotlinks, insert express code 1825P and click on the relevant link.

Learning objectives

- The judiciary and the other branches of government
- The judiciary and the political process
- The judiciary and federalism

The court packing bill

President Franklin D. Roosevelt, in response to the Supreme Court overturning several of his New Deal measures, proposed to appoint an extra Supreme Court justice for every justice over the age of 70.5 years. This would have meant six more justices. It ended in the Supreme Court becoming more amenable to his legislation.

The judiciary and the other branches of government

In the US, the separation of powers ensures that not only is power divided between the executive, the legislature and the judiciary, but also that they provide checks and balances for one another.

Under the terms of the US Constitution Congress can change the Supreme Court's jurisdiction. They can also propose constitutional amendments and if these are ratified they can reverse judicial decisions, as well as impeaching and removing federal judges.

Using the advice and the consent of the Senate, the president of the US has the power to appoint judges. It is important to remember that federal courts can only exercise judicial power; they cannot enforce or execute laws, as this is a power reserved for the executive branch alone.

The US judiciary plays a far more active role in the political process than judiciaries do in many other democracies. Federal courts are established by Congress and they receive their jurisdiction from Congress. It is the role of the federal judges to apply common, equity, statutory, constitutional, administrative, admiralty and maritime law. They also apply federal, criminal and civil law. Although they are bound by procedural requirements, they can exercise discretion. The Supreme Court itself has almost complete control over the cases it chooses to review. Although it may consider thousands of cases each year it usually concentrates on fewer than 100.

With the Constitution over 200 years old, the argument continues between those who believe that judges should only interpret the document literally and those who believe they should not or cannot do so in modern society.

The judiciary and the political process

In the US the Supreme Court does not have the degree of separation from government that the British court system enjoys. In many respects it is considered to be a political institution and, as such, it comes under enormous pressure and criticism. In some cases this has prompted presidents to instal more conservative justices in order to reflect public opinion, a prime example being President Nixon's criticism that the Warren Court was too soft on criminals.

The court also finds itself under pressure from interest groups, a notable example being abortion. The Roe decision brought about the formation of a number of pro-life groups and these in turn spawned the creation of several pro-choice groups. Justice Blackmun, who wrote the Roe decision, even received death threats. As we have seen, the Supreme Court may make a judgement, but it lacks the power to enforce it, hence when segregated schools in the south were declared illegal there was still strong opposition to desegregation.

The Supreme Court has a key role to play in the democratic process. It is there to overturn government restrictions on the right to vote, to safeguard the rights of citizens to join organisations, to ensure freedom of speech and freedom of the press. The fact that the court is unelected is seen by many to be a virtue. Justice Jackson said in West Virginia State Board of Education vs Barnette in 1943:

The very purpose of a Bill of Rights was to withdraw certain subjects from the vicissitudes of political controversy, to place them beyond the reach of majorities and officials and to establish them as legal principles to be applied by the courts.

Jesse Choper, author of *Judicial Review in the National Political Process,* was firmly of the opinion that the job of safeguarding a citizen's rights needed to be given to the Supreme Court and not to any other government institution. Choper believed that this should be the case because the Supreme Court itself does not have political responsibility. It is insulated from majoritarianism and in effect it is aloof from the political system, so the Supreme Court is not beholden to anyone and in particular the need to remain popular. It does not have to reflect popular views and, as a result, it can be objective. This alone makes the court special, as elected representatives no matter how many promises they make can never be truly objective.

The judiciary and federalism

For decades the Supreme Court has always seemed to interpret the Constitution that favoured an extension of federal authority. But once there was a majority of Republican-appointed justices they began to switch their allegiance towards the states (this was during the federalism revolution in the Rehnquist period 1986 to 2005). The justices were clear in their support of the 10th Amendment to the US Constitution, which provided that: 'The powers not delegated to the United States by the Constitution, nor prohibited by it to the states, are reserved to the states respectively, or to the people.'

It is important to appreciate that this system of dual sovereignty is central to American federalism. In a landmark case in 1985 (Garcia vs San Antonio Municipal Transit Authority) the Supreme Court reversed the constitutional rule that some government functions should be reserved to the states. The court held that 'the Constitution does not carve out express elements of state sovereignty that Congress may not employ its delegated powers to displace'. Many believe that this undermined the nature of the 10th Amendment, but consistently the courts have been looking at the Constitution and defining the limits that the Constitution places on federal government power.

The Low Level Radioactive Waste Policy Amendments Act (1985) required states to either implement federal instructions, or to be liable for waste generators' damages. There was a landmark case (New York vs United States 1992) which in effect restored the 10th Amendment. The court said:

State governments are neither regional offices nor administrative agencies of the United States. Congress may not simply commandeer the legislative processes of the states by directly compelling them to enact and enforce a federal regulatory programme.

In 1995, in United States vs Lopez, the Supreme Court restrained Congress from relying on its constitutional power to regulate interstate commerce in order to ban the possession of guns in school zones, unless it could clearly show that the conduct involved commercial channels or interstate economic activity. They enforced constitutional limits on Congress to enact legislation.

In the period 1996 to 1997, Printz vs United States invalidated many of the provisions of the Brady Handgun Violence Prevention Act (1993). This required local police to conduct background checks on those wishing to purchase a gun. In the same period in Vacco vs Quill and Washington vs Glucksberg, the Supreme Court upheld New York and Washington statutes that banned doctors from assisting their patients to commit suicide. In effect, they backed the power of the states.

INTERNET RESEARCH

There is an excellent collection of information on Supreme Court decisions dating from the 1990s at the Cornell University Law School website. To see this, go to www.heinemann.co.uk/hotlinks, insert express code 1825P and click on the relevant link.

Learning objectives

- The development of the rights of states
- The development of the rights of individuals

The development of the rights of states

While the Founding Fathers created the House of Representatives to express the majority popular will, with its members elected directly by the people on the basis of numerical representation, the Senate was created to represent the equal sovereignty of the states. States were represented in the Senate, irrespective of the population, thereby safeguarding states' rights, the equality of each state and counterbalancing the representative system.

The judiciary, over the years, has also played a vital role in ensuring that the rights of the states have been upheld according to the Constitution. There has always been a tension between the relative power of state legislatures and the federal government. At varying times one has had the upper hand and power. In effect, the Supreme Court has operated as a safeguard against federalism. However, it is important to note that there is a difference between federalism and a dominant federal government.

The Warren Court period (1953–69), led by Chief Justice Earl Warren, not only expanded civil rights and liberties, but also judicial power and the power of federal government.

The Rehnquist Court in the decades following Reagan's New Federalism, failed to impose any meaningful legal limits on federal power compared to the states. Instead it seemed to be content to allow the political process to determine the parameters of congressional authority. In the last couple of decades the situation has somewhat changed, with the Supreme Court reclaiming the role as the arbiter of federalism disputes and finding in favour of the states rather than federal regulations. This has proved to be somewhat controversial; the critics claim that the Supreme Court has no business in striking down federal regulations to protect states' rights and that the Founding Fathers intended the people to decide where congressional authority should begin and end.

Many believe that given the opportunity citizens would transfer most state powers to the federal government, as they only care about outputs or the policies the government adopts. The fear if this were the case would be that federal power would impose majority values on home state laws with which they disagree. However, many US citizens dislike federal government and do not trust Congress.

Those who favour state rights feel that it is the states that can provide populist legislation, more closely matching the preference of the local people. The passage of any federal law tends to open the door to unwanted federal regulations and there are concerns about how the federal government will exercise its authority. The key problem is that congressional statutes are often vague, which leaves too much room for manoeuvre for the executive. Citizens tend to trust state governments more than federal government and citizens do care about government processes. They like to be involved directly in law-making (such as via ballot initiatives) and many wish to resist federalism.

Often the Supreme Court will give mixed messages. Justice Stephen Breyer, in opposing the Supreme Court's decision to strike down part of the Violence against Women Act (in the US vs Morrison), said: 'Congress, not the courts, must remain primarily responsible for striking the appropriate state/federal balance.'

Back in 1985 the Supreme Court said: 'State sovereign interests are more properly protected by procedural safeguards in the structure of the federal system than by judicially created limitations on federal power.'

The development of the rights of individuals

This is a potentially complex subject and it would be advisable to look at the relevant sections in the 'Civil Rights and Liberties' chapter on page 252 to see how government institutions and the Constitution have a role in defending rights, as well as current issues. The following table outlines some of the key decisions made by the Supreme Court over a period of time in relation to key civil rights and liberties.

Civil right or liberty	Key judgements by the Supreme Court
Rights of racial minorities	Brown vs the Board of Education of Topeka (1954) – law in Kansas broke 14th Amendment Swann vs Charlotte-Mecklenberg Board of Education (1971) – extended ban on segregated schools Adarand Constructors vs Peña (1995) – struck down government affirmative action Gratz vs Bollinger (2003) – the university's admission programme was unconstitutional
Rights of arrested persons	Gideon vs Wainwright (1963) – under the 14th Amendment guaranteed the right to legal representation Miranda vs Arizona (1966) – under the 5th Amendment the right to remain silent was extended
Capital punishment	Furman vs Georgia (1972) – the death penalty violated the 8th Amendment Atkins vs Virginia (2002) – execution of mentally-ill patients was unconstitutional Roper vs Simmons (2005) – unconstitutional to extend death penalty to those under 18 Baze vs Rees (2008) – the court rejected an appeal that execution by lethal injection would violate the 8th Amendment, as it was a cruel and unusual punishment
Abortion rights	Roe vs Wade (1973) – Texas law forbidding abortion was unconstitutional under the 14th Amendment Webster vs Reproductive Health Services (1989) – supported Missouri state law, forbidding abortion if it was not to save the life of the mother Planned Parenthood of Southeastern Pennsylvania vs Casey (1992) – Pennsylvania law upheld, requiring a married woman to tell her husband that she was seeking an abortion Stenberg vs Carhart (2002) – a Nebraska law banning partial birth abortion was struck down Gonzales vs Carhart (2007) – this upheld the Partial Birth Abortion Ban Act of 2003
Freedom of religion	Engel vs Vitale (1962) – struck out New York State law, requiring school prayers, as it violated the 1st Amendment Wallace vs Jaffree (1985) – declared Alabama law allowing silent meditation in school to be unconstitutional Lee vs Weisman (1992) – prayers in public school graduation ceremonies unconstitutional Epperson vs Arkansas (1968) – Arkansas wrong to ban teaching of Darwinism Edwards vs Aguillard (1987) – unconstitutional for Louisiana to demand the creation story to be told alongside evolution theory Allegheny County vs American Civil Liberties Union (1989) – a Pennsylvanian Christmas display infringed the 1st Amendment, as it only had religious figures Zelman vs Simmons-Harris (2002) – supported Ohio's school voucher programme

Civil right or liberty	Key judgements by the Supreme Court
Freedom of speech, the press and expression	Buckley vs Valeo (1976) – part of the Federal Election Campaign Act (1974) limiting expenditure for presidential candidates was unconstitutional, as it limited freedom of speech Rankin vs McPherson (1987) – supported the non-sacking of an individual who made comment about the Reagan assassination attempt on the grounds that it would infringe the 1st Amendment Texas vs Johnson (1989) – a law forbidding the burning of the US flag was unconstitutional United States vs Eickman (1990) – Flag Protection Act (1989) was unconstitutional Reno vs American Civil Liberties Union (1997) – Communications Decency Act (1996) was unconstitutional as it infringed 1st Amendment Ashcroft vs Free Speech Coalition (2002) – Child Pornography Protection Act (1996) was unconstitutional
Gun control	United States vs Lopez (1995) – Gun-free School Zones Act (1990) was unconstitutional under Article I, Section 8 Printz vs United States (1997) – Brady Act (1993) was partly unconstitutional, as it required background checks by local law enforcement within five days DC vs Heller (2008) – it was held that the 2nd Amendment's protection of an individual's rights to possess a firearm for private use extended to a collective right, applying to state regulated militias

INTERNET RESEARCH

The more recent Supreme Court rulings can be found at its website. To see this, go to www.heinemann.co.uk/hotlinks, insert express code 1825P and click on the relevant link.

The Supreme Court and the Constitution

The Supreme Court is the primary instrument by which the US Constitution has been updated over the years. It has the ability to interpret the provisions of the Constitution and has therefore been instrumental in the growth in the protection of individual rights (in the 1950s and 1960s) and the increasing dominance of the federal government over the power of the individual states. However, most of this has been driven by the executive and the legislature and the Supreme Court has allowed it.

Above the main entrance to the Supreme Court building is written 'Equal justice under law'. The Supreme Court is the final arbiter of the law; it aims to ensure that US citizens receive the promise of equal justice and effectively functions as the guardian and interpreter of the Constitution.

There are few other courts in the world that have this degree of authority over the interpretation of a constitution. According to the nineteenth-century French political writer, Alexis de Tocqueville:

> *The representative system of government has been adopted in several states of Europe, but I am unaware that any nation of the globe has hitherto organised a judicial power in the same manner as the Americans. A more imposing judicial power was never constituted by any people.*

We have already seen that the US Constitution has proved to be a strong and flexible document. It balances individuals' rights to freedom and society's need for order. In their role of protecting and interpreting the constitution the Supreme Court can invalidate legislation or executive actions, which the court believes are in conflict with the Constitution.

The Constitution does limit the court for dealing with cases and controversies. When the Supreme Court rules on a constitutional issue the judgement is virtually final. The decision can only be altered by a constitutional amendment or a new court ruling.

Chief Justice Marshall wrote in 1819 in McCulloch vs Maryland: 'We must never forget that it is a Constitution we are expounding, intended to endure for ages to come, and consequently, to be adapted to the various crises of human affairs.'

The judicial review function of the Supreme Court is the key way in which the judiciary deals with the constant problem of balancing citizens' rights, separation of powers and federal arrangements. Ultimately they are the means by which disputes have to be sorted out either between individuals and government or between branches and levels of government.

The court itself comprises nine individuals with their own distinct opinions and approaches. Most of the enormous numbers of cases that are brought before the court are never heard; they are denied *certiorari*. This means that the losing party in a lower court cannot ask the Supreme Court to make the situation more certain or clearer. Over 90 per cent of all cases are appealed in this way and the others need the court to hear the cases using a statutory appeals process. The decision whether or not to grant *certiorari* usually rests on seven questions.

- How fundamental is the Constitutional issue?
- How many similar cases have been or are being argued?
- Is there a conflict of opinion in lower courts?
- Does the lower court decision conflict with an earlier Supreme Court decision?
- Are there any significant individual rights involved?
- Has the lower court followed usual judicial proceedings?
- Does it involve the interpretation of a statute that has not yet been examined?

Learning objectives

- The Supreme Court and the Constitution
- Dealing with issues within the Constitution

Dealing with issues within the Constitution

The following is a list of some recent Supreme Court decisions and their interpretation of the Constitution in each case.

18 April 2007 Abortion case

In a 5–4 decision the Supreme Court ruled on its first significant abortion case since Justices Roberts and Alito took their seats. It also allowed a nationwide ban on a specific procedure for the first time. The procedure, known as partial-birth abortion or intact dilation and evacuation, was banned by federal law in 2003. In his opinion for the court, Justice Kennedy said that the ban does not violate a woman's right to an abortion. Siding with Kennedy were Justices Alito, Scalia, Thomas, and Chief Justice Roberts. Justice Ginsberg, writing for the minority, called the decision the phalanx of an assault on abortion. Pro-choice activists said they feared the ruling would open the floodgates to restrictive state laws; pro-life activists, such as Senator John Boehner (R-OH), hailed the decision as setting the stage for 'further progress'. The case is Gonzales vs Carhart.

30 April 2007 Car chases

The Supreme Court in an 8–1 decision made it clear that if someone is injured while the police pursue them, the police cannot be held responsible. In the case of Scott vs Harris, Victor Harris was being pursued by sheriff's deputy Timothy Scott. After six miles and ten minutes of pursuit in populated areas, Scott decided to stop the pursuit by using a technique whereby the police car hits the vehicle in a precise location forcing it into a spin. The manoeuvre was not performed precisely enough and Harris's car overturned and crashed. Harris was left with quadriplegia, and he sued Scott, saying his 4th Amendment rights were violated by the use of excessive force. After the justices reviewed Scott's on-board video tape, however, they concluded that even if Scott used deadly force, the real question was whether the force was reasonable. They concluded it was. Only Justice Stevens dissented.

INTERNET RESEARCH

The US Constitution online website is an excellent source to keep up to date with issues about the US Constitution. To see this, go to www.heinemann.co.uk/hotlinks, insert express code 1825P and click on the relevant link.

28 April 2008 Voter ID requirements

The Supreme Court upheld an Indiana law that requires all voters to provide a photo ID in order to vote. The provision, opposed by Democrats because of fears that it would disenfranchise poor voters who cannot afford an ID, has exceptions for those religiously opposed to being photographed or who cannot afford an ID, but the law requires such persons to file an affidavit with a circuit court after an election; their provisional ballots would not be counted unless the affidavit was filed within 10 days. The affidavit would have to be filed prior to each election, a particular sticking point. The court, however, recognised the need of the state to prevent election fraud and found the provisions to not be too onerous. The court acknowledged that some voters might be turned away or fail to cast a ballot, but that the number would be small considering the law's purpose to maintain the integrity and reliability of elections. In the dissent, it was noted that the amount required to procure an ID exceeds the inflation-adjusted amount of a poll tax that a previous court had found to be unconstitutional prior to the passage of the 24th Amendment. The judgement of the court was joined by three justices with three more joining a concurring opinion, and three joining the dissent.

Boumediene vs Bush 2008

This was a writ of habeas corpus made by a civilian court on behalf of an individual held in detention at Guantanamo Bay. The Supreme Court held by a 5–4 majority that prisoners being held there had a right to habeas corpus under the Constitution and that the Military Commissions Act (2006) unconstitutionally suspended that right.

13 July 2008 Guantanamo prisoner rights

Rebuking Congress, the Supreme Court, in a 5–4 decision, ruled that prisoners at Guantanamo Bay retain their habeas corpus rights. Writing for the slim majority, Justice Anthony Kennedy noted that 'The laws and Constitution are designed to survive, and remain in force, in extraordinary times.' The Justice Department issued a statement that the ruling would not affect the current schedule of trials.

Contemporary issues concerning the role of the Supreme Court

As far as those on the liberal side of the political divide in the US are concerned the Supreme Court is very much a conservative institution. Recently it has upheld federal anti-abortion laws, cut back on free speech rights for public school students, enforced procedural requirements for bringing and appealing cases and limited schools' abilities to use racial measures to achieve or preserve integration. The majority of death penalty cases have produced decisions in favour of the prosecution and it certainly appears that the majority of the decisions made by the justices have been split along ideological lines. Many of the decisions have been decided on a 5 to 4 majority, reflecting the conservative versus the liberal justices. The conservatives, led by Chief Justice John G. Roberts Jnr, are in the majority, with the four liberal justices often marginalised. The balance of power is often held by Justice Anthony M. Kennedy, invariably siding with the conservatives. This will undoubtedly have implications for a Democrat president and a Democrat-dominated Congress.

Many commentators have pointed to the dangers of the conservative leanings of the Supreme Court. The president of People for the American Way, Ralph Neas, who had tried to stop both Chief Justice Roberts and Justice Alito from being nominated, said: 'The court has shown the same respect for precedent that a wrecking ball shows for a plate glass window.'

While liberals may worry about the composition of the Supreme Court, other groups are more supportive. Robin S. Conrad, of the National Chamber Litigation Center, who handles Supreme Court cases for the US Chamber of Commerce, said: 'It's our best Supreme Court [term] ever.'

There are also concerns about just how many cases the court is considering. In the term that began on 2 October 2006 and ended on 28 June 2007 just 68 cases were decided; the fewest since 1953 when there were just 65. There seemed to be a problem in finding the four judges necessary to hear each case. By the time the new term opened in October 2007 changes were afoot, largely because there were major cases looming. The court had decided to listen to three arguments a day rather than two.

Possibly the most important issue revolved around Guantanamo Bay and the detainees. The court decided that the detainees had a constitutional right to go to federal court to challenge their continued detention. Justice Kennedy said: 'The laws and Constitution are designed to survive, and remain in force, in extraordinary times.'

The Supreme Court decision overturned a provision of the Military Commissions Act (2006) that had stripped federal courts of jurisdiction over habeas corpus petitions from the prisoners (Boumediene vs Bush 2008).

The Supreme Court also overturned the District of Columbia's handgun ban, ruling that the 2nd Amendment protects the individual's right to own a gun for private use (DC vs Heller 2008).

On elections they upheld a voter identification law from Indiana, which required voters to present a current state or federal photo identification to cast a ballot. It had been challenged as an unconstitutional burden on the right to vote. The court also rejected a constitutional challenge to New York State's methods of choosing candidates to run in judicial elections. It overturned an appeals court ruling that had ordered the state to replace a direct primary election with a nominating convention system.

Learning objectives

- Contemporary issues concerning the role of the Supreme Court

The Supreme Court also rejected a challenge to Kentucky's method of execution (lethal injection) in Baze vs Rees (2008). It was claimed that the injection posed an unconstitutional risk of pain and suffering. In a second decision about the death penalty, the court ruled that the Constitution prohibited the death penalty for child rape. It held that death was a disproportionate penalty when the death of the victim was not the result of the crime.

According to Professor Philip Davies, of De Montfort University, the Supreme Court is often used to rule on problems that are avoided by Congress. Speaking in 2005, Davies believed that Congress often found it impossible to try to tackle difficult issues, particularly contentious ones such as abortion, capital punishment and segregation, and left it to the courts to resolve the matter.

He viewed the Supreme Court as comprising judges who have good records. They are individuals who tend to be loyal to the law and are not influenced by politics. For this very reason the president cannot depend on them to return a result favourable to him.

Others claim that the Supreme Court has far too much power for an unelected body. Certainly it can specifically or implicitly overrule, ignore or modify judgements that have been made in previous cases. They are unelected justices, but it is often argued that although they may have too much power it is justified.

The swing voter

Although Anthony Kennedy was appointed by the Republican President Ronald Reagan, he acts as the swing vote on many social issues. He has relatively moderate leanings and has come to prominence in a number of 5–4 decisions.

The power of the Supreme Court has certainly been in evidence over the years. Many see the Supreme Court as being a political body, as its members are appointed by the president, who is a politician, and confirmed by other politicians, the Senate. The power of the Supreme Court should not be overestimated, however, and even the most activist of justices cannot raise issues of their own. They can only look at cases that have been brought forward from lower courts. Ultimately their power relies on the support of the legislature and the executive.

In the landmark Brown case (1954) even though the court ruled against racial segregation in schools it took three years for the president, Eisenhower, to send troops to Little Rock in Arkansas to escort African-American children into school. Even then racial segregation did not end until the Civil Rights Acts of 1964 and 1968 and the Voting Rights Act of 1965 were passed by US Congress.

INTERNET RESEARCH

The *New York Times* carries a very succinct and reasoned summary of each of the Supreme Court terms decisions. To see this, go to www.heinemann.co.uk/hotlinks, insert express code 1825P and click on the relevant link. Click on the 'US' button and select 'Washington'.

Provided the power of the Supreme Court is used responsibly it can ensure that citizens have protection from government decisions that may not be in their best interests. Even after the terrorist attacks in 2001, a crisis period for the US, the Supreme Court protected rights and liberties against a potentially tyrannical response by government. The Supreme Court continues to perform its duties, as the Founding Fathers of the Constitution would have expected, within their intentions and limits. It did seem that the Roberts Court was beginning to veer to the right during the 2006 to 2007 term, with several conservative rulings. But the 2007 to 2008 term saw some liberal victories, including the Boumediene and worker discrimination cases. This illustrates that the court is complex and each justice can be quite independent.

The Judiciary and the President

Is the Supreme Court influenced by the president and by democratic control?

According to Robert Scigliano (1971) there is a clear institutional relationship between the president and the Supreme Court. In Seigliano's words The Founding Fathers saw the judicial and executive branches as: 'An informal and limited alliance against Congress.'

In fact most of the increases in the presidential and judicial powers have come at the expense of Congress. The Supreme Court has tended to be reluctant in challenging executive power and has seemed to silently assent to the expansion of presidential powers.

Presidents can impress their philosophy on the Supreme Court through judicial appointments, although opportunities are rare. A president can also use the Office of the Solicitor General to advance his agenda. They can bring negative sanctions against the Supreme Court, using the bully pulpit to initiate legislation or try to overturn a judicial decision through a constitutional amendment.

In the case of the Constitution, the president is often in a better position to take advantage of ambiguities. Presidents have a relatively short period of time to make their mark and they have pushed the boundaries of their power in response to social and political problems. They can take unilateral action.

Certainly the rise of the Office of the Solicitor General has been a major influence. It helps the court in controlling what appears before it, in effect defining the significant issues of the day. However it is the Supreme Court that controls its own calendar or schedule. Traditionally the post of Solicitor General has been responsible firstly to the court, rather than the president, but now presidents are using it as a resource to advance a case or a position. Solicitor Generals have become increasingly partisan and are used to help further an administration's policy goals and to serve as a check on the court.

Decision-making in the court, however, is influenced by a broad range of political, social, legal and attitudinal factors. On the one hand the attitudinal factor suggests a justice's own policy preferences, but in reality they should also reflect a broader range of views and attitudes towards policy and issues.

As far as the Supreme Court is concerned, democracy needs popular participation in decision-making and judicial reviews can be seen as a way of achieving this. It can impose accountability on government and it enables those who wish to challenge officials to participate in the decision-making processes. Democracy is far more than just majority rule: courts play a vital role in preserving the essential conditions of democracy, such as freedom of choice, fair trials, personal liberties and the ability to engage in democratic politics.

However there are those who would accuse the Supreme Court as being just one of the many anti-majoritarian devices in the US democracy. It should not be allowed to override democratic majorities (neither should a presidential veto, unequal population representation in the Senate, Congress committees, or the electoral college).

What are the weaknesses of the judicial nomination process?

Presidential appointment of judges

Theoretically, once a justice has been nominated by the president and confirmed by the Senate they are no longer directly accountable to any other branch of government (although they can be

Learning objectives

- Is the Supreme Court influenced by the president and by democratic control?
- What are the weaknesses of the judicial nomination process?

Question topic material

Note that these topics are not written in essay format, but they do include ideas, concepts and information and practices that you would need to think about if similar questions came up in an exam.

impeached). Presidents can use their power to shape the ideological balance of the Supreme Court and influence its decisions. Fortunately presidents often do not achieve this, even when they carefully select their nominees. However, appointing judges that reflect the president's political stance means that each president, when they have the opportunity, will leave a political legacy in the Supreme Court, which lasts considerably longer than their own administration. President Dwight D. Eisenhower was disappointed with two of his Supreme Court nominations, Earl Warren and William Brennan. He later called Warren: 'The biggest damned fool mistake I ever made.'

Truman was also less than pleased with one of his nominees, Tom C. Clark. Truman said: 'He hasn't made one right decision that I can think of. It's just that he's such a dumb son of a bitch.'

A more recent prime example is David Souter, who was appointed by the Republican President George H. W. Bush. He normally votes with the liberal wing of the Supreme Court.

Evidence does still suggest that many of the justices reflect the views of the president who selected them. Often when they do not reflect the views of the president the selection was made on other criteria, such as regional ties or religion.

The election of judges

The question is often asked as to whether in a constitutional republic like the US that is governed by the rule of law, it is better to have justices appointed by the executive or elected by the people. As far as the election model is concerned, judges could resemble legislators or at least policymakers and if they are to be truly independent then they have to be independent of the other branches. Judges cannot be independent if they have to worry about re-election; instead it is better to hold those accountable for the appointment if judges fail to do their jobs.

If there were direct elections voters would be likely to select a judge on partisan grounds. In selecting the judges the executive has enormous advantage; it can evaluate each and every potential candidate. Voting for judges would bring severe doubts about their impartiality. Many of the elections would be arbitrary and based on personality, rather than expertise. An appointment model is far more likely to reduce factors such as self-interest, judges feeling pressure to conform to popular opinion, or favour those who contributed to their campaign.

Alexander Hamilton, in *Federalist Papers* No. 78, wrote:

> *If the power of making [periodical judicial appointments] was committed to the people, or the persons chosen by them for the special purpose, there would be too great a disposition to consult popularity to justify a reliance that nothing would be consulted but the constitution and the laws.*

Alexis de Tocqueville wrote:

> *Under some [state] constitutions the judges are elected and subject to frequent re-election. I venture to predict that sooner or later these innovations will have dire results and that one day it will be seen by diminishing the magistrate's independence, not judicial power only but the democratic republic itself has been attacked.*

Peter Webster in the Florida State University *Law Review*, 1995, argued that in order to ensure the independence of judges, appointment with a long tenure is still the best way of selecting and retaining them. However, the advantage of this appointment process is also its key weakness. The system promotes judicial independence but at the same time, once the confirmation process has been completed, there is no significant check on the activities of a judge.

5.11 Politics and the Judiciary

Can the judiciary be politically independent?

In theory courts should be independent. In practice this certainly means that they should not be subject to political pressure, but independence should extend beyond this.

Blondel (1995) suggested that courts should be free from the: 'Norms of the political and social system itself.' In other words, they should be separate, rather than necessarily independent, and they should not be: 'Independent bodies striving for justice or equity.'

The actual independence of the judiciary varies from country to country. In some cases, such as Argentina in the 1970s, difficult judges who stood in the way of the military Junta were murdered.

More commonly, however, pressure is applied to the judiciary in other ways. The first way in which the judiciary can be influenced is the method of appointment. Some are literally appointed, as in the US, by the president and confirmed by the Senate. Others are elected. Appointment, however, has its problems, as it is seen as a way of possibly rewarding allies and that some judges are appointed on the grounds of their similar views to the present government. Electing judges suggests that they will be more representative of the citizens. But it does mean that elected judges acquire their position more on their political ability than their technical ability.

It does not necessarily follow that appointed judges follow any particular party line. Dwight D. Eisenhower, a conservative US president, appointed Chief Justice Earl Warren. Warren proved to be remarkably independent and was instrumental in advancing civil rights in the United States. A similar set of circumstances occurred when Justice Warren Burger was appointed Chief Justice by President Nixon. It was Burger who demanded that crucial evidence be handed over in the Watergate scandal. Equally, the appointment of Justice David Souter by George H. W. Bush was later considered to be a mistake. Liberal senators voted against his appointment, as he was considered a traditionalist and was expected to be a conservative. But once Bill Clinton became president Souter certainly moved to the middle ground.

Subject to good conduct, judges must be allowed to hold their post for a reasonable amount of time. They should not be able to be removed if the complexion of a government changes. Some countries get around this by allowing their judges to serve a fixed term. In the Supreme Court they serve for life, or at least until they choose to retire. In theory they can be removed, but this has never happened to date.

Judges also need to be neutral, at least in the political sense. However neutrality and independence can be interpreted in many different ways. In India forty years ago the judiciary found Prime Minister Indira Gandhi guilty of electoral malpractice and disqualified her from holding office. She responded by ordering mass arrests and imposing emergency rule.

Judges are often accused of being out of touch with society, unsympathetic to minorities and hostile to new ideas. They are also resistant to major changes in government and many parts of the New Deal put forward by President Roosevelt were struck down by the Supreme Court.

Should the judiciary keep out of politics?

Alexis de Tocqueville wrote: 'Hardly any question arises in the United States that is not resolved sooner or later into a judicial question.'

The US Supreme Court has been involved in many controversial issues. They have ruled on the death penalty, working standards, abortions and a host of other social and political issues.

Learning objectives

- Can the judiciary be politically independent?
- Should the judiciary keep out of politics?

Too old?

Justice Paul Stevens was born in 1920 and he will be 90 in 2010. He was appointed by Republican President Gerald Ford in 1975. He is the oldest and longest-serving current member of the Supreme Court.

The US Supreme Court is both judicial and political, as it considers legislation and action that comes before it and must interpret them according to the Constitution, thereby making political choices. Chief Justice Hughes once said: 'We are under the Constitution, but the Constitution is what the judges say it is.'

To a large extent the nine justices of the US Supreme Court have to be aware of the current political climate. They need to be aware of public opinion and the views of the media, not to mention election results. Their judgements are worthless unless they have consent. In other words, this means that their views have to be broadly in line with the other two branches of government.

It is, therefore, a question of judicial activism or judicial restraint.

Judicial restraint

Judicial restraint refers to the fact that the Supreme Court should not impose its views on the executive or the legislature unless they are certain that the Constitution has been violated. They should be passive, avoid conflict and allow the other parts of government to focus on social improvements. They should stay out of political arguments.

Anthony Kennedy, a member of the Rehnquist Court in 2000, stated that it was not his function to spend the rest of his life answering major questions and then suggesting the answers to Congress. He believed that individuals such as himself, who have lifetime positions and are not elected, should not take a public stance on issues that should be the preserve of the political branches of government.

Judicial activism

On the other hand there are those who believe that the Supreme Court should engage in judicial activism. A prime example was Chief Justice Earl Warren. He ruled on the rights of criminals and desegregation of schools. Many of his decisions radically changed US society and there were calls for him to be impeached. A similar case was the Burger Court, when judges were accused of making decisions that should have been left to elected representatives.

The Supreme Court sees itself primarily as the guardian of individuals' liberties and civil rights. Joan Biskupic, a commentator on the Supreme Court, wrote: 'Gone is the self-consciously loud voice the court once spoke with, boldly stating its position and calling upon the people and other institutions of government to follow.' By this she means that courts in recent years have been less likely to strike down federal and state laws.

The role of judges in political systems has certainly increased. It was only a few decades ago when politicians would effectively ignore the judiciary. Increasingly, across the world, judges have strayed into areas that would normally have been the province of governments, parliaments and state legislators. They have struck down laws and regulations that elected representatives had championed and seen through into law. International and transnational courts have added to this process, including the European Court of Justice and the European Court of Human Rights.

5.12 Judicial Activism and Conservatism

Is judicial activism the best way to check the executive?

In a parliamentary democracy, such as Britain, the primacy of the legislature should be unchallenged. But as we know, it is challenged by the executive, as the constitutional theorist Dicey wrote: 'Parliament has, under the English Constitution, the right to make any law whatever, and further, no person or body is recognised by the law of England as having a right to override or set aside the legislation of parliament.'

Judges, therefore, need to take into account the other branches of government when they make a decision. In a political system such as the US, where power is fragmented, the judiciary is more willing to decide against those in power. In other words, the more fragmented a political system is the more likely the judiciary will be effective. Often the key is whether or not there is a written constitution, as this will determine whether the courts have judicial review.

Judges not only need to be able to make independent decisions, but they must also be willing to do so. It should be possible for judges to make decisions because their preferences, motivations and interpretations differ from those of the executive. The tenure appointment procedures and salary protection all contribute toward ensuring a free-thinking judiciary.

A prime example was the US Supreme Court's ruling in the Hamdan case. It temporarily limited the president's power in the war on terror. For many it was also seen as a victory for the separation of powers, as it reinforced the view for the executive that the judiciary would not even ignore a president's wartime powers. The president responded quickly by pushing through the Military Commissions Act (2006). It was controversial and it put the Supreme Court in a position where it would have to decide once again just how far the executive could go. Over the years there have been power struggles between the three branches of the US government and the Hamdan case will certainly not be the last. The Boumediene case (2008) overturned the military courts.

Partisanship and ideology are important factors in the selection of judges. It is widely held that these factors ensure that there is a link between courts and the rest of the political system. In other words, the views of the people are reflected indirectly in the work of the courts. In most of the presidential campaigning in recent years (and to some extent the Senate) judicial appointments have been a key issue.

What are the conservative criticisms of the Supreme Court?

As far as conservatives are concerned, the Supreme Court should only make a limited contribution to the political process and only have a small role to play in government.

Policymaking and law-making

Conservatives would view the liberal Warren Court and the Burger Court to have been wrong in involving themselves in policymaking. Conservatives tend to be of the opinion that judges have little specialist knowledge of policy and as they have no direct contact with those who will be affected they have little idea about how lives can be affected by their decisions.

Learning objectives

- Is judicial activism the best way to check the executive?
- What are the conservative criticisms of the Supreme Court?

The Hamdan case

This was the legal case brought by Salim Ahmed Hamdan against the US Secretary of Defense, Donald Rumsfeld, on the issue of detainees at Guantanamo Bay being tried by a military commission. In its adjudication, the Supreme Court held that the military commissions lacked the power to proceed because they violated both the uniform code of military justice and the General Convention.

Conservatives also believe that those who wrote the US Constitution never intended the judiciary to make laws. All that was intended was that Supreme Court justices should interpret the Constitution along the lines originally envisaged by the Founding Fathers. Conservatives suggest that justices should objectively interpret and be guided by the text itself and supplementary writings by the Founding Fathers. If this approach is ignored then the justices are likely to misinterpret and not reflect the wishes of the citizens. In effect, this is strict constructionalism; in other words, a justice should take the literal text and interpret it entirely on how the authors intended that it should be read. Consequently, those who take this view are implacably opposed to judicial activism.

A prime example was the Supreme Court's decision in 1965 in Griswold vs Connecticut. The court decided that citizens have a right to privacy and that the state cannot prevent them from buying information or materials related to contraception. A strict constructionalist would claim that the Constitution does not list rights of privacy and that there is nothing in the Constitution that provides for this. Consequently, as there is no constitutional right the case should have had a different outcome.

In Roe vs Wade (1973) the Supreme Court once again found that citizens had a substantial right to privacy and that the state was limited in its ability to stop women from having abortions. Again strict constructionalists have consistently argued that no such right exists within the Constitution.

Strict constructionalists would suggest that they are firm supporters of democracy and that courts should limit themselves to the specific language of statutes and the Constitution. Each time that the Supreme Court rules that legislation is unconstitutional it is in fact ruling against a democratically elected body, responsible to the citizens of the US. They are telling that elected body that they cannot do what they wish or what their voters desire. The conservative would see the Supreme Court as violating key principles of democracy.

System of appointment and term of office

There are other issues that conservatives feel uncomfortable with, the first being the way in which Supreme Court justices are chosen. They are appointed by a president and confirmed by the Senate. The public may have an indirect influence over the appointment process, but Supreme Court vacancies are not filled by contested elections and the US citizen cannot cast a vote for or against a nominee. The second area of concern is Supreme Court justices' job security. Supreme Court justices, under Article III of the US Constitution: 'Shall hold their offices during good behaviour.'

It was never made clear what good behaviour meant and in practice federal judges are appointed for life.

The Supreme Court, in its interpretation of the Constitution, has a degree of finality to it. While policy and legislation in the US can be changed as an integral part of the legislative process either by majority vote in Congress or within the legislature of the state, it is not so easy to change a constitutional interpretation made by the Supreme Court. In many cases the Supreme Court's decision can only be reversed by amending the Constitution.

Contrast the importance of judicial appointments in different political systems

A study in Britain commissioned by the Lord Chancellor's department examined judicial appointments models in six countries: France, Italy, Spain, Portugal, Germany and the Netherlands.

The two different models identified in the study were:

- judicial self-governing bodies (or higher councils of the judiciary) who control the judicial appointments process
- less formalised institutions in charge of judicial appointments.

Four of the six countries studied were found to have judicial self-governing bodies (or higher councils of the judiciary): France, Italy, Portugal and Spain. The operation of each of these systems is examined in the following table.

Country	System used
France	France has instituted a self-governing body to control the judicial appointments process. The body responsible for judicial appointments in France is the Conseil Superieur de la Magistrature (CSM), which consists of 12 members, comprising: 5 elected judges, 1 public prosecutor, 1 councillor of state chosen by his or her peers and 3 individuals, of whom one each are nominated by the president of the Republic, the Senate and the National Assembly. The CSM also has as ex officio members: the president of the Republic and the minister of justice.
Italy	Italy's self-governing body to control judicial appointments is the Consiglio superior della magistratura (Csm). The Csm consists of 33 members, comprising 20 judges elected directly by the judiciary, 10 lawyers or university law professors nominated by parliament, and a number of ex officio members: the president of the Court of Cassation, the Prosecutor-General of Cassation and the president of the Republic.
Spain	Spain's self-governing judicial appointments body is the Consejo General del Poder Judicial, which consists of 21 members, comprising 12 judges and 8 lawyers with more than 15 years experience (all appointed by parliament), and the president of the Supreme Court as an ex officio member.
Portugal	Portugal's judicial self-governing body is the Conselho Superior da Magistradura (CSM), which consists of 17 members, comprising 7 judges elected directly by the judiciary, 1 judge nominated by the president of the Republic, 7 non-judges nominated by parliament, 1 non-judge nominated by the president of the Republic and the president of the Supreme Court as an ex officio member.

In Germany, there is a less formal system with a number of the Länder (regional governments) having judicial appointments boards, which are made up of members of the judiciary, members of the Länd parliament and members of the bar, in varying numbers. Nominees for appointment to the judiciary are recommended by the Länd minister of justice.

Learning objectives

- Contrast the importance of judicial appointments in different political systems

In Holland, at the time of the study, they were operating a combined system of judicial appointments, where 50 per cent of judges are recruited from recent university graduates and the remaining 50 per cent are appointed much later in their legal career. However, Holland has reformed its judicial appointments procedures. They have merged the appointments process for younger recruits with the appointments process for more senior members of the legal profession, to create a single judicial selection committee comprising members of the judiciary, a representation from the Justice Department and external representation (e.g. a journalist, university professor or member of the bar).

Earlier studies commissioned by the Law Society for England and Wales considered judicial appointments systems in Australia, Canada, the United States, New Zealand and all the European Union countries. The report of the review identified four principles which underpin, to different degrees, different judicial appointment mechanisms.

- Competence
- Independence
- Accountability
- Representativeness.

The study concluded that:

- appointment systems which utilise elections place an emphasis on accountability and representativeness, but sacrifice a degree of judicial independence
- systems based on appointments by the executive branch of government place an emphasis on competence and independence, at the cost of a degree of accountability and representativeness.

The four key issues bear more investigation and the key points are summarised in the following table.

Issue	Explanation and implication
Competence	Kate Malleson claimed that the use of different appointments systems has little effect on the overall competence of judges appointed. She cited a study by Mary Volcansek and Jacqueline Lafon (1988) which suggests, with reference to judicial appointments systems based on elections and those based on independent commissions, that 'there is no evidence to support the proposition that any one of these systems produces a better judge than do the others. Academic background and prior judicial experience tend to be approximately the same for judges selected under each system.'
Independence	Malleson notes that 'the aim of reducing political patronage in the appointment process is a central one behind the adoption of commissions in many countries'. It has also been suggested that, in the US context, the governor of a state still exercises partisan influence over an appointments process undertaken by a commission. Malleson suggests that, even under an independent commission, political considerations still play a role in appointments, although commissions are acknowledged to significantly reduce the element of partisanship in the appointments process.

Issue	Explanation and implication
Accountability	The need for accountability in the judicial appointments process has been cited as an argument against the creation of a commission. It is argued that an appointments commission made up of members not drawn from the executive or legislature has no direct line of accountability to parliament. In response to this position it is argued that the composition of the commission may be the decision of a member of the executive, through which the commission can be held accountable, or that the commission may include a member of the executive. Malleson notes that 'it is correct to say that the individual accountability of the minister who can be said to carry full personal responsibility for the decision is weakened under a commission system'.
Representativeness	Studies in the US reflect a wide range of opinions about the effect of different appointment systems on the composition of the judiciary. Among those who suggest that the use of independent commissions has an effect on the representativeness of the judiciary, the composition of the commission itself is viewed as an important factor in this process, with a representative balance in commission membership being viewed as the way to increase greater representativeness among the judiciary itself. It has been found that in relation to the representation of ethnic minority communities in the judiciary, the likelihood of members of ethnic minority communities being appointed relied more on the number of lawyers in that jurisdiction from ethnic minority communities.

Exam Café

Relax, refresh, result!

Relax and prepare

Questions for the exam are likely to be drawn from the following topic areas or similar. Use these to help focus on what areas of the subject you should be revising.

- Appointments to the Supreme Court, the power of judicial review and judicial independence, the politics of the court, the court and the protection of individual rights.
- Arrange a list of court cases which are relevant to the above headings. For example, Rasul vs Bush (2004) and Boumediene vs Bush (2008), which illustrate both the court's power of judicial review and its protection of individual rights. The case of Carhart vs Gonzales (2007) demonstrates an erosion of abortion rights and poses questions about Roe vs Wade (1973) in the future.
- Learn the first ten amendments of the US Constitution and appreciate the significance of the 14th in ensuring rights are enforced across all the states.

Refresh your memory

When revising this topic, try the following exercises. They will help you structure your notes and will give you a guide as to what you will need to know for the different papers. Remember to work through unit F853 first as this will provide the base you will need for F855.

- The Supreme Court's protection of individual rights.
- Draw a table which has the first ten amendments in one column and relevant Supreme Court cases in another. Focus on the more recent rulings (as above) as much as possible rather than landmark rulings from previous courts such as Warren.
- Examine the appointments of Roberts and Alito and the withdrawal of Miers. Consider the roles the president, the Senate Judiciary Committee, the Senate, pressure groups and the media.
- Look at recent 5:4 rulings from the court and identify the conservative, liberal and centrist voting blocs thereon. Identify key swing voters on the court.
- Define and use the following terms: judicial activism and passivism and strict and loose constructionism.
- Make a case for the Warren Court as a 'liberal activist' court, the Burger Court as a 'rootless activist' court and for 'conservative activism' in the early years of the Rehnquist Court and 'pragmatic passivism' thereafter. Attempt to define the political outlook of the Roberts Court thus far.

- Consider the power of the court within the context of democracy. Criticisms may focus on its lack of accountability and unrepresentative nature. Politicisation of the judiciary via presidential 'legacy' appointments is a key argument in this regard.
- Make a list of the constraints upon the court. These arguments are really useful as they can be used to justify the power of the court in a democracy and to counter accusations that the court is a political as opposed to a judicial institution. Similarly, the role of the presidency and the Senate also ensures there is a significant democratic input into its composition.

Exam tips

These are some reasons why students do badly in exams. They provide a guide to what you need to avoid and by implication what you need to do to perform well in the exam.

- They are too reliant on dated rulings, particularly from the Warren Court. It is worth noting that Brown vs Board of Education, Topeka (1954) is over 50 years old and the Burger Court Roe vs Wade (1973) over 30 years old. Consequently they give little insight into the role of the court today.
- Essays sometimes contain details of a long list of cases which are not always relevant to the question.
- In this regard, essays need to focus on the question. A question on judicial review is not the same as one on the judicial appointments.

Get the result!

These are some ideas to help you in your revision and to keep up to date with the latest developments in US politics.

- Use the Cornell Law Library online, the *Washington Post* and the *New York Times* to gain access to the most recent rulings from the Supreme Court and voting blocs.
- Refer to cases from the present session.
- Look up the website of the ACLU for an insight into contemporary issues relating to individual rights.
- Note that George W. Bush stated that he would not accept the judgement of the ABA on judicial nominees due to a perceived liberal bias. He preferred the recommendations of the conservative Federalist Society.
- Keep an eye out for retirements from the court. Some are anticipated in the very near future (Stevens and Ginsburg being the favourites to retire first). There will be a great deal of media coverage on the issues surrounding the appointment process at that time.
- Refer to statements from Obama about his view of the role of the court and his requirements for future selections.

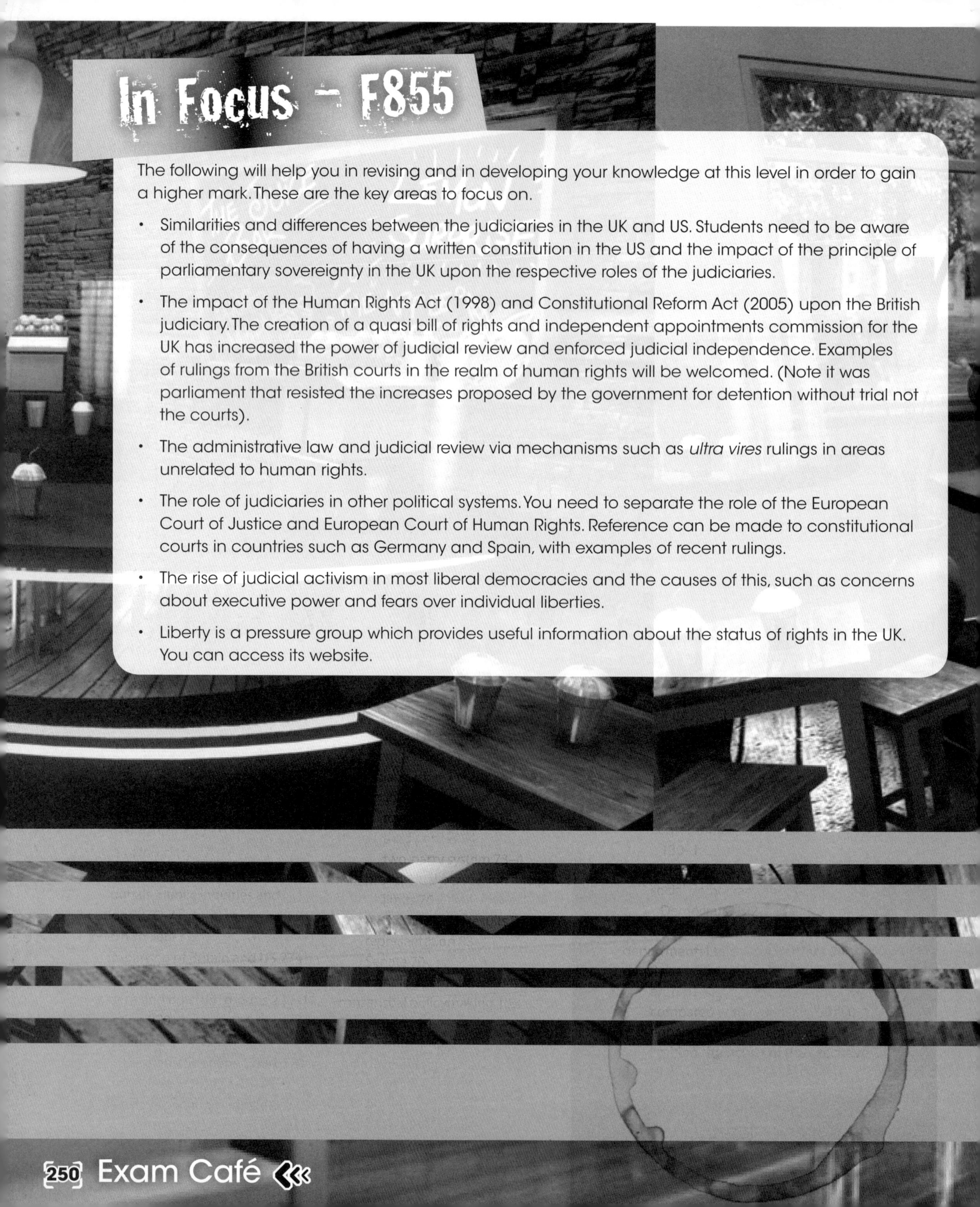

In Focus – F855

The following will help you in revising and in developing your knowledge at this level in order to gain a higher mark. These are the key areas to focus on.

- Similarities and differences between the judiciaries in the UK and US. Students need to be aware of the consequences of having a written constitution in the US and the impact of the principle of parliamentary sovereignty in the UK upon the respective roles of the judiciaries.
- The impact of the Human Rights Act (1998) and Constitutional Reform Act (2005) upon the British judiciary. The creation of a quasi bill of rights and independent appointments commission for the UK has increased the power of judicial review and enforced judicial independence. Examples of rulings from the British courts in the realm of human rights will be welcomed. (Note it was parliament that resisted the increases proposed by the government for detention without trial not the courts).
- The administrative law and judicial review via mechanisms such as *ultra vires* rulings in areas unrelated to human rights.
- The role of judiciaries in other political systems. You need to separate the role of the European Court of Justice and European Court of Human Rights. Reference can be made to constitutional courts in countries such as Germany and Spain, with examples of recent rulings.
- The rise of judicial activism in most liberal democracies and the causes of this, such as concerns about executive power and fears over individual liberties.
- Liberty is a pressure group which provides useful information about the status of rights in the UK. You can access its website.

THE JUICE BAR
LEMON SURPRISE
MANGO MADNESS
THE APPLE

6 Civil Rights and Liberties

Civil rights in the United States is most closely associated with the period 1955 to 1968, when reform movements fought to abolish racial discrimination in the southern states. As a consequence civil rights are more entrenched in the US than anywhere else.

The key civil rights and liberties cherished by US citizens are enshrined in the US Constitution (1787) and the Bill of Rights (1791), which consists of 10 key amendments to the Constitution.

These rights and liberties in the US have been further developed by the judiciary, the Supreme Court and organisations such as the American Civil Liberties Union, which funds cases believed to be fundamental to liberties. The key rights and liberties are clearly written down in the Constitution, however they can still be challenged, interpreted and sometimes enhanced by Supreme Court rulings.

The civil rights and liberties remain at the heart of US politics, and each piece of legislation proposed is measured for its impact on the Constitution and the Bill of Rights.

The Supreme Court aims to provide effective protection for majority and minority rights, whether for race, religion, gender, freedom of speech or expression.

The US system of protecting against the violation of the rights and liberties of its citizens is one of the most successful in the world. And given any violation of such rights and liberties the citizens can seek redress to petition the government under the 1st amendment of the Constitution. Apart from the constitutional right to redress, those suffering from such violation can seek help from pressure groups that are organised and expert at pursuing redress.

There are six key themes in this chapter.

- What are civil rights and liberties?
- Protecting rights
- Rights, liberty and citizenship
- Civil rights and liberties in the US (1)
- Civil rights and liberties in the US (2)
- Current issues

These are represented by the first six topics, and are supported by one question topic for F853, looking at the most common essay themes, and three F855 question topics, which again look at popular essay themes in the examination.

This chapter contains 10 topics in total, representing the following.

The chapter is rounded off with an exam café feature on page 278.

6.1 What are Civil Rights and Liberties?

Learning objectives

- What are civil rights and liberties?
- Rights
- Rights and duties of citizens

What are civil rights and liberties?

Both these concepts are principal features of liberal democracies. While Britain has a mix of legislation and other written guarantees, some of which have evolved over time, countries such as the US have a bill of rights, which is part of a written constitution that guarantees civil rights and liberties.

In effect, civil rights are positive obligations imposed on a government to protect citizens from illegal actions, whether these are committed by a government, agency or by another citizen. There are also certain areas of civil life in which the government can intrude to ensure that all citizens are treated fairly and there is equality of opportunity.

Civil rights are the obligations on government and civil liberties are, therefore, the protections that a citizen has against government intrusions.

Rights

Generally, there are three major types of rights, as listed in the following table.

Right	Explanation	Expansion
Natural	These are either God-given or law-given rights for all by virtue of human existence.	In the US Declaration of Independence these were defined as inalienable rights. John Locke argued that natural rights are life, liberty and property. They are not given nor can they be taken away by government. If they are violated then an individual should be able to protest or rebel.
Positive	These rights exist because they have been given to the individual by the state.	The question is often asked as to which rights should be given. They include bills of rights and written declarations in some countries.
Negative	Without a clear bill of rights it is difficult to know which rights exist, and in such cases a government could restrict rights through legislation.	If there is not a written statement about a right, it can still exist, but such rights lack the protection of positive rights, as they are not written down.

Since 1953 the United Nations has promoted its Declaration of Human Rights to encourage governments to incorporate them into their legal systems and to raise people's consciousness of them. Most modern democracies incorporate the following rights into their legal systems.

- Life and personal security
- Conscience, thought, expression and freedom of press
- Freedom of religion
- Political equality and the right to vote in free elections
- Political organisation and assembly
- Freedom of movement
- Equality in law
- Right to the process of the law
- Right to a fair trial.

There are, however, considerable arguments about where rights should or should not end and which are essential and which are not. These arguments focus on issues such as the right to work, to privacy and to own property. Some conservative groups add the right to life of unborn children; the more liberal approach focuses on a woman's right to choose.

Conservatives also favour the right of individuals to choose their own health and education provision, while liberals and socialists see state provision of these as being essential in upholding rights. Conservatives question the right for trade unions or organised labour to exist. This issue is less important for the Labour Party in Britain or the Democrats in the US.

In Britain, the Conservatives, particularly under John Major, focused on the rights, duties and expectations of citizens and the state by requiring performance targets for public services. Under the Citizens' Charter he set up clearer complaints procedures, the releasing of statistics and the penalising of failing public bodies. Labour has focused on the duties of citizens, and with the adoption of elements of the European Convention on Human Rights they have also focused on civil or citizens' rights. Parents are now held accountable for the actions of their children, families are penalised for the anti-social behaviour of family members, and the unemployed are expected to take a more active role in finding work. Citizenship classes have been brought into schools and individuals who wish to become naturalised British citizens are required to take citizenship examinations.

Rights and duties of citizens

The judiciary is the ultimate protector of the civil rights of citizens. Its position and role in this was substantially reinforced when the Human Rights Act (2000) was passed. For many this was a major turning point in law and politics; from that time on the judiciary would be far more active in the defence of rights.

A citizen is an individual who is formally recognised by a state as a member of that state, and as such is automatically granted certain rights and duties. Rights and duties are closely linked. If an individual is free to state their own opinions then everyone else has a duty to respect this right. Governments should protect the rights of citizens and punish those who fail to respect those rights.

The term 'human rights' is now used to indicate the rights of a citizen to equality of treatment. There are fundamental freedoms guaranteed by law, such as the right to a fair trial, freedom from slavery, freedom of expression and freedom from torture. In Britain most human or civil rights are guaranteed in common law and by the Human Rights Act, much of which is derived from the European Convention on Human Rights.

Along with these human and civil rights, citizens of Britain are expected to make their contribution to the state in the form of duties. In the 1980s, the British government of the time (the Conservative Party led by Margaret Thatcher) accepted the rights of citizens, but that these had to be counterbalanced by the duties of the citizens to the state and other citizens. Labour governments since 1997 have continued to hold this position, whereas in the past Labour Party policy stressed the state's duty to provide for citizens who could not provide for themselves. Typical duties of citizens now expected by the state are to:

- vote
- assist in law and order
- work
- provide for themselves in old age
- help the community
- be involved in social and political issues
- do voluntary work
- support charities
- take personal responsibility for one's actions (and that of the family and, perhaps, the community).

INTERNET RESEARCH

There is a website with a specific section on government, citizens and rights, explaining rights and responsibilities. To see this, go to www.heinemann.co.uk/hotlinks, insert express code 1825P and click on the relevant link.

6.2 Protecting Rights

Learning objectives

- Constitutions
- Bills of rights
- Legislatures and judiciaries

Constitutions

Britain has a tradition of freedom and liberty even though it lacks a written constitution. David Hume, writing in 1752, said: 'Her station as guardian of the general liberties of Europe and patron of mankind [are still maintained].'

The idea of framing a comprehensive statement on human rights within a constitution in Britain has been opposed for centuries. Britain is a signatory to the European Convention on Human Rights and Fundamental Freedoms, but the convention has not been incorporated into British law. British governments have had a negative approach to rights; the presumption is that individuals are free to do as they please unless it is expressly forbidden in common law or legislation. The rule of law is seen as the main safeguard on rights and liberties. There is still a demand for a written constitution, one that will adequately protect the rights of citizens. The view is that a written constitution would not only limit government, but if it was backed up with a bill of rights it would safeguard rights and liberties.

In the US the rights and liberties of citizens was central in the Declaration of Independence. Thomas Jefferson wrote: 'We hold these truths to be self-evident, that all men are created equal, that they are endowed by their creator with certain inalienable rights, that amongst these are life, liberty and the pursuit of happiness.'

The Constitution (1787) and the Bill of Rights (1791) incorporated separation of powers, checks and balances, a federal system and a bicameral legislation. It also incorporated:

- a writ of habeas corpus that could not be suspended
- a bill of attainder, which effectively meant that no individual without a trial could be held guilty of a crime
- that there should be no post facto or retrospective law
- the right of trial by a jury
- that any privileges or immunities of citizens of other states are the entitlement of the citizens of each state
- that there should be no religious tests or qualification for holding federal office
- that no law should impair the obligation of contracts.

The Constitution in the US provides written guarantees for both the states and individuals against intrusion by national government.

Bills of rights

Under threat

Many British freedoms have been under threat and some have been violated in recent years due to their status as negative rights.

While there is no written constitution or written bill of rights in Britain, British citizens enjoy freedom of movement, freedom from arbitrary arrest and police search, freedom of conscience in religious matters, politics and expression, freedom of association in peaceful protest; they also have the right to vote, stand for election, own property, have a fair trial, and not be subject to surveillance without legal process. There are also social freedoms regarding abortion, divorce, same-sex relationships and marriages.

The source of many of these rights derives from case and statute law, EU law and conventions, including the following.

- Magna Carta (1812)
- Habeas Corpus Act (1679)
- Bill of Rights (1689)
- Catholic Emancipation (1829)
- Sex Discrimination Acts (1975 and 1987)
- Race Relations Act (1976)
- Data Protection Acts (1984 and 1998)
- Police and Criminal Evidence Act (1984)
- United Nations' Declaration on Human Rights (1949)
- European Convention on Human Rights (1950)
- Human Rights Act (1998).

In the US the Bill of Rights is incorporated into 10 key amendments that were introduced in 1789. These are listed in the following table.

Amendment	Rights addressed
1	Freedom of speech, press, assembly and petition, also free exercise of religion
2	Right to bear arms
3	Prohibits troops from occupying a citizen's home in peacetime
4	No unreasonable searches and seizures
5	Indictment by a grand jury required for serious crime, prohibits double jeopardy, protects against self-incrimination, requires due process of law for government to take life, liberty or property, and prevents government from using private property without fair compensation
6	Provides for legal counsel for defence in a jury trial
7	Protects the right to jury trial in civil cases
8	Prohibits cruel and unusual punishments or excessive bail
9	Protects other unspecified rights
10	Reserves to the people or to the states all other powers that have not been granted to federal government or prohibited to the states by the Constitution

The 14th Amendment of the constitution extended basic liberties, focusing on the prohibition of states from interfering:

> *No state shall make or enforce any law which shall abridge the privileges or immunities of citizens of the United States nor shall any state deprive any person of life, liberty, or property, without due process of law; nor deny to any persons within its jurisdiction the equal protection of the laws.*

There have been four other amendments to the Constitution to extend rights. These are:

- Amendment 15 – the vote cannot be denied on account of colour or race
- Amendment 19 – the vote cannot be denied on account of gender
- Amendment 24 – the vote cannot be denied if a poll tax or any other tax has not been paid
- Amendment 26 – the right of all those aged 18 or more to vote.

In June 2006, the British Conservative Party leader, David Cameron, announced his support of an American-style bill of rights. He proposed that it should replace the Human Rights Act. His proposals were described as 'unworkable, confused, muddled, misconceived and dangerous'. Cameron believed that a bill of rights would be able to balance British traditions, rights and security. Behind his beliefs Cameron stated that current legislation was inadequate to fight against crime and terrorism and that the Human Rights Act had effectively prevented Britain from deporting suspected terrorists.

Legislatures and judiciaries

In Britain, parliament, through existing and proposed legislation, aims to continue to protect the rights and liberties of citizens. These rights are backed up by ombudsmen, citizens' charters and regulatory bodies. There are also administrative tribunals and more recently additional protection has been considered by the Scottish Parliament and by the Welsh and Northern Ireland assemblies. The courts in Britain, using the concept of the rule of law, ensure that all are equal under the law, no one is above the law and that the law is clear. All have the right to a fair and speedy trial by an impartial system. This is also supported by the increasing influence of European courts.

In the US, the amendments to the Constitution have been agreed by successive Congresses and mechanisms have been set up at both federal and state level to monitor and enforce rights. The Supreme Court has been active across a broad range of civil liberties issues. As we will see when we examine specific civil rights and liberties, the court has made many key judgements over the years. This has helped it to identify the amendments relating to each civil liberty and give clear interpretations as to the implications.

INTERNET RESEARCH

For the US Constitution and the amendments that make up the Bill of Rights, along with their implications, go to www.heinemann.co.uk/hotlinks, insert the express code 1825P and click on the relevant link.

Rights and liberties

In the US there is a more formal protection of individual rights than in Britain. The US Constitution, and specifically the Bill of Rights, sets out key freedoms, for example the 1st Amendment guarantees freedom of expression. Before the Human Rights Act came into force in Britain there were no clear protections. Many believe that a bill of rights is the way to deal with any potential problems that could arise between the individual and the state.

But even in the US a written statement of rights is meaningless if the government is unwilling or unable to enforce it. Many of the civil rights accorded to citizens of the US were not applied to African-Americans for generations and during the Second World War citizens of Japanese heritage were deprived of their liberty by being imprisoned. On the one hand, supporters of bills of rights, such as Thomas Jefferson, failed to see why a country would not adopt a bill of rights. He saw it as: 'what the people are entitled to against every government on earth, general or particular, and what no just government should refuse or rest on inference.'

In contrast the Conservative MP John Patten, former Secretary of State for Education, wrote:

> *Such documents are meaningless unless they exist within a country which has a political culture that renders them viable. The greatest protector of citizens' rights in the UK are citizens themselves. A protector of freedom in the end is the political culture, not some document, however weighty.*

The following table outlines the key ways in which liberties and rights of citizens are dealt with in both Britain and the US.

Issue	US	Britain
Bill of rights	First 10 amendments incorporated into the Constitution	No bill of rights, but there is protection under the Human Rights Act
Language and interpretation	Broad and unqualified interpretation dependent on the judiciary	Interpretation of Human Rights Act necessary, or with reference to European rulings, otherwise judicial interpretation
Freedom of expression	Guaranteed by 1st Amendment but not always extended to extreme minority groups	Under Article 10 of the Human Rights Act, but there are greater restrictions
Punishment	Favours police powers, tough regimes, and widespread use of the death penalty	Police power strengthened, no death penalty, need to balance right of accused and rights of victims
Women's rights	Obtained vote through 19th Amendment (1920) Anti-discrimination legislation brought in during the 1960s, although the equal rights amendment failed	Vote gained in 1918 and 1928 Anti-discrimination legislation brought in from the 1970s
Ethnic minorities	Although civil rights and anti-discrimination legislation came in during the 1960s, its application and enforcement is still patchy	Anti-discrimination legislation brought in during the 1960s and 1970s, but again patchy enforcement

Learning objectives

- Rights and liberties
- Citizenship

Citizenship

In Europe, the Maastricht Treaty introduced the idea of citizenship of the EU. Article 17 was subsequently amended by the EC Treaty: 'Citizenship of the Union is hereby established. Every person holding the nationality of a member state shall be a citizen of the Union. Citizenship of the Union shall complement and not replace national citizenship.'

In effect this not only accords fundamental rights to EU citizens, but also allows them freedom of movement around the EU. More broadly, citizenship is often seen as affording an individual or individuals, political rights. However it also implies that the individual has a range of responsibilities and duties and, in effect, a social contract with the state.

In the US citizens have the duty to serve on juries and pay taxes, males need to register for possible conscription into the armed forces and those who wish to become naturalised US citizens are required to make an oath of citizenship to defend the Constitution, to obey US law and to bear arms on behalf of the US if called upon.

Although the requirements for British citizens are not as overt, naturalisation takes place after six years, requiring an individual to be of good character, to communicate in English and have an intention to live in Britain or serve in the Crown Service abroad. There are plans to make the acquisition of British citizenship more exacting and that individuals have to earn citizenship.

There is no legal definition of a US citizen and no comprehensive list of the rights and duties of a US citizen in the Constitution. The 14th Amendment defined who a US citizen could be, but not what a citizen actually was. Citizenship is automatically awarded to those born in US territory, regardless of the nationality of their parents.

Citizenship can be withdrawn from an individual, but Congress's right to do this was limited by the 1967 Afroyim vs Rusk decision. US citizens have a number of rights and duties, including:

- freedom of movement
- right to a passport
- right to vote
- right of petition and to a referendum
- right to stand as a candidate in national and local elections
- right of access to public office
- right to protection
- linguistic rights
- non-discrimination rights
- a duty of allegiance to the state
- a duty to undertake military or alternative service
- a duty to pay tax
- a duty to make social security (national insurance) contributions.

The US Patriot Act (2001) was passed in the wake of the terrorist attacks on the US in September that year. It expanded law enforcement and counter-terrorism measures, both domestically and overseas. Many believe that the Act has had a massive impact on the rights conferred to citizens under the US constitution and its subsequent amendments, including:

- freedom of religion
- freedom of speech
- freedom of assembly
- freedom of the press
- freedom of deprivation of life, liberty or property without due process of law
- the right to public trial by an impartial jury
- the right to be informed of the facts of an accusation
- the right to confront witnesses and to have a lawyer
- freedom from excessive bail and cruel and unusual punishment.

US courts are suggesting that certain elements of the Act are unconstitutional. They have also recently ruled on the constitutional implications of individuals being held at Guantanamo Bay (Boudemiene vs Bush 2008).

INTERNET RESEARCH

For a summary of the Patriot Act, go to www.heinemann.co.uk/hotlinks, insert express code 1825P and click on the relevant link.

Learning objectives

- Race and religion
- Freedom of expression

Race and religion

For more than 150 years equality for African-Americans has been a key issue in US politics. Slavery was still constitutional after the Dred Scott case (1857). Forty years later, in 1896, the Supreme Court in Plessy vs Ferguson upheld the 'equal but separate accommodations for the white and coloured races'. Later cases relating to segregation include the following:

- Brown vs Board of Education (1954) – this involved the issue of how segregated schools violated the 14th Amendment.
- Alexander vs Holmes (1969) – this involved the issue of dual-school systems being unconstitutional.
- Swann vs Charlotte-Mecklenburg Country Schools (1971) – this involved the issue of bussing students into schools as a means of dealing with segregated schools.

On affirmative action the following cases involved key issues.

- Regents of the University of California vs Bakke (1978) – this reversed racial quotas and upheld affirmative action programmes as being constitutional.
- Affirmative action was under threat from the more conservative Supreme Court in decisions including Richmond vs Croson (1989) and Wards Cove Packing vs Atonio (1989).
- Adarand Constructors vs Peña (1995) – this ruled that affirmative action programmes needed to serve a compelling government interest.
- Gratz vs Bollinger (2003) – the Supreme Court ruled that the university's point system in their Affirmative Action Admissions Policy was too mechanistic and unconstitutional.

Racial gerrymandering was declared unconstitutional in the 1960s. In 1986, in Thornburg vs Gingles, legislative redistricting became the basis upon which minority representation could be maximised (known as affirmative racial or benign gerrymandering). In 1993 to 1996 three rulings struck down these majority–minority districts, holding that the use of race in drawing boundaries was unconstitutional.

The US comprises many different religious groups, some of them having fled their own countries in pursuit of religious freedom. Although religious freedom is an integral part of the 1st Amendment there have been a number of Supreme Court rulings that have created controversy, as can be seen in the following table.

Warren Court (1953–69)	Burger Court (1969–86)	Rehnquist Court (1986–2005)
Engel vs Vitale 1962 The court ruled: 'That it is no part of the business of government to compose official prayers for any group to recite as part of a religious programme carried on by government.'	Lemon vs Kurtzman 1971 This set three criteria to teach secular subjects, to serve a secular legislative purpose, to neither advance nor inhibit religion or foster an excessive entanglement with religion.	Edwards vs Aguillard 1987 The court overturned the law in Louisiana requiring public schools to teach creation science alongside evolutionary science.
Abington School District vs Schempp 1963 The court ruled that the Constitution requires neutrality between the state and the church. The state should: 'Neither advance or inhibit religion.'	Mueller vs Allen 1983 The court upheld tax deductions for school tuition fees, books and transportation.	County of Allegheny vs ACLU 1987 The court ruled against a nativity scene in a county courthouse.
Everson vs Board of Education 1947 The court stated: 'Neither a state nor the federal government can set up a church. In the words of Jefferson, the clause against establishment of religion by law was intended to erect a wall of separation between church and state.'	Lynch vs Donnelly 1984 The court ruled that a city's nativity scene display was viewed as having a secular legislative purpose that did not advance religion or entangle the city with religion.	Employment Division vs Smith 1990 The court ruled that state laws that interfered with religious practices that were not aimed at the religion were constitutional.
The accommodationist view, such as Sunday closing laws, does allow the government to make adjustments so that religious activities can be possible.	Wallace vs Jaffree 1985 The court ruled that a mandatory silence in public schools for meditation or voluntary prayer unconstitutional.	Lee vs Weisman 1992 The court decided that a school-sponsored prayer in public school violated establishment clause.
Engel vs Vitale 1962 Senator Sam Ervin (North Carolina complained that the Supreme Court: 'has made God unconstitutional'.	Grand Rapids School District vs Ball 1985 The court stopped a programme in parochial schools financed by federal funds and taught by public school teachers. In 1986 President Reagan said: 'The Good Lord, who has given our country so much, should never have been expelled from our nation's classrooms.'	Santa Fe Independent School District vs DOE 2000 The court ruled against prayers held by sports teams before a game.

Freedom of expression

The US Bill of Rights implies that no legislation should impact on the freedom of speech. In reality the situation is somewhat different.

- The Espionage Act (1917) and the Smith Act (1940) both restricted freedom of speech that might undermine government.
- The Schenck vs United States (1919) ruling upheld restriction of free speech if there was a 'clear and present danger' (changed to 'clear and probable danger' in 1951).
- In Brandenburg vs Ohio (1969) the court overturned the conviction of a white supremacist, who had advocated violence.

- In John Doe vs University of Michigan (1989) the court held that the university had responsibility to prevent discrimination but not at the expense of free speech.
- The arguments around the government's ability to stop the media from publishing stories are known as prior restraint. The government's right was affirmed in 1931 and the Supreme Court ruled that judges could not prevent the press from reporting about a case in 1976.
- Between 1957 and 1968 there were 13 cases involving obscenity, with 55 different opinions. Since then the Supreme Court has focused on what is offensive, on whether certain forms of pornography can be collected and on preventing minors from viewing obscene material.
- In New York Times vs Sullivan (1964) the court stated that statements about public officials are only libellous if deliberately malicious or reckless.
- On symbolic speech, involving the peaceful expression of unpopular ideas, a man's conviction for the burning of his draft card was upheld in 1968; in 1971 a state could not forbid particular words without the risk of suppressing ideas; and in 1989 Texan law on the banning of flag burning was ruled to be unconstitutional (Texas vs Johnson 1989).

The 1st Amendment is seen as the key dividing line between the liberals and the conservatives, but the Supreme Court has been consistent in its interpretation and the amendment is seen as a key to US democracy. In the Texas vs Johnson (1989) case, which declared the Texan law about flag burning as unconstitutional, the Supreme Court said: 'If there is a bedrock principle underlying the 1st Amendment, it is that the government may not prohibit the expression of an idea simply because society finds the idea itself offensive or disagreeable.'

Associate Justice Anthony Kennedy added: 'The hard fact is that sometimes we must make decisions we do not like. The flag protects those who hold it in contempt.'

When Congress passed the Flag Protection Act (1989) the Supreme Court found the legislation unconstitutional in US vs Eichman (1990).

INTERNET RESEARCH

For useful background to the Flag Protection Act visit the American Presidency Project. To see this, go to www.heinemann.co.uk/hotlinks, insert express code 1825P and click on the relevant link.

6.5 Civil Rights and Liberties in the US (2)

Learning objectives

- Rights of the accused
- Rights to privacy
- Women's rights
- Other rights
- Role of institutions and the Constitution

Rights of the accused

The 4th to 8th amendments to the Constitution focus on the rights of individuals accused of crimes. The concept of due process was applied to the states by the Warren Court interpretation of the 14th Amendment. The following were key decisions related to the rights of the accused.

- Mapp vs Ohio (1961) – illegally seized evidence had to be excluded as evidence. However, in Nix vs Williams (1984) evidence was allowed if it inevitably would have been discovered. The US vs Leon (1984) case established that if the police had acted illegally but believed they were acting constitutionally, then evidence was allowed. Arizona vs Evans (1995) allowed evidence obtained illegally as a result of clerical error and Illinois vs Wardlo (1999) allowed the police to stop and search someone who runs if they see a police officer.
- In Miranda vs Arizona (1966), 'prior to any questioning, the person must be warned that he has a right to remain silent, that any statement he does make may be used against him, and that he has the right to the presence of an attorney, either retained or appointed'. If the police do not follow this procedure then evidence can be excluded. New York vs Quarles (1984) allowed exemptions to self-incrimination when there were 'overriding considerations of public safety'. Arizona vs Fulminante (1991) held that involuntary confessions were admissible. In Dickerson vs United States (2000) the Miranda ruling was upheld.
- Gideon vs Wainwright (1963) found that an individual's conviction had violated the 14th Amendment's due process clause. He had asked for counsel (lawyer or attorney) but not received one. In Scott vs Illinois (1979) it was ruled that there was no need for an attorney when no sentence of imprisonment is imposed.
- In Furman vs Georgia (1972) the death penalty was ruled to be a 'cruel and unusual punishment' and violated the 8th Amendment. In Gregg vs Georgia (1976) the 1972 ruling was overturned. In Lockhart vs McCree (1986) it was ruled that jurors who oppose the death penalty can be excluded. In McClesky vs Kemp (1987) capital punishment was declared not to be cruel and unusual even though ethnic minorities were more likely to be given the death penalty. In Penry vs Lynaugh (1989) it was ruled that even if someone is mentally disadvantaged, but were proved to be competent to stand trial, they could be executed. In Stanford vs Kentucky (1989) it was declared that sixteen- and seventeen-year-olds can suffer the death penalty. Payne vs Tennessee (1991) declared that juries could hear victim impact evidence. In Buchanan vs Angelone (1998) it was decided that judges do not have to reveal evidence that could result in a life sentence rather than a death penalty.
- In Baze vs Rees (2008) two men in Kentucky had been sentenced to death by lethal injection. They argued that this would violate the 8th Amendment, which prohibited cruel and unusual punishment. The court rejected this challenge and upheld Kentucky's law by 7–2.

Rights to privacy

Usually privacy revolves around the abortion issue, however the concept of privacy itself does not appear in the Constitution. It has been developed and applied in the following cases.

- Griswold vs Connecticut (1965) ruled that it was unconstitutional to forbid the sale of contraceptives.

- Roe vs Wade (1973) struck down Texas law that only allowed an abortion when it would save the life of the mother.
- Webster vs Reproductive Health Services (1989) forbade the use of state funds or state employees to perform abortions.
- Rust vs Sullivan (1991) ruled that family planning services in receipt of federal funds could not counsel women regarding abortion. Planned Parenthood of Southeastern Pennsylvania vs Casey (1992) upheld the Roe decision. Madsen vs Women's Health Center (1994) protected women's right to enter an abortion clinic.
- In Stenberg vs Carhart (2000) the Supreme Court struck down a Nebraskan law that criminalised partial birth abortions, as it violated the due process clause of the US Constitution. In Gonzales vs Carhart (2007) the court refused to reverse the Stenberg vs Carhart ruling.

Presidents Reagan and George H. W. Bush were pro-lifers. President Clinton, on the other hand, lifted the ban on abortion counselling.

Women's rights

The struggle for equal status for women made considerable progress with the 19th Amendment in 1920. But there were still many hurdles to overcome that were largely addressed from the 1950s onwards.

- The National Organization of Women and the National Women's Political Caucus were created to advance women's rights.
- In Reed vs Reed (1971) the gender classification law in the equal protection clause of the constitution was struck down.
- In Frontiero vs Richardson (1973) married women in the armed forces were entitled to the same benefits as married men.
- Craig vs Boren (1976) struck down differential legal drinking ages.
- Rostker vs Goldberg (1981) upheld the draft that had been limited to males.
- Johnson vs Transportation Agency Santa Clara County (1987) ruled that the use of affirmative action to improve promotion prospects to address under representation was constitutional.
- Harris vs Forklift Systems (1993) made it easier to bring sexual harassment charges in the workplace.
- Since 1982 there have been a number of attempts to introduce an Equal Rights Amendment to the US Constitution. On each occasion it has failed to gain any degree of support.

Other rights

Specifically these relate to gay and lesbian rights, those with disabilities and discrimination against Native Americans.

- Bowers vs Hardwick (1986) ruled that privacy law did not apply to homosexual activity and in Lawrence vs Texas (2003) a similar ruling was made.

- Romer vs Evans (1996) ruled that Colorado law denying homosexuals protection against discrimination was against the 14th Amendment.
- The 1973 Rehabilitation Act made it illegal to discriminate against the disabled. The Education of All Handicapped Children Act (1975) gave all children the right to free education, regardless of their needs. Americans with Disabilities Act (1990) extended disabled coverage provided in the Civil Rights Act (1964).
- Native Americans did not become US citizens until 1924. The Indian Claims Act (1946) aimed to compensate Native Americans who had had their land confiscated. During the 1970s huge amounts of land were returned and the Sioux were given over $100 million for land that was confiscated in South Dakota.

INTERNET RESEARCH

There are two useful US government civil rights orientated websites: the US Commission on Civil Rights and the United States Department of Justice Civil Rights Division. To see these, go to www.heinemann.co.uk/hotlinks, insert express code 1825P and click on the relevant link.

Role of institutions and the Constitution

In the US the Supreme Court is the main branch of government that has the responsibility of ensuring citizens' freedoms are observed, as well as giving meaning to the freedoms. It has tended to refuse to make them absolute rights in the sense that they should not be beyond government regulation or observed regardless of the consequences. Consequently the amendments have never been interpreted in absolute terms. Rights to freedom of speech and the press are in fact limited.

Successive presidents, Congress, pressure groups and advisers have driven the campaign to defend rights in the US, primarily through legislation, although their decisions, policies and legislation are only as effective as the ability to conform with the Constitution, as interpreted by the Supreme Court. Also, the campaign only has an impact if there is the will and the way to enforce the legislation at both state and federal levels.

Issues associated with rights and liberties in Britain

Learning objectives

- Issues associated with rights and liberties in Britain
- Issues associated with rights and liberties in the US

During the Thatcher years (1979–90) there were doubts as to whether British citizens' rights and liberties were safe. It was felt that the government could damage these rights, as they were not clearly defined. Specifically, the government affected rights in the following areas.

- Official Secrets Act – this has been used by the government to silence the press and prevent them from criticising the government on the grounds that featuring a story would be damaging to the national security of the country (e.g. the Spycatcher case).
- The press faced the prospect of legal action from the rich or well-placed if they ran a story against the interests of such an individual. There were cases when the media was threatened with a slander or libel case. For example, Jeffrey Archer, the then deputy chairman of the Conservative Party, and Robert Maxwell, who was a media proprietor.
- The right to silence was removed for those arrested for a crime.
- The government sought to ban radio and television programmes they felt damaged the security of the nation, for example the government's attempts to silence Andrew Gilligan's claims that the Iraq weapons dossier was exaggerated in 2003.
- Sinn Féin (the political wing of the Irish Republican Army) representatives could not speak on television or radio.
- The police and security forces were given the right to listen into telephone conversations.
- Celebrities and members of the royal family found themselves subject to media intrusion (photographs, 'kiss and tell' stories, and frequent comments in the press).
- Citizens did not have the right to access information held by public bodies (such as hospitals, etc.).

The Labour Party believed that civil liberties was the fundamental goal in safeguarding individual or minority rights against state power. When the party took power in 1997 they added that citizens had responsibilities to the state to one another and to the well-being of the community.

The first key legislation of the New Labour government was the Crime and Disorder Act (1998). It was designed to tackle anti-social behaviour.

Criminologist David Wilson believed this legislation showed that the Labour Party was authoritarian. It was Wilson's belief that Blair's moral stance and his focus on individual responsibility was just a version of Thatcherism. The Labour Party had blindly followed Blair in the 1990s but later, as civil liberty issues came to the surface in the shape of terrorism and ID cards, there would be problems.

In 2005 a new package of terror measures was announced, the most radical for thirty or more years. Shami Chakrabarti, the director of the civil rights group Liberty, insisted that democracy was not just restricted to elections every five years. There were more fundamental issues, such as rights, freedoms and the rule of law. If rights, freedoms and the rule of law were ignored then democracy would descend into chaos, giving rise to mob rule.

The Labour Party viewed the judiciary as an obstruction to their proposed changes. After the 2001 election they announced changes to the role of the Lord Chancellor; paradoxically this would strengthen the independence of the judiciary. Labour gave the police more powers to arrest, to hold mandatory drug tests and DNA tests, and new dispersal orders (creating dispersal areas where police officers break up troublemakers and forcibly take under-16s home). All of these damaged liberties.

The freedom of the police to enforce the law and protect citizens was also affected, as Tony Butler, the former Chief Constable of Gloucestershire, pointed out in 2007. The mid-1990s had seen huge falls in the volume of crime, particularly burglary and car theft. There was flexible local police management. But more recently there had been a focus on performance management rather than combating crime. As a result drug-related and violent crime had not been successfully tackled and this gave rise to concerns.

Despite the changes, the Labour Party still claims to support the notion of civil liberties, maintaining that the Human Rights Act and the Freedom of Information Act have improved the government's accountability.

Issues associated with rights and liberties in the US

The Supreme Court continues to interpret the Constitution in the light of new legislation. The following list gives several examples of how the Supreme Court has ruled in terms of rights and liberties in recent years.

- In Ashcroft vs Free Speech Coalition (2002) the Supreme Court struck down parts of the Child Pornography Prevention Act (1996) largely because the Act was too broad and unconstitutional, as it banned images that were not actually children.
- In Ashcroft vs ACLU (2002) the court held that the Child Online Protection Act (1998) was not overly broad, as it only restricted material that was harmful to minors.
- In US vs American Library Association (2003) the court supported federally funded libraries in installing software to stop minors accessing pornographic websites.
- In Virginia vs Black (2003) the court overturned Virginia's law against burning the cross with the intent to intimidate as a violation of free speech. The state could still ban it if it were done to intimidate.
- In Scheidler vs National Organization for Women (2003) the Supreme Court stated that anti-abortion protestors could not be charged with extortion under the Racketeer Influenced and Corrupt Organizations Act (1970), as the protestors did not gain anything of value.
- In Republican Party of Minnesota vs White (2002) the court overturned Minnesota's ruling, which stopped judicial candidates from announcing their political or legal views. The court believed that it violated the 1st Amendment.
- In McConnell vs Federal Election Commission (2003) the court ruled that money given to political parties and not to candidates (known as soft money) did not violate the 1st Amendment.
- In Zelman vs Simmons-Harris (2002) the court supported the state school voucher programme that allowed poorer children to go to religious schools, signalling that it was not a violation of the establishment clause.
- In Locke vs Davey (2003) the court supported states withholding scholarship funds to students who wished to major in theology. It did not violate the Free Exercise clause.

- In McCreary County vs ACLU (2005) the court ruled that displaying the Ten Commandments in a courthouse was unconstitutional, but there was an opposite ruling in Van Orden vs Perry (2005).
- In Chavez vs Martinez (2003) the court held that suspects who had not been read their rights, but had made statements instead, could not claim violation of the 5th Amendment if their statements were not later used.
- In Missouri vs Seibert (2004) the court ruled that the police had violated the 5th Amendment by making a suspect confess before their rights had been read and then getting the suspect to repeat the confession.
- In Hiibel vs 6th Judicial Circuit of Nevada (2004) the court held that state laws requiring people to identify themselves to the police did not violate the 4th or 5th amendments as the question was not self-incriminating.
- In Crawford vs Washington (2004) the court held that using out-of-court testimony violated a defendant's right to cross-examine witnesses.
- There were a number of rulings on cruel and unusual punishment, specifically finding that executions of mentally disabled people were unconstitutional and minors under the age of 18 should not be sentenced to death, but upheld California's three-strike sentencing as being constitutional when an individual was given a long prison sentence for a series of petty crimes.

INTERNET RESEARCH

To see many of these court rulings in detail, go to www.heinemann.co.uk/hotlinks, insert express code 1825P and click on the relevant link.

6.7 Protecting rights and liberties

Learning objectives

- How are the rights of US citizens protected?
- What has been the effectiveness of the Supreme Court in protecting liberties?

How are the rights of US citizens protected?

In the US all three branches of government have a role to play in the protection of the rights of citizens. It is Congress's role to ensure the passage of appropriate legislation, it is the executive's role to ensure that the legislation is enforced, and it is the Supreme Court's job to interpret the legislation and how it affects the Constitution. As the US has a written constitution, which incorporates a bill of rights, the Supreme Court plays an important role in protecting the rights of the citizens.

Congress and the Supreme Court

Congress has been particularly active in securing advances for voting rights, equal protection, procedural due process, religious liberties and some areas of free expression. Congress has used its own initiative to protect rights by revising or eliminating provisions in older statutes that violated rights. It has also operated on its own initiative to secure rights, such as the Equal Pay Act (1963). Congress has also acted when it has felt that a Supreme Court decision or interpretation had not gone far enough by enacting statutes giving a greater level of protection, such as the Pregnancy Discrimination Act (1978) and the Civil Rights Restoration Act (1987). Congress has also moved to react to what it views as an improper Supreme Court interpretation of a constitutional issue. The Speedy Trial Act (1974) was enacted after a restrictive interpretation of the 6th Amendment.

Over the last 150 years the Supreme Court has issued an enormous number of decisions, aiming to properly defend individual and group rights. By the beginning of the 21st century the court was using three different standards, or levels of examination. It used:

- scrutiny to test a case for violations
- an intermediate level of scrutiny for those involving women and illegitimate persons
- a strict scrutiny for issues involving race, immigration and nationality.

Question topic material

Note that these topics are not written in essay format, but they do include ideas, concepts and information and practices that you would need to think about if similar questions came up in an exam.

The president and pressure groups

The US president is the most common catalyst for policy and some, such as Lyndon Johnson, initiated civil rights policies, while others, such as Ronald Reagan, held them up or set them back, as in the case of black civil rights, by restricting federal government roles. The role of the president in furthering civil rights was highlighted by Dwight D. Eisenhower. Stanford University's Kathleen Sullivan said: 'I think it was absolutely heroic of Eisenhower. He made the promise of the courts come true.' She was referring to the sending of troops to escort black students into a white school in Little Rock, Arkansas, in 1957.

Historian Taylor Branch, talking about the 2008 presidential election, suggested that even in the United States there were still not equal rights and that presidents tended to succeed when they mobilised the country to tackle fundamental principles of democracy.

In the US pressure groups also play a major role in promoting and monitoring citizens' rights. The NAACP continues to be at the centre of political debate and was the force behind the Brown vs Board of Education ruling in 1954. Pro-choice and pro-life lobbies continue to be engaged in the abortion debate. Numerous women's groups are still campaigning for equal pay and

The American Civil Liberties Union

The ACLU has been highly influential in the development of US constitutional law and steps in to provide legal assistance for cases where it perceives civil liberties to be at risk. In recent years it has been actively involved in challenging wire tapping without warrants and has opposed an ordnance in Pennsylvania that punished landlords who rented property to illegal immigrants and businesses that employed them.

job opportunities and the 2nd Amendment's right to keep and bear arms is solidly defended by the National Rifle Association.

What has been the effectiveness of the Supreme Court in protecting liberties?

Successes

In the US the Supreme Court considers cases that could impact on the Constitution. It can strike down federal laws or presidential actions that it considers to be unconstitutional. This has been primarily achieved through judicial review. But the outcome of many of the constitutional cases is dependent upon the composition and stance of the Supreme Court. Consequently, during the period of judicial activism (the Warren and Burger Courts), when the court was seen to be more liberal (e.g. Brown vs Board of Education and Roe vs Wade), civil rights tended to gain further protection. It is currently unclear what stance the Supreme Court will take now that it is more conservative.

Failures

In 1954 the Supreme Court undermined segregation in the US by reversing the separate but equal ruling. During the 1960s the court tended to favour affirmative action, but in later years its view on this issue was ambiguous and it has not moved to ensure equal treatment in issues such as education, housing and employment.

Although the court has not always acted to enforce positive legal protections, it has always conveyed the political message that executive power should always remain subject to the rule of law. This is particularly true of perceived wartime threats. Even before the reaction to the September 11 attacks, the Supreme Court had awarded reparations to those who had been interned during the Second World War.

The US government's counter-terrorism measures have adversely affected civil liberties and human rights, and although President Obama has pledged to close the US military detention centre at Guantanamo Bay, its mere existence energises those involved in civil rights and liberties and those who call for the Supreme Court to make a comprehensive ruling on the issue. Two major legal challenges that were brought before the court to determine the status of the detainees have failed, mainly on the grounds that the court lack the jurisdiction to hear the cases, although the Boudemiene vs Bush (2008) ruling casts doubt on this. The reason is that Cuba retains sovereignty over the military base; hence US courts have no power to check US government actions there.

The 2001 Patriot Act was labelled as being in violation of the 1st, 4th, 5th, 6th and 8th amendments. It has caused considerable controversy and there were grave civil liberty concerns. So far the Supreme Court has been reticent in addressing the implications of the Act. However, parts of the Act have come under attack and have been declared unconstitutional in some states. Critics claim that:

- it allows federal government to conduct surveillance on US citizens
- it allows the government to add DNA samples to databases
- it makes it more difficult to hold government accountable
- the police can enter private premises without the permission or knowledge of the owner
- it allows the Justice Department to develop additional legislation with little input from Congress.

6.8 The Constitution and Bill of Rights

Learning objectives

- Are civil rights and liberties best defended by a bill of rights or a constitution?
- Evaluate how the US Constitution and the first 10 amendments effectively protect rights and liberties

Are civil rights and liberties best defended by a bill of rights or a constitution?

United States

In the US, a citizen's basic freedoms are laid out in the first 10 amendments, often referred to as the Bill of Rights. Even the Declaration of Independence stated: 'We hold these truths to be self-evident, that all men are created equal.'

Egalitarianism is at the heart of the US system and mirrors the concepts of the American dream, in which an individual can use their skills in order to improve themselves and their family's life chances without reference to their background, colour or social standing.

It has not always been an easy task to enforce elements of the Constitution or the Bill of Rights, particularly in the case of African-Americans. It has needed enforcement of laws and the implementation of voting rights, which were only secured in the mid-1960s.

There is intolerance, if not persecution, of the political left in the US. During the early 1950s the McCarthyism witch-hunts against communist sympathisers sought to expose and root out supposed communist influence in US institutions. Even now, those who oppose the Patriot Act are branded as traitors and the treatment of terrorist suspects has been likened to the McCarthyism period.

Britain

Britain lacks a written constitution and a bill of rights, although much of this has been covered with the incorporation of the European Convention and the Human Rights Act. Nonetheless, British citizens lack an up-to-date, clear and unequivocal statement of their rights. During the Thatcher period many perceived that there was a disregard for freedoms, largely due to the preoccupation on national security. During the Blair and Brown eras legislation has been introduced specifically relating to terrorism and has had a marked impact on freedom.

In 2006 the British Conservative Party leader, David Cameron, suggested that the Human Rights Act should be replaced by a US-style bill of rights, although he stressed that Britain would still remain a signatory to the European Convention on Human Rights. As the convention would still apply and Cameron was strongly advocating his idea for a bill of rights, Lord Falconer reacted angrily to the suggestion, believing that it was ridiculous to suggest that problems such as crime and terrorism could be solved by simply introducing another undefined layer of rights.

Lord Goldsmith was of the opinion that a bill of rights would lead to more and not less confusion about how society should balance the need to protect individual liberties while protecting the public.

The human rights lawyer Michael Mansfield QC was equally critical. He believed that the Human Rights Act did not hinder investigation and prosecution of crime and that there were no examples of it doing this. He believed that Cameron's suggestion was misconceived and simply a sound bite for the media.

Nonetheless, in October 2007 Prime Minister Gordon Brown announced plans to reform the British Constitution with a new British bill of rights, building on the Human Rights Act. The view was that a British bill of rights and duties would give explicit recognition that human rights come with responsibilities. The director of Liberty, Shami Chakrabarti, warned that the government was yet to prove that a bill of rights was any better than Cameron's own proposal. She stressed that fundamental rights belong to all and not just to free-born Englishmen.

Evaluate how the US Constitution and the first 10 amendments effectively protect rights and liberties

The first 10 amendments to the US Constitution are collectively referred to as the Bill of Rights. They aim to protect individual liberties against government restriction and the interference of others, but they are not absolute. This is largely due to the fact that rights often collide and need to be balanced. Unsurprisingly, there is never agreement on where the balance should be struck.

The US civil liberties cannot be removed even if popular majorities either at national, state or local level votes to restrict them. The 1st Amendment, among other things, ensures that Congress cannot restrict freedom of speech, the press, peaceful assembly, petitioning for redress of grievances, free exercise of religion, but also that it cannot promote religion. The 1st Amendment has been used as a bulwark against successive US governments; however the courts have interpreted the 1st Amendment differently over the years. It continues to be redefined and reinterpreted.

Over the years courts have developed a series of tests to try to help find the right balance, such as the clear and present danger test (or clear and probable danger) and a bad tendency test, indicating that a speech could pose an indirect future danger.

The 4th, 5th and 6th amendments protect citizens from government intrusion, but even the term 'unreasonable search and seizure' has been a question of much debate in US courts. In 1989, for example, the Supreme Court felt that law enforcement employees and others should be subject to drug tests without search warrants, although a later court struck down extensions to this.

The 6th Amendment guarantees the 'right to a speedy and public trial, by an impartial jury'. Once again the exact meaning of the words speedy, public and impartial has been contested. This has meant that the trial judges had to rule on what information can be open to the media, how juries are selected, what evidence can and cannot be used, along with sentencing guidelines. Inevitably if an individual feels that they have not been treated fairly during the trial process they will appeal to a higher court. Ultimately the decision often arrives at the Supreme Court for them to determine and to interpret the Constitution and how it applies to that particular case.

In 1943 Robert Moses suggested that civil rights, even as they applied as far as the Constitution was concerned, were meaningless because it is impossible to 'legislate tolerance'. Milton Konvitz, a professor at Cornell's law school and an authority on constitutional and labour law and civil and human rights, was of the opinion that the term civil rights was no harder to define than concepts such as due process of law and equal protection under the law. All of those phrases could be found in the federal Constitution. It was the job of the courts and of Congress to define precisely what those phrases meant and to give them significance.

Rights and Liberties in Modern Society

Learning objectives

- How are rights and liberties protected in modern society?
- What is the effectiveness of the protection of rights and liberties in different political systems?

How are rights and liberties protected in modern society?

Civil rights are those that the government of a country is obliged to provide and liberties are the freedoms that protect individuals from government interference. Perhaps the most basic forms of rights and liberties revolve around equality, incorporating equal treatment in terms of gender, race, religion, the right to vote and freedom of speech.

Not all rights and liberties have been afforded to individuals without a considerable struggle and some are continually under threat, particularly due to the responses by governments to the terrorist threats.

Comparison of Britain and US

Although there are similarities in the range of rights and liberties in both Britain and the United States they are protected in radically different ways. In Britain, with an unwritten constitution, personal liberties are still extremely important and parliament takes the leading role in protecting the rights of citizens. It is a similar case in the US, but there is a written constitution and the Bill of Rights, which is comprised of the first 10 amendments. Both British and US courts play a vital role in interpreting and applying the law. Pressure groups and the media occupy an important position in protecting liberties by highlighting issues and abuses. They champion broad cases, as well as individual ones.

Britain, the European Union, along with the devolution of Scotland, Wales and Northern Ireland, has added other layers that seek to protect citizens' rights. To some extent this has always been the case in the US, with federal, state and local protective measures.

In the US the Constitution seeks to explicitly state rights and liberties. But in Britain rights and liberties tend to be based on the presumption that an individual can do as they please, provided common law or other legislation does not prevent it. Having a written constitution places the US Supreme Court in a unique position to interpret the precise implications of each element of the Constitution and the amendments.

Some feel, however, that an unwritten constitution provides inadequate protection, while others, such as A. V. Dicey, view this as a strength. A free parliament acts to protect freedoms as part of the rule of law, but in many cases it has failed to act when civil liberties have been threatened, particularly when the Conservatives extended police powers and the Labour government has sought to restrict trial by jury.

Although the US Bill of Rights laid out freedoms, such as due process of law, free speech and the right to legal representation, they were not effectively enforced until relatively recently. Due process was not recognised until the court cases Gideon vs Wainwright (1963), Mapp vs Ohio (1961) and Miranda vs Arizona (1966). Even equality, as contained in the 14th Amendment, took time to be enforced. It required Supreme Court action and the Civil Rights Act (1964) to end segregation and bring about affirmative action programmes.

In Britain courts tend to have less room for manoeuvre, as they have to operate within the legislation that has been passed by parliament. Even the European Convention on Human Rights and the Human Rights Act do not guarantee that any subsequent laws need to comply with them.

What is the effectiveness of the protection of rights and liberties in different political systems?

The World Audit Project produces a Freedom House Annual Survey, which monitors the progress or decline of human rights worldwide. Of particular note are the criteria upon which it bases its survey to determine whether civil rights and liberties are protected.

- Are there free religious institutions and free religious expression?
- Is there freedom of assembly and demonstration?
- Is there freedom of political organisation?
- Are there free trade unions or equivalents?
- Is there an independent judiciary?
- Does the rule of law prevail?
- Is the population treated equally under the law and are the police under direct civilian control?
- Is there protection from political terror, unjustified imprisonment, exile and torture?
- Is there freedom from government indifference and corruption?
- Is there personal autonomy, freedom from indoctrination and excessive dependency on the state?
- Are property rights secure?
- Are there basic social freedoms, including gender equality, choice of marriage partners and family size?
- Is there equality of opportunity or exploitation and dependency?

The US, for example, ranks very high on all counts, as does Britain. But there are other countries, such as Cuba, North Korea, Libya, Sudan, Turkmenistan and Uzbekistan, that rank extremely low on the civil rights survey. In Uzbekistan human rights activists have been jailed for long prison terms after less than fair trials. Turkmenistan has a repressive and authoritarian government. Human Rights Watch has criticised Cuba for having abusive legal and institutional mechanisms that deprive Cubans of their basic rights and in the Sudan government-backed militia groups have committed genocide against minorities in the Darfur region.

Paper rights

A bill of rights alone is not an adequate safeguard; culture, legislatures and the media, for example, all still have a major role to play in safeguarding rights.

In the US it is the US Constitution and especially the Bill of Rights that protects many civil liberties. The Constitution of Canada incorporates the Canadian Charter of Rights and Freedoms. In Europe there is the European Convention on Human Rights and in Britain, as well as being a signatory to the convention, the Human Rights Act (1998) incorporates the majority of the convention.

In China the Constitution of the People's Republic of China incorporates the Fundamental Rights and Duties of Citizens. In practice, however, dissidents are not usually protected by the rule of law. In India fundamental rights is in Part III of the Constitution. There are six fundamental rights to equality, freedom, protection from exploitation, freedom of religion, culture and education, and the right to constitutional remedies. Again in theory the Constitution of the Russian Federation guarantees a similar range of rights and liberties as in the US. But the state is still authoritarian and repressive, and freedom of expression, assembly and association are constantly under attack.

6.10 Grievances and Pressure Groups

Learning objectives

- How can citizens seek redress of grievance in different political systems?
- What has been the contribution of pressure groups in defending rights and liberties?

How can citizens seek redress of grievance in different political systems?

A redress of grievance is a remedy for a citizen's complaint about the administrative action taken by a public body (or an organisation funded by public finance). In Britain, there are several ways a redress of grievance can be sought.

Role of the judiciary and MPs

The judiciary is supposed to be a major defender of citizens' rights. But the judicial process may take months or even years, by which time the results of the problem may have had an enormous impact on the citizen and incur huge costs. It is possible for the judiciary to hear cases involving the exceeding of authority by a public body or public servant. This can include the police force or the government attempting to prevent a newspaper or broadcaster from publishing or screening a story that is critical of the government. The judiciary will rule on the case, by interpreting the law, finding the action either lawful or unlawful. If a citizen feels that a decision was wrong, they can appeal to the European Court of Human Rights (ECHR). If the ECHR finds in their favour the judgement of the British judge can be overturned. British courts are obliged to obey the decision of the ECHR. On average it takes five years and £30,000 to receive a ruling from Strasbourg, so the incorporation of the European Convention on Human Rights into British law has greatly improved things.

Constituents can enlist the support of their MP in their redress of grievance. While MPs do not have a wide range of powers, they can assist in a number of different ways.

- They can write on behalf of the constituent, outlining the complaint.
- They can directly bring up the case in the House of Commons.
- The case can be referred to a parliamentary select committee or an ombudsman by the MP. The effectiveness of ombudsmen has been variable and dependent upon the precise powers allocated to them.
- Written questions to the prime minister or a minister is also an option.

Role of the media

Instead of resorting to official and legal redress of grievance, the help and support of the media is an option open to the citizen, dependent on whether the media considers it to be an important enough case and an interesting one. It may also depend on the political bias of the newspaper or magazine in question. Some are openly critical of particular governments; others are openly hostile to all forms of government. While the citizen's case may be given media coverage, it may also mean that the case becomes associated with a particular political view.

Tribunals public inquiries, petitions

Administrative tribunals are government created, independent bodies that handle specific grievances. They cover areas such as tax, pensions, compensation and similar matters, and deal with complaints against employers (such as unfair dismissal, equal opportunities and racial discrimination) or government departments (including public bodies and agencies). Independent lawyers chair administrative tribunals. They have two specialists (experts in the field covered by the tribunal), along with two other members (called lay people). The lay people have been chosen for their abilities to fairly judge a situation. They also provide a cheap and relatively speedy resolution.

Citizens can convince the government to launch a public inquiry into the actions of government or a public body, but the government is not bound to implement the findings and recommendations of the inquiry.

Local councillors have the power to take up cases on behalf of citizens with a grievance, but will restrict their investigations and work on their behalf to the local authority. If the local authority is unable or unwilling to assist in providing a solution to the case the local councillor can refer the matter to the local government ombudsman (including complaints about housing, planning, education, social services, consumer protection, drainage and council tax).

In the US, the 1st Amendment specifically gives citizens the right 'to petition the government for a redress of grievances.' The concept dates back to 1215 with the Magna Carta. It was at Runnymede that the English barons compelled King John to sign the Magna Carta which placed limits on the king's powers. Although it did not explicitly mention the right to petition, it did touch on the need to be able to have a system in place that would rectify a wrong by voicing a grievance. Some 500 years later, this was a key issue in the American colonists' Declaration of Independence: 'In every stage of these oppressions, we have petitioned for redress, in the most humble terms; our repeated petitions have been answered only by repeated injury.'

The precedent for the right to petition for a redress of grievances originated in three English documents: the Magna Carta, the Petition of Right and the Bill of Rights (Declaration of Rights). Individuals, citizens' groups and corporations may request remedy or complain to and about their government without fear of punishment. Securing liberty and individual rights requires enforceable legal limits on all government power.

What has been the contribution of pressure groups in defending rights and liberties?

Pressure groups, rather like the media, are an alternative to more traditional forms of redress of grievance. They can be approached to help with the publicity of a case, or support in pushing the case. Sometimes new pressure groups have been created to carry a redress of grievance case forward. Although it cannot actually redress the grievance, it can bring significant pressure to bear on the government, the public body or the source of the problem. In some cases public inquiries have been authorised or the case taken up by MPs or councillors as a result of the intensity of feeling.

One of the overriding difficulties for pressure groups is actually getting started and gaining the initial publicity, particularly if the media is disinterested or opposed to the objectives of the pressure group. The key is to be seen to be winning the argument. Once this has been achieved the media will often switch its allegiance, or become interested in the case, giving it greater publicity and drive for a resolution to the grievance.

In the US there are differing views about the contribution that has been made by pressure groups. Some believe they have been beneficial to the government, while others feel that the ways in which they operate and influence are anti-democratic. President John F. Kennedy saw pressure groups as being essential: 'The lobbyists who speak for the various economic, commercial and other functional interests of this country serve a very useful purpose and have assumed an important role in the legislative process.'

On the other hand, President Woodrow Wilson was alarmed at the growing power of pressure groups and saw government slowly becoming subservient to them. He believed government was becoming 'the foster child of special interests not allowed to have a will of its own.'

Exam Café

Relax, refresh, result!

Relax and prepare

Questions for the exam are likely to be drawn from the following topic areas or similar. Use these to help focus on what areas of the subject you should be revising.

- Evaluate the role played by the Supreme Court in protecting rights and liberties.
- Examine how effectively the rights of citizens are protected in the United States.
- Evaluate the effectiveness of federal government in safeguarding rights and liberties.
- Evaluate the contribution of different institutions to the defence of rights and liberties in modern political systems.
- Discuss the view that rights and liberties are best defended when entrenched in a bill of rights or constitution.
- Analyse the contribution of pressure groups in defending rights and liberties.
- Contrast the effectiveness of the protection of rights and liberties in modern political systems.
- Use your notes from your study of the Supreme Court, British judiciary and constitutions in order to place rights in context. The Bill of Rights, European Convention of Human Rights, Social Chapter of the Maastricht Treaty and the EU's Charter of Fundamental Human Rights will also be useful points of reference.

Refresh your memory

When revising this topic, try the following exercises. They will help you structure your notes and will give you a guide as to what you will need to know for the different papers. Remember to work through unit F853 first as this will provide the base you will need for F855.

- Draw a table of three columns which outlines:
- the first 10 amendments
- relevant Supreme Court cases which have upheld these rights, for example free speech – upheld by Reno vs ACLU (1997) and Texas vs Johnson (1989).
- cases where rights have not been protected, for example Frederick vs Morse (2007) and Virginia vs Black (2003) which restricted free speech.
- It might help your understanding of the Bill of Rights if you can separate rights. The 1st Amendment relates to the individual political rights of free speech, freedom of the press, freedom from religion and the right to assembly. The 2nd is a 'stand alone' right to bear arms.

The 3rd Amendment is a historical anachronism and has no real purpose today. The 4th, 5th, 6th, 7th and 8th relate to the rights of the accused. The 9th is a broad catch-all amendment, which is highly relevant with regard to abortion rights, and the 10th relates to federal state relations.

- Consequently the 3rd and 10th are not that relevant to a discussion of individual rights and liberties.
- Note the importance of the 14th Amendment and its equal protection clause relating to issues relating to race and areas such as affirmative action in cases such as Bollinger vs Gratz (2003) and Adarand vs Peña (1995).

Exam tips

These are some of the reasons students do badly in exams. They provide a guide to what you need to avoid and by implication what you need to do to perform well in your exam.

- They do not question the adequacy of the Supreme Court as a defender of rights and liberties.
- They rely on dated cases that do not go beyond the Warren Court era.
- They are not able to comment on the role played by the other branches of government when the question demands they do.
- The notion of 'paper rights' is not considered thoroughly. This is the argument that a written statement of rights alone is not sufficient to ensure their protection.
- They do not separate the different roles played by the European Court of Human Rights and the European Court of Justice.

Get the result!

These are some ideas to help you in your revision and to keep up to date with the latest developments in US politics.

- Separate the protection of rights on the basis outlined above and consider the contributions made not only by judiciaries, but also by executives and legislatures, pressure groups and the media.
- Review developments since 9/11 and examine the implications of the Patriot Act and its subsequent renewal.
- Consider the impact of Supreme Court rulings with regard to those held on Guantanamo Bay without charge and access to a lawyer. (Rasul vs Bush (2004), Hamdi vs Rumsfeld (2004), Handan vs Rumsfeld (2006), Boumediene vs Bush (2008)).
- Evaluate the significance of the composition of the Supreme Court and the voting blocs on it. It will be useful to consider the impact of any resignations and appointments in this regard.
- Similarly assess the constraints upon the Supreme Court which might mean a ruling alone might not be sufficient to ensure that a right is safeguarded.
- Monitor Obama's measures in this area as an example of executive action in this regard.
- Use the website of the ACLU to get up-to-date examples of the most recent areas of concern for civil libertarians.
- Sites such as www.ReformthePatriotAct.org illustrate how the Act violates the 1st, 4th and 5th amendments and details the role played by Congress in the passage and renewal of the Act.

In Focus – F855

Covering certain areas will help you in revising and in developing your knowledge at this level in order to gain a higher mark. These are the key areas to focus on.

- The reform proposals from Brown and Cameron with regard to the introduction of a 'British bill of rights'.
- The rulings from British courts in relation to the European Convention of Human Rights.
- The role of parliament in cases such as attempts to extend detention without charge to 42 days.
- The significance and meaning of negative, positive and natural rights.
- The use of the websites of Liberty and Amnesty for additional material on rights.
- Read the *Economist* to monitor developments in the area of rights worldwide. Examples from beyond the US and UK will be rewarded.
- The importance of political culture and education could be considered against the impact of war and terrorist threats.
- The use of case studies in areas such as abortion might be a useful way in which to undertake comparative analysis and evaluation

Exam**Café**

Conclusion

10 steps to exam success

1 Fail to prepare, prepare to fail

Exam preparation is the key to success and it is vital you appreciate that there is more to preparation than simply reading through your notes. Detailed below are the steps that you can take which hopefully will ensure you have covered all the bases so that when you turn over the exam paper there will be no surprises and you will be able to do yourself justice.

2 Where to begin?

With the advent of the Internet, the amount of resources on line has increased. One of the best sites to access as an initial step in your revision programme is the exam board for the two units. On that website you will find past papers, mark schemes and the chief examiner's reports. Download as many of these as you possibly can. They are a vital resource, as will be explained later. Ask your teacher for copies of past papers if cannot access these on lines.

3 Morpheus: 'The Matrix is a system, Neo. That system is our enemy'

Not in this case it isn't! All examiners use a grid to set out their coverage of the specification, you should do the same. Set out the specification/syllabus in a spreadsheet. Break each topic down into headings and insert these into a spreadsheet. For example, the topic of pressure groups can be broken down into: types, factors which influence success/effectiveness and democratic theory. Use another column to mark when a question was asked on an aspect of the topic. In this way you can see how the paper is structured and the frequency with which questions appear and the sort of questions that the examiner is likely to focus upon.

Each paper for each exam board is likely to have its own favourites and the ways in which questions are varied across the paper. It may well be the case that you can prioritise certain questions as more likely to appear than others. So if you have not had a question on the electoral college for a while, it is reasonable to assume that you are more likely to get a question on this than on a topic which came up the last time a paper was set.

This of course leaves us entering the realm of question spotting. It is absolutely essential though that you do not put all your eggs in the one basket and solely concentrate a few aspects of a topic or on too few topics. Question spotting is not an exact science. Examiners may want to try to catch you out and repeat a topic that was on the previous paper.

Consequently, while it may be sensible to have a few favourite revision topics which you think are the most likely to appear, do not neglect other areas. These other topics may not be done as well as those in your personal 'premier league' but at least they may be there in case of emergency. So some breadth rather than depth is a good thing.

4 That's what I went to school for

The easiest way for you to learn is by being 'switched on' in the classroom. How many times do you walk out of a lesson and feel that you have not learned anything? Can you remember what you did in the previous lesson? Are your notes and file neatly ordered? If you can master these basics then at least you will have a reasonable knowledge base on which to build when it comes to revision, rather than starting from scratch. Thus school can be regarded as part of this process. They may even provide a revision programme for you which covers the essentials. Try to combine your programme with theirs.

5 Daytime Devil

A key part of the revision process is repetition. Going over topics several times will help you learn them and you will be able to recall facts and quotes far easier if you are really familiar with the material. This takes time. So start revising key topics as soon as possible.

How much time do you waste? This not only applies to the normal school day but to any study leave that you are given. Are you a late riser? Biologically, you are at your most receptive in a morning. A good morning session eases pressure on the rest of the day and allows you to do other things. Can you be sucked into daytime TV? Endless repeats of *Hollyoaks*, *Friends*, Jeremy Kyle and the Punk'd need to be resisted.

6 Keep it simple

Don't waste time devising the most intricate revision programme, cleaning a set of fountain pens you have not used for years, waiting until you have purchased a set of colour-coded post-it notes. Just make a set of simple notes using bullet points to cover all the key points. Try to reduce some quotes to a memorable size. These can add a lovely flourish to written answers.

Try working on a clear and tidy desk. It does make an enormous difference. I defy anybody to work in front of a television. Music can be OK providing it is ambiental muzak rather than the latest hardcore club classics played at maximum volume. Yes, there will be occasions when a break is required, in which case light stick and whistle may make an appearance in order to relieve tension. Has anybody ever revised well with their mates? Revision is simply a case of doing the hard slog in a quiet environment. You will know yourself what works for you and what doesn't.

7 Separate the wood from the trees

Students frequently look for alternatives and quick-fix solutions when it comes to revision. This may prevent them from doing the obvious. There are a host of text books, revision guides and Internet sites which provide the information that you need. The quality of each resource is variable, so you will have to make a judgement or rely on the advice of a teacher. The text book is an obvious starting point. Make sure you have read and noted the relevant chapter for a topic and then see how this relates to past exam questions. Try to do the same for handouts and information you have, such as journal articles. Try to combine these into one master revision sheet which will be in effect all you need to know for that topic.

If you simply highlight points on a handout that will mean that you have to read the whole handout again when you go over the notes. The preparation of these master sheets provides a quicker way to go over all the key points.

8 Practice makes perfect

Do as many test essays/questions as possible. It is vital that you get to grips with the timing of the exam. Make sure that you allocate time accordingly. Use school revision tests for this purpose. Try to write answers at home to exam questions and then see if you can apply the mark scheme to what you have written.

9 Ask for help

Keep on good terms with your teachers! If you encounter problems about a topic or the required exam technique, seek their help.

10 The Holy Grail of politics exams

Every chief examiner's report and mark scheme comments upon the need for students to refer to contemporary developments in politics. Make this a key part of your revision notes for each topic. Thus you may have comments about Obama as president, his impact on ideology, the latest rulings from the Supreme Court, etc. This will really set you apart from the other students and push up your mark levels. So read a newspaper online, such as the *New York Times*, read the *Economist*, listen to Radio 4, make the BBC News website your home page on the Internet. The little snippets of information you glean from these sources are little gems to use in an exam.

Index

Page numbers in *italics* refer to illustrations